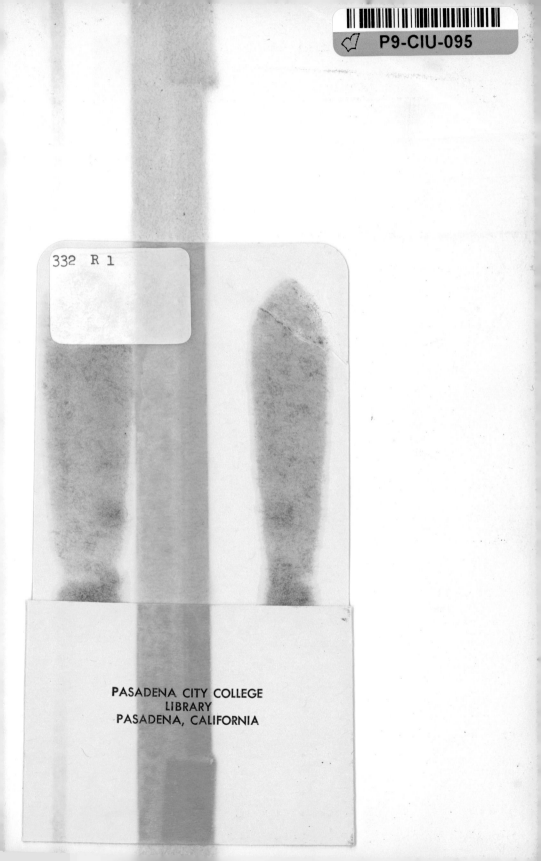

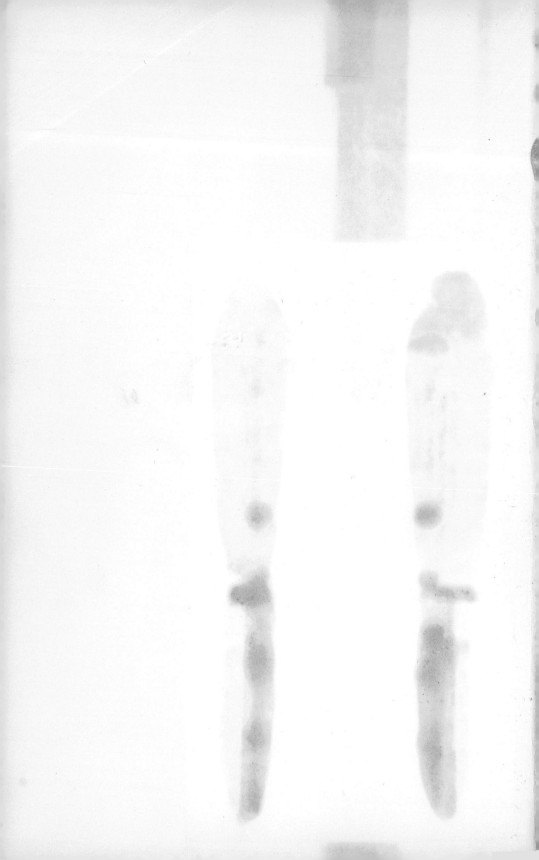

Managing your *own* MONEY

Managing your *own* MONEY

JEROME R. ROSENBERG

NEWSWEEK BOOKS, New York

Printed in the United States of America

First Edition 1979

Library of Congress Cataloging in Publication Data

Rosenberg, Jerome R
Managing your own money.

1.   Finance, Personal.   I. Title.
HG179.R675   332'.024   78-55215
ISBN 0-88225-261-5

Book design: Mary Ann Joulwan

Contents

Preface

F. SCOTT FITZGERALD said it more clearly than any other American writer: "The rich are very different from you and me." That difference does not lie, as Gatsby and Daisy thought, in the splendid quality of their shirts, nor in the obvious amount of money that they had. Thirty years of experience has convinced me that it lies in the fact that the active rich are superb record keepers. In fact, one of the American families whose wealth is proverbial requires its members to study record keeping along with whatever field they have chosen.

Experience has also shown me that too large a percentage of people, other than the industrious rich, cannot perform even relatively simple record-keeping functions such as reconciling the monthly bank statement to the checkbook. This does not derive from poverty or lack of education. In many cases, these are learned people doing sophisticated work in their own fields and making comfortable incomes. But they cannot hope to manage their money until they have understood the fundamentals of money. By this I do not mean economic or monetary theory. I mean the nuts and bolts of everyday money management.

When I was working on the annual *H. & R. Block Income Tax Workbook*, I became acutely aware that most of the publishing firm's employees with whom I was dealing were plagued by a hopelessness concerning money. They were constantly worried about finances and did not understand any of the basics of managing money. They were in better company than I had guessed.

At that time, a lawyer employed by a "Big-Eight" accounting firm in charge of executive financial planning for his firm's clients, spoke to the New York University Tax Study Group. The members of this group are tax partners of most major accounting and law firms in New York City. This man had worked with 150 chairmen and chief executives of major U.S. corporations on their personal financial problems. He observed that *not a single individual had done a satisfactory job of personal money management.* In the entire group of executives, only one had an acceptable will! Although that will was in proper form, the ownership of most of that executive's property was incorrectly defined, making his estate plan ineffective.

The speaker's findings reinforced my conviction that my years of professional experience could be of great value to the average family. I thought there was great need for a practical book on money, beginning with the fundamentals of money, then moving on to explain other subjects in money management. I could not promise to make the reader rich, but I could pass along my knowledge in handling what cash was available.

I accumulated material which I believed would be suitable for a complete nonprofessional treatise on personal money management. This research, and my many years in the "trenches", defending my clients in their battles with tax collectors and share-your-wealth promoters, form the basis of this book. This is a "how-to" book, and is written for the average reader who is not professionally trained to handle money.

Many people kindly offered help in writing this book and their efforts should not go without recognition. After completing the first draft of the book, I submitted individual chapters to experts to check for conceptual errors. Their suggestions whenever possible were included in the final manuscript. Of course, I am solely responsible for all the material as well as the opinions expressed.

The *Computing Your Net Worth* chapter was reviewed by my brother, Norton A. Rosenberg, who is engaged in public accounting. He deals regularly with the needs of the individual in borrowing money and other uses of net worth statements. My former accounting intern, Wayne Danson, CPA, examined both the *Cash Flow* and *Budgeting For the Future* chapters.

My old adversary and now my associate, Thomas J. McLoughlin, Esq., read and commented upon the *Tax Planning* chapter. Before his retirement last year from the Service, he was an Internal Revenue Agent assigned to the Large Case Branch.

Paul Rosenberg, Esq. reviewed *Estate Planning*, his specialty. Herbert Ernest, C.L.U. and Alvin Singer, C.L.U. undertook an examination of the *Life Insurance* chapter. Their suggestions were invaluable. Mr. Singer spent an inordinate amount of time on my personal insurance problems.

In addition, he reviewed the material on *Health and Casualty Insurance*. Mr. Ernest supplied computer runs of countless policies. I was fortunate in having additional computer output on insurance policies through the kindness of Charles E. Meyer and John D. McElwain.

I am also grateful to my own beloved personal insurance consultant, Alexander Crosthwaite, C.L.U., who died while I was writing this book.

My friend at the bank, William Glos, offered his kind help on the *Credit* chapter. One of the outstanding real estate people in New York State is my client and friend, Israel M. Dolgin, to whom go warm thanks for his suggestions for the *Real Estate* chapter.

N. Leonard Fox is a tax shelter expert who is very knowledgeable in real estate. He reviewed both the *Real Estate* chapter and *Leasing versus Purchasing*. Jerome Silverstein, a veteran auto dealer, reviewed the chapter on *Tangible Property*.

I am most grateful to Oliver R. Grace, one of the most respected members of the Wall Street community, for his interest and encouragement. Mr. Grace devoted countless hours in reviewing and contributing to my chapter on *Intangible Property*. My thanks, also, to my personal investment counsel, Gerald White, C.F.A. for his careful study of both the *Intangible Property* and *Futures* chapters. His comments on economic principles I found most rewarding.

Donald R. Wheeler, the well-known bond trader, supplied much of the detail concerning municipal bonds. His associate, Thomas F. Fricke, assisted in the presentation of the yield to maturity data.

To Mr. and Mrs. Duncan Bennett, my thanks for their permission to invade their financial privacy.

I would also like to thank Abe Lerner, my former literary agent, for his initial enthusiasm and assistance.

In 1968, I appropriated from the American Committee for the Weizmann Institute of Science, and particularly from its president, the late Meyer Weisgal, one of my most precious assets, my wife, Julia Daniels. We are the proud parents of Louise, age nine, and Daniel, age seven. I have used their given names for those of the profile family in this book. It seems inevitable that authors thank their spouses for help on books. There are meals missed, weekends ruined, parties and social engagements curtailed, and vacations not taken. But far beyond that, Julia's contribution to the book was immeasureable. I gave her my handwritten manuscript and she painstakingly read and considered each word, pruning and clarifying the text of each draft for me before she typed it, acting, in short, as my favorite "in-house" editor.

My senior editor on the *H & R Block Income Tax Workbook* was Bernard Hassan, now an author in his own right. He devoted his energies to reworking my material, simplifying it, making me rewrite where necessary and, as Al Garfin, Publisher of *Newsweek Books* would say, "translating my draft into English." I also wish to thank my other editors, Nat LaMar and Susan Suffes, for their extraordinary devotion to this book. My thanks also to Howard Gotfryd, who skillfully rendered my workpapers. And my deep appreciation is extended to Mary Ann Joulwan, who designed and executed the book's interior and jacket.

While I was writing this book, a colleague introduced me to a marvellous pocket calculator able to handle most basic financial decision computations in a few seconds. This calculator, which costs less than $30, was invaluable in doing the economic studies necessary for personal money management. My compliments to the people of Texas Instruments for developing the "Business Analyst."

The tax law and financial data used were current at the date the manuscript was finished. Let me caution you to watch for Congressional action on the tax laws. Insurance premiums, interest rates, prices of automobiles, and other examples using money change over a period of time, but principles of money management do not change rapidly. You should be able to work with any new set of values in dealing with your own affairs.

* * * * *

The world was at war when I was in my teens. All of us who remember those dark days of the summer of 1940 believed then that our civilization was at stake and time has, I think, confirmed that we were right. In those days, when we did not know whether the truly good things of life would survive the onslaught of barbarism, we never thought of money as anything other than a commodity or a means of exchange. Though I have handled money professionally all of my adult life, I have tried not to lose that perspective.

My wife spent those frightening days of 1940 in a London bomb shelter while the greatest air battle the world had ever known was fought above her. Because of her and my deep feelings about that period in our history, this book, for whatever it may be worth, is humbly dedicated to the 1,400 young airmen of the Royal Air Force who acted so valiantly to save Western civilization.

Jerome R. Rosenberg
J.D., CPA, LL.M (in Taxation)

New York
June 12, 1978

1
THINKING
ABOUT MONEY

Everyone in the modern world is involved with money and the money culture. Money operates in new and more complex ways almost daily. Yet, despite the fact that it surrounds us and has endless repercussions on our lives, few of us, no matter what our intelligence or education, have a thorough understanding of the ways in which it is used.

We all handle money in multiple forms. We think about it, talk about it, daydream about it, and sometimes have nightmares about it. Money gives us ulcers, breaks up marriages, and perhaps takes years off our lives. Many of us—and not the rich alone—are earning salaries that far exceed our own expectations. Money has given us access to services and material luxuries that would have astounded our grandparents. Yet most of us seem to have difficulty in understanding anything about money more complicated than the W-2 form which arrives every January.

Managing Your Own Money has been written for you, the average reader. You may be highly trained in a technical field. You may even be doing extraordinarily sophisticated work in an area that did not exist 25 years ago. But there is no reason to assume that skill in biochemistry, early Chinese history, or computer design confers any special sophistication in money matters. Having earned and spent money all your adult life makes you no more capable of handling it intelligently than listening to a symphony makes you a conductor of the Philharmonic.

Although some individuals seem to have a greater monetary aptitude than others, everyone must learn the *rules* of handling money. There is no reason to feel ashamed or defensive about not yet having learned these rules. If you have not studied Ukrainian or Urdu, you probably feel no shame about being unable to speak those languages. Think of money in the same way. You can allow it to remain a completely foreign and mystifying tongue or you can decide to study the basics of its "grammar and vocabulary." You may never go beyond the fundamentals, but you will be able to put what you have learned to the best possible use.

Managing Your Own Money can teach you the rock-bottom vocabulary of money and the basic concepts of money as a human activity and method of exchange. This is not, however, a book which can enable you to make a fortune by tipping you off to some obscure little paragraph tucked away in the tax laws. There *are* many details engineered into the laws by special-interest groups. These items are hot news one year and a dead issue the next, and they won't do much to improve your overall situation. When you have mastered the *concepts* in this book, the details can change and you will still have a structure into which you may fit new information.

Please don't start reading this book on April 1 in the hopes of some dramatic last-minute change in your last year's tax situation. If you are in dire financial distress, we cannot offer you immediate relief, and you should seek professional assistance from an accountant, your banker, or from one of the increasing number of professional money managers retained by corporations to counsel their staffs on personal money matters. But if you and your family are simply feeling the common financial stresses of our time, *Managing Your Own Money* can definitely help you on a long-term basis.

It may be that your income is so high or its sources so complex that you need the services of a professional. Throughout the book, we will point out certain areas in which the only intelligent response is to seek professional advice. But there are different kinds of professional advice available. Picking the right adviser is a major part of the game. Since almost every professional consultant charges you on a time basis, you can only profit by knowing what questions to ask, what questions you will be asked, and what documentation you will be expected to produce. If you are aware of these questions ahead of time, you will not only have saved yourself time and money, but will be more likely to gain the respect and cooperation of your consultant.

Perhaps you are not in the happy situation of having a substantial income from diversified sources. You may have the impression that our "model" family, the Smiths, are too far removed from your situation, and that the work involved in this book too complex. This is not true. The Smith family is *only* a composite and does not correspond point by point to many real families. You don't have to assume a medium-high income, an inheritance, royalties, rent from a vacation home, or income from a diversified portfolio to use this book. Even if you have only recently finished school and earn a very modest starting salary, you will find a great deal of useful advice here. You will be better off if you start out on the right foot. As to difficulty, the average high school graduate earning a moderately good living is quite capable of doing all the financial planning we suggest, and an eighth grade student should be able to do every arithmetical operation in this book.

Managing Your Own Money will show you how to curtail your expenses without having to resort to "two dozen little secrets" out of current magazines. You probably realize that altering your life-style could save you money and might even help you to cut expenses in half. Changing the way you live is as much a psychological decision as it is a financial one, and there are many excellent books which show you how to go about this. However, this book is not one of them. We hope to show you how intelligent planning can make it possible to maintain your standard of living while spending less. If you eliminate unnecessary or unwise expenditures, you automatically increase the money available for discretionary spending without having a single penny of new income. That is as good as a raise. You should also understand sensible ways in which to guard against the unexpected problems or disasters that can wipe out the resources of an unprepared family or individual—and most people *are* unprepared.

As you find yourself gaining greater control over your own money, you will become more confident in dealing with the economic stresses which we all face. If you need to deal with bankers or credit institutions, they will have greater confidence in you when they see serious evidence of your financial foresight and preparedness. And if you ever have to deal with an IRS audit, you will be able to defend yourself from a position of strength through knowledge and documentation.

Mastering the concepts in this book will take you some time. You cannot achieve all this in a weekend or even a month. There is nothing particularly difficult in this book, but it will present a new *conceptual framework* for thinking about money, so you must give yourself time to become accustomed to a new way of thinking.

Don't attempt to read the book straight through. Read a chapter at your own pace. If the going gets a little rough, skim or browse. *You* are in control here, and you should adjust your reading rate to *your* needs and *your* schedule.

Each chapter is written to stand by itself, but the chapters are arranged in a logical sequence in orrder to acquaint you with the concepts of handling money. If you will approach the chapters in the specific order we chose, you are likely to find them of greater use. You may find the first few chapters a little difficult if this is the first time you have been exposed to such ideas and methods. However, they are fundamental to the understanding of most of what follows. If you work through the book slowly and thoroughly, you will be rewarded.

As you do your initial browsing, you will see what looks like an awful mess of figures and documents that "only a CPA could handle." Don't be put off by first impressions.

Composers and conductors can look at a sheet of music and "hear" it by eye. Most of us must be content with taking the notes of a score one by one. Numbers and calculations that may seem hopelessly complex will prove very simple if you approach them step by step. Remember, this book uses only addition, subtraction, multiplication, and division. Even if you cannot perform those operations with confidence, you have no excuse in today's era of the decent ten-dollar calculator.

Begin your reading equipped with a little notebook for the questions that will occur to you as you progress. These questions will be answered at some point, and you may want to take notes or jot down the page on which the answers appear so that you can return to the material later. You will also be able to use the index to cross-reference these questions for greater understanding.

THE TOOLS OF THE GAME

Financial records have been kept in many ways throughout history. Much of our knowledge of ancient civilizations comes from inventories and invoices kept on baked clay tablets. Since this book is not intended to prepare you for professional practice, we are taking the stand that whatever works for you is good *if* it works. Do your calculations on an abacus—if you think you are up to that very sophisticated device—if that's your thing. Or you may prefer to skip the colorful and exotic. Modern money management uses a small group of tools and symbols which, while mundane, have been proven by trial and error over the years.

You can prepare your financial data most conveniently if you use the following tools: (1) four-column paper 8½" × 11" with three holes punched on the left; (2) a loose-leaf binder for 8½" × 11" sheets; (3) a calculator; (4) black pencils, either #2 or HB; (5) red pencils; (6) a pink eraser; and (7) a 6" ruler.

Columnar paper

Classifying and tabulating your figures on four-column paper helps avoid careless errors. Plain paper does not give you the convenience of uniform placement of your figures. (You can waste time and energy searching for a simple error made by a single figure out of line.) Four-column paper is relatively expensive and should be used only for serious work which will be retained permanently. Use scrap paper for tentative jottings and enter your corrected work on the columnar paper. As you see from this sample, there is nothing complicated about the paper, but there are certain conventions in its use. Notice that you do not use dollar signs, commas, or decimal points. You should use whole dollars in your records, dropping

		$1							
		$23			2 3				
		$456			4 5 6				
		$7,890			7 8 9 0				

the cents. The IRS and most financial institutions observe the practice of reducing, for example, $7.49 or less to $7.00 and increasing $7.50 or more to $8.00. This evens itself out in the long run. In any case, calculations will never be exact to the penny except in small and very tightly controlled circumstances. If you use this practice of "rounding off"—and you should—use it consistently.

Loose-leaf binder

The best-kept records are useless if you can't find them when you need them. Having to hunt around for them will put you in a sour mood for financial calculations and will use up energy that could be better used in record keeping. Get into the habit of keeping all permanent financial records in one place. A sturdy three-ring binder to hold the columnar paper is useful. Spend the few extra dollars for a high-quality binder, since you will be adding to it regularly and using it for years. You may want to use circular gummed reinforcements for the holes in the paper. You may also want to make copies of your records on a regular basis and keep them outside your home. Given the value that these records will eventually assume, especially in case of fire, you might want to keep the originals in a fireproof box at home and the copies in your bank safe-deposit box.

Calculator

Calculators are very useful in increasing accuracy and reducing mental fatigue. Judge for yourself how complex a calculator you are likely to need. If you are going to buy one for the purpose suggested in this book, be certain not to buy the machines intended for the special uses of engineers or physical scientists. For many people, the ten- or twenty-dollar model is sufficient. There are some very sophisticated operations, available to you when you reach the thirty-dollar range. For $50, you can get a calculator that stops just short of stroking your fevered brow. You may decide that your needs would be better served by a desk-top calculator with a tape (the term professionals use for the paper on which the figures are printed).

Be sure to take the time to master the machine. All calculators are amazingly simple considering their speed and the work they do. A wrong step, though, could have you "walking on air" with optimism or thinking of "ending it all" in despair over your financial status.

Whether you do the arithmetic yourself or use a calculator, a little manual checking on an unexpected figure makes sense. And no matter which way you work, make it a practice to repeat your steps at least once to confirm all answers. If you have ever watched professional auditors, you know that they sit very patiently going over every step they have made to see that they have neither omitted nor duplicated any figures. If you do your figuring on paper, all the steps are written out. If you have no tape in your calculator, this checking is an especially important step.

Pencils

If you don't use a pencil professionally, you may think of it as "just a pencil," and you may consider it unnecessary to be told what kind of pencil to use. The wrong pencil, however, will either smudge almost immediately or fade within a short time. If you use a #2 or an HB pencil, the figures will remain legible. And since in theory you are preparing permanent records with long-term implications, legibility is significant.

Sharpen a dozen pencils or so at a time. They lose their points quickly and nothing breaks a train of thought like a trip to the pencil sharpener every five minutes. Mechanical pencils are neither as sharp nor as clear as the #2 or the HB. *Red pencils* are used to verify information and to check the accuracy of figures. The color is chosen for its contrast to regular lead. (A substantial group of males cannot distinguish these colors. If you belong to that group, use whatever kind of pencil you can see as a contrast to black.) In general, use the red pencil to check for errors when your figures are not in balance. Instead of rewriting all the figures, simply make a red mark to indicate that you have verified a particular figure in the recalculation.

Eraser and Ruler

The kind of eraser on the average pencil is likely to tear your paper if you are not careful. Therefore, a small separate eraser is useful for corrections. You want what the stationers call a "pink eraser." The ruler not only makes underlining neater, it is a good guide to prevent your eyes from jumping from line to line as you read across the columns. A six-inch ruler is the most convenient size for this work.

A SYMBOL-MINDED APPROACH

There are five symbols commonly used in the preparation of financial data which you will find useful. These are (1) the single underline, (2) the double underline, (3) the dash, (4) two dashes, and (5) the tick mark.

Underline (single and double)

A single underline beneath a figure means a subtotal. The sum of all subtotals is a total. A double underline beneath a column of figures indicates that a final total has been reached.

	3 5	
	4 2	
	8 7	
Subtotal	1 6 4	
	2 3	
	3 9	
Subtotal	6 2	
Total (164 + 62)	2 2 6	

Use of Dashes

A dash after a total indicates that the arithmetic has been verified a second time. Two dashes (an equal sign) to the left of a figure mean that the figure has been proven to be equal to the total of the figures to the left or right.

					35						
					42						
					87						
					164 −						

			1ST		2ND		3RD		Total	
			35		42		87		164	
			0		23		39		62	
			35		65		126		= 226	

Note: The figure =226 means that the sum of the first, second, and third columns equals the total of the two individual items (which are the totals of these columns).

Tick mark

Use a tick mark to indicate that you have verified the accuracy of the figures from other sources. If you are interrupted for any reason while working, you may also use the tick mark to show where you left off.

					35 \						
					42 \						
					87						

Tick marks after *35* and *42* indicate that you have already made the transfer of figures elsewhere. The absence of a tick mark beside an *87* indicates that the figure has yet to be transferred. It may also mean that you have verified figures *35* and *42* from another source when rechecking figures; make tick marks red.

2
COMPUTING YOUR NET WORTH

HERE'S A LITTLE SCENARIO FOR YOU. It's been a good day and you are sitting quietly after dinner, perhaps savoring a drink or reading an interesting book. The doorbell rings. When you answer it, a man with a gun forces his way in. He has a look of crazed enthusiasm in his eye. As a captive in your own home, you discover that he is a state tax agent who has been working too hard. (It's nice to think that someone on the public payroll might work too hard.) The agent has gone off the deep end with dreams of glorious conquest because he has heard about the Swedish woman who proved in the courts that the law made her liable for 102% of her income in taxes. Perhaps he has also heard about Italy where, if the tax laws were taken seriously, taxes could add up to 110% of income for many people. It all sounds like pure heaven to him, and he has decided to raise public consciousness regarding the Tax Collectors' Liberation Movement. You're his first hostage. He will release you if you'll reveal your net worth so that he can calculate your liability along somewhat more foreign lines. If you're like most people, you couldn't come up with an accurate figure of your net worth if your life depended on it. Knowing your net worth is so basic to all serious financial planning that you will have earned back the cost of this book many times over if you work your way through this chapter alone. There are astute, hard-nosed individuals who tolerate no nonsense in their own line of work but who nevertheless entertain dangerous and infantile fantasies about their money. There are others no less competent but so modest that they underestimate their net worth substantially. One situation is as bad as the other, and both can cost you dearly.

The formula for determining net worth is very simple. The only difficulty lies in gathering the data and arranging it in manageable form. You calculate your net worth by taking the total of your assets and subtracting from it the total of your liabilities. The rest of this chapter will show you how to do this. If you are doing it for the first time, it may take a few hours. But once you have established the basic information, you will be able to update it quickly and efficiently whenever necessary.

Your net worth will make clear to you (1) the extent, cost, and value of your properties; (2) the source and amount of funds at your disposal for new investment; (3) your optimum borrowing capacities; (4) the cost (basis) of your assets for the most intelligent response to tax situations; and (5) your resources for liquidating liabilities. You will then be able to prepare for your retirement and plan your estate realistically. The more accurate your information, the greater control you will have over your money. Your comparative net worth over a period of years offers you a valuable yardstick by which to measure present transactions against future needs.

You may receive money as salary, interest, rents, royalties, bonuses, gifts, or from other sources. This money is *income*. If you save this income it is *capital*. You may also have other *assets*. These include all properties worth more than a nominal amount (say about $100) which can be converted with relative ease into cash. Your home, for example, is a substantial asset, perhaps the most valuable one you have. When your cash and other assets are greater than your debts (liabilities), you are in the enviable state of *solvency*.

Net worth is always computed as of a specific date. For the lay person, the best day for all practical purposes is the last day of the calendar year, December 31. That is to say, for you, your fiscal (financial) year is identical to the calendar year. (Businesses work on a different system, but your personal needs are different from those of a corporation.) There is not much point in preparing a statement that covers less than a 12-month span, since most of your taxes and benefits are computed on the basis of one year. Moreover, you cannot prepare a realistic budget on a week-by-week basis. A budget should cover at least a one-year period, broken down for easier handling into three-month or quarterly segments.

PREPARING YOUR WORKSHEET

Since this book deals with personal and family finances, we have selected a "model" family, Daniel and Louise Smith, in order to give you a full example of the preparation of a net worth statement. No model we could construct would ever correspond to everyone's needs, but we have attempted to provide a set of financial facts which have a general validity.

This model is intended for single individuals as well as for married couples. We have simplified the computations by not indicating whether the assets or liabilities are singlely or jointly owned.

To begin, review the checklist of liabilities and assets which follows. Check off all items which might possibly pertain to you. Read the pages which describe those items, show how to account for them, and provide a completed schedule. Prepare each of the applicable schedules according to the models. Then look at the net worth statement near the end of this chapter. When you are satisfied that you understand the preparation of the individual schedules, enter the totals onto your own net worth statement which you have prepared according to the model on page 52. In general, assets and liabilities have been listed in the order in which you should record them on your own statement. All of this material will be developed at greater length in later chapters. This checklist furnishes only as much information as you need now to set up your net worth statement.

NET WORTH CHECKLIST FOR DANIEL AND LOUISE SMITH

ASSETS

Cash
Due from stockbroker
Marketable and restricted securities
Mortgage receivable
Loans receivable
Prepaid interest
Individual retirement arrangement (IRA) and Employer pension plan
Life insurance (cash-surrender value)
Automobiles
Furnishings
Appliances
Real estate
Miscellaneous assets

LIABILITES

Mortgages payable
Notes Payable
Loans Payable
Due to credit card companies
Due for miscellaneous bills
Taxes payable
Deferred gain on installment sale

ASSETS

Cash

Cash consists of money in your checking account, your savings accounts, and cash on hand. Cash is the amount available in your checking account on your net worth date. Your checking account balance is your bank balance for that day less outstanding checks plus any deposits not yet recorded on your monthly statement. In other words, in computing net worth, balance your checkbook to December 31, the cutoff date. (We assume you are not doing the actual work on December 31!) If the January rent is due on January 1, it makes no difference to your calculations. It is *not* due on December 31. Observe this consistently.

Similarly, enter your savings bank balance *with interest credited through December 31*. If you have not had the interest credited for the last quarter of the year, estimate it. (You should have the interest owed you credited to your savings bank book(s) at least once a year.)

Cash in two-year time deposits can be counted with cash in your savings accounts even though you would forfeit some interest through premature withdrawal. Certain securities which are readily converted into cash (such as U.S. savings bonds and certain other federal and state bonds) should not be included with cash. They are better shown as marketable securities.

If the cash in your safe deposit box exceeds $100, list it. Also list cash in the house which exceeds $100. If you are holding cash for anyone else in your safe deposit box make certain that all such currency is in a separate envelope clearly marked with the owner's name. If you and your spouse keep personal monies separately in a joint box, mark these as well. Otherwise, in the event of a death, the tax authorities simply assume that any and all cash found in the box belongs to the deceased.

The following (page 23) is a cash schedule for the Smiths.

Due from Stockbroker

If at the end of the year your stockbroker owes you money for stock that has been sold or dividends that have not be remitted, you have an asset due from the stockbroker. On the other hand, if you maintain a margin account, in which the stockbroker lends you money against the value of your securities, you have a liability due to the stockbroker.

Brokerage account balances in a net worth statement are shown on the worksheet on page 24.

	1	2	3	4
Checking Accounts:				
Chemical Bank				
# 019-2028 65 (Daniel)			1156	
# 019-2084 13 (Louise)		211		
Cash in Checking Accounts				1367
Savings Accounts:				
Union Dime Savings Bank (Regular)				
# 295294-27 (Daniel)			2704	
# 293778-27 (Louise)			2654	
Manhattan Savings Bank (2 year)				
# 8-8-2676 63 (Louise)				
Balance per book 10/1/78	5253			
Add: 4th Quarter				
Interest not entered		88		
12/31/78 Balance			5341	
Cash in Savings Accounts				10699
Cash on hand (less than 100)				-0-
Total Cash				12066

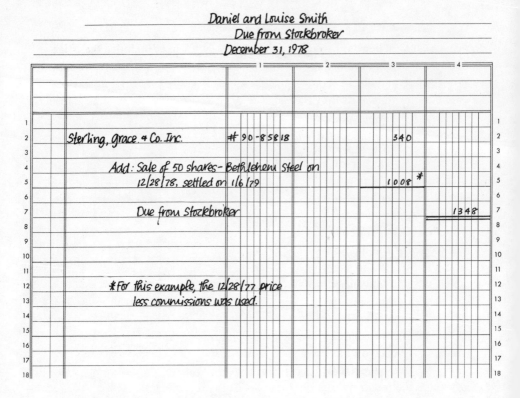

Daniel and Louise Smith
Due from Stockbroker
December 31, 1978

	1	2	3	4
Sterling, Grace & Co. Inc. #90-85818			340	
Add: Sale of 50 shares- Bethlehem Steel on				
12/28/78, settled on 1/6/79			1008 *	
Due from Stockbroker				1348
*For this example, the 12/28/77 price				
less commissions was used.				

Marketable and Restricted Securities

Securities are either *marketable* or *restricted*. Marketable securities may be sold through an exchange. Those which cannot be sold in this way are considered to have a restricted marketability. You should decide whether or not to list restricted securities in your net worth according to whether or not there is a future market for them. For example, you may own securities in a family business. These may be valuable even if you cannot sell them without a great deal of difficulty (such as obtaining specified agreements of the other parties involved). In such an instance you should list such securities as having a low priority among your assets.

Marketable securities are in the form of stocks, bonds, options, warrants, or convertible debentures. These are readily convertible into cash and may be sold on an exchange or through a stockbroker. U.S. Savings Bonds are also marketable securities and are redeemable at a bank. Thus, for purposes of net worth, include such bonds under marketable securities, although it is not necessary to update the interest being earned. The Treasury Department issues tables at banks, giving redemption values for Series E,F,G,J,K, and Freedom Shares at varying stages of maturity.

PURCHASES. When you purchase a security, your cost includes the price of the stock plus the broker's commission. When you purchase a bond, you do not include in the cost any amount that you pay for interest because the purchase usually takes place between interest dates. The interest you pay is subtracted from the first interest coupon you collect.

GIFTS. If you receive stock as a gift, it is generally valued at the cost of the stock to the person who gave it to you (the donor) plus any gift tax that may have been paid. The gift tax must not bring the cost to more than the fair market value of the security on the date on which you receive it. Even though you receive the stock as a gift and use the donor's cost on your net worth statement, you should also keep a record of the fair market value for the date on which you received the gift. This is necessary if you should sell the security at a loss. (The IRS requires that you use as your cost whichever figure is lower.)

Let's say that your uncle gave you 100 shares of Amalgamated Widget for a wedding gift. He told you that his shares cost him $800. At the date he gave you the shares, the fair market value was $750. If you sell the stock for $900, you have a gain of $100 ($900-$800). If you sell the stock for $700, you have a $50 loss for tax purposes ($750-$700). Since there is a loss, use the lower figure, whether it is the donor's cost or the fair market value, on the date of the gift. For your final net worth, convert the amount to fair market value.

INHERITED SECURITIES. Your cost for inherited securities is the value shown on the estate tax return of the deceased. For persons dying after 1979, the rule is different (See ESTATE PLANNING, page 155).

OTHER. A corporation may send you additional stock certificates, which is known as a stock dividend or a stock split. The corporation will usually notify you as to the tax consequence of receiving these additional certificates. In most cases, the exchange is tax-free so you would carry these additional shares in your net worth at cost. For example, you purchased 100 shares of Sweeney Todd Safety Razor Ltd. at $10 per share plus commission five years ago for a total price of $1,010. This year the company split its stock at 2 for 1 and you received 100 shares. On December 31 you own 200 shares, but your cost is still $1,010.

You convert your marketable securities into their value at the net worth date by an adjustment to your net worth.

In computing the value of securities you may use either the closing price as of December 31 or the mean price. The mean price is the high

Daniel and Louise Smith
Securities
December 31, 1978

No. of shares or par	Description	Date Acquired	Cost	Market Price *	Market Value
	Marketable Securities:				
300	Financial General Bankshares, Inc. Class A	11/23/77	2679	9.9375	2981
25	Mobil Corp.	12/27/74	916	63.6875	1592
50	National Distillers & Chemical Corp.	12/27/74	702	20.8125	1041
37	St. Regis Paper Company				
	Bought 25				
	Split 12/12/73 12				
	Total Shares 37	9/26/73	1222	30.5625	1131
75	U.S. Gypsum Company	11/25/75	1314	22.0625	1655
	Total Marketable Stocks		6833		8400
5 M	U.S. Savings Bonds Series E	12/15/65	3750	1464	7320
	Total Marketable Securities		10583		15720
	Restricted Securities				
10 00	Hopeful Manufacturing Corp.	9/15/75	10000	N/A	10000

* Mean prices of 12/30/77 used for stocks;
table of June, 1978 adjusted for estimated
increase to December, 1978 used for "E" bonds; and
cost of restricted stock used since market value
was not available (N/A).

26

plus the low for the last trading date in December divided by two. For example, a newspaper listing of your stock on December 31, 1978 might look like this:

	HIGH	LOW	CLOSE
Beefsteak Mines	63¾	63¼	63⅝

The closing price would be 63⅝, but the mean price would be 63¾ + 63¼ = 127 ÷ 2 = 63½. It is not important whether you use the mean price or the closing price. The fair market value is technically based upon the mean price. (Always save the first copy of the newspaper of the new year which shows the closing prices at December 31.)

The worksheet on page 26 shows how to list securities.

Mortgages Receivable

If you sell a piece of real estate and do not receive in cash the sales price minus the existing mortgage, you are said to be in receipt of a purchase-money mortgage. That mortgage is a *mortgage receivable*. You could also own a mortgage receivable by buying it from someone who already has a mortgage or by lending money and receiving a mortgage on a piece of real estate as security for the debt.

There are special tax rules for reporting profit from the sale of real estate. When you receive 30% or less of the selling price within one year, you may elect to report your sale on the installment method. This method allows you to include a portion of the gain in your income tax return spread over the period of the mortgage.

The installment method is applicable only to gains (profit) and never to losses. The gain from the casual sale of personal property over $1,000 paid to you by installments may also be reported for tax purposes on the installment method. For example, on September 15, 1975, Mr. Smith sold a piece of vacant land for $45,000. On the sale he paid commissions, legal fees, and other expenses totalling $2,500. When he inherited the land in 1965, it had a tax basis of $27,500. At the time he sold the land, he owed $17,000 on a first mortgage which he had taken out on his land. The buyer agreed to assume the first mortgage at the closing. The $28,000 balance owed Mr. Smith ($45,000-$17,000) was payable by the buyer as follows: $6,000 in 1975 (the year of the sale) and the remaining $22,000 over the next five years.

Payments	Due date	Date paid	Total Payment	Interest	Principal	Balance
	9/15/75					22000
1	3/15/76	3/11/76	3080	880	2200	19800
2	9/15/76	9/12/76	2992	792	2200	17600
3	3/15/77	3/10/77	2904	704	2200	15400
4	9/15/77	9/12/77	2816	616	2200	13200
5	3/15/78	3/8/78	2758	528	2200	11000
6	9/15/78	9/6/78	2640	440	2200	8800
7	3/15/79					
8	9/15/79					
9	3/15/80					
10	9/15/80					

Mortgage dated 9/15/75, due 9/15/80; interest 8%:

Terms of Sale - 9/15/75

Sales price			45000
Less, cost	12/15/70	27500	
Add, Expenses of sale- commissions, attorney's fees and other expenses		2500	
Total cost			30000
gain on sale			15000

Settlement:

Mortgage Assumed by Buyer	17000
Cash at Closing	6000
Purchase Money Mortgage	22000
Sales price	45000

Contract Price (Cash to Be Collected) — 28000

Gross Profit Percentage (gain and cash to be collected; 15000 ÷ 28000) — 54 %

Note: If mortgage assumed by buyer exceeds cost, excess is considered cash received in year of sale.

28

The unreported profit for tax purposes called *Deferred Gain on Install-ment Sale* is treated as a separate item. It is segregated from Net Worth under Liabilities. The computations are part of the mortgage receivable work paper.

At December 31, 1978, the Smiths reflected the transaction as follows:

		Year	Collection (100%)	Gain (54%)	Gain Remaining
Mortgage payments are taxed:					
(Deferred gain on sale)					
At Date of Sale		1975			15000
		1975	6000	3240	11760
		1976	4400	2376	9384
		1977	4400	2376	7008
		1978	4400	2376	4632
		1979			
		1980			

Loans Receivable

Moneys owed to you by friends or relatives and not secured by any for-mal agreement are shown as *loans receivable*. If there is a reasonably good chance of collecting on these loans, you should carry them on your net worth. Do not confuse loans receivable with accounts receivable. *Ac-counts receivable* are amounts owed to you by customers or clients for goods and/or services.

The following worksheet shows how to record loans receivable.

Borrower	Date of Loan	Due Date	Interest %	Amount of Loan
Wayne Danson	7/1/76	Demand	6%	2000
Ellen Emory	10/15/78	10/15/79	None	1200
Total Loans Receivable				3200

Prepaid Interest

Prepaid interest is interest paid in advance and is an asset, even though it cannot be converted into cash. You should show it as an asset because it represents an expense you will not have to pay in future years.

Discount on bank loans is considered prepaid interest. Suppose, for example, that you borrow $7,000 from the bank but have to pay back in installments $7,500. The $500 difference is the discount. When preparing your net worth statement, you would show a total liability of $7,500, which also includes the interest factor the $500 difference between what you borrowed and what you owe.

The prepaid interest ($500) on such a loan is reduced over the period of the loan. Suppose that the $7,000 you borrowed was taken in May with the term of the loan being one year. If you made a payment each month, you could simply reduce the prepaid interest by one-twelfth. Having taken the loan in May and preparing your statement as of December 31 of that same year, you have made seven monthly payments with five remaining as prepaid on December 31. Your prepaid interest at that date is $208, which you calculate by dividing $500 by the twelve months of the loan and multiplying by the remaining five months.

The Smith family borrowed money to purchase cars. They show their prepaid interest on their net worth statement on page 31:

Individual Retirement Arrangement (IRA) and Employer Pension Plan

Your Individual Retirement Arrangement (IRA) is readily available as cash, though there are tax penalties for the premature use of this money. When you enter these retirement funds in your net worth, be sure to include your current year's contribution as well as the earnings. Self-employed plans (HR-10) are also part of your net worth.

Most of the financial institutions which deal with pension plans will supply you with a statement of the value of your account as of the end of each year. If you have not received this statement by the time you are ready to compute your net worth, you may use your last year's balance plus your current year's contribution and an approximate earnings factor.

If, under the terms of your employer's plan you have vested rights (i.e., if you will receive a cash or insurance benefit at anytime you leave) count this as part of your net worth and include it in your net worth computation. If the end of your employer's plan year is not December 31, you may still use the figure submitted to you by the administrator of the plan at its year end.

	1	2	3	4
Citibank				
Loan to purchase Ford Station Wagon – 36 months				
4/4/77 Amount financed			3500	
Finance charges (13.38%)			769	
Amount of loan			4269	
(Monthly payment 118 57)				
Finance charges				769
Straight line amortization				
Finance charge ÷ 36 months				
769 ÷	36			
Amount of monthly write off			21	
	Months	Writeoff		
Year	Paid	for year		
1977	8	168		
1978	12	252		
Writeoff to 12/31/78				420
Prepaid Interest				349
GMAC				
Loan to purchase Oldsmobile Delta 88 – 36 months				
10/5/78 Amount financed			4000	
Finance charges (12.83%)			903	
Amount of loan			4903	
(Monthly payment 136 20)				
Finance charges				903
Straight line amortization				
Finance charge ÷ 36 months				
903 ÷	36			
Amount of monthly writeoff			25	
	Months	Writeoff		
Year	Paid	for year		
1978	2	50		50
Prepaid Interest				853
Total Prepaid Interest – 12/31/78				1202

An Individual Retirement Arrangement and an Employer Pension Plan are accounted for in the net worth statement as follows:

Daniel and Louise Smith
Retirement Plans
December 31, 1978

			1	2	3	4
1	Individual Retirement Arrangement (Wife)					
3	Manufacturers Hanover Trust Co.					
4	As per IRS form 5498					
6	Total value at beginning of 1978				4825	
8	Contributions for 1978				1500	
10	Earnings in 1978				334	
12	Total value – 12/31/78					6659
15	Employer Pension Plan (Husband)					
17	Money purchase plan					
18	totally vested					
20	Value of account per					
21	administrator's statement –					
22	12/31/77				18235	
24	Contribution for 1978 (6% salary)				1500	
26	1978 net earnings				1194	
28	Total value per statement – 12/31/78					20929

Life Insurance (Cash-surrender Value)

Ordinary life insurance policies have a cash-surrender value. This is the amount you would receive if you were to cash in your policy at a particular time. If you have been borrowing on your life insurance, you should consider the value of your policy to be its cash-surrender value minus any loans owed on it.

When you examine your policy, you will find a schedule showing the cash value for each $1,000 of face value after each year. For example, a $50,000 policy issued to a 38-year-old male under a typical cash-value schedule would be worth $9,800 on the tenth anniversary of issue ($196 per $1000 × 50). If you borrow against your policy to pay current premiums, your life insurance agent should be able to supply you with the after-premium net values.

Although the anniversary date of your insurance policy will probably not coincide with your calendar-year date for computing your net worth, you may use the value of your policy after payment of your last premium for purposes of computing your net worth.

Term insurance and employee group life insurance do not have value for net worth computations since these types of coverage have no cash-surrender value. Nevertheless, these policies should be entered on your schedule of insurance and carried at zero value. This is done in order to maintain a complete record of your assets.

Show your insurance policies on your net worth statement in the following way as shown on pages 34 and 35:

Automobiles

Your automobile should be entered on your net worth statement at cost. Later, you will convert it to fair market value.

If you traded in an automobile when you bought your present one, estimate the value of the old vehicle and add the trade-in value to your cost. If you are unable to judge the trade-in value, ask your dealer or look in the automobile-sales section of your local paper. Find the approximate model and year of your old car and use as its cost 75% of the advertised price of a comparable car. (Include under automobiles the cost of any motorcycles, motor scooters, mopeds, or tractors.)

If, at the time you purchased your automobile, you treated the sales tax as a separate itemized deduction on your income tax return, you should not include the sales tax as part of the cost of the car. If you use your au-

	1	2	3	4
				Net Equity
1) Canada Life				
Policy #		N1 357281		
Issued		11/20/68		
Insured		Daniel		
Owner		Louise		
Face Value		50000		
Minimum Payment				
Premium		791		
Interest paid on loan		5%		
Dividends purchase term				
insurance to cover loan				
Maximum loan				
Cash Value - 12/31/78			9119	
Loans Payable			8663	
Net Equity				456
2) Mutual of New York				
Policy #		901-05-29		
Issued		6/15/73		
Insured		Daniel		
Owner		Louise		
Face Value		50000		
Minimum Payment				
Premium		1086		
Interest paid on loan		5%		
Dividends purchase term				
insurance to cover loan				
Maximum loan				
Cash Value - 12/31/78			4095	
Loans Payable			2666	
Net Equity				1429
Subtotal (forward)				1885

34

Daniel and Louise Smith
Schedule of Life Insurance
December 31, 1978

					1	2	3	4	
								Net Equity	
1		Subtotal (forward)						1885	1
2									2
3		3) New England Mutual Life Insurance							3
4									4
5		Group Policy #		GSP		21723			5
6									6
7		Issued				10 1 1 76			7
8									8
9		Insured			Daniel				9
10		group Policy assigned to			Louise			.	10
11									11
12		Face Value				50000			12
13									13
14		No cash value						-0-	14
15									15
16		Total Equity						1885	16

tomobile partly for business and partly for pleasure, your net worth statement should show your car at cost, less whatever depreciation you have claimed on your tax return. If you have adopted the standard mileage rate for your business car on your tax return, you will not be required to reduce your cost by depreciation unless you change your method of computation. Once you adopt the standard mileage method for taxation, you should not change to actual expenses without professional advice.

Automobiles, depreciate in value over a period of time. In computing the fair market value of your automobile, you may use either comparable sales prices from the newspaper or your original cost, depreciating the value by a formula. One suggested formula consists of immediately reducing the cost of your car by 20% for dealer mark-up and depreciating the remaining 80% over a 48-month period (1.67% per month or 20% per year).

For example, the Smiths' automobile, purchased April 4, 1977, for $5,250 under this formula would be worth on December 31, 1978:

Cost		$5,250
Minus 20% markdown	$1,050	
Write-off to 12/31/78		
(21 months × 1.67% ×		
$5,250)	1,841	
Total depreciation		2,891
Fair Market Value		$2,359

The Smiths' other automobile, bought October 5, 1978, would be worth on December 31, 1978:

Cost		$6,000
Minus 20% markdown	$1,200	
Write-off to 12/31/78		
(3 months × 1.67% ×	301	
$6,000)		
Total depreciation		1,501
Fair Market Value		4,499
Total Value of Automobiles		$6,858

Automobiles are shown on the net worth statement as follows:

Daniel and Louise Smith
Automobiles
December 31, 1978

				1	2	3	4
1)	1977	Ford LTD II	Squire Station Wagon				
		Purchased			4/4/77		
		Dealer			gotham ford		
		Cost (Excluding sales tax)					5250
2)	1979	Oldsmobile Delta 88 Sedan					
		Purchased			10/5/78		
		Dealer			Crest Olds		
		Cost (Excluding sales tax)					6000
		Total Cost of Automobiles – 12/31/78					11250

Furnishings

Under furnishings, you should include not only furniture in the various rooms of your home, but also your stereo equipment, television sets, and typewriter. Draperies, easily removable lighting fixtures, and wall shelving which is not built-in may also be considered furnishings. It is not necessary to account for furnishings which cost less than $100 including sales tax.

If in a single year you redecorate your home and enter the sales tax as a separate item on your tax return, you should not consider the sales tax as part of the cost of the furniture. On the other hand, if you itemize your deductions and you claim your sales taxes based upon the IRS chart, you should include sales taxes as part of the cost of your furnishings.

Note: A list of furnishings is essential in case of theft, fire, or casualty. Such a schedule will be of considerable assistance in proving the claim with your insurance company as well as with the IRS. (In case of a casualty loss, a detailed schedule of your furnishings, even without the bills, will generally be given evidentiary weight by an IRS examining officer.)

A schedule for listing furnishings follows on page 39.

Appliances

Consider as an appliance any piece of equipment which is relatively easy to disconnect from a power source. If a device operates by electricity, gas, or oil and can be completely removed from its fittings within a half-hour, you may consider it an appliance. (Ordinarily, your oil burner or gas furnance is considered a home improvement and should not be listed with appliances.)

If your refrigerator, stove, dishwasher, and other appliances were included in the purchase price of your home you should list the costs of these separately and reduce the cost of your home by their total cost. Although a television or a stereo might seem to fit the definition of an appliance, these items should be included with furnishings, as should a typewriter.

Appliances are shown as follows on page 40.

Real Estate

Real estate may consist of a principal residence, a vacation home, or land and buildings owned for investment or business.

	Description	Vendor	Date Purchased	Cost
Garden				
	Lawn furniture	Sears	7/31/74	422
Living Room				
	Sofa	W.-J. Sloanes	8/10/74	650
	2 Lounge chairs	Gimbels	8/15/74	310
	Coffee table	R.H. Macy	8/17/74	185
	Paintings	C Ree - Co.	10/12/74	273
	Draperies and shades	R. Walters	12/16/74	415
	Wall unit	Frankart	1/10/75	240
	Pioneer stereo	Grand Central	5/9/75	315
	Rug	R.H. Macy	6/10/75	450
	Miscellaneous	Various	estimated	400
	Total Living Room			3238
Foyer				
	Consul table	Village Antiques	1/18/76	245
	Indian rug	Lord - Taylor	1/18/76	346
	Lamps	Bowery Lighting	2/17/76	122
	Total Foyer			713
Master Bedroom				
	King-size bed and board	Head Bed	10/10/74	356
	Chest (2)	Gimbels	1/10/75	420
	Night stands	Sachs	1/17/75	460
	Dressing table	Sachs	1/17/75	255
	Chair + ottoman	R.H. Macy	2/18/75	225
	Lamps	R.H. Macy	2/18/75	198
	Draperies and shades	R. Walters	4/9/75	380
	Zenith TV set	Crazy Eddies	9/24/76	358
	Carpet	Allen Carpet	4/15/75	372
	Betamax VCR	Barco Business Machines	12/23/77	950
	Total Master Bedroom			3974
	Total Furnishings - 12/31/78			10847

		Description		Vendor	Date Purchased	Cost
	1.	GE Refrigerator Model TFF 24 RV		Hampton Sales	7/20/74	808
	2.	Magic Chef 5-Burner gas Range		RH Macy	7/25/74	230
	3.	Kitchen-Aid Dishwasher		Hampton Sales	9/30/74	310
	4.	Kenmore garbage Compactor		Sears	10/15/74	225
	5.	GE. garbage Disposal		Korvettes	12/14/74	152
	6.	GE gas Dryer Model DDE 7200 N		Gimbels	2/15/75	195
	7.	GE Clothes Washer Model WWA-8420 N		Gimbels	2/15/75	269
	8.	Excellence chest Freezer		RH Macy's	2/22/75	170
	9.	Hoover Vacuum Cleaner Model Celebrity II		Korvettes	5/10/76	168
		Total Cost of Appliances – 12/31/78				2527

If you own land, you are said to have a *fee interest* in the real estate. This means that the property is yours against all persons and that you have a right to transfer the land forever. If you do not own the land but own a building on leased land, you have a *leasehold interest*. Any buildings which you erect on the property usually revert at the end of the lease term to the owner of the land at that time. The party who pays the rent is the *lessee* and the one who collects it is the *lessor*.

Buildings are termed "improvements to land." If you erect a building on someone else's land, the building is a *leasehold improvement*. Such improvements, which may not be readily converted to cash, are nevertheless part of your net worth. (Real estate may consist of land with or without improvements.)

For purposes of net worth, your residence should be carried at the price you originally paid for it plus improvements. Later, you would convert it to fair market value. If you constructed your own home, you should include in its cost all items except those that may be easily removable.

A mortgage is a lien on real estate. In computing your net worth, deduct any mortgages directly from the total value of the real estate. Mortgages may be self-liquidating or they may have a "balloon" at their due date. These are discussed in detail in the chapter on Real Estate.

Note: The Financial Publishing Co., 82 Brookline Avenue, Boston, Massachusetts 02215, will supply you with a schedule of mortgage balances, principal, and interest charges. This amortization schedule would help you in calculating your net worth and in preparing your tax return.

IMPROVEMENTS. Improvements are capital expenditures incurred after purchasing real estate. An improvement adds to the value of the property or extends its life. Improvements should not be confused with repairs. Changing the plumbing system of your house is an improvement, but repairing damaged pipes is not. A new bathroom or driveway is an improvement, as are extensive remodeling, landscaping, fencing, paneling, or room extensions. Treat local assessments for sidewalks, streets, or sewers as improvements. If you are in doubt, treat the item as an *improvement*.

If you sell your home, you will find it advisable (especially if you make a substantial profit) to put the question of improvements vs repairs into the hands of a professional. The tax regulations are so intricate that you should not try to unravel them yourself. If you supply such an adviser with your schedule of costs, he or she should be able to determine fairly easily the acceptability of your accounting for tax purposes. Keep these records on a chronological basis. Whether or not an item is properly capitalized is not as important as the consistency of your treatment of it.

The workpaper on page 42 shows the Smiths' equity in their residence at December 31, 1978.

THE VACATION HOME. In computing your net worth, treat your vacation home in the same way you treat your principal residence. Adjust your net worth to conform with your tax return. For example, if you rent out your vacation home for 14 days or less during the year, you do not have to

	1	2	3	4
Residence – 72 Elm Street				
Anytown, N.Y.				
Purchased – 7/15/74				
Purchase price			72500	
Legal fee to William Black, Esq.			500	
Security Title Company – Title				
insurance, search, mortgage				
tax, and recording of deed				
and mortgage			544	
Preparation of mortgage – legal			75	
Title Company closer			35	
Cost of Residence				73654
Improvements				

Date	Vendor	Description	Amount	
8/21/74	A. Bainter	Painting	2400	
12/3/74	Siebert Electric	Electrical work	468	
12/10/74	Wm. Hoffman	New gutter & labor	265	
1/17/75	S. Abbruzzi	Storm windows	1210	
4/9/75	Mayrin Paving	Asphalt paving	219	
4/23/77	Pelham Lumber	Material for porch	227	
5/22/77	P.H. D'Angelis	Porch construction	538	

	1	2	3	4
Total Improvements				6827
Total Cost of Residence – 12/31/78				80481
Less, mortgage payments				
Union Dime Savings Bank				
8½% interest; due in 25 years				
payable monthly by 15th		44287		
original mortgage (7/15/74)		55000		
Mortgage Balance – 12/31/78				51587
Equity in Residence – 12/31/78				28894

42

Daniel and Louise Smith
Vacation Home
December 31, 1978

		1	2	3	4
Vacation Home					
	Vermont				
Purchase price	12/13/73 (includes legal + other costs)				
	Land			7500	
	Building (includes furnishings)			25000	
	Total cost				32500
Add: Improvements					-0-
	Total cost – 12/31/78				32500
Less, Depreciation claimed for Taxes:					
	Cost of Building		25000		
	Life		25 years		
	Method		Straight Line		
	Annual Depreciation		1000		
	1974			1000	
	1975			1000	
	1976			1000	
	1977			1000	
	1978			1000	
	Total Depreciation Claimed				5000
Tax Basis of Vacation Home – 12/31/78					27500
Less, Mortgage Payable					
	Bellows Lake Trust Company				
	7⅛% interest; due in 25 years				
	Payable Quarterly				
	1/15, 4/15, 7/15, 10/15			577 63	
	Original Mortgage (12/13/73)		26000		
	Mortgage Balance – 12/31/78				23837
	Equity in Vacation Home – 12/31/78				3663

43

make any adjustments to the cost of your vacation home; and you are not required to report the rent received as income for tax purposes. In this case, no deductions are allowed other than the itemized deductions for interest, taxes, and casualty losses.

The Smiths do not use their vacation home personally. It was purchased as an investment. It appears on their net worth statement on page 43 (to simplify, the furnishings were not allocated separately).

TOOLS. For the average person tools do nor represent a substantial item of net worth. In general, ignore tools worth less than $100, but include under *appliances* such tools as power saws, drills, and landscaping machinery. If you are engaged in a business operation in which you do maintain and use expensive tools, include these as a separate asset and reduce their worth by whatever depreciation you claim for tax purposes.

Miscellaneous Assets.

You may possess miscellaneous assets that are convertible to money but which do not immediately come to mind. Your statement should reflect business investments, trust interests, security deposits, insurance claims, and other assets.

BUSINESS INVESTMENTS. The value of your personally owned business interests and partnership interests is part of your net worth. Starting with the book value of these interests, you would convert them to fair market value by adding appreciation of assets or by reducing for depreciation. In the event there is goodwill, you may need professional advice in order to compute the value properly.

TRUST ASSETS. Trusts are complex legal entities which will be discussed in detail under Estate Planning. We assume that if you are a beneficiary or remainderman of a trust that you will already have some sense of the trust. The income (life) interest and the remainder interest of a trust have ascertainable values. Imagine, for example, a trust with a corpus of marketable securities with a fair market value on December 31, 1978 of $30,000. If we use the IRS gift-tax tables computed at a 6% rate, the value of a life interest in that trust for a 35-year-old female would be about $26,300, with a remainder interest worth about $3,700. For a male life tenant of 35 the life interest would be about $25,000, with a remainder interest worth $5,000. If you have an interest in such a trust, use the IRS tables available from any local IRS office.

SECURITY DEPOSITS. You have probably advanced money to your landlord, the telephone company, or a utility company as security deposits. These should be included in your net worth. In many states, such deposits earn interest, and the party holding the deposit is required to pay you the interest annually. Public utilities usually refund security deposits once you have established a record of prompt payment over a certain period.

A rent deposit returnable at the end of your lease is an asset. Include this in your net worth statement even if your landlord has the option of applying your deposit to the last month of rent. Most leases provide for the return of the deposit to avoid an adverse tax effect on the landlord.

INSURANCE CLAIMS. Insurance companies frequently take a long time to settle property damage and personal injury claims. These claims are assets. If you have a pending claim which will be settled for the calendar date of your net worth statement, make a *reasonable* estimate of the amount you hope to recover. Err on the side of conservatism in this.

OTHER ASSETS. If you have a collection of coins or stamps and think that it may be of serious value, have it appraised by a reputable appraiser. If the collection is not insured, such an appraisal may be your only proof of ownership in case of casualty losses such as fire, theft, or flood. A complete loss is limited to the extent of your cost for tax purposes. Once you have had an appraisal made, carry new additons to the collection at cost.

Do not overlook any possession that may be of value in a compilation of net worth: this includes jewelry, works of art, old or rare books, patents, and copyrights. If you are uncertain as to how to estimate the value of any property for net worth purposes, ask yourself these questions:

If I were under no compulsion to sell this property, what might a willing buyer pay me for this? If I had a year in which to sell this property, what is the maximum amount I could obtain for it?

Jewelry		
Engagement Ring, Acquired June, 1966	1000	
Watch and Bracelet, Acquired Sept. 1977	415	
Total Miscellaneous Assets – 12/31/78		1415

LIABILITIES

Liabilities are debts owed at the date of your net worth statement. They include mortgages, notes payable, loans payable, money due credit card companies, money due for miscellaneous bills, and taxes payable.

Mortgages Payable

For the average American, the mortgage is usually the most substantial liability. A mortgage is a lien on your property held by the person or institution who lent you the money to buy it. Of course, after you buy real estate you can refinance the old mortgage or acquire a new one. When a mortgage is recorded at the county clerk's office, it puts on record that claim or lien against the property. As the borrower, you also sign a note acknowledging the liability. The note is the debt on the property, and the mortage the lien. A mortgage on your real estate reduces the amount of the property's value that you can claim as an asset.

Mortgages can be held on properties other than real estate. If you buy a car on the installment plan, the lender has probably recorded a chattel mortgage against the car. In this case, however, treat the chattel mortgage as part of notes payable, a separate category on your net worth statement.

The mortgages directly reduce the value of the real estate and are included on the real estate workpapers.

Notes Payable

A *note* is a promissory agreement usually between two parties, the maker and the payee. The *maker* is the person who borrows the money and, as evidence of the debt to the payee, executes the note. A *guarantor* pledges to the payee that if the maker fails to pay the debt the guarantor will pay it. A *co-signer* or *co-maker* of a note is a guarantor. An *endorser* of a note is another party to the note. When you cash your paycheck at the supermarket, you, the payee, sign your name on the back of the check. When the supermarket signs its name below yours on the back of the check, it becomes the endorser.

If you owe money on your automobile or have borrowed from a bank by signing a note, you have a liability for notes payable. You do not offset your note on the automobile directly against the asset, because you are personally liable on the note. On the other hand, on your residence mortgage there is little chance that the value of the property will be less than the mortgage. In most cases, the mortgagee does not seek to collect the

		1	2	3	4

Citibank

4/4/77 - Loan to Purchase Ford Station Wagon

Terms:

Months		36	
Annual Percentage Rate		13.38%	
Monthly Payment		118 57	
Amount Financed		3500	
Finance Charges		769	
Amount of Loan			4269
Paid:			
1977	8 months x 118 57	949	
1978	12 months x 118 57	1423	
	Total Paid		2372
	Balance Due - 12/31/78		1897

GMAC

10/5/78 - Loan to Purchase Oldsmobile 88

Terms:

Months		36	
Annual Percentage Rate		12.83%	
Monthly Payment		136 20	
Amount Financed		4000	
Finance charges		903	
Amount of Loan			4903
Paid:			
1978	2 months x 136 20		272
	Balance Due - 12/31/78		4631
Total Notes Payable - 12/31/78			6528

47

excess due him or her over what your residence would bring at a foreclosure (auction) sale.

Caution: If you are a guarantor of a note, you have an obligation to repay it if the payee is unable to collect the debt from the maker. Thus, acting as a guarantor of another's debt is a serious undertaking. Under the terms of the debt, the payee may not be required to press the maker for the money, but could, without any delay, begin collection proceedings against you.

The Smiths owe money on both of their automobiles. They executed notes which are reflected on their net worth statement on page 47.

Loans Payable

Loans payable are debts owed by you for moneys borrowed. These loans are not evidenced by notes and therefore are carried as separate debts.

Due to Credit Card Companies

At your net worth date, include among your liabilities the amounts due to credit card companies. Include not only the unpaid bills, but also the total amount of the charge tickets that have not yet been billed.

The Smiths' unpaid credit card charges at December 31, 1978 are shown as follows:

Credit Card	Date of Bill		Amount
American Express	12/26/78	68	
Charged & unbilled		34	102
Master Charge	12/27/78	76	
Charged & unbilled		31	107
Mobil	12/21/78	123	
charged & unbilled		27	150
Total Due Credit Card Companies – 12/31/78			359

Due for Miscellaneous Bills

On your net worth date, you will possibly owe money for fuel, tuition, utilities, and the like. Using the previous month's bills as a base, prepare a realistic total of your debts. The Smiths show their unpaid bills this way:

Daniel and Louise Smith
Due for Miscellaneous Bills
December 31, 1978

Vendor	Date of Bill		Amount
N.Y. Telephone			
unbilled 12/5/78 - 12/31/78	Estimate		40
Con Edison			
unbilled 12/8/78 - 12/31/78	Estimate		60
Lord & Taylor	12/22/78	48	
Charged & unbilled		53	101
B. Altman & Co.			
Charged & unbilled			39
Bloomingdale's			
charged & unbilled			42
Exxon			
Charged & unbilled			61
Total Due for Miscellaneous Bills - 12/31/78			343

Taxes Payable

You may owe for income taxes, real estate taxes, and personal property taxes on the net worth date. These taxes may be assessed or may be due for underpayment of estimated taxes. "Assessed" means that you have received notice that there is a tax due but you have delayed the payment.

If you have outside income and have not paid sufficient estimated income taxes, set up an *estimated liability*. The theory is that you have had the cash available from the extra income. Therefore, set up the liability. This liability should not be set up unless it is in excess of $100.

To do this calculation, estimate your tax bracket and apply the bracket to that part of the income on which you did not pay estimated tax. For example, you received $3,000 income from your late mother's estate. You have been notified that you must report this income on your current year's return, but you made no estimated payment on this income. Last year your federal tax bracket was 25% and your state bracket was 6%. By multiplying $3,000 by 31% (25% + 6%), $333 is a fair estimate of the liability you will have to pay at the next filing date. Caution: Since your state tax is a deduction on your federal tax return if you itemize your deductions, the effective rate of tax is computed as follows:

Federal tax bracket	25%	
State tax bracket	6%	
		31%
Minus tax benefit for state taxes as a deduction on federal return (25% × 6%)		1.5%
Effective Tax Bracket		29.5%

Remember, the exactness of your estimate is not as important as the concept to understand that there is tax owed on the money in the bank and this tax should be considered a liability.

If, as the result of a prior year's IRS audit, you owe additional tax that has not been paid by the net worth date, you should set up the liability together with the interest for the amount owed.

DEFERRED GAIN ON INSTALLMENT SALE

The deferred gain on the installment sale of land is a segregation of net worth for profits not as yet realized. See *Mortgage Receivable*.

THE NET WORTH STATEMENT

After you have completed all of the individual schedules which realistically pertain to your assets and liabilities, you are ready to transfer this data to your net worth statement.

After the Smiths prepared their schedules of assets and liabilities, their net worth as of December 31, 1978 looked like this (see page 52).

CONVERTING NET WORTH TO FAIR MARKET VALUE

After you have completed your net worth statement, you should prepare a separate computation converting the net worth statement from historical cost (what you originally paid for certain items) to their fair market value (what they are currently worth).

In general, you need to convert only your home, real estate, automobiles, and marketable securities. If, however, you think that it is applicable, you can convert any other item to market value by entering the difference between its historical cost and what you realistically believe the item to be worth as of the date of your statement. (Notice, for example, that the net worth statement shows marketable securities at cost; the schedule also contains the market value of the securities as of December 31.)

The conversion to fair market value need not be excessively exact unless you are planning something very specific. To convert your home to its fair market value for general purposes, be guided by the price of comparable homes in your immediate area. (Unless you are in the market to sell your house, an exact figure is not necessary.)

The Smiths' assets adjusted to fair market value are on page 53.

COMPARATIVE NET WORTH STATEMENTS

Your net worth statement for any given year shows your fund of wealth at a specific date. If it is done on a one-time basis, it may have value for you in forcing you to a greater awareness and realism regarding your money. Such statements disclose their real value, however, when they are used comparatively. In this way, you discover whether you are progressing, standing still, or falling behind financially. The remainder of this book will deal with reasonable courses of action that you may take on the basis of the information you have now gathered. You may at first be depressed by what you have discovered because you may never before have had a realistic approach to your money. Don't jump to conclusions too soon. Above all, *don't become pessimistic*.

Daniel and Louise Smith
Net Worth
December 31, 1978

Assets

	1	2	3	4
cash				12066
Due from stockbroker				1348
Marketable securities				10583
Mortgage receivable				8800
Loans receivable				3200
Prepaid interest				1202
Individual retirement arrangement				6659
Employer pension plan				20929
Cash surrender value- life insurance			13214	
less, loans payable			11329	1885
Automobiles			11250	
less, notes payable			6528	4722
Furnishings				10847
Appliances				2527
Residence – cost		73654		
improvements		6827	80481	
less, mortgage payable			51587	28894
Vacation home- cost		32500		
Less, accumulated depreciation		5000	27500	
less, mortgage payable			23837	3663
Restricted securities				10000
Miscellaneous assets				1415
Total Assets				128740

Liabilities and Net Worth

	1	2	3	4
Due to credit card companies			359	
Due to miscellaneous bills			343	
Total Liabilities			702	
Deferred gain on installment sale of land			4632	
Total Liabilities and Deferred gain				5334
Net Worth - 12/31/78				123406

Daniel and Louise Smith
Conversion of Cost to Market Value
December 31, 1978

	1	2	3	4
Net Worth (at book value)				123406
Add, appreciation				
	Market Value	Cost	Appreciation	
Marketable securities	15720	10583	5137	
Residence	100000	80481	19519	
Vacation home	40000	27500	12500	
Totals	155720	118564		37156
Subtotal				160562
Deduct depreciation				
	Market Value	Cost	Depreciation	
Automobiles:				
Ford	2359	5250	2891	
Oldsmobile	4499	6000	1501	
Totals	6858	11250		4392
Net Worth (at market value) – 12/31/78				156170

	Assets	1978	1977	Differences— Addition (Reduction)	
1	Cash	12066	10959	1107	1
2	Due from stockbroker	1348	1196	152	2
3	Marketable securities (market)	15720	16701	(981)	3
4	Mortgage receivable	8800	13200	(4400)	4
5	Loans receivable	3200	2000	1200	5
6	Prepaid interest	1202	601	601	6
7	Individual retirement arrangement	6659	4825	1834	7
8	Employer pension plan	20929	18235	2694	8
9	Cash value—life insurance (net of loans)	1885	852	1033	9
10	Automobiles (net of notes)	330	2103	(1773)	10
11	Furnishings	10847	10847	-0-	11
12	Appliances	2527	2527	-0-	12
13	Residence (equity at market value)	48413	47525	888	13
14	Vacation home (equity at market value)	16163	11664	4499	14
15	Restricted securities	10000	10000	-0-	15
16	Miscellaneous assets	1415	1415	-0-	16
17					17
18	Total Assets	161504	154650	6854	18
19					19
20	Liabilities and Net Worth				20
21					21
22	Due to credit card companies	359	483	(124)	22
23	Due for miscellaneous bills	343	276	67	23
24					24
25	Total Liabilities	702	759	(57)	25
26	Deferred gain on installment sale	4632	7008	(2376)	26
27					27
28	Total	5334	7767	(2433)	28
29					29
30	Net Worth at Market Value	156170	146883	9287	30
31					31

Keep reading and learning. If you had any difficulty in completing the net worth statement (beyond the annoyance of bringing together and organizing many facts and figures for the first time), work it over again. Look at it from many angles, recalculate, and study the statement carefully until you develop a real "feel" for it. It's your money, and you should make yourself comfortable with the record which reflects it.

The Smiths prepared a statement of their net worth as of December 31, 1978, just as they had done for 1977. You can see that the model, once established, retains a validity as long as there is no drastic change.

3
CASH FLOW

THERE ARE ALWAYS CERTAIN WORDS which through endless repetition and imprecise usage eventually acquire a certain semimystical significance. Words like these gain currency for serious reasons, even if they come to be used as meaningless cliches. Unfortunately, "cash flow" has joined the list of such words.

Cash flow is basic to the financial planning of corporations as well as individuals and families. Charting your cash flow means, simply, knowing where your money is coming from and where it is going. Cash flow is just as important as net worth to you in intelligent and successful budgeting, tax and estate planning, and in making all important monetary decisions. If you are not accustomed to working with figures charting your cash flow will be time-consuming, tiresome, and frustrating.

Cash, of course, does not literally *flow* but you will have no trouble understanding the metaphor if you will visualize your cash as the tide of the ocean, flowing in and flowing out. If you attempt certain financial acts when the flow is working against you, you will probably not succeed; but if you can go with the flow your chances of success are much greater. Cash flow measures the money you receive and spend over a specific period of time. Generally, this means the 12 months of the calendar year. Cash flow traces the movement of your money during this time.

Since taxes usually play an important role in your monetary life, your cash flow is always set up with tax considerations in mind. Thus, at the same time you compute your cash flow you will be able to prepare many of the necessary schedules for your tax return. If your return is professionally prepared these schedules will reduce the time you spend in gathering information. The more information you are able to submit to the preparer and the more specific your questions, the greater the benefit to you at the lesser expense.

If you are to summarize your annual transactions accurately it is essential that you learn to classify items of cash inflow (receipts) and cash outflow (disbursements).

CASH INFLOW AND INCOME

Cash inflow and income are not the same. Cash inflow includes income as well as items (such as borrowings) which do not affect income. Income, on the other hand, may include the value of non-cash items which do not affect cash inflow. (Suppose, for example, that you are awarded a vacation trip for having exceeded a sales quota. This results in no cash inflow but is taxed as income.) Preparing you cash inflow will help you with tax questions even though inflow and income are not normally identical.

Cash inflow (cash receipts) usually comes from five main sources:

1. Income from salary, interest, or dividends
2. Realization of an asset (e.g., the sale of your car)
3. Loans from banks and other institutions or individuals
4. Gifts or inheritances
5. Refunds of expenses previously paid (e.g., income tax refunds)

CASH OUTFLOW AND EXPENSES
(DISBURSEMENTS)

Cash outflow and expenses are not the same. Cash outflow includes both expenses and items that do not affect expenses, such as repayment of the principal on your home mortgage. On the other hand, expenses may include items which do not affect cash outflow, such as depreciation.

Cash outflow (cash disbursements) is usually directed to four purposes:

1. Payment of an expense (e.g., rent, electricity)
2. Liquidation of a liability or debt (e.g., payment on account of your car loan or home mortgage)
3. Purchase of an asset (e.g., buying a television set)
4. Making gifts

NET WORTH

You must also learn to recognize the difference between an item affecting your net worth and one that relates to your income. *Net worth* is the value of your assets after deducting all your debts, while net income is what remains after all expenses of the year have been deducted from your total or gross income. An example of an individual's net worth as of December 31, 1978 and income for 12 months is shown on the following worksheet:

		1	2	3	4
	Net Worth – December 31, 1978				
	Assets:				
	Cash			1000	
	Securities			2000	
	Total Assets				3000
	Less, Liabilities				1200
	Net Worth – December 31, 1978				1800
	Income for the 12 Months Ended December 31, 1978				
	Income:				
	Salary			15000	
	Less, expenses			14000	
	Net Income for the 12 Months Ended December 31, 1978				1000
	Transition from Income to Net Worth				
	Net Worth – January 1, 1978			800	
	Net Income for the 12 months ended December 31, 1978			1000	
	Net Worth – December 31, 1978				1800

CHART OF ACCOUNTS

Before assembling any data for your cash flow statement, you must establish your personal chart of accounts. A chart of accounts is a listing by title of the various items of cash inflow and outflow custom-made to your needs. This chart allows you to organize all necessary financial information into categories reflected on the cash flow statement.

Most of the accounts referred to in the chart of accounts are self-explanatory. Complete descriptions of accounts relating to assets and liabilities are found in Chapter 2. Descriptions of certain income and expense accounts follow the listing in this chapter.

The following chart of accounts (see pages 59 and 60) is a relatively complete profile of the Smith family whom we have already chosen. Again, remember that it does not make any great difference whether or not you fit exactly into their particular description. You are not doing bookkeeping here. Instead, you are learning concepts and the *method* of preparing financial statistics. When you understand the Smiths' chart, take what you have learned and adapt it to your own needs.

Every account on your chart must have some form of constant identification. If you prefer, you can use names for the accounts and rewrite the name of an account each time you make an entry. However, it is much more professional—and in the long run, much faster—to write out the name of each account once and refer to it thereafter by an identifying number. Don't try to memorize the number. Refer instead to the chart, just as professionals have to do with all but the most frequently used accounts. (And don't lose the chart!)

If you are adept at systems, you can devise your own, or you may wish to adopt the three-digit number series which follows. The sequence has been set up to facilitate the preparation of the cash flow statement:

1. 100 series for assets
2. 200 series for liabilities
3. 300 series for net worth
4. 400 series for self-employment income and business expenses
5. 500 series for other income
6. 600 series for tax deductible expenses
7. 700 series for personal expenses.

If you do not have self-employment income, you may want to rearrange the number series using the 400 series to designate another category, or

Account No.	Name of Account		Account No.	Name of Account
	Assets			
100	Cash — Chemical Bank, checking (Husband)		295	Deferred gain on
105	— Chemical Bank, checking (Wife)			installment sale of
110	— Union Dime Savings Bank (Husband)			real estate
115	— Union Dime Savings Bank (Wife)			
120	— Manhattan Savings Bank (Wife)		300	Net worth
125	— On hand			
130	Due from stockbroker			
135	Marketable securities			**Income**
140	Restricted securities			
145	Mortgage exchange		500	Salary (Husband)
147	Mortgage receivable		510	Salary (Wife)
150	Loans receivable		520	Dividends
155	Prepaid interest		530	Interest income - savings
160	Individual Retirement arrangement (Wife)		540	Interest income - other
165	Employer pension plan (Husband)		550	Vacation home - Rent income
170	Cash surrender value - life insurance		555	G.I. Pension
175	Automobiles		560	Sale of securities
180	Furnishings		562	Cost of securities sold
185	Appliances		565	Capital gains and losses
190	Residence (includes improvements)		570	Gifts received
192	Vacation home		580	Sale of automobile
194	Reserve for depreciation - vacation home			
198	Miscellaneous Assets			**Tax Disbursements**
				Vacation Home:
			600	Depreciation
	Liabilities		602	Real estate taxes
			604	Interest Expense
200	Mortgage payable - residence		606	Repairs
210	Mortgage payable - vacation home		608	Heat & Electric
220	Notes payable - Citibank		610	Caretaker & Janitor
225	Notes payable - GMAC		612	Gardening
230	Due to credit card companies		614	Insurance
240	Due for miscellaneous bills		616	Advertising
250	Loans payable - insurance companies		617	Telephone
260	Loans payable - others		618	Supplies - Misc.
270	Taxes payable			

Account No.		Name of Account		Account No.		Name of Account	
		Tax Disbursements - other				Personal Expenses	1
							2
3	620	Medical - Drugs		700		Cash checks	3
4	622	- Insurance		705		Food stores	4
5	624	- Doctors, etc.		707		Auto - gas - oil	5
6	630	Taxes - State Income		710		- repairs and misc.	6
7	632	- Local Income		712		- insurance	7
8	634	- Federal Income		715		Department stores	8
9	636	- Real Estate		718		Tuition	9
10	638	- gasoline		720		Child care	10
11	640	- Sales		725		Life insurance	11
12	642	- FICA		727		Casualty insurance	12
13	644	- Misc.		730		Electric	13
14	650	Interest paid - Residence Mortgage		732		Telephone	14
15	652	- Insurance companies		734		Fuel oil	15
16	654	- others		736		Landscaping	16
17	660	Contributions - cash		738		Repairs	17
18	662	- Property		740		Supplies	18
19	664	Casualty losses		745		Laundry - cleaning	19
20	670	Political contributions		750		Allowance - mother	20
21	675	Business expenses (Husband)		752		Restaurants	21
22	680	Business expenses (Wife)		754		Travel	22
23	682	Safe deposit box		795		Miscellaneous	23
24	685	Tax return preparation					24

you may decide not to use the 400 series at all. Again, what you do in this regard is not important as long as you are consistent. The 400 series is excluded from the Smith's chart. Notice also that within each series, many numbers are not used. This allows you to expand within the series without having to set up an entirely new set of books. (You will sometimes see account numbers inserted between a <   > . Thus, No. 700 and < 700 > both refer to the account "cash checks.")

Note: If you are dealing with an item of less than $25 and you are uncertain of its category or account title, treat it as miscellaneous income if it is an inflow item, or as miscellaneous expense if outflow.

OBSERVATIONS ON CHART OF ACCOUNTS

As you study the Smiths' chart of accounts, remember that most of these accounts probably have nothing to do with you, at least in your current state. If there are additional accounts which do affect you, add them, by all means. If you are uncertain about where the added items belong, begin by classifying them into one of the seven major groups listed.

Numbers in the 100 (assets) series are assigned more or less according to the readiness with which an asset may be converted into cash. In the 200 (liabilities) series, secured debts such as mortgages are listed first and others in order of relative importance. (There is no significance to the fact that there are five numbers between some accounts and two between others. These are random numbers designed to leave room for expansion.)

The "salary income" (500 and 510) for both husband and wife reflects salary after all deductions for income tax, medical coverage, and the like have been taken. You may prove the accuracy of your employer's W-2 Form Wage Statement by the gross-up method. (See page 62.) In this method, you take the actual cash you received, add back all the deductions and then prove your gross wages. Thus, you may adjust the salary account for the deductions so that the salary recorded in cash inflow will be the gross amount of your wages.

The appearance of an item under one category on the sample chart should not be taken as final. The vacation home, for example, could be looked at as an activity with either personal or strictly investment-related uses. The husband's G.I. pension may or may not be taxable. Child care may bring you a tax credit (which is more valuable than a deduction, since it reduces the tax itself rather than the taxable income) but is included here under personal expenses. All these categories and their alternative interpretations will be dealt with in the chapter on TAX PLANNING.

Now that you have prepared your chart of accounts, you are ready to assemble the documents you need to construct your cash flow statement. Maintaining a checking account, whether at a commercial bank or a savings bank, is vital to doing your cash flow. Otherwise you will be bogged down with numerous pieces of paper and a good deal of guesswork.

If you do not maintain a checking account now, you should give serious thought to opening one to aid next year's cash flow document. Deposit your entire salary in the account. From it draw all the necessary checks for expenses and savings, as well as for your cash needs. Even though you may be required to pay for each check, it is generally easier to ac-

	1	2	3	4
Net wages				
	Periods	Amount Paid	Net Wages	
	14	724	10136	
	3	615	1845	
	6	787	4722	
	1	678	678	
	24			
Total Net Wages				17381
Add:				
FICA Maximum (17700 × 6.05%)			1071	
Federal withholding tax			4361	
State withholding tax			1637	
Local withholding tax			108	
Other withholding from wages:				
Disability benefits			15	
Hospitalization insurance			436	
Total withholding from wages				7628
Total Wages				25009
Gross wages per form W-2				25000
Difference				9

The difference is accounted for by the rounding off of net wages. Any difference up to $15 is acceptable.

count for your money if the records are made in a single book for receipts and disbursements. An overlooked tax-deductible item may easily equal the cost of using more checks.

If you maintain a checking account, you may assemble your data in several ways. For cash inflow, review your checkbook stubs and prepare a schedule from the stubs showing the source of the deposits. If you did not enter the cash deposits on your stubs and if you have not kept your bank deposit slips, then you will have to accept the bank statements as your record. It is also a good idea to mark on the bank deposit slip, to the left of the amount deposited, the source of the deposit, abbreviating where necessary. In any event, the source of the deposit should always be entered in your checkbook.

If you check covers more than one expense item, you should indicate the allocation on the check stub. If, after assembling your data for this year you find your checkbook has insufficient room for notations, order your next book with three checks to a page. These provide sufficient room for making notations on the stubs. Instead of carrying this large checkbook with you, you can carry a few spare checks from the back of the book for an emergency. The pocket-type checkbook is satisfactory only if you use only a half-dozen or so checks a month because it affords little room in the check register for any detail.

In ordering your checks it is a good idea to ask for them to be prenumbered. This saves writing in the numbers by hand and makes it easy to sort your cancelled checks in numerical order. Many banks automatically prenumber your checks so that you can tell at a glance from the bank statement what checks are outstanding. (Of course, if you have used other, unnumbered checks for emergency purposes you will not find these checks in order.) In any event, you must still refer to your checkbook to reconcile your bank statement. The correct way to do this is shown on page 90, in BUDGETING FOR THE FUTURE.

If the mortgage payment on your home includes not only principal on the mortgage plus interest but, in addition, a payment of escrow for taxes, you should break down the payment into the three accounts: Mortgage payable (200), Interest (650), and Real estate Taxes (636). You may charge the escrow for taxes immediately to the real estate tax account, although for tax purposes only the amount actually paid for real estate taxes is a deduction. The escrow is only an advance payment of real estate taxes to the mortgagee. Thus, you will later need to adjust the real estate tax account for tax purposes.

If you do not have the breakdown of the principal and interest payments on your mortgage, set up a new account, Mortgage Exchange (145), and charge the entire payment to this account. Later, when you have obtained the breakdown from your mortgagee, you may adjust your records. You should have an amortization schedule of your mortgage. If your mortgagee has not supplied you with a schedule showing the breakdown of principal and interest over the entire period of the mortgage, you may either prepare your own mortgage amortization schedule or obtain one at a reasonable price from the Financial Publishing Company, 82 Brookline Avenue, Boston, Massachusetts 02215. Send them the correct mortgage principal balance, the interest rate, and the monthly or quarterly payment for interest and principal. From this information they can furnish you with the schedule.

THE TAKE-OFF: CASH RECEIPTS

Starting with your cash receipts, list by the categories established in your chart of accounts the source of your deposits for the year. There is no limit to the number of four-column sheets you may use. (See pages 66 and 72.)

The take-off of figures from your source, whether a checkbook, duplicate deposit slips, or other documentation, requires concentration in order to prevent error. Therefore, plan to do your take-off at a single sitting when you are in a relaxed mood. If you average about 25 checks and deposits a month, a year's take-off and addition of the columns will require about three hours.

The miscellaneous column is used for the occasional source of receipts, those which may occur only two or three times a year. After taking off the receipts, add each column and insert the grand total of the receipts as indicated. This total should prove to (tally with) either your checkbook or bank statements.

Your net salary (take-home pay) should be checked against your Form W-2 or Wage Statement. If you have not received your Form W-2, check your last paycheck vouchers for cumulative totals. You can delay proving your Form W-2 until a later date.

Corporation stocks usually pay dividends quarter-annually (four times a year). Bonds, on the other hand, pay interest semiannually (twice a year). If you have held a stock for the whole year, a glance at the listing of the securities will tell you whether or not you have received the correct number of dividends.

ERRORS IN THE TAKE-OFF

Errors in transcribing figures are commonplace. Surprising as it may seem, many certified public accountants are extremely careful rechecking all their calculations because they have never mastered simple arithmetic. This is understandable when you consider that accounting deals with *relationships* rather than with the mechanics of arithmetic.

Therefore, if your receipts do not prove to your source document, follow these rules:

1. If the difference is less than $100, treat it as an addition to or subtraction from "miscellaneous personal expenses."

2. If the difference is an even amount, such as $200, re-check additions (footings).

3. If the difference can be divided by 9, you have probably made a transposition error. (For example, taking off a $29 item as $92 results in a difference of $63 (92 − 29 = 63.) Since 63 is the difference and is divisible by 9, you would recheck the take-off for some transposition in figures. *Transposition errors are always divisible by 9.*

4. If the difference is an odd amount, such as $32, it is possible that you failed to list a deposit. Count the total entries from your source document and compare the total to your take-off to make certain you have not missed an item or that you have not shown more items than you should.

For easy reference, a chart showing errors, probably in transposition, is shown below:

Difference: (may be divided by 9)	9	18	27	36	45	54	63	72
Correct number	43	57	25	15	38	28	81	91
Number taken off	34	75	52	51	83	82	18	19

Remember, if your difference is divisible by 9, check your take-off from the checkbook against the columnar paper, looking for a transposition. If you are dealing with differences of over $100 you would check for the transposition of at least a three-digit number (such as $372 for $732).

If at the end of your figuring you still end up with what appears to be a substantial difference between the accounts, charge the difference to a new account called "suspense" and number it 800. If the difference shows you have more cash inflow than you should, the suspense-account balance will be treated as a subtraction to arrive at your correct cash balance. If the difference shows more cash outflow than you should have, you would treat the suspense account as a receipt account. This balances out the accounts. It is better to deal with a large suspense item than to stop your financial work before it gets off the ground, so to speak. The chances are that somewhere along the way you will find the error and be able to clear the suspense account.

1978	Account	Amount	Net Salary <500>	gI Pension <555>	Vacation Home Rent Income <550>
3|8	J. Buyer – Mortgage receivable		724	41	700
	Principal <147>	2200	615	41	700
	Interest <540>	528	724	41	700
			724	41	550
8|11	I. Dolgin – Sale of		724	41	375
	Automobile <580>	1300	724	41	375
			724	41	575
9|6	J. Buyer – Mortgage receivable		615	41	200
	Principal <147>	2200	724	41	375
	Interest <540>	440	724	41	550
			724	41	700
9|8	Mutual of New York – Refund		724	41	900
	of Alan Aron, MD Bill		724		
	Paid 7|10 <624>	120	615	492	6700
			724		
9|14	W. Danson – Interest		724		
	on 2,000 loan		724		
	1 year at 6% <540>	120	787		
			787		
		6908	678		
			787		
			787		
			787		
			787		
			17381		
	Total Receipts	31481			

Daniel Smith
Cash Disbursements
For the Calendar Year 1978

			Miscellaneous	Cash Checks <700>	Cash Checks (con'd). <700>	Union Dime Mortgage <145>	
1978	Account		Amount				
4/11	Internal Revenue Service			35	fwd 1340	443	1
	Balance 1977 Tax	<634>	472	35	35	443	2
				35	35	443	3
4/11	N.Y.S. Income Tax			35	35	443	4
	Balance 1977 Tax	<630>	127	50	35	443	5
				35	70	443	6
5/15	T. Jones, CPA			35	35	443	7
	Tax Return Preparation	<685>	225	35	35	443	8
				35	35	443	9
5/15	Union Dime Savings Bank			35	70	443	10
	(Daniel)	<110>	1000	35	35	443	11
				35	35	443	12
8/25	Crest Oldsmobile Deposit			35			13
	on 1979 auto	<175>	300	35	1795	5316	14
				35			15
10/5	Crest Oldsmobile			35			16
	Balance cash	2120		35			17
	Sales tax in			35			18
	above	420		35	American		19
	for auto	1700		35	Express	Mobil	20
	sales tax	<640>	420	100	(Restaurants)	(Auto)	21
	auto	<175>	1700	35	<752>	<707>	22
				35	43	60	23
11/14	Allstate Insurance			35	28	75	24
	Add'l. for Olds	<712>	21	35	17	63	25
				35	25	48	26
11/14	Allstate Insurance			35	40	39	27
	Auto Insurance	<712>	952	35	38	61	28
11/14	Aetna Casualty			35	56	62	29
	Homeowners'	<727>	346	35	22	83	30
11/14	Mutual of N.Y.			35	40	86	31
	Disability Income	<727>	115	35	23	215	32
12/13	Federal Insurance			35	67	123	33
	Excess Liability	<727>	50	35	37	136	34
12/13	Cash - Travel	<754>	400	35			35
12/13	Chemical - Safe Deposit	<682>	11	35	436	1051	36
							37
				6139	fwd 1340		38

In general, if you arrive within $100 of proving your total, whether receipts or disbursements, you have done an acceptable calculation.

THE TAKE-OFF: CASH DISBURSEMENTS

Unfortunately, the number of items of your cash disbursements will usually far exceed the number of your deposits. By looking at your checkbook stubs or other receipts, you will get an idea of your recurring expenditures. Do not use a separate column for an item paid once or twice a year, such as a safe-deposit box rental fee. Such disbursements would be included in the Miscellaneous column. (See pages 67, 69, 70, 71, and 73.)

Certain disbursements may cover more than one account. For example, your American Express charges may include not only restaurants but department stores, travel expenses, and other items. If you have failed to allocate the charges in your checkbook to the various accounts and you recall that substantially all of the charges went to restaurants, allocate the payments to restaurants. On the other hand, if there are certain payments that can be charged directly to the travel account, by all means do so. You should, however, remember for the future to make your allocations at the same time as you draw the checks.

You will notice that the mortgage payment has been shown as a monthly figure without reflecting the amounts for interest and principal. This was done in order to show later how allocations are made after the take-off is done. If you can break down your mortgage payments from your checkbook initially, do so rather than wait until your summary sheet has been done.

There is no fixed order in the take-off. You set up the money columns as they are required for account categories that you believe will have more than two or three entries for the year. You create a column with a heading as required, with the exception of the vacation home disbursements. All of the disbursements affecting the vacation home are gathered separately on one or more sheets of columnar paper to facilitate the preparation of your cash flow statement and tax return. Since each column of the paper has 40 lines, you would need only one-half of a page to account for the usual monthly bills.

Keeping tax considerations in mind for the take-off of items which may require details for your tax return, use the description column as well as the money column. You will find this helpful for doctors' bills and contributions even though you may not be able to take the medical-expense deduction or be required by the IRS to account for cash contributions.

1978		Medical – Doctors & other Amount <624>	Telephone <732>	Con Edison <730>	Citibank (Auto Loan) <220>
1/12	Robert Murphy, MD	40	32	43	1 19
			27	51	1 19
4/11	Irving Wallach, DDS	50	31	53	1 19
			43	46	1 19
5/14	Jerome Shack, MD	1 10	28	49	1 19
			25	57	1 19
7/10	Alan Aron, MD	150	42	65	1 19
			33	103	1 19
9/12	American Opticians	43	41	112	1 19
			27	115	1 19
		393	36	62	1 19
			44	48	1 19
			409	804	1428

1978		Real Estate Taxes – Residence <636>	Dep't Stores <715>	Dep't Stores <715>	Community Center (Child Care) <720>
			218	fwd 11 56	11/12 350
4/11	Receiver of Taxes State, County, Town	416	222	37	4/11 350
			15	158	9/12 550
			72	18	1250
			36	37	
6/12	Receiver of Taxes Village Tax	402	82	26	
			135	28	
			42	37	
			18	142	
9/12	Receiver of Taxes School – 1st half	593	43		
			29	1639	
			46		
12/13	Receiver of Taxes School – 2nd half	593	36		
			82		
			65		
		2004	15		
			fwd 11 56		

Daniel Smith
Cash Disbursements
For the Calendar Year 1978

	1978		Contributions Amount <660>	Drugs & Medicines <620>	Food Stores <705>	Exxon (Fuel Oil) <734>	
1	1/12	Community Church	75	12	115	80	1
2	1/12	United Fund	25	18	122	110	2
3	1/12	Channel 13	30	7	83	96	3
4	5/14	Cancer Research Institute	25	32	58	82	4
5	8/11	Prevent Blindness	15	14		68	5
6	8/11	Red Cross	15	8	378	53	6
7	9/14	PTA	10	6		47	7
8	9/14	Community Church	75	4		43	8
9	12/13	Red Cross	25	21		46	9
10	12/13	Volunteers of America	15	15		44	10
11	12/13	Salvation Army	15			56	11
12	12/13	100 Neediest Cases	15	137		65	12
13	12/13	Westchester Hospital	15				13
14	12/13	New York University	25			790	14
15	12/13	Disabled Veterans	15				15
16							16
17			395				17

				Mother's Allowance <750>	Magazines (Business) <675>	GMAC (Auto Loan) <225>	
18							18
19							19
20							20
21				300	42	136	21
22				300	59	136	22
23				300	43		23
24				300	17	272	24
25		Political Contributions					25
26			<670>	1200	161		26
27							27
28	10/12	Mandrake for governor	25				28
29	10/12	Rand for Congress	25				29
30							30
31			50				31

Daniel Smith
Disbursements - Vacation Home
For the Calendar Year 1978

1978	Total	Mortgage Payable Interest <604>	Principal <210>	Heat & Electric <608>	Caretaker-Janitor <610>	Gardening <612>
1/12	578	456	122	110	31	12
4/11	577	454	123	106	116	31
7/10	578	452	126	103	87	53
10/12	577	449	128	95	32	14
				83	14	3
	2310	1811	499	52	31	4
				45	42	106
				43	6	18
				41	3	13
		Real Estate Tax		54	21	6
			<602>	63	89	
8/11	Town Treasurer		486	76		260
					472	
				871		

	Repairs <606>	Insurance <614>	Advertising <616>	Telephone <617>	Supplies & Misc. <618>
	26	292	24	7	13
	41	54	42	7	63
	32		42	7	4
		346	24	7	6
	99		24	7	13
			21	7	8
				7	12
			177	7	16
				7	7
				7	4
Total Disbursements:				7	
				7	146
Vacation Home	5251				
				84	
All Items	31298				

Louise Smith
Cash Receipts
for the Calendar Year 1978

	1978	Account	Miscellaneous Amount	Net Salary <510>	Dividends Payor	<520>
1	6/8	Union Dime Savings <115>	1100	307	St. Regis	15
2				307	Nat. Distillers	20
3	10/10	Union Dime Savings <115>	1200	307	Mobil	24
4				307	Beth. Steel	25
5	12/13	Union Dime Savings <115>	1500	307	U.S. Gypsum	30
6				307	Nat. Distillers	20
7			3800	307	St. Regis	15
8				307	Beth. Steel	25
9				307	Mobil	24
10				307	U.S. Gypsum	30
11				307	St. Regis	15
12				307	Nat. Distillers	20
13				307	Beth. Steel	13
14				307	Mobil	24
15				307	U.S. Gypsum	30
16				307	St. Regis	16
17				307	Nat. Distillers	20
18				307	U.S. Gypsum	30
19				307	Beth. Steel	12
20				307	Mobil	26
21				307		
22				307		434
23				307		
24				307		
25				307	* Actual 1977 Dividends	
26				307		
27						
28				7982		
29						
30						
31						
32		Total Receipts	12216			

Louise Smith
Cash Disbursements
For the Calendar Year 1978

	1978	Account		Miscellaneous Amount	Food Stores (+ cash) <705>	Food Stores (+ cash) <705>	Personal <795>
1	6/12	Mony			88	fwd 2844	23
2		Insurance Cost	<725>	970	64	75	18
3		Interest	<652>	133	48	93	23
4					42	87	14
5	10/15	Ellen Emory	<150>	1200	54	83	18
6					102	78	22
7	11/14	Canada Life			101	91	18
8		Insurance cost	<725>	-0-	129	124	16
9		Interest	<652>	138	57	106	31
10					52	103	18
11	12/13	Manufacturers Hanover			87	73	23
12		Individual Retirement			86	82	16
13		Arrangement	<160>	1500	63	75	18
14					89	73	46
15				3941	72	86	38
16					56	93	27
17					87	94	36
18					93	83	18
19					84	76	22
20		Union Dime			103	92	
21		Savings Bank			75	58	445
22		<115>			87	93	
23				200	93	105	
24				200	90		
25				200	78	4767	
26				300	63		
27				300	93		
28				200	104		
29				300	87		
30				300	86		
31				200	92		
32				200	79		
33				300	81		
34				300	43		
35					62		
36				3000	74		
37							
38					fwd 2844		
39		Total Disbursements:		12153			

Certain expenses (child care, for example) may qualify for a tax credit and not a deduction. Therefore, these expenses are recorded in the personal section of your chart of accounts only to make their reconciliation to taxable income less complicated.

PROOF OF CASH

Now you have finished your take-off of cash receipts and disbursements. Before going on to the actual preparation of the cash-flow statement, you should substantially prove your cash balances in your checking account, starting with the beginning of the year. A workpaper showing how the proof is on page 75. If there is a difference of $100 or more between your take-off and your closing cash balance, locate the difference. If your difference is less than $100, increase or decrease your miscellaneous personal expenses as required in order that your ending cash is in balance. Do not change your take-off figures. Make the change on the Statement of Cash Flow (see page 83).

The checking account balances are one part of your total cash balance. All of your cash is accounted for in the cash flow, whether in checking accounts, savings accounts, or certificates of deposit. (The rule is that if you could convert a bank account into currency within one business day, with or without a forfeiture of interest, include the balance under cash.)

ADJUSTMENTS TO THE RECEIPTS AND DISBURSEMENTS

The financial information obtained from your checkbook substantially completes the information that you require for your cash flow statement. However, in order to make the statement more meaningful, you should make adjustments to information as follows (see pages 77 and 78):

CASH RECEIPTS

1. Transfers between bank accounts are eliminated because they do not increase receipts or disbursements. The transfers do not affect cash flow.

2. Transfer refunds of disbursements to offset expenditure (e.g., a medical-expense refund is not shown as a receipt, but as a reduction of expense).

3. Wages are increased to reflect gross earnings before withheld taxes and other deductions.

Daniel and Louise Smith
Proof of Cash Balances
December 31, 1978

	Daniel	Louise	
Chemical Bank - Checking Accounts			
Balance 1/1/78	973	148	
Add, Receipts	31481	12216	
Subtotal	32454	12364	
Less, Disbursements	31298	12153	
Balance, 12/31/78	1156	211	
Union Dime Savings Bank (Daniel & Louise)			
Manhattan Savings Bank (Louise)			
			Louise
Balance 1/1/78	1583	3255	5000
Add, Deposits	1000	3000	-0-
Subtotal	2583	6255	5000
Less, Withdrawals	-0-	3800	-0-
Subtotal	2583	2455	5000
Add, Interest for year	121	199	341
Balance, 12/31/78	2704	2654	5341
Summary of Cash Balances			
		12/31/77	12/31/78
Checking Accs. (Daniel)		973	1156
" " (Louise)		148	211
Savings Accs. (Daniel)		1583	2704
" " (Louise)		3255	2654
" " (Louise)		5000	5341
Total Cash		10959	12066

75

4. Cash transactions not reflected in the checking account are included (such as savings account interest and a G.I. pension check that was cashed but not deposited).

5. Savings account deposits not flowing through the checking account are added to the cash flow. For example, a gift of cash deposited to a savings account should be shown in the adjustment column.

CASH DISBURSEMENTS

1. Refund of previously received income is not a disbursement but a reduction of receipts. A refund of a rental deposit would offset the rental income from a vacation home reported in cash receipts.

2. Transfers between bank accounts are eliminated because they do not increase receipts or disbursements. The transfers do not affect cash flow.

3. Withheld taxes and other deductions reducing wages are added back to receipts, and the withholdings are reflected as expenditures.

4. Allocation of expenditures not reflected in the checking account are included in the cash flow. For example, a check drawn at the food store may also have included cash. If the exact amount of cash is unknown, an estimate of the cash should be made and a transfer from the amount expended at the food store is required. Payments on a mortgage may also require allocation. When you do the take-off of disbursements, you may not have the exact amounts chargeable to mortgage principal and interest. Charge the entire payment to *mortgage exchange* at first. Then, use the adjustment column to allocate the correct amounts to principal and interest. If you do not have exact figures for allocations, estimate them and make the corrections at a later date.

CASH FLOW SEQUENCE

The chart of accounts' numerical sequence is set up to facilitate the preparation of the cash flow statement. An additional benefit of the chart of accounts is that the tax data is arranged in logical sequence.

While you have all the necessary financial data in the receipts and disbursements workpapers, before transferring the information to the cash flow statement, you should consider what accounts you will need. The reason for using account numbers is to allow you in advance to list the required accounts. (See page 79.)

			Account	Daniel	Louise	Adjustment= Increase (Decrease)
1.	Eliminate receipts from savings accounts - (included in cash balances)					
		Daniel	<110>	-0-		
		Louise	<115>		(3800)	(3800)
2.	Transfer medical expense reimbursements:					
		Dr. Aron 9/8	<624>	(120)		(120)
3.	Increase salary receipts to reflect withholdings Daniel:					
	gross salary - 25000					
	Deposits 17381					
		withholdings	<500>	7619		7619
	Louise					
	gross salary - 10000					
	Deposits 7982					
		withholdings	<510>		2018	2018
4.	Add to cash balances savings bank interest					
		Union Dime Savings	<530>	121	199	661
		Manhattan Savings	<530>		341	
	Total Adjustments to Receipts			7620	(1242)	6378

77

Daniel and Louise Smith
Adjustments to Disbursements
December 31, 1978

			Account	Daniel	Louise	Adjustment-Increase (Decrease)
1.	Eliminate checks to					
	Savings accounts					
	(included in cash					
	balances)					
		Daniel	<110>	(1000)		(1000)
		Louise	<115>		(3000)	(3000)
2.	Reduce Medical for Reimbursements					
		Dr. Aron 9/8	<624>	(120)		(120)
3.	Record Withholdings from Salary					
	(per form W-2 or payroll voucher)					
		FICA	<642>	1071	605	1676
		Federal Income	<634>	4361	1053	5414
		State Income	<630>	1637	356	1993
		Local Income	<632>	108		108
		Disability Benefits	<727>	15	15	30
		Hospitalization	<622>	436		436
		Misc. (Rounding of am'ts.)	<795>	(9)	(11)	(20)
Total –	Daniel	7619				
	Louise	2018				
	Total	9637				
4.	Allocate Mortgage Payments					
	Total paid 443×12 5316		<145>	(5316)		(5316)
		Interest	<650>	4428		4428
		Principal	<200>	888		888
5.	Reflect cash included in					
	Food stores- estimate					
	$25 per week × 50 weeks					
		cash	<700>		1250	1250
		Food stores	<705>		(1250)	(1250)
		Total Adjustments				
		to Disbursements		6499	(982)	5517

78

Daniel and Louise Smith
Account Number Sequence
December 31, 1978

		1 <100>	2 <200>	3 <500>	4 <600> to <618> (Vacation Home)
1	"R" is a cash receipt item	R 147	220	R 540	604
2		R 147	225	R 580	606
3	"Unmarked" is a cash	110	210	R 540	602
4	disbursement item	175	200	R 540	614
5		175		R 500	608
6		145		R 555	616
7		R 115		R 550	610
8		R 115		R 510	617
9		R 115		R 520	612
10		150		R 500	618
11		160		R 510	
12		115		R 530	
13		R 110		R 530	
14		R 115			
15		110			
16		115			
17		145			

	<620> to <649>	<650> to <699>	<700> to <725>	<726> to <799>
23	R 624	685	712	727
24	634	682	712	727
25	630	660	725	754
26	640	670	700	752
27	624	675	707	732
28	636	652	715	730
29	620	652	720	750
30	R 624	650	705	734
31	624		725	795
32	642		725	727
33	634		705	795
34	630		700	
35	632		705	
36	622			

The sequence is done by listing account numbers by series (100, 200, etc.), and then in the order in which they appear on the workpaper. Thereafter, you know order of the accounts for the cash flow statement.

You may also go back to the chart of accounts and indicate what accounts you have used by a red circle around the account number. Since you will be using the chart of accounts for a number of years, change the symbol used each year.

Included in the account sequence are the accounts used in the adjustment workpapers. Do not forget to include these accounts in your listing.

THE CASH FLOW STATEMENT

The final product of all your statistical efforts is the cash flow statement. All of the activities of all your cash accounts for the past calendar year are now going to be set forth in logical sequence in this statement.

If you approach the cash flow statement that appears in this book as a comparison or a criticism of your own fiscal life, you are making a substantial error. The statements here are for the moment fairly realistic, but the prices of goods and services change so rapidly that these may seem almost quaint by the time you read this book. Don't concern yourself with whether or not our "model" couple underpaid or overpaid for an item. And don't feel that you are deprived in income, goods, or services. Many of the elements included here—especially the vacation home—were included more to introduce to you certain ideas regarding real estate, tax planning, depreciation, installment sales, and investment opportunities than to describe a real family situation.

The diversity reflected in our model statement is intended to familiarize you with the broad concept of receipts and disbursements. While the figures used are as realistic as possible, the many variables in federal, state, and local tax situations make it imperative that you not consider these figures as being in any way authoritative.

Many questions will occur to you as you prepare your cash flow statement. The statement, however, should not become too subtle or refined at this stage, and especially not before you have worked your way through subsequent chapters of this book. The only purpose, here, in preparing the statement is to help you acquire a method for setting up a logical presentation of your cash flow. You cannot absorb this just by reading, and you will probably *not* get everything right the first time. If after all your efforts your figures do not balance, use account 795 (Miscellaneous Personal Expenses) to add or deduct your differences. *Do not abandon finan-*

cial planning because you can't tie in the numbers. The effort and even, sometimes, the frustration are well worth getting for a clear understanding of where your cash is coming from and where it is going.

Your cash flow statement does not aim to tell you whether you did right or wrong in your financial life. It does aim to tell you clearly what your cash did over each 12-month period.

SETTING UP THE CASH FLOW STATEMENT

First, working from the chart of account numbers in numerical order, outline your statement without descriptions. When you have completed the numerical order, you may then add the names of the accounts as was done in the models. Then, transfer your figures from the take-off workpapers, checking to see that you have not omitted any accounts in going from one set of papers to the next. It frequently happens that people leave out an account here or there when first putting an account sequence in numerical order. You may want to skip a line between entries so that you can squeeze a forgotten account into its proper place.

As you set up the cash flow statement, you do not have to enter the individual balances in cash accounts since you have already proved the cash. Begin the statement with your *total cash on hand* at the beginning of the period. Then, add the receipts for the period to the opening cash.

When you add the cash receipts of the year to the total of the opening cash, you will know what cash was available for the period covered by the statement. (Let's assume one year.) Then, take the total of the disbursements for the same period and subtract this from the cash available. You thus arrive at the cash balances for the end of the period. Since you have proved the cash balances previously, the cash flow statement ideally now presents all the accounts in a logical order.

Each column of the statement proves itself. Each page may be cross-footed to prove the correctness of the combined totals. Cross-foot by adding crosswise all totals on the page. These should agree with the combined total in the last column.

Your cash flow statement is not intended to be a work of art, and it is an historical document only in the most limited technical sense. Since the information is assembled according to a logical order, you can also trace your errors through the same logic. Even the most highly paid professionals work in pencil so that corrections can be made easily. Remember also that a mistake is sometimes the most valuable teacher.

Here are the preliminary steps for the preparation of the statement:

1. Take off (i.e., write in) receipts and disbursements from the original sources.
2. Add receipts and disbursements.
3. Prove cash.
4. Make adjustments to receipts and disbursements.
5. Arrange accounts in numerical sequence.

Then, lay out the statement of cash flow in the following order:

1. Four money columns are used: one for each spouse, one for adjustments, and one for combined total.
2. Opening cash balance is recorded from proof of cash.
3. Account numbers for receipts are listed in numerical order from the account sequence workpaper.
4. Account titles are added from the chart of accounts.
5. Amounts are transferred from take-off workpapers of each spouse's receipts.
6. Total of receipts is verified to proof of cash.
7. Adjustments to receipts are transferred from workpaper and total is verified.
8. Combined Total column is completed and cross-footed.
9. Total cash available is computed.
10. Disbursements repeat steps 3 through 8.
11. Subtract disbursements from cash available to arrive at cash balance at end of year.

You should use at least one sheet of columnar paper for receipts so that you can start the disbursements on a separate sheet. Make certain that the adjustments decreasing the receipts or disbursements are in parentheses. The plus adjustments have no sign and are automatically added to the total of the account balances for the spouses. For example, the amounts eliminating the transfers between bank accounts decrease the totals and, therefore, the figures are in parentheses. Adding the withheld taxes to wages increases the account and is not in parentheses.

Since cash disbursements usually require a number of sheets, you should not carry forward the Cash Available total until the last page. This gives you an extra line on each page and reduces the chance of a possible transposition error in carrying the balance from one page to another.

Account No.	Account	1 Daniel	2 Louise	3 Adjustments– Increase (Decrease)	4 Total
	Cash – January 1, 1978	–	–	–	10959
	Cash Receipts – 1978:				
110	Cash – Union Dime (Husband)				
115	Cash – Union Dime (Wife)		1100	(3800)	-0-
			1200		
			1500		
147	Mortgage Receivable	2200			4400
		2200			
500	Salary – Husband	17381		7619	25000
510	Salary – Wife		7982	2018	10000
520	Dividends		434		434
530	Interest Income – Savings			661	661
540	Interest Income – Other	528			1088
		440			
		120			
550	Vacation Home – Rent Income	6700			6700
555	G.I. Pension	492			492
580	Sale of Automobile	1300			1300
624	Medical – Doctors, etc.	120		(120)	-0-
	Total Cash Receipts – 1978	31481	12216	6378	50075
	Total Cash Available (to page 4)				61034

When bringing forward the disbursement subtotals to the top of the next page, re-add the columns across (cross-foot) to be certain you have not made an error in transferring.

Before leaving this chapter look over the Smiths' cash flow, account by account. Now study *your own* cash flow. See if you can remember some of *your own* key figures. On a separate sheet spend a few minutes and test

Daniel and Louise Smith
Statement of Cash Flow
For the Calendar year of 1978

Account No.	Account	Daniel	Louise	Adjustments- Increase (Decrease)	Total
	Cash Disbursements:				
110	Cash - Union Dime (Husband)	1000		(1000)	-0-
115	Cash - Union Dime (Wife)		3000	(3000)	-0-
145	Mortgage Exchange	5316		(5316)	-0-
150	Loans Receivable		1200		1200
160	Individual Retirement Arr't.		1500		1500
175	Automobiles	300			2000
		1700			
200	Mortgage Payable - Residence			888	888
210	- Vac. Home	499			499
220	Notes Payable - Citibank	1428			1428
" "	- GMAC	272			272
602	Vacation Home - R.E. Taxes	486			486
604	- Interest Exp.	1811			1811
606	- Repairs	99			99
608	- Heat & Electric	871			871
610	- Care & Janitor	472			472
612	- Gardening	260			260
614	- Insurance	346			346
616	- Advertising	177			177
617	- Telephone	84			84
618	- Supplies & Misc.	146			146
620	Medical - Drugs	137			137
622	- Insurance			436	436
624	- Doctors, etc.	393		(120)	273
630	Taxes - State Income	127		1993	2120
632	" - Local Income			108	108
	Forward	15924	5700	(6011)	15613

84

Account No.	Account	Daniel	Louise	Adjustments-Increase (Decrease)	Total
	Forward	15924	5700	(6011)	15613
634	Taxes — Federal Income	472		5414	5886
636	— Real Estate	2004			2004
640	— Sales	420			420
642	— FICA			1676	1676
650	Interest Paid — Residence Mtge.			4428	4428
652	— Insurance Co.		133 ⎫ 138 ⎭		271
660	Contributions	395			395
670	Political Contributions	50			50
675	Business Expenses (Husband)	161			161
682	Safe Deposit Box	11			11
685	Tax Return Preparation	225			225
700	Cash Checks	1795		1250	3045
705	Food Stores	378	4767	(1250)	3895
707	Auto — gas + oil	1051			1051
712	— Insurance	21 ⎫ 952 ⎭			973
715	Department Stores	1639			1639
720	Child care	1250			1250
725	Life Insurance		970		970
727	Casualty Insurance	346 115 50		30 ⎫ ⎪ ⎪ ⎭	541
730	Electric	804			804
732	Telephone	409			409
734	Fuel oil	790			790
	Forward	29262	11708	5537	46507

85

Daniel and Louise Smith
Statement of Cash Flow
For the Calendar Year 1978

Account No.	Account	Daniel	Louise	Adjustments—Increase (Decrease)	Total	
	Forward	29262	11708	5537	46507	1
						2
750	Allowance — Mother	1200			1200	3
752	Restaurants	436			436	4
754	Travel	400			400	5
795	Miscellaneous		445	(20)	425	6
						7
						8
						9
	Total Disbursements	31298	12153	5517	48968	10
						11
						12
						13
	Summary					14
						15
						16
	Cash Balances - January 1, 1978				10959	17
						18
	Add, Receipts - 1978				50075	19
						20
	Cash Available				61034	21
						22
	Less, Disbursements - 1978				48968	23
						24
	Cash Balances - December 31, 1978				12066	25
						26

your memory of gross salary, federal withholding tax, food stores, and several of your other large items. (It is not necessary to memorize exact numbers, and recall within $100 is quite acceptable.) This exercise is to "tune in" your mind financially. If you have no ability to do these types of exercises you'll need to do more paper and pencil work.

On your own statement, if the figures for an account do not seem to be within the range of an amount you thought should have been received or disbursed, go back to your checkbook or other source to verify the correctness of your take-off. Of course, correct your statement. Short-cut the correction through the adjustment column so that you don't have to redo either the receipts or disbursements. Use your red pencil on the take-off workpaper to note that you have made a later correction.

4
BUDGETING
FOR THE FUTURE

MOST OF US TEND TO RESIST BUDGETS. Like diets and New Year's resolutions, they are often elaborately planned but rarely carried through.

You may rationalize your resistance. Budgets are only for big business and government. The only individuals who need budgets are the financially troubled. You may be probably reading this book because you are meeting your needs on a week-to-week basis and have a few dollars left as purely discretionary money. With this in mind, you convince yourself that you can get by without a budget.

My practice over the last 30 years has brought me into constant contact with wealthy private individuals. People get rich and stay rich by being willing to keep tight control over their finances. Such people do not like financial surprises. Even if they do not prepare a budget themselves, they do not begrudge the time and expense required for the preparation of a budget. In fact, so as to keep abreast of constantly changing business and tax situations, such people often have budgets prepared semi-annually and even quarterly.

Obviously, this is contrary to the notion that budgets are for the financially disabled, for such people rarely have the sources of cash that would make a budget meaningful. The better off you are financially, the more you need a budget. If budgets have seemed difficult and arbitrary to you in the past, they should no longer.

The suggestions in this book are not intended to provide a one-shot solution. We are dealing with lifetime approaches to money. Keep in mind that the difficulty of the first year or two will be rewarded in later years. Consider the assistance that your budget will be in the preparation of next year's cash flow and tax statements. You will realize quickly that each separate piece of information ties in with many other pieces to form a picture that will become increasingly clear to you.

Budgets, when used in tandem with other financial documents you will prepare, will not only help you to understand the feasibility of your goals, they may open your eyes to new financial opportunities. Budgets can help you reduce taxes, create capital for new or expanded ventures, develop your investment portfolio, and make realistic projections for your retirement and estate planning needs. Budgets are also indispensable for refinancing, one of the least understood methods of improving immediate cash flow. Refinancing, discussed in detail in a later chapter, can help reduce the immediate pressure of cash needs and give you the breathing space necessary to put your financial house in order.

If you have already completed a cash flow statement, preparing a budget will not be an arduous task. The first time you set up a budget, be stingy in the amount of money you expect to receive, but be quite generous in your expectations of expenditures. Your budget should cover a period of time no shorter than three months. It is difficult to control expenses over a shorter period. You may eventually switch to a semi-annual or annual budget, depending on the predictability of your financial situation. But in starting out, you will find the quarterly budget better since it will give you much more rapid feedback concerning the differences between your projected and actual finanical status. Plan, then, to prepare two or three budgets on this basis.

Prepare your first budget immediately after preparing your cash flow statement. If you have decided for whatever reason to forego the cash flow statement, you can still attempt the quarterly budget, but you will lack sufficient data against which to test the accuracy of your projected figures.

If you find that your cash outflow is equal to or exceeds your cash inflow and you can survive fiscally only by borrowing, a budget is an absolute necessity. In a consumer-oriented society such as ours, with constant inducements to buy beyond our needs, the budget's main enemy is compulsive buying. Merchandisers have developed very sophisticated marketing techniques to induce us to make impulsive and often useless purchases. Be realistic in setting up your budget. Set aside a specific cash resource for this spending, and withdraw slowly from the habits of compulsive buying.

Before you begin a budget, there are certain terms that you should recognize. Sources of receipts are divided into active and passive. Active sources of receipts are wages, income from self-employment, personal service income, and earned income. Passive sources include dividends, interest, proceeds on sales of assets, rentals, and other investment income.

Income in one category may sometimes shift to the other. For example, a vacation house rented for a three-year period and requiring no management on the part of the owner would be classified as passive. The same house rented on a weekly or monthly basis and requiring frequent inspections and caretaking would be classified as active. In general, the active receipts require your personal efforts whereas the passive require little effort for their cash flow.

One goal in budgeting may be to build up the ratio of passive receipts to active ones by using excess cash (savings). The "coupon clipper" is a person whose receipts are substantially from passive investments. (Bearer bonds come with interest coupons that must be removed to be cashed semi-annually; thus, the term "coupon clipper.") A frequent buyer and seller of securities is engaged in an active enterprise. A casual investor or an investor in long-term bonds is involved in a passive activity. Active receipts generally may be subject to wide fluctuations in amounts and passive receipts are generally subject to smaller changes.

Budgetary disbursements are generally accounted for in two ways: by the nature and by the categories into which they fall. The nature of the disbursements is divided into fixed and variable. Fixed disbursements are those over which you have little immediate control. The monthly payment on your mortgage is a fixed disbursement. Unless you go through refinancing, you will be saddled with the same amount over an extended period. Electrical costs, which may vary seasonally, are fixed expenses since you can do relatively little to reduce the amount expended during a given budget period.

Variable disbursements are those you have the ability to control, for example, your vacation budget or, to some degree, your clothing budget. Bringing your variable expenses under control first and then attacking your fixed expenses is generally the most acceptable step-by-step approach to sound financial planning.

If you are uncertain whether the nature of a disbursement is fixed or variable, ask yourself this question: "Must I commit myself to the amount of this disbursement over the budgetary period without the item fluctuating within a 25% range?" If the answer is yes, then its nature is fixed. If you cannot answer the question either way, treat the disbursement as fixed and work on controlling the amount at a later time.

Categories of disbursements deal with actual breakdown such as those for tax, personal items, and investment.

Tax disbursements affect the computation of taxable income: real estate taxes, medical expenses, contributions, interest, and other deductions.

Personal items include food, payments of principal on your mortgage, charge accounts, and other disbursements for living expenses having no tax implications.

Some expenditures fall between the tax category and the personal category. If that is the case, treat the entire expenditure as a tax disbursement unless the tax allocation is insignificant (less than 15%). Tax and personal disbursements may be either fixed or variable.

Investments are the sources for financial projections. They are divided into real estate; tangible property (i.e. machinery); and intangible property (i.e. securities). Separate chapters have been devoted to these three main headings for investment. For the present budget, investments are included in the excess cash or savings category.

BALANCING YOUR CHECKBOOK

Doing your budget without comparing the projected figures to your later actual disbursements is doing half the job. To be accurate, your checkbook must be balanced (reconciled) monthly to your bank statement.

As soon as possible after you receive your monthly bank statement, do your bank reconciliation as follows:

1. Put cancelled checks into numerical sequence.

2. Assemble out-of-sequence checks and debit and credit memos in order of date.

3. Using a red pencil, verify figures of cancelled checks to your checkbook. Place a red tickmark next to the amount in your checkbook. Note on a separate sheet the date, number, payee, and difference of any check figures that do not agree with checkbook. If you have failed to enter any checks in your checkbook, note this on the sheet.

4. Verify out-of-sequence checks and debit memos to your checkbook, then collate by date with the numerical checks. Note any errors or omissions separately.

5. Check deposits from bank statement to checkbook. Make certain all credit memos have been added to your checkbook. Note any errors or omissions separately.

6. List any checks that have not cleared the bank at the date of your bank statement. Your red pencil is of great assistance in quickly locating the outstanding checks. List the outstanding checks by check number and amount. Do the same for deposits entered in your checkbook but not yet credited on the bank statement.

7. Review the bank statement for any debit or credit memos that you have failed to enter in your checkbook and note the unentered items.

The bank reconciliation formula is as follows:

Balance per bank statement (end of period)		XXX
Subtract: Outstanding checks:	XX	
	XX	
	XX	XX
Subtotal		XXX
Add: Outstanding Deposits		XX
Balance Per Checkbook, Tentative		XXX
Subtract: Debits Unentered	(X)	
Add: Credits Unentered	X	X
Correct Checkbook Balance		XXX
Add (or subtract) errors as follows:		
		X
Checkbook Balance (end of period)		XXX

If you are still unable to reconcile the bank statement there are three possibilities: Either the arithmetic in your checkbook is wrong, or you made a mistake verifying the checks and deposits to your bank statement, or the bank made an error.

After rechecking your arithmetic and deposits, compare the optical scanning figure (located below your signature on each check) to your checkbook. If you are unable to locate any differences, gather your checks, checkbook, and bank statement and take them to your bank.

If you have not reconciled your checking account for a period of time, use the bank statement balance at the beginning of the period for a tentative opening checkbook balance. Using that balance in your checkbook, do the arithmetic computations from the beginning of the month right up to date. Strike a balance after the check, which is the last date reflected on your bank statement. Then treat checks of the prior period as unentered debit memos, and treat deposits of the prior period on the current statement as unentered credit memos. Make the adjustments for errors and omissions at the end of the current page in your checkbook.

PAYING YOUR MONTHLY BILLS

You cannot, of course, begin to have any reasonable idea of a budget if you do not have control over the payment of bills. If you live alone or are the only adult member of the household, you already exercise some control over the bill situation as the only person responsible for contracting them. If there are two adult members of the household, it is imperative that they both know the state of the family finances. Both miserly and spendthrift ways tend to vanish when both parties function as real partners, equally responsible for expenditures and savings. This holds true even if there is only one wage-earner in the partnership.

The procedure described below should take no more than two hours each month. It is the method used by business concerns to pay their bills and is the same whether or not the company uses a computer.

There are compulsive bill-payers who believe they must pay bills by return mail or their credit will suffer. This is a myth. A good record of paying your bills regularly each month by the date due *is* the important factor in your credit rating.

The bulk of a month's bills should generally be paid sometime between the 10th and 15th day of the following month. If you find that most of your credit-card companies and department-store accounts require payment before this date, establish a bill-paying period earlier in the month. If this is not feasible, you will probably be able to change the due date of your billing by requesting a new account number from your creditors, explaining that you are seeking to establish a specific billing cycle. To effect a 10th to 15th day payment period, your credit-card bills should be due the 20th day to avoid finance service changes.

For the procedure outlined below you will require an 8½″ × 11″ alphabetical sorter folder, available at most stationery counters. This file holds your unpaid bills, current budget, schedules of insurance payments, and all other papers that will be needed at the end of the month. Buy a second, legal-size alphabetized accordion file for retaining your paid bills on an annual basis. These folders will last for years. For tax purposes you are required to retain only three years' bills. Thus, if you file your return by April 15 you can destroy any documents older than the three prior calendar years. Do *not* destroy those documents and schedules necessary to prove the basis of assets which may be sold in the future, such as your home and securities.

As you receive the bills and receipts during the month, place them in alphabetical order in the unpaid file folder, which you should keep handy. At your convenience, sometime between the 10th and 15th day, follow the procedure below.

If you are sharing bill-paying duties with a partner, you may alternate responsibility for the various steps.

1. Remove bills in alphabetical order, collating receipts with the credit-card or department-store billings. Verify to statement, check arithmetic, and remove remittance slip. Encircle in red pencil correct amount to be paid. Mark bill with account number. Assemble bills with retained part of bill (showing amount to be paid encircled in red on top), the creditor-provided envelope, and the creditor's remittance slip.

2. Date sufficient check stubs and checks for number of bills to be paid. Draw but do not sign the checks. Prepare any required envelopes. Write the account numbers on the check stubs. Remove checks from checkbook and place on top of the documents.

3. Sign each check after verifying its correctness, put the payment date on the bill, then insert the check and remittance slip into the envelope. File the paid bills.

4. Seal the envelopes and attach the postage.

5. Run a tape of the checks from the checkbook and deduct the total from the opening balance. Recheck the tape and affix to the last current page in the checkbook. Insert the correct balance on that page. If the checks drawn did not complete a page, compute to the last check and double underline so that you do not deduct the amount a second time. It is not necessary to enter the check balance on each page of the checkbook. If no tape is available, however, the balance will have to be figured for each page.

Sometimes the cash balance at the beginning of the payment date is insufficient to cover all the checks required. Draw all the checks even though your checkbook will show an overdraft, and hold up mailing the envelopes containing those checks equaling the overdraft until such time as funds are available.

PREPARING YOUR BUDGET

To prepare your budget, head up the four-column paper as follows:

COLUMN	DESCRIPTION
1.	Prior Year 1/1/78 - 3/31/78
2.	Projected 1/1/79 - 3/31/79
3.	Actual 1/1/79 - 3/31/79
4.	Difference

Using your cash flow statement, consolidate accounts, whenever possible by combining accounts or transferring groups of accounts to subschedules. This will simplify the budget preparation. For example, if your monthly mortgage payment consists of principal, interest, and escrow, you may use a single account, "Mortgage". The accounts for a vacation home or investment property would be transferred to a sub-schedule. The objective is to cover your budget on a single page.

The order or sequence follows your cash flow statement. Account numbers are necessary because of the third column's requirement for actual figures. Incidentally, the four quarterly budgets' "Actual" columns may be combined at the end of the year to supply you with your cash flow computation exclusive of the cash proof and adjustments.

A new account, "Reserve for Contingencies," has a function similar to that of the suspense account in the chart of accounts. Its main purpose is to cover these unforeseen expenditures that tend to destroy a person's faith in budgets. Experience will dictate the percentage you will want to set aside. For the Daniel and Louis Smith example, approximately 25 percent of excess cash was designated for the reserve.

The budget may also include a savings factor. In the example, the excess cash is assumed to be available for savings. This is an operating budget covering the fixed and variable disbursements resulting in excess cash. To simplify, goals for the excess cash have not been set forth.

After you have worked with several consecutive quarterly budgets, you will be able to pick up the projected figures easily. Notice that for budget purposes withheld taxes are ignored since they are not a part of your direct cash flow and are treated as year-end adjustments. This is because the cash is not received by you. If the withholdings for FICA, federal, state, and local income taxes change, adjust the projected figures.

If you have been receiving substantial tax refunds each year because of excess withholding, consider increasing your exemptions to the prior year's actual tax. Remember that refunds do not include interest for the period covered by your return. If interest is paid, it covers the period subsequent to the due date of the tax return. On the other hand, if you have made a habit of treating this refund as a form of enforced savings, wait a year or two until you have established real control over both your money and your spending pattern. Then begin to save in a way that pays you interest, instead of letting the IRS hold your money.

If you find that you must pay substantial additional taxes each year, consider decreasing your exemptions to increase the tax withheld to approximate your prior year's actual tax. If you have an unusual item of income or deduction during the year (such as a capital gain or casualty loss), do not hesitate to change your withholding tax immediately for the balance of the year to extend the effect of the change over the current year instead of waiting until you file your return. Most employers will permit you to contribute additional moneys for withholding taxes necessary to cover any substantial increase in your tax during the year. This allows you to include the amount on your Form W-2 without filing estimated tax returns. You also benefit in that the additional state tax becomes a current-year tax deduction without your having to remember to pay this tax before the close of the year.

In looking at the sample budget it is important not to be overwhelmed by the calculations and figures. You are studying a completed budget and it looks like a forest of numbers rather than individual trees.

You will note there are double checkmarks on some accounts. These refer to a supporting schedule, which shows the individual breakdown of the account. This is done to accommodate a budget summary in a one-page statement for ease of understanding. Experience will help you to determine whether you want to use schedules or to complete your budget on several pages in account order. Make this choice after you have worked with a summary budget and supporting schedule for several quarters.

OBSERVATIONS ON THE BUDGET

The budget is prepared in two stages:

1. Actual figures for the comparative prior year's quarter, together with projected figures for the current year's quarter.

2. Actual figures for the current year's quarter.

Budget

For the Three Months Ended March 31, 1979

Account No.	Account	1/1/78 to 3/31/78 Actual	1/1/79 to 3/31/79 Projected	Actual	Difference Increase (Decrease)
	Receipts:				
147	Mortgage Receivable (Ppl.)	2200	2200	2200	-0-
540	" " (Int.)	528	350	352	2
500	Salary- Net (H)	4235	4200	4202	2
510	Salary- Net (W)	2149	2150	2147	(3)
520	Dividends	114	104	138	34
530	Interest- Savings	165	160	167	7
W	Vacation Home (sch.1)	434	920	1221	301
555	Misc. (G.I. Pension, etc.)	123	120	123	3
	Total Receipts	9948	10204	10550	346
	Disbursements:				
W	Housing (sch. 2)	1762	2000	2266	266
W	Automobiles (sch. 3)	699	1200	1237	37
705	Food Stores	1088	1100	1187	87
715	Department Stores	445	400	388	(12)
750	Allowance - Mother	300	300	300	-0-
725	Life Insurance (Prem. + Int.)	-0-	-0-	-0-	-0-
727	Casualty Insurance	-0-	-0-	-0-	-0-
W	Personal (sch.4)	1343	1570	2619	1049
	Total Disbursements	5637	6570	7997	1427
	Tentative Cash Excess (Deficit)	4311	3634	2553	(1081)
	Less, Reserve for Contingencies	—	900	-0-	(900)
	Cash Excess (Deficit)	4311	2734	2553	(181)

Account No.	Account	1/1/78 to 3/31/78 Actual	1/1/79 to 3/31/79 Projected	Actual	Difference Increase (Decrease)
	Schedule 1 — Vacation Home				
550	Rent	2100	2700	2900	200
	less,				
210/604	Mortgage (Ppl. & Int.)	578	580	578	(2)
602	R.E. Taxes	-0-	-0-	-0-	-0-
606	Repairs	26	50	23	(27)
608	Heat & Electric	319	350	364	14
610	Caretaker	234	250	246	(4)
612	Gardening	96	100	78	(22)
614	Insurance	292	300	313	13
616	Advertising	24	30	32	2
617	Telephone	21	20	24	4
618	Supplies & Misc.	76	100	21	(79)
	Total Deductions	1666	1780	1679	(101)
	Cash Flow — Vacation Home	434	920	1221	301
	Schedule 2 — Housing				
200/650	Mortgage (Ppl. & Int.)	1329	1330	1329	(1)
636	Real Estate Taxes	-0-	-0-	-0-	-0-
727	Insurance	-0-	-0-	-0-	-0-
730	Electric	147	200	184	(16)
734	Fuel oil	286	300	293	(7)
738	Repairs	-	100	460*	360
736	Landscaping	-	-0-	-0-	-0-
740	Supplies	-	20	-0-	(20)
—	Misc.	-	50	-0-	(50)
	Total Housing Costs	1762	2000	2266	266
	Schedule 3 — Automobiles				
220	Notes Payable - Citibank	501	500	501	1
225	" " - GMAC	-0-	400	408	8
707	Gas & oil	198	200	236	36
710	Repairs & Misc.	-	100	92	(8)
712	Insurance	-0-	-0-	-0-	-0-
	Total Automobiles	699	1200	1237	37

* New appliance- window
  air conditioner

Account No.	Account	1/1/78 to 3/31/78 Actual	1/1/79 to 3/31/79 Projected	Actual	Difference Increase (Decrease)
	Schedule 4 - Personal				
160	Individual Retirement Art.	-0-	-0-	1000	1000
620	Medical - Drugs	37	50	47	(3)
622	" - Insurance	-0-	-0-	-0-	-0-
624	" - Doctors, etc.	40	100	150	50
630	Taxes - State Income	-0-	-0-	-0-	-0-
632	" - Local Income	-0-	-0-	-0-	-0-
634	" - Federal	-0-	-0-	-0-	-0-
640	" - Sales	-0-	-0-	-0-	-0-
660	Contributions	130	120	75	(45)
675	Business Expenses	42	50	48	(2)
685	Tax Return Preparation	-0-	-0-	150	150
700	Cash Checks	470	500	455	(45)
720	Child Care	350	350	350	-0-
732	Telephone	90	100	94	(6)
752	Restaurants	88	200	126	(74)
754	Travel	-0-	-0-	-0-	-0-
795	Miscellaneous	96	100	124	24
	Total Personal	1343	1570	2619	1049

Stage one requires that you merely transfer figures from your cash flow or prior year's budget to the current budget. If you have no prior figures, you will, of course, have to use estimated figures. Do not devote more than an hour to completing the prior year's quarterly figures. The projected figures require careful effort. Estimate each category of receipt and disbursement using the prior actual figures as a starting point and increasing or decreasing them according to your anticipated financial status.

Stage one should be started sometime between the middle of the last month of the prior budget period and the middle of the first month of the quarter. Thus, a January 1, 1979, through March 31, 1979, quarterly budget should be prepared between December 15, 1978, and January 15, 1979, to be of real use. After you have had one prior quarter's experience, the total time for stage one should take no more than two hours. Unlike the cash flow statement, there are no cash balances at the beginning and end of stage one of the budget. The budget is a self-contained unit which measures money changes within a fixed period.

The categories of budget reporting, or "accounts," should reflect a logical sequence in the order of your individual needs. The Smiths' budget simply represents a profile to help you understand budgetary concepts. Try to use the accounts established for the Smiths until you have gained experience in working with your own budget.

Stage two, the completion of the actual figures for the quarter, may be worked on at various times before the end of the quarter. Thus, at the end of the first month, you may begin an analysis similar to the cash flow take-off. The second and third month's figures would be added later, and the cumulative totals transferred to the budget. The final figures should await the last month's bank statement for total accuracy.

The "Difference Increase (Decrease)" column is the result of subtracting the actual figures for the budget quarter from the projected figures. Decreases of both receipts and disbursements over budgeted figures are in parentheses so that you can see at a glance whether the big differences are cash pluses or minuses. A decrease in a receipt is the opposite of a decrease in disbursement, so that a decrease of a receipt has the same affect on cash as an increase in a disbursement. You will recognize this if you read the difference column of the Smiths' budget.

Your actual figures for the quarter may serve as a basis for your cash flow statement at the end of the year. Except for the savings' bank interest, all the budget figures will have flowed through the checking accounts. If you prove your cash each quarter, you may combine the four quarterly actual figures for a final cash flow. By joining two four-column sheets side by side, you can do your cash flow as follows:

COLUMN	DESCRIPTION (ACTUAL FIGURES)
1.	1/1/79 to 3/31/79
2.	4/1/79 to 6/30/79
3.	7/1/79 to 9/30/79
4.	10/1/79 to 12/31/79
5.	Total for Year (Col. 2 to 5)
6.	Adjustments
7.	Combined total.

In doing your own budget, keep in mind the following remarks on specific accounts in the sample budget.

Salary. The amount is recorded as *net*, after withheld taxes and deductions, since for budget purposes cash was not received. This will appear as a cash flow adjustment at the end of the year.

Vacation Home. Net cash is treated as a receipt since the vacation home is treated as an investment. Thus, if result was a deficit in cash, the account would be transferred to disbursements, showing the net cash deficit,

Savings Interest. This is included with cash receipts, although if the amount is not substantial this item may be ignored.

Reserve for Contingencies. This is a conservative estimate to cover those items which tend to destroy confidence in budgets, such as the unexpected replacement of a washing machine, unexpected medical expense, or any other contingency, which even the most accurate forecast could not project. In the Smiths' budget, approximately 25% of the balance of cash was allocated to this reserve. In your budget the reserve serves as a buffer to ease the burden of accuracy for a nonfinancial person to arrive at an acceptable "bottom line," or cash balance. You will notice in the Smiths' example that the reserve for contingencies was actually used to absorb most of the increases in expenditures over what had been projected.

Housing (Schedule 2). Additional accounts were provided, which were not in the chart of accounts, for such items as repairs, landscaping, supplies, and other miscellany. For the cash flow year, these expenses were minimal and were paid out of pocket money. No adjustment was made for these items at the year-end. For the budget, these accounts were added, though it was unnecessary to assign account numbers. As is shown by the figures, the item included in the repair account was for an appliance and was footnoted. On the annual cash flow, this would be an adjustment.

Personal Taxes and I.R.A. (Individual Retirement Arrangement). (Schedule 4). In the prior year, the Smiths filed their returns in early April. In the current year, since their actual disbursements combined with an increase in receipts became apparent in the middle of March, they decided to file their returns at the end of March. The Federal return showed an overpayment. Mrs. Smith made two-thirds of her allowable I.R.A. contribution in the amount of $1,000 at the end of March. In addition, the tax preparer was paid the annual fee. The payment of these items was within the Smiths' control and could easily have been made in the subsequent quarter.

The payment of the I.R.A. is an effective use of budgeting for the future. In the prior year the I.R.A. contribution was made in December. The I.R.A. account earnings are deferred from present taxation. Making the payment early in the year increases the earnings without any immediate tax cost.

A word about the symbols: The dash indicates that there were no figures for this account in the *entire* prior year's cash flow; the dash-zero-dash indicates that there have been figures for this account in one or more quarters in the prior year. This is a signal to you as you project the next quarter that you may have to forecast some amount. For example, Schedule 3, Automobiles, Account #225, notes payable: G.M.A.C. started payments late in the prior year; the "—0—" is a signal that some amount may be required in the projected column.

Finally, always leave some unused lines, as the Smiths did here, so that substantial receipts or disbursements for which there was no account set up in the original budget may be added later on the summary page.

Reviewing the differences between projected receipts and actual receipts, the summary shows an increase of $346 over the projection. The only substantial difference was the cash flow from the *vacation* home. Schedule 1 shows immediately that this was due mainly to an increase in rental, together with small individual decreases in disbursements. Thus, of the total increase in cash flow from the vacation home, two-thirds was attributable to receipts and one-third to a reduction in actual disbursements. Learning to appreciate these relationships builds your understanding of the conceptual nature of figures.

The disbursement section of the budget shows two major areas of difference. *Housing* was up $266 and *personal* increased by $1,049. The *housing* schedule shows that the increase was due to appliance purchases. The *personal* increase was due to the early payment of the I.R.A. contribution and the tax preparation fee. These payments would usually be made in the second quarter but were made at the end of March because the funds were on hand.

The *automobiles*, *food stores*, and *department stores* were well within acceptable budgetary parameters.

Interestingly, the bottom-line results of the Smiths' budget shows a difference of less than $200 in actual against budgeted figures. This is less than a 10% difference, which is extremely good projecting. Differences between projected cash excess (or cash deficit) within a range of up to 25% are considered acceptable. The key to a sound financial plan is to grasp clearly the concept behind the receipt and disbursement of money so that you know where your money goes. As you work with the budget you will develop expertise in meeting your goals by shifting the impact of disbursements over which you have some measure of control.

Once you have budgetary control of your disbursements, you should be able to achieve any reasonable predetermined monetary goals.

There is no fixed percentage of receipts that a person should spend to cover housing, food, life insurance, recreation, clothing, and saving. You set your own percentages. The standard formula of 25% for housing fails to take into account differences in housing costs from one area to another. You are already committed to a housing cost whatever the percentage of your total receipts. The only substantial change you might make would be to refinance or to move. The decision to do either of these is highly personal and should be made only after you have carefully studied the entire outflow of your disbursements.

The only rule you *must* follow is classically simple: receipts must exceed disbursements if you wish to remain solvent. The percentages are accurate and may be used if it serves your purpose to compare them with published data of persons in the same economic range as yourself.

The Smiths spend 21% of their combined receipts for housing and 12% to maintain their automobiles. The automobiles as a percentage of receipts was 1% more than was spent at food stores (11%). If the Smiths consider the automobile percentage too high, they might consider the following question:

1. Should they try to manage with one car, or a smaller second car, or participate in a car pool?

2. Should they consider extending auto note payments from 36 months to 48 months? (See Chapter 9, CREDIT, for carrying costs of installment obligations.)

Daniel and Louise Smith
Cash Flow – Actual Percentages
For the Three Months Ended March 31, 1979

		Actual	Percentage
Total Receipts		10550	100%
Disbursements:			
Housing		2266	21
Automobiles		1237	12
Food Stores		1187	11
Department Stores		388	4
Allowance – Mother		300	3
Life Insurance		–0–	0
Casualty Insurance		–0–	0
Personal			
Individual Ret. Art.	1000		9
Cash Checks	455		5
Child Care	350		3
Other	814		8
Total Personal		2619	
Total Disbursements		7997	76
Excess Cash		2553	24%

3. Should they eliminate the collision feature of their automobile policy and reduce premium costs? Increase the deductible? Change companies? (See, Chapter 8, HEALTH AND CASUALTY INSURANCE.) Note that no insurance was paid in this quarter and still the percentage was relatively high.

4. Are the cars performing at top efficiency? What is the gas mileage? Should they use cheaper gas? Are regular tune-ups helpful?

A word of caution before you conclude that the Smith's automoblie costs are out of line because of the percentages. Mr. Smith may be required to commute a long distance with no public transportation. Mrs. Smith may need an automobile for her job and for general mobility.

These questions are not intended to focus on automobile costs as such. But you cannot make any serious consideration of major changes in your budget without asking similar questions of each item of importance. Each budget profile is highly personal and must accurately reflect the particular situation of the individuals involved.

## 5

TAX PLANNING

OLIVER WENDELL HOLMES ONCE REMARKED that taxes are the price we pay for civilization. There may be a certain element of fatalism in the idea that death and taxes are the inevitable, but it is exactly this fatalism that you must overcome if you want to find yourself in the most favorable tax position.

You can only reduce taxes by knowing the law and by foresight, re-cord-keeping, and serious financial planning. *It is your responsibility to minimize your own taxes.*

This chapter is not meant to be an exhaustive guide to taxes. It is only meant to stimulate your thinking along the lines of realistic tax planning. If you have some truly exotic tax situation, chances are you would auto-matically seek professional assistance. By commenting on the major items that make up the tax liability for the majority of citizens, I will try to show you patterns of thought that can help to reduce your taxes. Where professional advice is a necessity, I will say so.

America's entire tax system is based on the taxpayer's assessment of his or her own tax, with the Internal Revenue Service (IRS) serving as the government's audit agency. The IRS is charged by law with issuing in-come tax regulations, maintaining taxpayers' accounts and collections, auditing a set percentage of the returns (automatically or at random ac-cording to the level of income), and suggesting legislative changes. Tax changes are sometimes made by Congress late in the year, retroactive to the beginning of the year. Normally, these changes are liberalizations of the laws. For the purposes of your tax planning, however, it is wise to work on the assumption that there will not be any adverse changes affect-ing you.

It is important for you to understand general procedures of the IRS, if only to set your mind at ease. If you make an innocent mistake in your interpretation of the law, the only penalty imposed is payment of the additional tax, and interest computed from the due date of the return. The IRS may also differ with you on your interpretation and disallow a part or all of your deductions.

By and large, most people comply with the rules of the game, and statistics bear this out. In an average year, with more than 75 million individual returns filed, fewer than 1,000 tax cases go to criminal court and another 1,000 cases are tried in the civil courts. You also have the right to take tax issues to court on your own behalf, and if an issue is considered worthy, it can go as high as the U.S. Supreme Court.

You may have heard some horror stories about IRS abuses, especially in the areas of collection. These abuses do exist, but the IRS makes every effort to correct them. Most experienced tax professionals agree that the auditing done by the IRS over the years has generally been conducted on a fair and reasonable basis. If you have difficulties with the attitude of a particular IRS employee and you have been acting in good faith, these problems can almost always be resolved by meeting with a supervisor or by appealing the findings. Under no circumstances should fear of retaliation enter into your dealings with the IRS.

There is no such thing as an annual list of troublesome taxpayers. Each year's tax returns are selected for examination independently and without reference to previous returns. If you have been examined on a particular item in the past and have satisfied the IRS in that regard, you may very well be able to prevent a subsequent examination on that issue by writing to your district office, stating that the issue was resolved in your favor in a previous year and requesting that the current return therefore not be audited for that reason. It is the IRS's policy that wherever possible it will not reaudit the same issue previously resolved in a taxpayer's favor.

As you can conclude from the statistics we quoted, almost all tax controversies are settled within the IRS. (Remember that this means settled to the satisfaction of the *taxpayer*, who has the right to appeal to the courts.) The Appeals Division of the IRS is the level of appeal before the courts, and as such, it is staffed with experienced personnel, most of whom are lawyers as well as accountants.

The Appeals Division has settlement authority under what is called the "hazards of litigation" doctrine. This means that the IRS gives great consideration to the possibility that it could lose part or all of the case if it were appealed in the courts. If, therefore, your return is audited and you are unhappy with the terms of the auditor's proposal to close your case, you should definitely request a conference with the auditor's supervisor. (This is usually dealt with immediately.) Then, if you cannot reach an agreement with the supervisor and you consider the amount involved substantial enough to warrant further appeal, do not hesitate to appeal further. Your appeal goes to the District Appeals Office. Such appeals are scheduled for times that are mutually convenient for you and the IRS. The appeals officer almost always allows a delay of several months to enable you to gather documentation and arrange to take time off for a personal appearance. If it ever becomes necessary for you to undergo this appeal system, you will probably find that the IRS will conduct itself in the highest traditions of our public service and will do its best to see that you are treated as fairly as is consistent with the tax laws.

To avoid the experiences just referred to, there are two cardinal rules that you must bear in mind and act upon. (1) Tax planning begins on the first day of your tax year. (2) You should know your approximate tax for a given year by the end of the year.

After you have completed your tax return and submitted it along with the supporting schedules, it may nevertheless fail to meet certain criteria (Discriminant Function, or DIF). The service center then selects your return for possible examination and it is individually reviewed at the district office by an experienced classifying officer who decides whether it should be audited. At a third stage, an audit supervisor or examining officer may decide the return does not require an audit. (Experienced revenue agents working in this area begin to develop almost an "instinct" for returns whose potential tax deficiency makes them worth auditing.) The classifier also determines whether the return should be examined either in the office or in the field. The complexity of the return and the issues selected for audit determine the experience level of the IRS personnel employed on the examination.

For these reasons, it is imperative for you, in preparing your return, to make neat and complete presentations of the figures and facts on which you relied in determining your tax liability. Even though the IRS in many cases does not require documentation to be attached to your return, experienced practitioners know that an "out-of-line" item which might cause the return to be selected for audit should be supported by attached documents. This is done in the belief that the individual classification system would reject the return from being audited. Thus, a "flagged" item later found to be substantially correct by the IRS's system may be returned to the files without audit. This saves the IRS production time and, more important, helps you avoid the time, effort, and worry usually expended on undergoing a tax audit. You should particularly consider attaching documentation to your return for such items as an unusual medical expense, a large property contribution, or casualty loss.

Frequently, the IRS makes inquiries about returns, and in such instances you must have an exact copy of the original available. Therefore, if you prepare your own return, do not forget to make a photocopy for yourself. (A professional preparer is required to furnish you with a copy of your return.) Also, be sure to secure your original return with two staples at the top. You should keep on hand at least the prior three years' returns, the period of the statute of limitations.

THE TAX FORM

Form 1040, the U.S. Individual Income Tax Return, is a compromise between the needs of the IRS and the capabilities of the average citizen. This form is constantly being redesigned to cope with changes in the laws, and to make comprehension easier. Unfortunately, the complex demands of the tax laws are such that many intelligent and educated people do not feel that the contents of the form are sufficiently intelligible to the non-professional. Part of this reaction, however, comes from the anxiety many individuals feel when attempting to do taxes at the last minute.

Unfortunately Form 1040 does not completely set forth in logical accounting-statement terms the computation of taxable income and the final balances paid or overpaid. If the form were prepared as a series of additions and subtractions, it would be easy for you to transfer your data directly from workpapers or documents to the form itself.

Since the form requires you to go from page one, to schedules, to page two and to schedules, and then back to page two, you should appreciate that you require a bridge between the raw data and the form itself. This bridge is called a tax worksheet. This worksheet is obligatory in preparing any but the simplest tax return. It is the transition step between all of your raw material and the tax return itself, and it therefore contains notations, references, and all information necessary to support the position taken on your return.

It would be worth your while to request from your district IRS office a free copy of their excellent book, Publication 17: *Your Federal Income Tax*. This book is usually published after the end of the current tax year. The 1979 edition will be used for preparing 1978 returns. Along with your prior three years' returns, you should also save the corresponding copies of Publication 17.

Publication 17 represents the IRS's view of the interpretation of the tax statutes. In most cases, it is correct and is supported by law and the courts. However, Publication 17 is not intended to be all inclusive. If, during the year you faced an unusual and substantial tax problem and find an adverse view of your situation in Publication 17, don't be content with that. Buy one of the excellent commercially published tax guides. If you are still not satisfied with the answer, seek professional help. Remember, professional services on tax matters are deductible.

If the tax form were in a *logical* sequence, this order would follow:

1. Income *less*
2. adjustments to income *equals*
3. adjusted gross income *less*
4. flat standard deduction or excess itemized deductions *equals*
5. tax-table income.
6. Tax-rate computation *plus*
7. additional taxes *less*
8. credits *plus*
9. other taxes *equals*
10. tax *less*
11. payments *equals*
12. balance due or overpaid.

Your tax worksheet is prepared according to the above sequence.

WHEN TO DO YOUR TAX PLANNING

Tax planning is the substance of what you pay or do not pay the IRS. Your tax planning time begins on or before January 1 of any given year and ends December 31 of that year. The tax planning period does not start *after* the year-end because by then it is too late to effect any meaningful reductions. Before December 31, you should have a fair knowledge of what your tax liability will be for federal, state, and local income taxes. You should consider the tax form itself as a remittance slip to be completed at some time during the filing period; but the real work of doing the figures should be done periodically *during* the year. If you have prepared cash flow statements or budgets, most of the detailed work needed to prepare your tax worksheet will have already been done. Completing the form is the procedural step in meeting the IRS's requirements.

The IRS checks all mathematics on your return, and therefore, in preparing it you should redo all arithmetic at least once. In order to take advantage of any "legislative grace" items (deductions, exemptions, and credits), you must maintain adequate records such as checks supported by bills, a complete diary, appraisals, and receipts. These will all go to make up the tax file which you should keep for yourself, so that when you do your final tax projection (which later becomes your tax worksheet) you will have these important documents immediately at hand. Data to retain will be discussed with the various items that make up your return.

Pertinent provisions of the Revenue Act of 1978 affecting your 1978 return have been included in the discussion of various items. A summary of these provisions, effective in 1979, are at the end of this chapter.

SALARY

A cash-basis taxpayer (if you are not one and you certainly already know it) pays taxes on salary when paid, not when earned. Thus, if your year-end bonus for 1978 is computed and paid to you on January 2, 1979, you would not report this bonus on your 1978 return. You have the use of the tax difference between the taxes withheld from your salary and your actual tax liability from January, 1979 through April 15, 1980. Of course, your employer would be required to withhold immediately FICA (social security) taxes, and this offsets to some degree the gain on this deferment of taxes. On the other hand, if you did not reach maximum FICA salary by the end of 1978, the tax deferment might be substantial. In fact, you may have reasons for wanting to include the 1978 bonus on your return. For instance, if you sustained a business loss or an unusual deduction in 1978, you might want to show more income for that year. Timing is all-important, and whatever position you take, you must understand the tax consequences. As another example, if you receive January vacation pay in the prior December, it is taxable in the current year. If you request a salary advance to be repaid in a subsequent tax period, the advance is not subject to tax when received.

Your tax *rate* depends on your taxable income. The rates are progressive and go up rapidly for single taxpayers—approximately 2% per $2,000 of income in the lower brackets. For 1979 the brackets will widen. Even a small change in brackets may be worth one or more dinners in a fine restaurant ($2,000 x 2% = $40 plus the state tax benefit). Don't overlook such a simple method of saving some tax dollars.

Remember what was said earlier about the gross-up method of proving your W-2 form. Simply because a computer prepared the form is no reason to assume that it is correct. Computers simply take literal-minded orders from people, some of whom are not always the brightest or most scrupulous.

The law limits the maximum tax rate on salary to 50%. In general, the salary is reduced by one-half of capital gains before November 1, 1978 and certain other items. The 50% limitation applies to highly paid individuals showing taxable incomes of over $55,200, if filing jointly, and $40,200 if filing separately.

INTEREST AND DIVIDENDS

Savings-bank interest and corporate interest are taxable when credited, regardless of whether or not you have a right to receive the cash without a penalty. The payer is required to supply you with a statement of the correct interest amount to be reported for the tax year.

You should be alert to the benefits of tax-exempt bonds, particularly if you have taxable certificates of deposit.

There are a number of corporations which pay dividends that are partially or wholly tax-free. In addition, a part of a dividend may be considered entitled to the capital-gains treatment. These corporations make certain that their registered stockholders receive this information. If your stock is held by your broker or bank, make certain that you receive it. If you own stock in a public utility or mutual fund, you may also have dividends that are not fully taxable. Write a postcard to the Stockholders' Relations Department of the corporation in which you own stock, if you are uncertain of the tax status of your dividends.

Sometimes it is difficult to figure out the amount of a dividend entitled to special treatment. The company's notice may state that 19¢ or 19% of the dividends are tax-free. Read the notice carefully if the exact amount is not stated on Form 1099 distributed after the close of the year.

STATE AND LOCAL INCOME TAX REFUNDS

A refund of state or local income taxes is income, and the amount does not offset the itemized deduction. Therefore, if you are in a higher bracket, you might consider leaving the overpayment as a credit towards your next year's state or local income tax.

For high-bracket taxpayers, the advantage of the deduction in one year at the maximum personal service income tax rate of 50% may be offset by a following year's refund being taxed at 70%. This is so because the refund is not subject to the maximum tax of 50%.

If, in the prior year, you used the flat standard deduction (called "zero bracket amount"), a refund of that year's state or local income taxes is not reportable this year. You had no tax benefit in the prior year; therefore, there is no income to report currently.

ALIMONY RECEIVED AND PAID

Alimony must be paid under a written agreement. Alimony received is income. Alimony paid is an adjustment to income, which means the payment is deductible whether the payer itemizes or not. The amount deductible by the payer is required to be included in income by the payee.

Many tax disputes arise between former spouses over the amount of alimony one should report as income and the other should claim as deduction. For example, a voluntary increase in alimony not incidental to a decree is *not* deductible.

If you are involved in alimony, be certain that your agreement states clearly what amounts are reportable and who shall claim the personal exemptions for the children. The agreement should also spell out the amount to be considered alimony and the amount to be treated as child support. Periodic payments in discharge of a support obligation are alimony even when characterized as a payment for property rights. If part of the money is for repayment of interspousal gifts, state this clearly. Due to the complexities and the possibilities of serious financial consequences, this is an area for competent professional advice. (Don't ask "your friend the lawyer" who specializes in real-estate closings.) If your alimony agreement fails to spell out clearly the tax status of both parties, the IRS becomes a stakeholder in your disputes. As a result, you and your ex-spouse may both be subject to costly litigation to resolve the issues and there may be substantial losses on either or both sides. Once you have arranged a satisfactory, professionally supervised, written agreement, be sure that your end of the transaction is in accordance with the agreement.

BUSINESS INCOME AND FARM INCOME

A personal-service business (one not dealing in merchandise) should generally adopt the cash-basis method of reporting income and expenses. In a merchandise business where inventories are involved, the IRS permits a "hybrid" method of tax accounting, whereby the sale of merchandise, purchases made, and inventories are on the accrual basis (i.e., when they are earned or incurred). Other income and expenses are permitted to be treated on the cash basis. Since timing is a basic theorem of tax planning, your method of reporting determines when you pay the tax.

When you start a business, you should consult a professional to determine whether the form of the business should be sole proprietorship, general or limited partnership, or regular or Subchapter S corporation. Each of these forms has specific tax attributes, and unfortunately, the decision is not an easy one. If you expect to make a substantial investment, sustain beginning losses, or, happily, large profits, you should first read the IRS Publication 334, *Tax Guide for Small Business*. The IRS also publishes a tax guide for farmers. These guides are updated annually and are free on request. After familiarizing yourself in general with the way individuals, partnerships, and corporations function under the tax law, you will be able to raise specific questions for a professional to answer. The tax law permits several choices. Once the choice is made, it could be costly to you to change the form of organization.

CAPITAL GAINS AND LOSSES

Since Congress has in recent years made a number of changes in the capital gains provisions, you should be aware of the law at the beginning of the year. Any changes made in the statute during the year and effective for the current tax year will generally not affect you adversely. This was certainly true in the case of the Revenue Act of 1978. For example, long-term capital gains incurred after October 31, 1978 are includable in income at 40%, whereas prior gains were subject to a 50% inclusion. The holding period for long-term capital assets is more than one year and the net capital loss allowed against ordinary income is $3,000 per year.

Some of the capital asset concepts to remember include the differences between long-and short-term capital asset transactions:

1. Holding period for long-term treatment is over one year. (i.e., from January 2, 1977 to January 3, 1978 is long-term, but from January 2, 1977 to January 2, 1978 is short-term.)

2. Net long-term capital gain through October 31, 1978 is included in income at one-half the gain. Subsequent gains are included at 40% of the gain.

3. Net long-term capital losses are reduced 50% before applying against income.

4. Net capital gains are subject to tax rate limitation of 25% on the first $50,000 gain and 35% excess over $50,000 gain.

5. The untaxed portion of capital gains is a tax preference for 1978.

Excess capital losses not allowable against your current income may be carried over to your returns for subsequent years.

The importance of offsetting capital-asset transactions within the same year cannot be overemphasized. Thus, a taxable gain early in the year on the sale of your home should trigger the following questions: Is my basis (cost) correct? What improvements, furnishings, appliances, etc., have I failed to include in the basis? Did I increase the cost for transfer taxes, commissions, legal, survey, advertising, telephone calls, etc? Did I increase my interest and real estate tax deductions for closing charges against the sales price, or decrease the same for credits to me? Am I subject to the new $100,000 exclusion rule?

You should compute your gain almost immediately after the closing of the sale of your home. If you sold your house at a loss, such loss is not deductible. You should, however, either report the transaction either on Schedule D, showing no loss and indicating that it was a personal loss, or report the transaction on a statement attached to your return. Do not wait until after the end of the tax year to compute your gain. The chances are that a gain computed early will be reduced later because you might recall a new roof or some other item.

After realizing a capital gain, whether that gain is from the sale of your home, or from the sale of a personal, business, or investment asset, *carefully review all business and investment assets to determine if there are any unrealized losses.*

If there are losses, you should make every effort to realize them before the end of the year. Generally, you should try to take these losses in December. If the stock to be sold is a favorite one, you may *repurchase* the stock either 31 days *before* you sell the same stock or 31 days *after* its sale. This 31-day rule is called the "wash-sale rule" and prevents your taking losses and immediately repurchasing the same security.

Despite widespread belief to the contrary, the sale of your stock in December for a tax loss will not cause an immediate price rise in the market, so that if you repurchase the stock in January on the 31st day, you will pay a premium. With rare exception, you will find that the repurchase price of a wash-sale security in January will probably cost you less than the December trading price after adding two brokerage commissions. In other words, you probably won't have a cash loss.

There is no requirement, of course, that you retain a loss security (one on which you are planning to take a tax loss) until December. If your forecast at the time of the gain suggests that the loss security has little chance of any appreciation to the end of the year, do not wait to sell it, and then use the funds to improve your portfolio position.

The date for determining the holding period of a security is the trade date and not the settlement date. The loss on a security is a current-year loss so long as the trade date is December 31, even though there is a following-year January settlement date. But a capital gain to be reported in the current year must settle on or before December 31. You cannot realize gains after December———(the exact date changes each year) unless your broker can arrange a cash transaction, which may be difficult.

If you sell your personal residence at a gain and reinvest part or all of the proceeds in a new residence, you *must* defer all or part of your gain. You cannot elect to pay the capital-gains tax if you reinvest substantially all of the proceeds in a new residence. IRS Form 2119 will be of great help in making all the calculations.

If you sold your house after July 26, 1978, and you were 55 years old or older, up to $100,000 of the gain may be excluded from income. In addition, any capital gains is not subject to the minimum tax on preferences. For persons 65 years old or over who sold before July 27, 1978, there are special rules and exemptions on the sale of a residence.

The basis of property you sell is generally your cost. Basis subtracted from sales proceeds measures your gain or loss. If you forget the basis of a security, do as follows:

1. Examine the certificate for the date issued.
2. Assume your trade date to have been two months prior to the date of issue.
3. Check your local library's microfilm for the newspaper showing the stock quotations for that trade date.
4. Use the mean price for the day (high plus low divided by two). Add a point ($100 per 100 shares sold) for an approximate commission.
5. For any stock dividends or stock splits to date of sales, adjust the per-share price.
6. Multiply the per-share price by the number of shares sold to arrive at your basis.

If you cannot accomplish any of the steps listed above, write to the corporation and ask for the issuance date of your certificate, the stock price range for that month, and for any price adjustments for stock splits and stock dividends to date.

If you inherited securities or received them as a gift, see ESTATE PLANNING, page 155, and COMPUTING YOUR NET WORTH, page 19.

Gain on the sale of depreciable property (i.e. a building, an automobile used for business, machinery) may be subject to recapture. This means that part of your gain is taxed at less favorable, ordinary income rates. For more about recapture see Chapter 6 (REAL ESTATE) and Chapter 11 (TANGIBLE PROPERTY).

PENSION AND ORDINARY INCOME

Fully taxable pensions and annuities are reported on the first page of Form 1040. Where a part of the payment includes your own cost, the excludable portion is shown on Schedule E.

If you have a choice between accepting an annuity or a lump-sum distribution from a qualified plan, calculate the tax as follows. *Lump-Sum Tax Treatment*: Capital gain's for pre-1974 contributions, and ordinary income for post-1973 contributions, or special 10-year averaging. *Annuity Tax Treatment*: Straight tax rates.

Remember, capital gains in 1978 are subject to the 15% minimum tax on preferences. On the other hand, on a $20,000 lump-sum distribution, using the special formula, $10,000 is tax-exempt. Within 60 days, you may also roll over a lump-sum distribution tax-free to an IRA account.

The tax treatment of pension plan distributions is complicated and you may want to seek professional help.

RENTAL INCOME

If you own rental property, you should use the cash-basis method of reporting income and expenses. An *improvement* to property may be subject to a depreciation deduction based on the total cost of the improvement even though you have not yet paid the total amount due under the contract. You may elect to charge as an *expense* any item of less than $100, even though technically the expenditure was an improvement. An appliance purchased for rental property is eligible for the investment credit; an improvement to real estate generally is not eligible.

Before the end of the year, review the repair and other expense needs of the property. Determine if, for tax purposes, you should accelerate its reparation and pay for it in the current year.

Rent received in advance is current income, and you may wish to postpone receipt until the new year. Tax deferment is perfectly legitimate and should always be a consideration when dealing not only with rental property but all items of income and expense. A December expense reduces any tax amounts due in April. On the other hand, an expense in January cannot be a tax benefit for at least another year to 15 months.

If you have refinanced investment real estate during the year, any mortgage tax paid is a deductible item. The balance of the refinancing costs (attorney's fees, surveys, and services charges) are prorated over the life of the mortgage.

PARTNERSHIPS, ESTATES, TRUSTS, AND SUBCHAPTER S CORPORATIONS

A Form K-l is usually supplied to all parties with taxable transactions relating to partnerships, estates, trusts, and small business (Subchapter S) corporations. The format of Form K-l changes each year, and you must be certain to understand how each figure relates to your taxes. A partnership loss may be a combination of two or more figures from Form K-l. If you are not clear as to how to report an item, you should communicate directly with the preparer of the form.

DEPRECIATION

Depreciation is the deduction allowed over a specific period of time for the cost of a tangible asset of a certain kind. The rates and methods of depreciation have little relationship to reality, but represent instead an attempt by Congress to stimulate or slow down investment in depreciable property.

The following example of the tax choices on the purchase of a $6,000 automobile intended entirely for your business use will enable you to decide whether to try to compute the depreciation yourself or turn it over to a professional. You should probably be able to handle most of the questions once you are aware of the kinds of property which qualify for depreciation and have tried out the various methods to see which are the most advantageous.

You may depreciate your business vehicle over a period of three, four, or five years, depending on the type of vehicle and its useful life in *your* business. You can use one of three methods to depreciate.

In Straight-Line depreciation taken over a four-year life, you would divide the $6,000 cost by four to allow $1,500 depreciation in each of four tax years. In theory, if, at the end of the four years the value of the automobile exceeds 10% of its cost (i.e., more than $600), you are required to reduce the cost on which the depreciation is calculated by such excess. In most cases, this is simply too small an adjustment to make. If you followed the same straight-line method over a three-year period, the depreciation would allow $2,000 for each of three years. For a five-year period the depreciation would be $1,200 a year.

If you wish to use the Standard Mileage Allowance method, check Publication 17 first to see if you qualify. With this method, you would deduct 17¢ per mile for the first 15,000 miles put on your vehicle, and 10¢ for each succeeding mile. If, in the course of business you drove 18,500 miles, your deduction for depreciation repairs, gas, and oil (but excluding parking and tolls) would be

$$15,000 \text{ miles} \times 17¢ = \$2,550$$
$$3,500 \text{ miles} \times 10¢ = \underline{\quad 350}$$
$$\text{Total deduction } \underline{\underline{\$2,900}}$$

So, if your actual costs, including straight-line depreciation, did not exceed the standard mileage, you would not compute depreciation at all for your business automobile.

You may want to use the Double-Declining-Balance method for a new automobile. If this is done for a four-year period, each year being a full year, you will compute it as follows:

1st year: $6,000 ÷ 4 years × 2 =	$3,000
2nd year: $6,000 − $3,000 ÷ 4 years × 2 =	$1,500
3rd year: $6,000 − $3,000 − $1,500 ÷ 4 × 2 =	$750
4th year: $6,000 − $3,000 − $1,500 − $750 ÷ 4 × 2 =	$375
Total cost:	$6,000
Total depreciation allowed:	5,625
Balance left (Salvage)	$ 375

The Sum-of-Years-Digits method applies (in this case) a four-year-life to a diminishing rate: 1 year + 2 years + 3 years + 4 years = 10 years. Ten years becomes the denominator of the fraction:

1st year: $6,000 \times {}^4/_{10} =$	$2,400
2nd year: $6,000 \times {}^3/_{10} =$	1,800
3rd year: $6,000 \times {}^2/_{10} =$	1,200
4th year: $6,000 \times {}^1/_{10} =$	600
Total depreciation:	$6,000

The following compares the methods over a four-year life:

	1ST YEAR	2ND YEAR	3RD YEAR	4TH YEAR	TOTAL
Straight-Line	$1,500	1,500	1,500	1,500	6,000
Double-Declining	$3,000	1,500	850	375	5,625
Sum-of-Years	$2,400	1,800	1,200	600	6,000

You may choose any of these methods and subsequently change to straight-line depreciation, provided you make the necessary adjustments.

There have been many arguments between taxpayers and the IRS regarding the useful life, salvage value, and repair costs of business assets. To reduce controversy in this area, the Asset Depreciation Range (ADR) allows up to 20% shorter lives for certain depreciable assets. If you have purchased substantial business assets, it may be worth your while to adopt this method. (For further details, see IRS Publication 534.) Also, for an asset likely to have a six-year useful life or longer, Congress has allowed a little gift called "bonus depreciation." This allows a 20% deduction on cost in the first year of new tangible business property in addition to regular depreciation. This bonus is limited to $10,000 *of cost* ($20,000 on a joint return).

The basis of most tax shelters is the benefit derived from depreciation and amortization. Amortization is to intangible property what depreciation is to tangible property. For example, an improvement to your landlord's real estate is considered an intangible since you do not own the property. You can amortize the improvement over the remaining life of your lease if you use the property for business or investment purposes.

Remember, larger depreciation deductions delay the impact of tax to later years while the investment credit is a reduction in the tax itself and need never be repaid unless the asset in question is disposed of prematurely. Interest earned on the deferment of tax is a cash flow item. The cost of real estate includes the mortgage on the property. Real estate generally is not subject to the investment credit.

Once you have elected a rate or method of depreciation, you may adopt a new system if the facts should change. You may not change to an accelerated method of depreciation, declining balance, and sum-of-years-digits after the first year.

INVESTMENT CREDIT

There is an arithmetical relationship between useful life, method of depreciation, investment credit, and tax rates. Obviously then, the availability of the investment credit is important in determining the amount of useful life you should claim for property. On a $6,000 automobile used for business, a 10% credit against the tax itself is available if the useful life is seven years or more. If the useful life is reduced to five or six years, the investment credit is reduced to 66⅔%. If the useful life is three or four years, the credit is 33⅓%. No credit is allowed for a useful life of less than three years If there are substantial savings involved (and this is for you to determine), either do the computations carefully yourself or consult a professional.

ADJUSTMENTS TO INCOME

Adjustments to income are deductions allowed which do not affect your eligibility to claim the flat standard deduction. These items also reduce the 1% to 3% of adjusted gross income medical-expense limitations for drugs and other medical costs, thus allowing a larger medical-expense deduction. (See page 125.) They also reduce the charitable limitations.

Adjustments to income include: employee moving expenses; employee business expenses; Individual Retirement Arrangement; self-employed retirement plan; forfeited-interest penalty; alimony paid; and disability income (sick pay). You may claim the above deductions against income and also elect to claim your zero bracket amount (standard deduction).

MOVING EXPENSES

If you are planning to move to another city early in the year, you should be totally familiar with the moving expense requirements before you go to contract on a new home, sell your old home, or incur any expenses involved in the move. To be eligible for the moving expense deduction, the distance between your old home and your new job location must be at least 35 miles more than the distance between your old home and old job location. In addition, you must be employed for at least 39 weeks during the 12-month period after your move.

Deductible moving expenses include travel; moving household goods; house-hunting trips; temporary quarters; and cost of selling the old residence or of disposing of the old lease. There are no limitations on the first two items, but the last three together may total not more than $3,000 overall, with house-hunting and temporary quarters limited to $1,500.

Even though you are paid your salary on the cash basis, you may elect to deduct your moving expenses in the year you are reimbursed by your employer, provided you have paid the expenses *before* the due date of the return for the reimbursement year. Also, you may claim moving expenses even if at the time you filed your return you failed to meet the standard work requirement. You can do this by later filing an amended return (Form 1040X) or reporting as income the amount of your deduction claimed in the year in which you failed to qualify. These options permit a perfect opportunity to save some money. IRS Publication 17 has an excellent example of computing the moving expense adjustment as well as explanation of the IRS's interpretation of the law.

EMPLOYEE BUSINESS EXPENSES

Taxpayers have been battling the IRS over the question of "T&E" (travel and entertainment) expenses for a long time. So far, T&E disputes have been avoided or at least more easily settled by keeping good records. Although the IRS does allow you some expenses merely on trust—don't forget how wide an area of comparison they have to observe—there is still no substitute for an intelligently maintained diary with supporting documents wherever possible. In the past few years, the IRS has made it a policy to allow all reasonable amounts for T&E when these are supported by proper documentation. Don't buy the myth that tells you to take a greater deduction in hopes of finally getting away with a good chunk of it in the event of a review or an audit. This is acceptable neither to the IRS nor to any knowledgeable practitioner. Remember, the IRS auditor will have seen perhaps thousands of comparable expense statements and will therefore know what is reasonable.

If you keep accurate and intelligent records of expenses you will probably be entitled to a "no change" on T&E, meaning "return accepted as filed." By keeping correct tabs on expenses as they occur, you will probably come out ahead, since one tends to forget the dozen or so little expenses of a dollar here and there unless they have been written down.

In general, you should keep the following details in your records. *Travel* requires receipts for transportation and lodging, with food and other costs totaled daily. Dates of trips, places visited, and the business purpose of each trip should all be carefully listed. *Entertainment* requires receipts for expenditures over $25, with others totaled daily, giving date, place, business purpose, and names of person(s) being entertained. Collate your business expense documentation with your diary. It would also be wise to consider attaching a letter from your employer regarding the company's expense account policy. This, together with other factors such as reasonableness of amounts and professional appearance, may prevent an audit of your return. Even if attaching the statement does not prevent an examination, you may impress the examining officer with your understanding of the IRS's record-keeping requirements. The statement from your employer is needed to preclude the assumption that you are illegally taking a double deduction. In addition, the statement serves to prevent your claiming a business-expense deduction for an expenditure that was reimbursable by your employer but for which you voluntarily decided not to seek payment. Do not be embarrassed to request from your employer, on a periodic basis, reimbursement for job-related telephone calls, transportation, stationery, and incidental expenses. Remember, $1 spent by you on business may cost you from 50¢ to 75¢ after tax benefit. The same $1 spent by your employer costs you nothing. Do everything in your power to convince your employer to bear all business expenses rather than have you pay any expenses out of your compensation.

If your employer reimburses you for home entertainment, don't fail to include in the per-person meal charge the wine and liquor costs and incidental expenses such as extra help, a share of utilities, invitations, postage, etc., in order to arrive at a figure which appears fair to you and reasonable to the IRS. In some areas, depending on your job status, $12 per person (including you and your spouse) is acceptable for dinner at home. In other areas, $25 per person is considered reasonable. Work up the figures yourself on a workpaper and use this to document the per-person amount claimed.

Employee business expenses are claimed as adjustments to income or as itemized deductions. An adjustment-to-income deduction does not affect your claiming the standard deduction and is more beneficial to you.

Employee business expenses allowed as adjustment to income are: travel away from home, outside salesperson's expenses, and transportation expenses (excluding commuting). All other employee business expenses are claimed as itemized deductions. Make certain your business expense schedule attached to your return is neat, complete, and mathematically correct.

INDIVIDUAL RETIREMENT ARRANGEMENT
AND SELF-EMPLOYMENT RETIREMENT PLAN

Payments to your Individual Retirement Arrangement (I.R.A.) or HR-10 (self-employment retirement plan), should be made as soon as possible after the beginning of the year. You are permitted to make partial payments during the year and you may make your final I.R.A. or HR-10 payments up to the due date of the return.

By making your payments early in the year, you earn income which is not currently taxable. If you borrow money to make your contribution to the plan, the interest is deductible.

If your employer does not cover you with a qualified retirement plan, you should certainly consider establishing an I.R.A. The maximum payment for an eligible spouse is $1,500. However, if your spouse is not working, you may contribute up to $1,750 divided equally between the two of you.

Establishing a retirement plan is no more difficult than starting a bank account. You may participate through a bank, an insurance company, through mutual funds, or by buying special U.S. bonds through your place of employment. The money may be invested in cash, stocks, bonds, insurance policies, or other property. Participation in an I.R.A. or HR-10 is an excellent tax-planning device. You should be alert to "front-end loads" when investing in your retirement plan. This means that if you terminate the plan in the early years, the proceeds are reduced substantially for origination costs. This is especially true if the I.R.A. is administered by an insurance company.

INTEREST PENALTY FOR PREMATURE
WITHDRAWAL OF SAVINGS

You are required by the IRS to report the gross income credited from all saving accounts. If you withdraw your savings prematurely and are required to forefeit a part of the interest, the penalty for early withdrawal is deductible in computing your adjusted gross income. In other words, you are actually only paying tax on the *net* amount you received. You should be notified by your bank as to what these amounts are.

SICK PAY (DISABILITY INCOME) EXCLUSION

The IRS allows disabled persons who were not 65 by the end of the year and who did not reach mandatory retirement age by the beginning of the new year to claim up to a $5,200 tax deduction.

Even though you may be eligible for the disability income exclusion, you may, under certain circumstances, elect not to exclude this income from your return. For instance, if your disability is such that you believe your life span will be insufficient to allow you to receive the cost of your annuity, you would elect not to exclude the disability income. This would be done so as to treat the disability income as subject to the credit for the elderly.

In recent years sick pay exclusion has been changed substantially. If you are receiving any form of sick pay for a prolonged period, study IRS Publication 522 for both the prior and current year. If you become ineligible, do not assume that such ineligibility will automatically continue for the next year.

ITEMIZED DEDUCTIONS

The remaining part of your income after all the adjustments have been allowed is called the Adjusted Gross Income (AGI). The AGI determines the floor on medical expenses, and the ceiling on charitable deductions.

The broad categories of itemized deductions are: medical expenses, taxes other than federal income tax, interest expenses, contributions, casualty losses, and miscellaneous employee and investment expenses. If the total of your itemized deductions is not within the amounts allowable as a standard deduction, you would elect not to itemize. If you make a mistake and forget a deduction, you may rescind your election by filing Form 1040X before the three-year statute of limitations expires. Home ownership and a state income tax generate sufficient deductions to itemize.

Your standard deduction (zero bracket amount) is determined by your filing status (see page 133):

	SINGLE AND HEAD OF HOUSEHOLD	MARRIED JOINT RETURN	MARRIED SEPARATE RETURNS
ZERO BRACKET AMOUNT	$2,200	$3,200	$1,600

The annual tax tables reflect whatever the zero bracket amount is for a given year. Therefore, your itemized deductions are reduced by the amount otherwise allowed to you. This difference is called your excess itemized deductions. To arrive at your tax table income, you reduce your adjusted gross income by your excess itemized deductions.

Taxable income has been redefined to exclude the zero bracket amount, since that allowance has been built into the tax tables. Therefore, taxable income is determined by simply subtracting your personal exemptions from your tax table income.

MEDICAL EXPENSES

Because of the floor on medical expense deductions, the failure to time your medical expenses properly within a given year could mean the total loss of any tax benefits. Thus, if your Adjusted Gross Income is $25,000, your drugs must exceed 1% of that amount ($250) to be eligible for just the first-level computation. Assume, for example, that your drugs for the year cost $450. Your eligible drug expense would be $200 ($450 − $250). If your doctor's bills totaled $500, your total eligible medical expense would be $700 ($500 + $200). Against the $700 is applied a second limitation—3% of adjusted gross income. The 3% rule ($25,000 times 3%) requires eligible medical expenses to exceed $750 before any amount is allowed. In this example, therefore, none of the drugs or doctor's bills results in a tax deduction. Medical care insurance premiums are the one item not subject to this limitation. Your Blue Cross and major medical premiums are allowed without regard to the floor percentage up to one-half the amount paid and not in excess of $150. If your premiums total $475, you can claim $150 without regard to any percentage limitations, and $325 is included with other medical expenses.

Understanding the above rules, you realize that substantial medical expenses, including dentists, nurses, and hospitals, should be confined to a single tax year whenever possible. Thus, if you are undergoing dental rehabilitation requiring a long treatment period, you should consider, if possible, paying for the dentistry in a single year. You should request that your doctor perform substantially all medical services in that year also. This is done so that each year's bills will not be subject to the floor limitation, thereby saving you substantial money. The IRS and possibly your state are subsidizing your medical expenses to the extent of your tax bracket. Remember to reduce your medical expenses by the amount of any reimbursement. Otherwise it may be income to you in a later year.

Tax-return instructions do not require you to submit medical expense documents. However, if your expenses are unusual in amount or nature, you should consider making full disclosure by separate statement. A copy of a substantial medical, dental, or hospital bill attached to your return could prevent an audit. Especially if you have been in and out of the hospital during the year, a statement showing the hospitals, dates of admission, and lengths of stays will assist the classifier in determining whether your return is worthy of audit.

You can deduct for the transportation costs of medical visits. If you use your automobile, the standard mileage rate is 7¢ per mile plus parking and tolls. If you claim the standard mileage, consult the current year's edition (1979 edition for 1978 returns) of IRS Publication 17 to determine the rate allowable for the year involved.

If you pay medical expenses for a person who qualifies as your dependent but who is not necessarily a personal exemption, you may be able to deduct such medical expenses. Suppose, for example, that you provide more than 50% of your mother's support and her interest and other income outside of social security is $1,200. You are not entitled to a deduction for a personal exemption because her gross income was $1,200, but she is still your dependent for medical. Therefore, any of her medical expenses which you pay directly (*not* expenses which she pays from *your* funds) may be included in your medical expenses.

TAXES

Refunds of state and local income taxes are treated as items of income and are not an offset against the taxes withheld for the current year. There is one exception to this: if you claimed the zero bracket amount last year, any refund of last year's state income tax is not includible in income.

A tax refund is always includible in the tax year in which it is received. An unusual deduction such as a casualty loss with the resultant effect of a substantial overpayment of this year's state income tax may not automatically call for a refund. You may consider using the overpayment as a credit toward next year's tax if (1) you have a floor limitation on substantial medical expenses for next year; or (2) you are subject to 50% maximum tax on earned income (see page 136). Remember also that a tax refund raises the tax bracket of your *unearned* income.

Your state and local income tax deduction includes withheld taxes, the balance of prior year's taxes, all estimated tax payments made within the year, and additional taxes paid for prior years. By December 31 of the current year, substantially all of your state and local income taxes should be paid in order to claim the maximum deduction on your federal return. Your employer should be able to arrange in early December to credit additional amounts to your withheld taxes by depositing your personal check to his withholding tax account; or, you can pay a single estimate to the state at the year's end. Even if you cannot find a state estimated-tax form, send a check with a letter. Mark the bottom left of your check with your social security number and write *Estimated tax* 19—.

Foreign income taxes may either be claimed as a deduction or as a credit. In general you claim the taxes as a credit. However, there is always the rare case in which the foreign tax limitation may reduce the amount you paid, so that after taxes you would benefit more by claiming a deduction instead of a credit. Prepare your tentative tax worksheet, electing the credit. If the entire credit is not allowable, compute your tax liability on a separate workpaper with foreign taxes treated as a deduction.

Real estate taxes due in January of the following year and paid the preceding December are a current year's deduction. If you bought or sold a house, you have either an additional real estate tax deduction or a reduction of the tax paid. The closing statement of the purchase or sale reflects the real estate tax adjustments. If you sold a house, a credit to you as seller reduced your deduction, and a debit increases the deduction. The reverse is true if you are the buyer.

A portion of an assessment (local benefit tax) on a piece of real estate may be deductible to the extent it covers maintenance, repairs, or interest. Ask your local real estate tax collector for this breakdown.

General sales tax is usually computed using the IRS tables. These tables are changed annually. In most cases, the tables are liberal in their allowance. If you had unusual sales tax expenses, due to purchases of appliances or clothing, you may, of course, use the exact amount paid for the year. Even though you use the IRS tables, you may claim additional general sales tax if you purchased an automobile, a boat, an airplane, and/or a home (including a mobile home and materials for building a home). The tables are relatively easy to use. For example, a New York City resident with Adjusted Gross Income (AGI) of $26,000 computes the sales tax deduction for a family of four (1977 table):

1. Deduction for first $19,999 of AGI (per chart) $212
2. Over $19,999 and less than $50,000 equals $6,001
3. 2% is allowed for each $1,000 over $19,999. For $6,001 the excess is 12%; since $1 extra in the $6,001 permits an additional 2%, the total allowed is 14%
4. $212 × 14%   30
5. Tentative deduction for New York State sales tax ($30 + $212) $242
6. Per IRS footnote, add New York City % to above ($242 × 103%) 249
7. Total allowable deduction for general sales tax ($242 + $249) **$491**

If the AGI exceeds $50,000, you add 1% for each $1,000 or fraction over $49,999. And if the AGI exceeds $99,999, you do the calculation starting at Step 1 using 210% of the table plus the footnote.

The gasoline tax deduction is also computed by using the IRS table. You approximate your year's nonbusiness automobile mileage and multiply by the rate. For example, a Michigan resident drives 15,000 nonbusiness miles for the year. At a tax rate of 9¢ the gasoline tax deduction is $115. Remember to include mileage for all automobiles driven during the year for which you paid the tax on gas. Although the IRS permits a larger deduction if your records support it, most people use the table. This deduction has been eliminated after 1978.

Annual local personal property taxes based on the value of property are deductible. If part of the tax is based on other than value, such as automobile weight, that portion is not deductible.

Nondeductible federal taxes include federal income taxes, FICA, estate and gift taxes, and excise taxes.

INTEREST

Generally, a creditor will supply you with the information necessary to support your interest deduction. If you pay interest in advance for a period extending beyond the tax year, you must prorate the interest over the period involved. For example, on December 1 you paid $500 interest in advance on a loan due in 12 months. In the first tax year only 1/12 ($42) of the $500 is deductible. The subsequent year's deductible is the balance of $458. You must have *paid* the interest on your debt (or as co-signer against someone else's debt) to claim the interest legitimately.

Any payment for the use or forbearance of money is considered interest. Thus, "points" paid by you to a lender (even if called premium charges, loan fees, or other names) are treated as deductible interest.

Installment credit finance charges for the year are usually stated on the December bill. If you have paid an installment obligation, and cannot compute the interest factor expressed as an annual percentage rate that is based on the unpaid monthly balance (1) add up the monthly installment payments for the year and (2) multiply the total by 12%. The result is an approximate interest deduction which, in the absence of exact percentages, should be acceptable to an examining officer.

If you bought or sold a house during the year, there is an interest factor to consider from the closing statement. Interest paid to life insurance companies on minimum deposit insurance is deductible.

There is a limitation on the amount of interest allowed for investment purposes. If this interest exceeds $10,000 for the year, you should seek professional assistance.

CONTRIBUTIONS

If, in a particular year, the ratio of your contribution deduction to your AGI exceeds the function factor established by the IRS, there is a good chance that your return will be selected for audit. Therefore, if your large charitable contribution is in property, you should attach to your return copies of all receipts and appraisals. Present your contribution schedule and supporting data in an orderly fashion, designed to convince the classifier that you knew what you were doing when you claimed the deduction.

If part of your real property is being used by the public, you might consider donating the property to your community. You are entitled to a charitable donation to the extent of the fair market value of the gift. Donations to the community for beautification purposes are also deductible. You should be aware that the first category of charitable organization is the federal, state, or local governments.

You should be selective in choosing the charity to which you donate used personal property. Most public charities which accept clothing, furniture, and other personal property are devoted to seeing that the disadvantaged receive the benefits of your donation. Unfortunately, individual charities have varying degrees of tax knowledge about how to evaluate your gift. One charity may not appraise your gift at all while another may have an appraisal committee that treats each gift as a valuable antique. If you believe a charity has undervalued your gift, ask to speak to the appraiser and explain the rule that fair market value is the price at which a willing buyer and a willing seller would exchange the property. In other words, the price paid at the thrift shop's annual bazaar is usually not representative of the true value of good-quality used clothing. And remember, because of your tax bracket an increase in the sale value by $1 means 30¢ in your pocket. It is unfortunate that some of the most worthwhile public charities will do nothing to assist you in the matter of proper valuation, leaving solely to you the burden of substantiating your claim. Your charitable intentions are in no way diminishéd by seeking a tax benefit, nor are you belittling your gift by maximizing its tax value.

If you are donating substantially appreciated property (e.g., a valuable painting) to charity, make certain that you use recognized appraisers. The

IRS maintains an art advisory council to assist in the proper evaluation of property for tax purposes. It is interesting to note that you would seek the highest value for a painting donated to charity. On the other hand, if the same painting were included in an estate of which you were the sole beneficiary, it would be to your advantage to seek the lowest valuation because the low value reduces estate taxes.

CASUALTY AND THEFT LOSSES

If, during the taxable year, property you own is damaged, stolen, or destroyed, you would probably qualify for the casualty loss deduction. After reading IRS Publication 17, if you are still uncertain as to whether your loss is deductible, you should seek professional help. The casualty loss area is constantly being litigated. If your loss appears to be non-deductible, there may be a case pending with your factual pattern. On the other hand, if the IRS says your facts are within their view of casualty losses, by all means claim the deduction.

The amount deductible is the value of the damaged or destroyed property limited to its tax cost. This amount is reduced by insurance plus a $100 deductible. The aftermath of any disasters or accidents to property should be photographed to establish the damage for tax purposes.

The value of a tree destroyed in a storm may be established according to the species and the tree's diameter. Your local landscape firm would probably have a book establishing this value and they can supply you with a letter of confirmation. The cost of cleaning up and carting away the debris is also part of the casualty loss deduction.

EMPLOYEE, INVESTMENT, AND MISCELLANEOUS EXPENSES.

Employee business expenses, tax counsel fees, political contributions (1978 only), custodial fees, and other expenses incurred in connection with income-producing property are deductible. However, to be deductible, these expenses must be paid during the tax year.

If you own marketable securities and follow the price changes in a daily newspaper, the cost of the newspaper is an expense incurred in connection with your income-producing property. Of course, this kind of expense must be reasonable. Thus, $60 a year for financial publications purchased in order to follow a $5,000 securities portfolio would be considered an ordinary and necessary expense.

All legal, accounting, and other professional fees in connection with income, estate, and gift taxes are deductible. Professional fees paid to produce taxable income are usually deductible; however, legal fees paid to acquire property are not currently deductible. The amount paid is added to the cost of the property. If the property is depreciable, the capitalized fees are recovered over the useful life.

If you have a custodian account at your bank, you must allocate the fee paid between taxable and exempt income. The fee allocable to tax-exempt income is not deductible. However, if the income is subject to state and local taxes, you may be entitled to a deduction at those levels.

Although substantial changes were made several years ago in the office-in-home deduction, you should *carefully* consider whether you are eligible. Test yourself with these questions: (1) Do you provide space at home for your business or for the convenience of your employer? (2) If so, is the space used on a regular and exclusive basis (storage space and child-care facilities not having to be exclusive)? If the answer to both questions is yes, you may qualify for the office-in-home deduction.

The deduction is limited to the amount of income received from business use of the home without regard to expenses allowable as itemized deductions, (interest, taxes, and casualty losses). Of course, only the prorated share of the office is deductible. Depreciation is allowable on the office and its furniture. Costs includible and excludible in computing operating expenses as the basis for allocation are as follows:

INCLUDABLE	EXCLUDABLE
Rent	Purely personal household
Heat and light	Painting non-office rooms
Painting office	Repairs of non-office rooms
Painting outside of house	Repairs of non-office appliances
Repairing roof	Landscaping
Depreciation of house	Lawn care
Depreciation of office furniture	Depreciation of household goods

For a complete discussion of office-in-home, request IRS Publication 587.

If you have paid *any* expenditure you believe may have tax significance, first check IRS Publication 17. If Publication 17 states that the item is not deductible and you are still not satisfied, consult one of the private tax guides. If the amount is significant you should definitely seek professional help. Remember, if you are in a question area, your problem may already be in litigation. Or it may have been settled by the courts but the IRS may choose not to agree with them. (The IRS is not required to acquiese to any court decision other than that of the Supreme Court.) Therefore, there are many tax areas wherein for a period of time uncertainty exists.

EXEMPTIONS

A dependent is a person who may qualify as a personal exemption (in 1978 worth a $750 tax deduction) if you provide support and if his or her income is limited. For 1979, this exemption is increased to $1,000. If you meet this criterion, study the actual requirements carefully to determine if by changing one or more facts in your situation you would be entitled to a personal exemption for a dependent. For example, in order for your mother to become your personal exemption her income for 1978 must be $750 or less. (Her social security income does not count towards the $750.) Savings bank interest is includable as part of her income. Therefore, if her income is $750 or more for the year because of savings bank interest, consider asking her to transfer part of her bank balance to Triple A municipal bonds. The interest on tax-exempt bonds is *not* subject to the income test. You have met one criterion for claiming her. Next is the more-than-50%-support requirement. If you are not certain whether you meet this test due to the complicated method of figuring support, request Form 2038 from your IRS district office. In this form the computations are clearly set forth. Even if you fail the more-than-50% support test because your brother and sisters also contribute to your mother's support, she could still qualify as your exemption if you supply more than 10% of her support and if the other contributors mutually agree to your claiming her as an exemption. (The contributors may mutually decide to alternate the right to claim the mother as an exemption each year.)

It is important to remember that you should study the rules for exemptions before the year's end. An exception to this is your child who marries late in the year. Let's say that you paid for your child's summer school and that his or her new spouse worked last summer. If the couple file a joint return, you cannot claim your child as a dependent. On the other hand, if they file separately, you are entitled to your child's personal exemption if the other qualifications are met. It is up to your ingenuity as to how to satisfy the young couple for their personal monetary loss.

Maintaining a student in your home during the school year, although not a personal exemption deduction, may qualify as a charitable contribution if certain criteria are met. If you have in your home a foreign or American student who is neither a dependent nor a relative, you should study the precise qualifications early in the year. Apply the tests to your own tax picture and make every attempt to change your fact pattern to conform to the requirements. As a valid deduction this item is worth up to $50 a month during your tax year.

The qualification requirements for divorced or separated parents are complicated. If you support a child, whether you are the custodian parent or not, you should study the tax rules for personal exemptions carefully. For example, a noncustodial parent who provides at least $1,200 support a year may be entitled to the personal exemption for the child, even though a written agreement may state otherwise. The rule in this case requires the custodial parent to establish that his or her child-support payments exceeded the amounts paid by the other parent. The IRS will allow only one parent to claim the exemption. To be entitled to the deduction your records must show (1) fair value of rental if furnished to the dependent; (2) clothing, medical, and educational expenses; (3) out-of-pocket expenses (allowance and cash); (4) proportionate share of food and nonlodging household costs; (5) vacation and special expenditures; (6) the cost of furniture, appliances, or an automobile (after 1977).

In computing total support, you do *not* consider (1) income and social security taxes paid by dependent on own income; (2) scholarships (includes schooling for handicapped); (3) funeral expenses; and (4) life insurance premiums.

FILING STATUS

Your filing status determines the percentage of your taxable income that you must pay in tax. As a taxpayer, you fall within one of the following filing status categories listed by tax rates:

1. Married, filing separate returns
2. Single
2. Head of household
4. Married, filing jointly
5. Certain widows/widowers.

On a taxable income (not *tax-table* income) of $20,000, the tax differences for these categories are substantial:

	TAX	EXCESS BRACKET
1. Married, filing separate returns	$5,350	45%
2. Single	4,442	34
3. Head of household	4,098	31
4. Married, filing jointly	3,484	28
5. Certain widows/widowers	3,484	28

Obviously the choicest bracket is "married, filing jointly." You are considered to have been married for the entire year if you are married by or on December 31. (A Christmas wedding has paid for many a honeymoon in tax savings.) If your marital status is not clear (i.e., if you are not divorced or legally separated) you may file a joint return.

Determining head of household status requires meeting three requirements: (1) you are unmarried on December 31, (2) you maintain a household, and (3) your household has a resident relative (except a parent who may have his or her household). "Unmarried" means a legal separation. An interlocutory decree of divorce is not a legal separation.

A "single" taxpayer is one who does not fit into any other filing status.

Married persons earning approximately the same salary and having substantial medical expenses may find that a tax savings results from using the "married, filing separate returns" tax table. Married taxpayers filing separate returns are not "single" taxpayers.

A widow or widower can continue to use the "married, filing jointly" tax table for two years after the tax year in which his or her spouse died if the following conditions are met: (1) the widow or widower did not remarry by or on December 31 of the year of death of spouse; (2) he or she claims a dependent child; and (3) he or she maintains a household for that child. You may file a joint return for yourself and your deceased spouse in the year of your spouse's death; and such tax is payable out of your spouse's estate to the extent of the spouse's income. Of course, you may still be personally liable for the tax on the joint return.

TAX COMPUTATION

If you did not itemize your adjusted gross income (AGI) is your tax-table income. If you itemized your deductions, the tax-table income is your AGI *less* itemized deductions *plus* your zero bracket amount. The tax tables give effect to personal exemptions and the zero bracket amount.

The tax tables are used by single, head of household, and married persons filing separately *up to* a tax-table income of $20,000. Married persons filing jointly use the tables for an income of up to $40,000. All others, including those who must itemize deductions or with exemptions exceeding the table, use Schedule TC (Tax Computation). Those using special tax computations should also use the TC schedule.

SPECIAL TAX COMPUTATIONS

ALTERNATIVE TAX (FOR 1978 ONLY)

If you had net long-term capital gains and your tax bracket exceeds 50%, the alternative tax computation may save you money. To compute the alternative tax where the long-term capital gains do not exceed $50,000

1. compute taxable income;
2. reduce taxable income by includable long-term capital gain deduction (the 50% reduction);
3. subtract step 2 from step 1 for ordinary income;
4. compute tax on ordinary income;
5. add 25% of long-term capital gains
6. add steps 4 and 5 to get your alternative tax.

If your net long-term capital gains exceed $50,000, the excess is taxed at a maximum rate of 35%. The alternative tax computation may be combined with the 50% maximum tax rate on personal service income (see page 136).

SCHEDULE G INCOME AVERAGING

If your taxable income for the present year has substantially increased over the prior four years, you may qualify for income averaging. This tax computation method is a tax-bracket reduction formula and, therefore, saves you money. To see if you may qualify for income averaging

1. compute the current year's taxable income;
2. add the prior four years' taxable income (including your spouse's separate income, if unmarried in any year), adjusted to tax-table income by the zero bracket amount;
3. multiply the total of step 2 by 130% (the income-averaging markup) to give base-year taxable income;
4. subtract step 3 from step 1 for averageable income. If the result of steps 1 minus 4 exceeds $3,000, you may elect income averaging.

You then compute the tax as follows:

1. Compute tax on base-period income (Step 3 above).
2. Compute tax on total of base-period income plus 20% of averageable income (Step 4 above).
3. Subtract step 1 from step 2 and multiply the difference by 4.
4. Add steps 2 and 3 for tax using income averaging.
5. Compare with regular tax computation to confirm the tax benefit.

Income earned outside the U.S. and excluded during the base years is added back to base year's taxable income.

Premature distributions under HR-10 plans are excluded in computing the current year's income subject to averaging.

If you live in a community-property state and for the current year expect to file a separate return from that of your spouse, you will have to reduce your taxable income for the current year by any excess of includable, earned community-property income not otherwise taxable to you.

FORM 2555—FOREIGN-INCOME EXCLUSIONS

If a part of your wages was from excluded sources because you were a resident of a foreign country or were abroad for 510 days out of an 18-month period, you compute your tax on Form 2555.

The 1978 Revenue Act contains relief provisions and new elections.

If you have foreign earned income, you are in this category. Follow the media and be certain to obtain IRS Publication 54, *Tax Guide for U.S. Citizens Abroad.*

MAXIMUM TAX

If your tax bracket exceeds 50%, you may qualify for the 50% maximum tax on personal service income. This benefit is applicable as follows:

FILING STATUS	TAX-TABLE INCOME EXCEEDS
Single	$40,200
Head of household	40,200
Married	55,200

You do not qualify if you are married and filing separately or if you elect income averaging.

Since the allocation formula requires the use of the Adjusted Gross Income figure, any reduction in nonearned income increases the percentage of taxable income subject to the 50% maximum rate. Therefore, state and local income tax overpayments should be credited to estimated tax and not be refunded. Medical and casualty reimbursements should be used to reduce expenses in the year incurred. Tax preferences such as the long term capital gains deduction prior to November 1, 1978 reduce the income subject to the maximum tax. Every effort should be made to reduce nonearned income.

GENERAL TAX CREDIT

If you use the tax tables, a general tax credit has already been built into the table. If you use Schedule TC (Tax Computation), the general tax credit is the greater amount arrived at by taking 2% of your taxable income after subtracting either (1) the flat standard deduction, or (2) $35 for each exemption. This credit may not exceed $180.

ADDITIONAL TAXES

You may be required to pay additional taxes on your current year's income if you (1) received an accumulation from a trust, (2) use the special 10-year averaging method for lump-sum distributions from qualified retirement plans or use the multiple recipient method, (3) sold a residence prematurely on which you had previously claimed the new-residence tax credit, or (4) made an excess contribution to your HR-10.

CREDITS AGAINST TAX

In your tax planning, you should carefully consider trying to accumulate credits against your tax. Unlike a deduction, a credit is a dollar-for-dollar reduction in the tax itself. Thus, in the 38% bracket, a $1 credit is worth almost $3 in deductions. Credits are currently available for political contributions, the elderly, child care, investment, foreign tax, work incentive (WIN), new jobs, and residential energy credits.

Political Contributions

You may claim political contributions either as an itemized deduction or as a tax credit. Half of your contribution, with a limit of $50 if married or

$25 if single, may be used as a tax credit. If you are married and have made the maximum $200 contribution ($100 if single) and if your tax bracket exceeds 25%, the deduction method will probably work better for you. If you gave less than the maximum and you are in a higher-than-25% tax bracket, the credit will probably be better for you.

If you are in a lower-than-25% bracket, always claim the credit. In a bracket over 25%, the deduction generally results in greater savings unless you contribute less than the maximum. After 1978 the deduction has been eliminated and the credit has been increased.

Credit for the Elderly

If you are over 65 and your social security does not exceed $2,500 if single or $3,750 if married (and if your spouse is 65), you may qualify for this credit. The credit is 15% of maximum retirement income after reduction for excess earned income.

Credit for Child-care Expenses

The child-care credit has no income limitation. It is available to you if (1) you are employed or looking for work; (2) you maintained a household for a qualifying individual (personal exemption dependent under 15, other dependent if handicapped, or a handicapped spouse); (3) your expenses were necessary for you to be employed; and (4) payment is made to other than a dependent. The amount deductible is limited to 20% of child care or $400 credit for one qualifying individual and a maximum of $800 credit for two or more individuals. If you are married your spouse must be gainfully employed, a full-time student, or be handicapped for you to qualify for the child-care credit.

INVESTMENT CREDIT

A 10% investment credit is available. The credit is applied to the cost of new and used tangible business property having a useful life of at least three years. Your automobile or furnishings used in your employment or business may qualify for the investment credit. Certain structures are also eligible for the investment credit. There are limitations on the individual, partnership, and Subchapter S levels. Carrybacks to prior years and carry-overs to subsequent years are available. Study IRS Publication 572 if you have problems or questions in this area.

FOREIGN TAX CREDIT

The foreign-tax credit is allowed against your U.S. tax for any payments made to a foreign government for income taxes. Not all foreign-tax payments qualify as income taxes, and there has been special pressure on Congress to liberalize this credit. If your foreign taxes are substantial, make certain that you obtain IRS Publication 514 before you prepare your final return. Since most states do not allow the foreign-tax *credit,* compute both credit and deduction results to see which will offer you the more favorable position.

The foreign tax-credit computations are complicated. If your foreign tax withheld from dividends is less than $25 and this is your sole payment of foreign tax, you should consider ignoring both the deduction and credit possibilities and reflect the dividend income as the net amount of cash you actually received.

WORK INCENTIVE PROGRAM

If you employ household help who have been receiving federal assistance payments, you may be permitted 20% of their wages, up to $1,000 per employee, as a tax credit. This program was designed by Congress to encourage average households to employ disadvantaged persons. In order for you to qualify, the employee must have received the federal payments consistently during the 90-day period prior to being hired by you. In addition, the person must have worked for you for more than 30 days on a substantial full-time basis. Only the wages paid during the first 12 months of employment are eligible.

This credit is an excellent opportunity for both tax savings and social benefits. There appears to be no reason why you cannot combine the child-care credit with a WIN credit for a substantial tax advantage. These rules were changed for 1979 (see page 153).

NEW JOBS CREDIT

Up to $100,000 tax credit is available for creating new jobs. This credit cannot exceed 25% of the total wages paid subject to federal unemployment insurance.

This credit is 50% of the total of all eligible wages in excess of 102% of total eligible wages for the prior year. Wages up to $4,200 are eligible, even though the amount of wages subject to federal unemployment insurance may be higher. Obtaining this requires professional assistance.

RESIDENTIAL ENERGY CREDITS

For energy-saving expenditures made on or after April 20, 1977, a 15% tax credit (up to $300) is allowed in 1978. The money must be spent on your principal home. It is allowed to renters. An additional credit is allowed for solar—and wind—energy machines.

OTHER TAXES

Before arriving at your final federal income tax, you must add up your liability for certain other taxes. These other taxes include (1) self-employment tax (social security), (2) tax on preferential income and deductions (minimum tax), (3) investment credit recapture, (4) social security tax on tip income not reported to employer, and (5) uncollected employee social security tax on tips.

These additional taxes (except for the social security) affect relatively few taxpayers. However, you should have a general knowledge about each in the event that in the current year by some chance you might be liable for one or more.

MINIMUM TAX ON PREFERENCES

If you receive certain items of income or claim certain deductions which have been classified as preferences, you may be subject to the minimum tax at a 15% rate. There are eight items of tax preference for 1978:

INCOME
1. Capital gains deduction (excluding residence gain after July 26, 1978).
2. Stock options (excess of value over price at exercise date).

DEDUCTIONS
3. Accelerated depreciation on real property. (For the difference between rate-used and straight-line, see Depreciation, page 343.)
4. Depletion (percent allowed on gross income from mineral interests less cost remaining of property).
5. Excess amortization (affects limited number of facilities which claim fast tax write-off).
6. Accelerated depreciation on leased property (excess over straight-line rate).
7. Excess itemized deductions (difference between 60% of your AGI less itemized deductions adjusted).

8. Intangible drilling costs (cost of drilling a successful well less limited amortization of such costs).

Add up these items of tax preference. If they total in excess of $10,000 ($5,000 if married, filing separately), you must file the minimum tax schedule. You are allowed a deduction of the greater of $10,000 or one-half of your regular tax against the tax-preference income. The balance is subject to the 15% minimum tax. For 1979 there have been changes in the minimum tax (see page 153).

If you had net operating losses, deferment of the minimum tax is permitted.

INVESTMENT CREDIT RECAPTURE

The purchase of tangible property used in business may qualify for the 10% investment credit. At the time you claim the investment credit, you elect a useful life to which the maximum 10% rate is applied.

If you dispose of the asset before the estimated useful life ends, you must recompute the investment credit. You make this computation in the year in which the disposition takes place. For example, you purchased an automobile for business purposes. In the year of purchase you estimated a five-year useful life. You paid $6,000 for the automobile. Your investment credit in the year of purchase was $400 ($6000 × 66⅔ × 10%). Three years later, your company gives you an automobile and you sell your business car. Since you estimated a five-year life for this asset but disposed of it in the third year, you are required to recapture part of the $400 investment credit originally claimed. The tax on recapture would be $200 computed as follows:

Investment credit claimed (5-year estimated life, $600 × 66⅔ × 10%)	$400
Investment credit properly allowed (3-year actual life,—$6.000 × 33⅓ × 10%)	200
Tax on recapture	$200

In your current year's return, you would repay the $200 investment credit recaptured.

If you traded in your business automobile prematurely, you may have a recapture tax on the old one and an investment credit allowed on the new automobile.

SOCIAL SECURITY TAX ADJUSTMENTS

You are required to pay a social security tax of 8.10% on your first $17,700 of self-employment income. (Any wages earned within the year from a previous employer and on which FICA has been paid may reduce this base.) There are special rules for farmers computing the self-employment tax.

Tips are subject to both income tax and, if in excess of $20 a month, to social security tax. If you did not report these tips to your employer, you must include the income on your return. You are required to pay both the income tax and the social security tax on the unreported tips. If your employer reported the tips on your W-2 Form but failed to withhold your share of the FICA, you must pay this tax with your income tax return.

TAX ON PREMATURE DISTRIBUTION
INDIVIDUAL RETIREMENT ARRANGEMENT (I.R.A.)

If you receive a distribution from your I.R.A. before you reach age 59½ (or become disabled), you pay a 10% additional tax. The amount received is included in gross income and the 10% tax is a penalty for premature withdrawal of the savings.

PAYMENT OF TAX

Your total federal income tax is the tax computation reduced by credits and increased by any other taxes. Your liability to the IRS on the filing date is determined by subtracting your or your employer's payments from the tax. The excess or reminder of tax over payments is required to be paid by April 15 following the close of the previous calendar year. Refunds are paid, without interest, within 45 days. (Interest is due thereafter.) Payments made by you later than April 15 are subject to interest in addition to a penalty if your payment is delayed without reasonable cause. If you failed to pay sufficient withholding estimated taxes or other payments you may be subject to the penalty tax for underestimation. The due date for your 1978 return is April 16, 1979.

The following are also considered additional tax payments: excess of FICA over the limitation from two or more employers; credit for non-highway use of fuels (motorboat, tractor, and/or other vehicles not used on highways); tax paid on your behalf on dividends paid you by a regular investment company (if this applicable, a notice is sent to you).

Earned-income credit is also an additional tax payment. You qualify for this if the greater sum of your earned income or Adjusted Gross Income (AGI) is less than $8,000 and if you maintain a household for a child who is under 19, for a full-time student, or for someone who is disabled. If you are married you must be filing a joint return. This credit is computed on 10% of the first $4,000 of earned income reduced by 10% of income over $4,000. Credit is eliminated at $8,000 of earned income. This credit has been liberalized for 1979.

UNDERESTIMATION OF TAX

If you failed to pay proper estimated taxes on the installment dates, you are penalized 6% per successive quarter. This penalty applies if you owe 20% or more of the final tax, without regard to the minimum tax.

You avoid the penalty, if your payments are equal to your prior year's tax (excluding tax preferences). There are special formulas for avoiding the penalty for first, second, and third quarters by annualizing your income, computing the tax due for each quarter, or by recomputing the prior year's tax using the current year's exemptions.

If your return shows that you owe 20% or more of the tax and you can avoid the penalty by one of the exceptions, you should include Form 2210 with the return. It is not necessary to complete the entire form if you are not subject to the penalty because the current year's withholding plus your estimated tax are equal to or exceed the prior year's tax. Complete only the four columns of Exception 1.

Complete Form 2210 if you are subject to the penalty. You pay the penalty on the due date of the return.

TAX SHELTERS

Tax shelters are the legal means by which you avoid tax by claiming deductions now which you will report as income in later years. In other words, a tax shelter is an investment designed to defer current taxes.

Tax shelters are devised mainly in real estate through the depreciation deduction, but they have been set up for motion pictures, record companies, in publishing, airplanes, computers, coal mines, and for the acquisition of any property where the deduction is at least equal to or more than the cash required for investment. The law in recent years has substantially reduced the effectiveness of tax shelters although you can be assured that new and unusual tax shelters can always appear.

The cardinal rule for investing in a tax shelter is: *first determine the economic upside.* If you cannot make a profit other than tax benefits, you can be certain that your tax-shelter investment will be attacked by the IRS, which has established groups of experienced revenue agents to audit tax shelters. The fact that reputable firms of professionals are involved does not guarantee that the IRS will approve the shelter. Read the legal opinion on the tax aspects of a proposed shelter carefully. Count the number of sentences that read something like "The IRS *might* hold. . . . " and then, after consulting with your adviser (who should not be receiving a commission from the promoter, and who should receive a fee from you whether or not you buy), make your own decision. Never rush into a deal on Saturday afternoon because it must close on Monday morning.

There is a widespread belief among experienced tax practitioners that you should rarely invest in a tax shelter unless your Federal tax bracket is in excess of 50%, and then you should restrict the deductions to that bracket or above. In other words, if your bracket is 50% a tax shelter should not reduce it below 50% (tax-table income of $55,200 if married and filing jointly).

The actual tax-shelter dollars are the excess of deductions over cash outlay. Congress in many instances has approved certain tax shelters to stimulate and encourage the private sector to develop low-income housing and other projects currently viewed as socially desirable.

RECONCILIATION OF CASH FLOW TO TAX WORKSHEET

If you have completed your cash flow or your actual budget for the year, your tax worksheet has been substantially completed. In general, you may need the following further information to complete your return: taxable stock distributions, costs of assets sold, other income items such as partnership income not included in cash inflow, property contributions, casualty loss calculations, exemptions, and other deductions not related to cash outlay, such as gasoline tax and sales tax.

PREPARING YOUR TAX WORKSHEET

Your tax worksheet is the transitional step between your tax data and the tax form (Form 1040).

The cash flow of "Daniel and Louise Smith" is used as the basis for the accompanying worksheet, which has exactly the same form that you would use for tax projections, with one exception: your projection would compute your state and local income tax liability before the federal tax. (If there is any balance due at the year's end in your state and local income tax, you may pay that balance by December 31 and receive a current-year deduction.)

On your tax projection, you may wish to round off amounts to the nearest $100 ($236 becomes $200 and $250 become $300). This is perfectly permissible and aids you in telling quickly the difference between the tax worksheet figures and the tax projection figures. In addition, by rounding off to the nearest $100 on the projection, later changes are easier and neater to make.

After you have completed your own tax worksheet, you need only transfer the data to the tax form, attach Form W-2 and a check (if necessary), and sign the return. Be sure to recheck all your calculations, and if it is a joint return, your spouse must also sign.

TAX WORKSHEET FOR THE SMITHS

The Smiths' tax worksheet and accompanying schedule contain almost all the tax data and computations necessary to complete their Form 1040, U.S. Individual Income Tax Return. The worksheet brings down the final balance of tax due or overpaid which must be compared with the Form 1040.

The source of each document supporting the items of income and deductions is referred to on the worksheet. In general, the basic workpaper for the worksheet is the cash flow statement. Occasionally, because further details are required (e.g., payers of dividends and interest), you would use the cash receipts and adjustment workpapers. In addition, the non-cash items such as capital gains and losses and depreciation must be added to the cash flow figures.

For future reference, the date you began your worksheet preparation should appear in the top left-hand corner of the first page. If your basic documentation is organized, the worksheet should require about one evening's work.

Since many states permit spouses to elect separate state returns after filing joint federal returns, you should show the spouse responsible for the production of income by either an (*H*) or a (*W*). You and your spouse might elect to file separate state returns if each of you had a separate income and if the tax-rate table for your state was the same whether you are single or married. On the other hand, if both you and your spouse work and one of you had large capital gains while the other had large capital losses, you should consider filing a joint state return. Remember to review your state and local tax return options each year.

Your income sources are derived from the cash flow statement, the net worth statement, payer documents (i.e., Form W-2 and Form 1099) and from receipt data. Supporting schedules such as the cash receipts workpaper and individual net worth accounts may also be required to amplify the information needed for the tax form.

Note that all interest income received by or credited to the Smiths was taxable. They owned no tax-exempt municipal bonds. The $5,000 U.S. Savings Bond Series E carried in the net worth has an interest-appreciation factor each year. The Smiths, however, have never elected to report current E Bond interest. When the bond is redeemed, they will report the entire interest earned on the bond. You may elect to report all the accrued E Bond interest in one year and thereafter report the interest as earned. Thus when you redeem the bonds, there will be no interest to be reported. In most cases, however, you would probably be in a lower tax bracket when you redeem the bonds, and thus, a current reporting of E Bond interest would work to your tax disadvantage. U.S. interest received by check or by coupon collection is taxable. Your state may exempt U.S. interest. However, this exempt U.S. interest does not include interest paid on delayed U.S. tax refunds.

The Smiths' dividends are received only by the wife since the securities are registered in her name. Therefore, the $200 dividend exclusion available to married couples has been reduced to the $100 limitation for one spouse. Whether the securities should be jointly owned is discussed under Estate Planning. As a general rule, securities should be in the name of the owner.

Capital gains and losses require additional documentation. The cash flow shows only proceeds received from the sale of securities. Additional information is required for cost of securities sold, prior year's capital-loss carryover, installment sales' recognized gain, and recapture of gain from depreciable property as ordinary income.

The cost of the security sold was obtained from Mr. Smith's prior year net worth workpaper "marketable securities." The information is also available from the broker's purchase slip or statement.

The installment sale for the Smiths was set forth in the workpaper on Mortgage Receivable. The real estate sold by the Smiths is being paid for by the purchaser over a number of years. The original sale qualified as an installment sale. Each year part of the principal payments received on the mortgage includes gain to be reported currently. The mortgage receivable payments were received prior to November 1, 1978; therefore the 60% capital gains deduction was not available. Future years collections will be subject to the 60% deduction even though the sale took place before November 1, 1978.

The post-December 31, 1978 net capital loss offsets the earlier gains.

The financial information for the Smiths' vacation home requires its own separate schedule. Since there was no personal use of the home during the year, the Smiths did not have to allocate any of the expenses between tax-deductible and personal items. All the figures, with three exceptions, were derived from the cash flow statement. The additional amounts to be added to expenses were cash outlay for miscellaneous supplies and repairs, inspection trips, and depreciation.

Petty cash items for hardware, landscaping, and repairs made during the year should be added to expenses. Retain these receipts in a separate folder in your paid-bill file so that you can run up a total when creating your tax worksheet.

After each tenancy, Mr. or Mrs. Smith personally inspected the premises for damage and in order to ascertain the condition of the home for the next tenant. The transportation costs of these inspection trips was computed at the standard mileage rate, plus tolls.

Depreciation is an allowable expense to cover the cost of tangible property over its useful life. Land is not subject to depreciation. When the Smiths acquired their vacation home for rental purposes, they allocated the cost of the property between land and building. The original useful life was determined to be 25 years and the method for depreciation adopted was straight-line. Therefore, a 4% (100% ÷ 25) depreciation charge each year of the cost of the building is made against taxable income.

Medical expenses may be subject to three different limitations:

1. Health insurance premiums: $150 allowable in any case where premiums exceed $300 (otherwise, 50% of amount paid). Excess included in other medical expenses. Includes Medicare, Blue Cross, and major medical. Does not include premiums for solely disability payments.

2. Drugs: excess of expenses over 1% of AGI to other medical expenses.

3. Other medical expenses: excess premiums and drugs together with doctors, dentists, hospitals, and all expenses for medical treatments. This total is reduced by 3% of AGI for allowable amount of deductible medical expenses.

The Smiths received the benefit of only $150 of health insurance premiums.

The deduction for taxes was derived from the cash flow statement, Forms W-2, the sales tax table, and the gasoline tax table. A separate schedule shows how the Smiths computed their general sales-tax allowance from the IRS tables. The sales tax paid on the automobile purchased is allowed separately. Remember, if after completing your return you are required to change the AGI, redo the sales tax only if the AGI change is significant. The mileage for the gasoline tax allowance (1979 not allowable) is the personal mileage less business use (inspection trips to the rented-out vacation home) mileage. The balance of the prior year's state and local income taxes is a current deduction.

The interest-expense deduction figures were obtained from both the cash flow and net worth statements. Interest paid in advance is not a current deduction and must be prorated. There is a net worth workpaper for interest paid in advance which shows how the deduction for interest paid on both automobile notes was computed.

The contributions made out-of-pocket and in property must be added to the cash flow figure. Generally, the IRS accepts up to $1.50 a week for out-of-pocket contributions or $78 for the year. The clothing contribution was supported by a receipt which includes the appraisal. The Smiths did not have any casualty losses this year.

Miscellaneous deductions came from the cash flow statement. There were no cash outlays. Except for Mr. Smith's business subscriptions, all business expenses were paid by the employers. There were no additional expenses to be claimed. The political contribution option indicates that the Smiths saved money by claiming the payment as a credit. The option worked in favor of the credit since the contribution was less than the $200 maximum allowed and the Smiths' tax bracket exceeded 25%.

The total of the itemized deductions must be reduced by the zero bracket amount of $3,200 if a married couple filing jointly are computing their tax according to the tax table. The tax-table income is the Adjusted Gross Income less the excess itemized deductions. The Smiths used the tax table to calculate the correct tax, including the general tax credit. Schedule TC is used for computing the tax for those ineligible for the tax table.

The Smiths took four exemptions for the current year. Although Mr. Smith paid $1,200 to his mother as an allowance, this was not more than 50% of her support. Mr. Smith's brother, Norton, also contributed to their mother's support. The exemption is subject to a multiple-support agreement, since the mother's gross income for 1978 did not exceed $750.

Daniel and Louise Smith
Tax Worksheet
Calendar Year 1978

		1	2	3	4
1	Income:				
2	Wages				
3	(H)	Acme Manufacturing Corp. (W-2)		25000	
4	(W)	May's Food Stores, Inc. (W-2)		10000	
5	Total Wages				35000
6	Interest Income				
7	(H)	Union Dime (form 1099)		121	
8	(W)	Union Dime (form 1099)		199	
9	(W)	Manhattan Savings Bank (form 1099)		341	
10	(H)	J. Buyer (Mtge. Rec. - Cash Receipts)		968	
11	(H)	W. Danson (Loan - Cash Receipts)		120	
12	Taxable Interest				1749
13	Dividends				
14	(W)	(Cash Receipts and forms 1099		434	
15	Less. Exclusion (W only)			100	
16	Taxable Dividends				334
17	Capital gains (or Losses)				
18	(H)	1975 Installment Sale of Land			
19	gain to be reported				
20	(Mtge. Receivable Workpaper - chapter 2)			2376	
21	(W)	100 Kaiser Industries - sold 5/12/78	1819 *		
22	cost 12/27/74	455	1364		
23	(W)	50 Bethlehem Steel - sold 12/29/78	1008 *		
24	cost 9/26/73	1704	(696)		
25	(* Examples use 1977 prices on sales dates.)				
26	Total Capital gains			3044	
27	Less. 50% Deduction for Long Term (No post 10/31/78 gains)			1522	
28	Net Long Term Capital gains				1522
29	(H)	Vacation Home - Net Rental / Income			
30	(Real Estate Workpaper - chapter 10)				711
31						
32	Total Income				39316
33						
34	Less. Adjustments to Income:				
35	(W)	Individual Retirement Arrangement			1500
36						
37	Adjusted gross Income (forward)				37816

149

Daniel and Louise Smith
Tax Worksheet
Calendar Year 1978

	1	2	3	4
Adjusted Gross Income (forward)				37816
Itemized Deductions:				
Medical Expenses				
Drugs		137		
Less. 1% of Adjusted Gross Income		378		
Drugs Allowable			-0-	
Health Insurance Premiums		436		
Less, 50% limited to 150 (Below)		150		
Includable Insurance			286	
Doctors, Dentists, etc.			273	
Medical Transportation (300 mi. × 7¢)			21	
Includable Medical			580	
Less, 3% of Adjusted Gross Income			1134	
Medical Allowable			-0-	
Health Insurance Premiums—Maximum				150
Taxes				
State Income: Balance 1977		127		
Wtx 1978 (H)		1637		
Wtx 1978 (W)		356	2120	
Local Income Wtx (H)			108	
Real Estate Residence			2004	
Sales Tax — 1977 Table			504	
— Auto Purchased			420	
Gasoline Tax —Mileage less Vermont				
Trips re. Vacation Home (16500 mi × 8¢ table)			109	
Total Taxes				5265
Interest Expense				
Mortgage Residence			4428	
Life Insurance : Canada Life		133		
Mony		138	271	
Automobiles —Citibank (Prepaid int. Workpaper-ch.2)			252	
—GMAC (" " " -ch.2)			50	
Total Interest Expense				5001
Contributions— By check			395	
Out-of-pocket (52 weeks × $1.50)			78	
Property (Clothing to Irvington House)			125	
Total Contributions				598
Subtotal (forward)				11014

	1	2	3	4
1 Adjusted Gross Income (forward)				37816
2 Subtotals of Itemized Deductions (forward)				11014
3				
4 Miscellaneous Deductions				
5 Business Expenses (H)			161	
6 Safe Deposit Box			11	
7 Tax Preparation Fee (1977 return)			225	
8 Total Miscellaneous Deductions				397
9				
10 Total Itemized Deductions				11411
11 Less, zero Bracket amount				3200
12 Excess Itemized Deductions				8211
13				
14 Tax Table Income				29605
15				
16 Exemptions (4 - Mother claimed by brother this year)				
17				
18 Tax per Tax Table (filing jointly)				5296
19				
20 Less, Credits				
21 Political Contributions (50 × 50%)		25		
22 Child Care (1250 × 20%)		250		
23 Total Credits				275
24				
25 Federal Income Tax				5021
26				
27 Less, Payments wtx (H)			4361	
28 wtx (W)			1053	
29 Total Payments				5414
30				
31 Balance (Overpayment - to be refunded)				(393)

This year Norton will claim the exemption for the mother and the following year it will be Daniel's turn for the exemption. Daniel will send Norton a Form 2120, Multiple Support Declaration, for him to attach to his return.

The Smiths' top tax bracket is 32% (tax-table income less $3,000). That initial tax computation is reduced by the credits for political contributions and child care. There were no other taxes due. The Smiths have a qualifying child in a nursery school. The $250 credit does not exceed the $400 limitation. Review each item of credit and other taxes to be certain you understand them and their applicability to *your* taxes.

After you have completed your own tax worksheet, you need only transfer the data to the tax form, attach Form W-2 and a check (if necessary), and sign the return. Be sure to recheck all your calculations, and if it is a joint return, your spouse must also sign.

The federal income tax for the year is reduced by the Smiths' payments, and the excess will be refunded. The Smiths do not reasonably expect their next year's estimated tax to be $100 or more. No estimated tax is required for the subsequent year even though they had outside income not subject to withholding taxes.

REVENUE ACT OF 1978

In November, 1978 President Carter signed the Revenue Act of 1978, the Energy Tax Act, and the Foreign Earned Income Act. Those provisions affecting your 1978 return have been discussed previously. The changes effective for 1979 returns are summarized in alphabetical order, as follows:

1. Capital gains: eliminated alternative tax computation.

2. Earned income credit: increased to 10% of first $5,000 of earned income; credit phased out between $6,000 and $10,000; starting July 1, 1979 integrated with withholding tax tables.

3. Entertainment: eliminated deduction for yachts, hunting lodges, and other similar-type facilities. Country club expenses are still deductible.

4. Gasoline tax deduction: eliminated state gasoline tax deduction for non-business automobile use.

5. Investment credit: increased amount of credit allowed against tax in excess of $25,000.

6. Job credit: changed to targeted jobs tax credit; credit equal to 50% of first $6,000 qualified first-year wages; encourages hiring of handicapped, certain Vietnam veterans, and disadvantaged persons.

7. Maximum tax: eliminated reduction of personal service income by capital gains deduction.

8. Minimum tax: became two taxes; one is an add-on to regular tax; the second is an alternative tax; add-on tax eliminated preferences for capital gains deduction and excess itemized deductions; alternative tax adds to taxable income capital gains deduction and excess itemized deductions. Alternative minimum tax has $20,000 exemption; eliminated from excess itemized deduction preference are state and local taxes.

9. Personal exemptions: increased to $1,000 for each eligible dependent.

10. Political contribution: eliminated deduction; credit increased to $100 on a joint return and $50 on a separate return.

11. Rate cuts: widened tax brackets to ease inflationary trend of taxable income.

12. Tax shelters: extended "at risk" rules to everything except real estate.

13. Unemployment compensation: benefits may be taxable if adjusted gross income is over $25,000 on a joint return and $20,000 for a separate return.

14. WIN credit: changed to be similar to new targeted job credit.

15. Zero bracket amount: increased to $3,400 for married filing jointly; $2,300 for single and $3,000 for head of household.

There are other changes made in the tax law for 1979 but these changes will either come to your attention in the tax computation or not be applicable to you. The 1978 estate tax changes will be discussed in Chapter 6.

CONCLUSION

After you have completed your tax worksheet and tax return, you may want to seek professional assistance to review your work. A professional preparer can audit the return and make suggestions for both additional savings and your written presentation. If you prepare your final return yourself, the professional fee for tax preparation is substantially less than if the professional did the entire job for you.

This chapter has been designed to make you *think* about your taxes during the entire year instead of suffering through a state of acute anxiety for the last two or three weeks of every year. Items of income and expense that affect most individuals were chosen to alert you to the general problems involved, help you solve some of these problems, and suggest where to go for help from others. First and foremost, you must organize your own tax affairs. Without the right facts, the best tax professional is of little or no use.

## 6

ESTATE PLANNING

IN THE 19TH CENTURY, the average English or French reader of fiction knew far more about the importance of estate planning than most of us do today. Every good writer from Jane Austen to Anthony Trollope knew that the question of inheritance was a burning issue for the middle and upper classes and wrote accordingly. Louis Auchincloss among today's serious writers knows well how to cover the hidden dramas inherent in estate planning. But then, Auchincloss works as a practicing lawyer as well as a novelist.

Today wealth and property are more widely distributed throughout our society than ever before. One need neither have a penchant for fiction nor be a lawyer in order to be concerned with these questions. Almost every reader of this book has a serious interest in the question of estate planning. Yet the average reader may continue to think that serious estate planning is for *"them,"* rather than for himself. When you have finished reading this chapter, it is hoped that you will not simply again relegate this question to the realms of the multi-millionaires, but will realize that intelligent estate planning may be the best thing you can ever have for your survivors and heirs. (Writers casting around for a good theme might find this helpful too.)

Once you realize that you should *plan* your estate, it may seem to you that the complexities of your business affairs are so great that a fortune can be spent sorting things out. It is true that later developments may diminish the validity of certain solutions, but this should not discourage you. You may be surprised to find that the same problem patterns arise in rich, middle-income, and poor families. It is rare to find a genuinely unique situation.

The solutions suggested in this chapter may not prove perfect in all respects, but *planned solutions* will always be more satisfactory than chaos, even when extensive adjustments have to be made. Remember also that your family may be emotionally less capable of coping with what may now seem simple problems, due to the emotional distress caused by your death. The tax and financial considerations may not work out perfectly, but when you weigh in the human elements, a carefully planned estate will generally produce satisfactory results.

MAKING YOUR WILL

The basic tool of estate planning is the will, the written testimony of your wishes regarding the distribution of your money and property. The will is supported by legal powers which you delegate to individuals or to institutions who will be bound contractually to carry out your plans after your death. The will is an extremely personal document and as such, the law will allow only you or your attorney to prepare it. The execution of your stated wishes is enforced by the probate court. This judicial enforcement of wills is a cornerstone of individual and property rights in all free societies.

The disposal of money and property is only one purpose of a will. The other major (and many times sole) purpose of a will is the provision for the welfare of individuals. If, after your death, it is found that you have left no valid will, the state will intervene through the laws of intestacy and will decide which person or institution is to administer your estate and to whom and in what proportion your assets are to be distributed.

Wills can be very simple. You may decide to write yours out in longhand and sign it as testator. This is called a holographic will, and it can be valid even without witnesses. (If someone, however, wishes to legally challenge your capacity to prepare this form properly, such a will may prove complex in the end.)

Usually, a will is typewritten, dated on the day of its execution, and signed by its testator. Witnesses (adults) then attest to the authenticity of the signature by signing the will themselves. The witnesses must not be mentioned in the will, nor should they be persons who could take an intestate share of your estate if you fail to provide a valid will. Most states require two witnesses and they must both be present when the will is executed. An attorney will usually provide a third witness so that the inability to locate one of the witnesses after the testator's death will not delay the probation of the will. Thus, any two of the three witnesses will suffice.

It is not usually required that a notary be present when the witnesses sign the will, but many states permit having a notary at the signing to take acknowledgement from the witnesses. These acknowledgements may later be used as a substitute for the personal appearance of witnesses in the probate court. This is called a self-proving will.

Though the will is the basic document of this process, it is really the final step in planning your estate. Your planning should not be limited to monetary and property considerations. There are human repercussions to a will, and you should think these out carefully and gather your information sensibly and sensitively.

In the event of your unexpected death, if your children are minors, your failure to prepare a will may bring about a family catastrophe or at the very least cause serious psychological damage to your children. A healthy child can survive the death of a parent emotionally, but he or she may ultimately find that the emotional loss is the least of the problems. Every professional can cite instances of parents taking leave of their children and telling them that in the *remote* chance of an accident, Uncle John would be their guardian. The children abhor Uncle John, but until now they have held their peace in deference to their parents' obvious fondness for him. The children now tell the parents that they would rather have *anyone* but Uncle John, and the parents, surprised, realize they will have to change the will when they return. But suppose they *don't* return?

Perhaps this example is a little too melodramatic for your taste, although you have read it often enough in the newspapers. And you have also certainly heard of a surviving parent dying whether from accident, disease, or grief after the death of his or her spouse. With the increasing frequency of divorce, there are more single parents these days than ever. Such parents should be doubly aware of the problem.

Let us suppose all your near relations likely to be named guardians by the court in the event of your intestate death adore your children and are, in turn, adored by them. In the event of a common disaster, taking both parents or the single, divorced parent, ignorant but well-intentioned neighbors have been known to come into the homes of deceased parents and, in the interim pending a court decision, discuss in front of the children the possibility of *their* being named guardians. Or relatives will quarrel among themselves over this question if there is no will. If your own good sense does not tell you how possible or even probable the above situations are, any professional estate planner can quickly tell you that they are commonplace.

Don't hide the possibility of your death from your children. They *are* thinking about it. They do not think about it the way you do because you most likely have experienced more of death. But to the child who has never faced the question experientially, the possibility may loom so large and awesome as to prevent talking about it. Mention death to your child when you think the child has reached an appropriate age. Bring what you know about your child to bear in selecting the proper moment. If you feel incapable of doing this without some guidance, consult one or more of the many books published over the last few years on death and dying. Once you have brought the question of death out into the open and have, however casually, discussed the child's needs, fears, and personal reactions, you will have provided some relief and a measure of certainty for him or her. Your knowledge of the personalities involved should help you make suggestions to your child about guardians, but you should listen seriously to your child's view and give it great weight. Children old enough to discuss this question often have surprising insights into their own needs in such a situation. You may be startled by certain perceptions of adult relatives and friends, but do not be defensive or aggressive in this matter. Above all, don't take offense at the candor of the child's remarks. It is this candor that you should be eliciting above all else. In the event of a common disaster, the situation will be far less traumatic if your child can confidently name the person or persons appointed as guardians in your will and know how to reach that person. (It is rather improbable that a young child will know the name of your estate-planner.) If your will provides for virtually nothing more than these circumstances it will have served its most important human function.

It may occur to you and your spouse that the person or persons who would be perfect emotionally and psychologically as guardians would be incompetent to handle the financial management of your estate. This problem can readily be solved. Different states use somewhat different terminology, but basically it is possible to separate the functions of individuals into guardians of minor children (or incompetents) and guardians of property. Business and investment acumen (or the lack of it), lifestyle, and marital status inconsistent (or consistent) with the needs of the children may be serious reasons for the separation of these functions.

If you have not given intelligent forethought to these questions, after your death court proceedings may be necessary to resolve your lack of preparation. Such battles are expensive and the cost is usually borne by the estate. So do your best to choose wisely and well in the planning of your will and with the informed consent of all involved. This can save your heir(s) a great deal of money.

As the following section will make clear, the preparation of a will requires specific legal expertise. Unless your family and estate needs are so basic or your knowledge is so sophisticated that you are capable of preparing your own will, you would be well-advised to retain the services of a lawyer. The fees for the preparation of a will are usually reasonable, and these should be settled before you retain the lawyer's services.

In general, a will provides the following material in sequential order:

1. Name of testator, domicile, capacity to make a will and revocation of prior wills and codicils (changes made in a will without the need for an entire new will)

2. Payment of administration expenses and testator's debts

3. Specific legacies (personal and real property existing at the time of death bequeathed to named persons)

4. Cash legacies

5. Bequest of balance of personal property

6. Bequest of residuary estate (entire balance remaining)

7. Appointment of guardian for minor child or incompetent

8. Common disaster provision (which spouse deemed to survive)

9. Appointment of executor (if trusts involved, appointment of trustee) and executor's successors

10. Powers of executor (and trustee) in addition to those provided by law

11. Special instructions

12. Date executed and signature of the testator

13. Signatures and place of residence of witnesses (not required to be notarized).

In addition to a will, an estate planner may use a trust to carry out a testator's family requirements. A trust is a legal entity consisting of four parties: a settlor (donor), trustee (fiduciary), beneficiary (life tenant), and remainderman (*corpus donee*). The "parties" need not be different individuals. A settlor may also be the trustee and the beneficiary. For example, a trust is created when A gives property in trust to B as trustee for the lifetime of C, and at C's death the property passes to D. Party A could have named himself or herself as trustee and beneficiary. Party A could then have provided for a termination of the trust when he or she dies. The trust instruments vary as to the settlor's purposes.

A trust may be *inter vivos* (established during the settlor's lifetime) or testamentary (established at the settlor's death). A trust may be revocable (a legal power retained by settlor to terminate the trust) or irrevocable (no power is retained by settlor to terminate the trust). Under the tax law a trust may be simple (all its income required to be distributed annually) or complex (any other stipulations).

Using a standard form of trust to solve a personal problem is like buying a suit or dress off the rack. You can wear it but without alterations and adjustments it never feels or looks quite right. Just as the trained fitter or dressmaker can make the appropriate adjustments to clothing, a lawyer, using standard form trust agreements, makes the adjustments necessary to suit your individual needs. The language of trusts is complicated, and for centuries courts have been required to interpret special provisions in wills and trusts which are unclear. To cover contingencies and with the knowledge that the settlor may not be alive or capable of interpreting what his or her wishes were at the time the trust was executed, the drafter of the trust instrument inserts language to cover the situations most likely to occur during the life of the trust. Don't be afraid of lengthy trust documents. Ask your lawyer to explain, in plain language, the legal purpose of each clause. Do not accept the answer that is frivolous if you don't understand a clause.

If the trustee is a financial institution, it is customary for the trustee to retain the lawyer who drafted the trust as attorney for the trust. Similarly, if one of the executors of an estate is a financial institution, the lawyer who prepared the will is usually retained as attorney for the estate. If you do not necessarily want the attorney who prepares your trust or will to be retained at a later date without a free choice on the part of the trustee or executor, you should consider naming a financial institution as successor fiduciary with an individual as primary fiduciary. Of course, as successor trustee or executor, the institution may request a judicial accounting before accepting the fiduciary relationship. The cost of the accounting could offset any benefit from negotiating the legal fees. You may discuss a waiving of the formal accounting during your lifetime. In any event, a trustee or executor should request a statement in writing of legal costs before engaging the attorney. Even if you are beneficiary, you might request the fiduciary to settle legal costs prior to performance by the attorney.

Probate legal costs are generally equivalent to a statutory executor's commission. Thus, on a probate estate (excluding property which passes to heirs outside the estate) of $350,000, in many states the executor's commission would be $10,875, computed as follows:

4%	on first	$ 25,000	equals $1,000
3½%	on next	125,000	equals 4,375
3%	on next	150,000	equals 4,500
2%	over	50,000	equals 1,000

Total executor's commissions $10,875

All commissions on an estate over $300,000 are computed at 2%.

You may find that you are advised to use an *inter vivos* trust as a solution to the high costs of administering an estate in which a trust is required. A trust can be established during the testator's life with a minimum fund (corpus) of as little as $10. Some states require no funding for *inter vivos* trusts. This is known as a *dry trust* since the substantial corpus will not be forthcoming until the death of the testator. The will provides that at the testator's death a fixed amount or percentage of the residuary estate is to be distributed to the trust [for example, Trust F/B/O (for benefit of) Mary Jones, Chemical Bank, Trustee, U/T/I (under trust indenture) dated December 15, 1978, John Jones, settlor]. The use of trusts in solving your family's personal needs depends on the nature of the problems and on the assets available for a corpus donation.

Trustees' commissions on an annual basis may be paid in some states on the value of the trust as follows:

½%	on first	$300,000	equals $1,500
¼%	on next	500,000	equals 1,250
⅕ %	on excess over	800,000	equals $2 per $1,000

On a trust of $350,000 the annual fee would be $1,625 ($1,500 on the first $300,000 plus $125 on the next $50,000). In addition, when principal is paid out, the trustee receives 1% of the value of the distribution.

YOUR HEIRS

You are probably convinced that your family and friends, those for whom you want to provide through your will and trusts, are unique. *They* are, but your circumstances are almost certainly not. The following pages will most probably delineate for you a category which will basically describe the type of person or persons likely to be your heir or heirs.

The first four categories cover the surviving spouse. Please note that the term *spouse* is used precisely, because it can refer either to husband or wife. Although current statistics indicate that the surviving spouse is almost always a widow, the following sections in no way imply that the deceased is invariably male and the person provided for is invariably female. The principles discussed here have equal validity for husband and wife. A wife, especially if she has any money, income, or significant property of her own (and this is increasingly the case) requires her own will for the protection of her husband and children in the event of her predeceasing him or them. A widow, especially one with children, must also have a will, and for any woman with a disabled spouse, a will is an absolute necessity. If you, the reader, are male and married, encourage your wife to work her way through this book, realizing that in any case she should also prepare a will as carefully as you should.

The Innocent Spouse

Make a realistic appraisal of your spouse's capacity to handle your estate's business and investment matters and if you conclude that your spouse has little capacity to act with intelligence and prudence in decisions affecting money, you have an *innocent spouse* who must be protected. This means that the proceeds of insurance and other assets of value must be invested according to the foreseeable needs of this spouse and other beneficiaries.

The term "innocent spouse" refers only to competency in monetary matters and not to career achievement in the arts, sciences, or other nonfinancial areas. The term need not even denote a person with a lack of training in business and investment matters. He or she may simply have no desire to function in these areas. The importance of making this determination involves not only the monetary cost of solving estate problems but also the complication of others' being involved in the decision-making process.

As a general rule, if possible, your spouse should be sole executor of your estate. But if you believe your spouse to be innocent in the ways of the business and investment world, you should consider assisting him or her with a co-executor. A co-executor may be a knowledgeable friend or a financial institution. The friend should be trusted and respected by your spouse in addition to having the acumen to make monetary decisions. Depending on the size of your estate, you can appoint one or more co-executors. (By statute in most states, up to three full executors' commissions may be paid.) You may also name an individual and a financial institution as co-executors. In appointing a financial institution you gain the double advantage of permanency as well as expertise in the management of estates and money. Although many financial institutions have not achieved reasonable investment performance records over the past five years, this fact alone should not deter you from making such an appointment. There is a saying among estate planners that no bank or trust company has been known to lose the entire residuary value of an estate through mismanagement. Unfortunately, the same cannot be said of individuals.

A very important practical reason for selecting a financial institution as co-executor or trustee is its employment of young trust officers. These officers specialize in guiding an innocent spouse, and they operate under the supervision of experienced senior personnel. The availability of a "willing ear" with the time to listen is a very important consideration in selecting the co-executor. A close friend may develop urgent business problems and not always be able to afford the time necessary to assist the innocent spouse in the managing of your estate. The established reputations of trust departments have been built upon the value of the services they render. Their fee schedules are usually established by statute, but if there are sufficient funds involved and if the institution is to undertake other than a pure executorship, you may during your lifetime enter into a fee agreement as to postmortem supplemental services.

If you decide upon a financial institution as co-executor, you have the additional benefit of a review of your attorney's estate plan by persons specializing in this field. Their services are usually performed at no cost to you and provide a valuable assistance to your attorney. Frequently, the vast experience of personnel may suggest alternative solutions to personal tax problems. The institution will work with your attorney. (If it did not do so, this would in most states constitute unauthorized practice of law.)

If your gross estate exceeds $500,000, you should consider using a three-person team for your estate plan: accountant, lawyer, and banker. If liquidity is a problem or if insurance is a factor, an insurance consultant will be a necessary member of the team. Depending upon the complexity of the estate, the planning team may be expanded to include an investment counsel, a tax lawyer, and other specialists.

If, due to cost factors, you decide against two co-executors, you may appoint a financial institution as substitute co-executor in the event your valued friend fails to qualify, dies, or is incapable of continuing as co-executor. In some states, a clause in your will may permit the substitute executor to accept the fiduciary relationship without a formal judicial accounting. This exonerates the successor from legal liability arising from the lack of the accounting.

The innocent spouse receives the designated share of your estate out-right. Trusts are not required to solve the innocent spouse problem. How-ever, if very substantial assets are involved or if specific reasons dictate, trusts may be utilized. The solution, therefore, to the innocent spouse problem, is the introduction of competent assistance to serve in a fiduci-ary capacity.

The Spendthrift Spouse

A spendthrift spouse may also be an innocent spouse, but it is more likely that he or she has had a successful business career. The spendthrift spouse is characterized by the compulsion to spend two dollars for every dollar of income. Therefore, prolonged supervision of a spendthrift spouse is required in estate planning. The legacy to a spendthrift spouse must be legally segregated and placed in an entity managed by a trust.

The organization of a trust is treated by the law in the same fashion as a partnership or corporation. The characteristics of each organization are different, but common to each is a binding agreement supported by a stat-ute among the parties involved. For example, (1) each may sue or be sued in the name of the entity, (2) each may own property in its own name, and (3) the life of the entity is determined by agreement or statute.

The trust for the spendthrift spouse may be established during your lifetime (*inter vivos*) or at your death (testamentary). The trust's provi-sions may or may not qualify for the marital deduction allowed in the computation of your taxable estate. You may use two or more trusts for a spendthrift spouse, each containing different authority for the trustee, in-come distribution requirements, standards of invasion of corpus (princi-pal), and investment guidelines. One trust may qualify for the marital de-duction and the other not.

A simple qualifying trust for a spendthrift spouse requires all income of the trust to be distributed quarter-annually. The corpus may be invaded by the trustee for the beneficiary's (spouse's) benefit in case of need for health, welfare, and education. These purposes are said to have ascertain-able standards legally. Therefore, an outrageous request for corpus based upon the spouse's married level of living may be denied by a trustee as failing to meet the ascertainable standards. On the other hand, the trustee has wide descretion in applying the standards of health, welfare, and/or education. The standards are designed to protect the spendthrift spouse, not to turn the trustee into a Scrooge. For a trust to qualify for the marital deduction, your spouse must have the power to designate by will who shall receive the balance of the corpus at his or her death. If you and not the spouse have the right to appoint the trust property, the trust does not qualify for the tax benefit of a marital deduction.

Even where the spouse is not considered a spendthrift, if a substantial legacy is involved, the trust is an excellent vehicle for relieving your spouse of the major responsibility for financial management. The trustee of a spendthrift trust should be an independent person or, as is more usually the case, a financial institution. Your spouse may be one of the trustees, provided there are two other trustees and the spouse is not granted the right to consent to the invasion of principal.

The question frequently arises as to whether adult children should be trustees of a spendthrift spouse's trust. In general, the answer is no. Since the children are probably the remaindermen of the trust, they are placed in a position of voting on a principal invasion which adversely affects their personal financial interest. You must be absolutely positive that the children have the independence of mind to serve as trustees. If possible, avoid placing them in the invidious position of being between the trust and your spendthrift spouse.

The Disabled Spouse

The disabled spouse requires extraordinary medical expense and supervision. The trust device which applies to the spendthrift spouse may not in many instances be suitable for you to provide properly for both a disabled spouse and for your children. The possible shorter life-span of the disabled spouse is the crucial factor in determining the proper course. Tax considerations are important also because one suggested solution is to waive the marital deduction provisions. The disabled spouse's legacy would be in trust for life with the remainder going directly to the children. The additional tax cost of losing the marital deduction may be partially offset by the savings of probate expenses. More important, however, is the assurance that at the spouse's death the remainder interest will vest in the children.

You might also omit the disabled spouse from your will with the understanding that a waiver of the spouse's intestate share will be filed after your death. A disabled spouse whose mental condition would not permit such waiver of intestate share would require a trust. The omission of a disabled spouse is a satisfactory solution where adult children are trustworthy to carry out your testamentary desires. In addition, because of the economic standards for social benefits, a disabled spouse may not qualify unless the income of the spouse is minimal. In most states, children have no legal obligation to support a needy parent. In the proper family framework a lack of income and assets on the part of a disabled spouse will in fact allow for the use of excellent medical facilities not otherwise available. If at first this solution goes against your moral conviction, weigh the economics in favor of your children. On the other hand, you may still use a trust device for the benefit of your disabled spouse.

How you should provide for the disabled spouse requires a careful analysis of future needs that are not always foreseeable. For this reason, the trust may be insufficient to provide properly for future monetary requirements.

In most states, a spouse is entitled to at least one-third of your estate. This is known as the intestate share. A spouse cannot be disinherited. On the other hand, children may be omitted from your will and they have no statutory rights to a share of your estate. The scene in a film of the family lawyer reading the wealthy decedent's will and informing the family that "son John" has been left one dollar because of his immoral lifestyle is rarely fact. To save lawsuit costs, the testator would omit "son John" entirely. Otherwise, John might argue that under modern conditions his lifestyle is acceptable and that his father lacked the mental capacity to execute a proper will.

The spouse's intestate share may be fully or partly waived after the testator's death. This must be done generally within six months of death.

The Former Spouse

A former spouse has no claim (other than for unpaid alimony) against the estate unless such a claim is established by a contractual right. However, there are many instances where generosity decrees that provision be made for a former spouse. This wish may be fulfilled by the same trust device used for a spendthrift spouse. If you are remarried, a testamentary trust for a former spouse may possibly have adverse effects on your present spouse. Unless you have both come to an agreement on this matter that you are fairly certain your death would not change, you may wish to consider a cash legacy, an annuity, or an *inter vivos* trust. An annuity is an amount of money, generally a fixed sum, paid for a given period. Your estate requires sufficient assets in order to purchase such an annuity from an insurance company, and an annuity is subject to inflation although insurance companies have special types of annuities which adjust for increased earnings. The annuity for the former spouse purchased after your death avoids any further dealings by your estate and family with that individual. If the former spouse dies shortly after the estate acquires the annuity, no refunds would be made to the estate. Also, after the death of the former spouse, there is no remainder interest in an annuity. This type of annuity is the least expensive. There is no guaranteed period of time over which a simple annuity is paid. The cost of setting up an annuity depends upon the age of the former spouse. Above all, remember, if you choose an annuity provision for a former spouse, to make certain that you have not been generous at the expense of your present family.

A cash legacy to a spendthrift former spouse offers short-term help. If the former spouse is financially independent, you would normally omit any bequest at all. However, there may be special personal reasons that override this consideration. You might make special provision in an insurance policy for the former spouse, but since the ownership of life insurance should be in the name of your present spouse, the use of life insurance to fund this payment may be difficult. Thus, from the standpoint of sheer practicality a cash bequest is the easiest solution. This may present a problem, however, with your present spouse. For that reason, the *inter vivos* trust presently established with a minimal sum to be later funded at your death appears to be a proper solution. If you later change your mind, you can redo your will and lose the minimum corpus in the trust. The trustees should be independent, responsible persons who would have no conflict of interest with the beneficiary, and you can provide that the remainder interest after the death of the former spouse go to your beneficiaries.

The advantage of the trust over an annuity for a former spouse is the retention in the trust of all or part of the principal for your family. However, if you provide for invasions of principal for ascertainable standards of health, welfare, and/or education, there may be little corpus remaining. In addition, an annuity may pay larger amounts of income than a prudent trustee may earn for the trust. The annuity also requires no third involvement or separate trust tax returns. The annuity is a gambling decision on a personal level unless corpus invasion powers are permitted in a trust. In that case, if the sole purpose of using a trust is to leave a remainder interest to the family, a trust with invasion powers is also a gamble. There is no way in the foreseeable future to determine what invasions of corpus will be required.

Revocable trusts may also be used in a former-spouse situation. During your life you can revoke the trust at any time. The trust would provide the income as distributable to you during your lifetime and at your death a second life tenant (former spouse) receives a life interest. At the death of the former spouse, the principal is paid to your family. Since the trust is treated for tax purposes as a testamentary disposition, the advantage lies in separating the administration of this trust from your probate estate. The problem is that the trust requires you to have sufficient assets now to fund it; and your income tax return treats the income as earned by you. The trust return during your lifetime simply shows the amounts as being earned by you as a grantor.

The Friend

A friend, for estate planning purposes, may be considered a spouse without legal status (in other words, a *revocable spouse*). The same solutions for the innocent, spendthrift, or disabled spouse problems are equally applicable to a friend; but since a friend has no intestate share or marital deduction benefits, those parts of the discussions are inapplicable.

Cash bequests, trusts (*inter vivos* and testamentary), and annuities are the generally accepted postmortem benefits conferred upon a friend. Because of the revocable nature of the relationship, take great care in the present funding of these provisions. Life insurance is another solution to funding the needs of a friend after your death. Term insurance is the most suitable for this relationship.

Your relatives may have different notions of morality and may find provisions for a friend repugnant, especially when the friend may profit at their expense. A will which has been carefully and professionally prepared may dampen any litigious enthusiasms your relatives may have.

The Minor Child

In most marriages, prime consideration is given to the needs of the minor children. You must always be aware of the possibility of a parental common disaster. The joint deaths of parents of minor children unfortunately is not so remote, as statistics bear out. Most estate planners have personally encountered in their professional practice the minor children of common-disaster parents who either died together or within a relatively short time of each other.

Unless your estate exceeds $500,000 you should consider omitting the minor child from any share in your estate and leave your spouse your entire residuary estate. If your estate is considerable or if you have children from a former marriage, you might leave one-half of your estate outright to your spouse and the balance outright or in trust to your children of the former marriage. Or, you may leave the entire estate to your spouse in trust for life, one-half being subject to a power to appoint by his or her will and the other half paid directly to your children upon your spouse's death.

Even if the child is not to be included in your estate as a primary beneficiary, you must provide for the common-disaster situation. If the child is too young to receive outright distribution, then his or her share should be left in trust.

The income of the trust for the benefit of a minor is paid over to the guardian or is applied for the child's benefit until the child's age of majority or age 21. (In most states majority occurs at age 18.) After majority the income is usually required to be paid directly to the child at least annually. You may withhold the payment of principal for any period that doesn't violate state law. A typical period coincides with specific ages. Thus, distributions of one-third of principal at ages 21, 25, and 30 would terminate the trust on the child's 30th birthday. Any combination of ages or percentages that you believe will best suit the child's future needs is acceptable.

The trust for the child also provides for invasion of principal for the purposes of health, welfare, and/or education. In addition, invasions (e.g., $5,000 a year) are usually allowed to pay for a marriage reception, set up housekeeping, or as a business investment. A limitation of amounts withdrawn for these purposes is usual.

The new Orphan's Exclusion provision requires you to consider special trust provisions for your children in the common-disaster or single-surviving parent situation. The Orphan's Exclusion is similar to the marital deduction and operates in the estate of the surviving parent as a deduction equivalent to $5,000 times the difference between age 21 and a child's age at date of death. Thus, a child, age nine at the death of the last parent gives rise to a $60,000 deduction ($21-9 = 12; $5,000 \times 12 = $60,000$).

The requirements for this deduction are the same as for a marital deduction. There is an exception which allows the deduction if the trust remainder passes to another person if the child dies before the youngest child of the decedent attains 23 years. You qualify here if, under the terms of the trust, the remainder passes to other children and the youngest is under 23. Most parents, however, would hesitate to use that form of trust for a child. You may use a single trust for all your children. The rules are complicated and require a lawyer.

You might still consider the type of trust that terminates proportionately at specific ages, making the rights of the child nonterminable. In other words, death before the age of final distribution (and after your youngest child reaches age 23) terminates the trust and the remainder passes to those appointed by the adult child's will.

You also might consider using two trusts, one setting forth a maximum deduction formula terminable at age 23 with the second naming the specific remainder interests if the child dies before final distribution. This would eliminate the child's power of appointment by will. If your and your spouse's combined estates exceed $250,000 (including life insurance) you should give careful thought to framing your estate plan in the event of a common disaster to qualify for the Orphan's Exclusion.

The use of your state's Gift to Minors Act is not a substitution for a testamentary trust. This act permits bank accounts and securities to be registered in your child's name; and at 21 (in most states), the child has a legal right to the gift property. If you use this act for making gifts to your child, you should not be the custodian named in the registration of the account or security. For estate tax purposes, if you die before the child reaches age 21 and you made the gift, naming yourself as custodian, the value of the property at your death is includable in your taxable estate. Therefore, your spouse or someone else should be the custodian for such gifts made by you.

Generally, single gifts of cash or securities in excess of $10,000 to a minor should be made in trust. Since there are income, gift, and tax implications with respect to powers and other terms in an *inter vivos* trust, you should consult an attorney before transferring property to such a trust.

The Innocent Child

The innocent child has reached majority in age but is still immature or naive in the ways of the financial and business world. This child may have an outstanding career in the arts or the sciences and still be considered "innocent." The innocent child's share could be left to the child outright, naming a financial institution as executor of your estate. In that case, you may hope that a relationship will develop whereby the child uses a custodian arrangement with the institution. You also might consider naming your investment adviser as an executor, granting sufficient powers to the adviser to diversify the estate's investment.

The innocent child problem may also be solved by using a trust, either *inter vivos* or testamentary. The trust could be for the life of the child with the remainder to your child's children. However, the 1976 estate and gift tax changes may cause a tax penalty on the trust at your child's death.

The innocent child requires professional assistance, but not personal supervision. For this reason, you should consider involving the child with custodian operations, your investment adviser, and your other professional advisers. Thus, at your death, you are basically bequeathing your advisers to your heir. Unfortunately, only large institutions have the time and patience to "wet-nurse" the innocent child. Therefore, unless you have total confidence in a plan to ultimately leave the innocent child's share to him or her outright, a trust is the best solution.

The Spendthrift Child

The spendthrift child is found not only in rich families but in middle-class families as well. A spendthrift spouse and a spendthrift child may not evidence the same symptoms. You may be startled to discover that the spendthrift child has abhorrence of material things. Or, he or she may be overgenerous in sharing what has not been earned. The object of the spendthrift child may not be personal satisfaction, but a quest for social acceptance by the sharing of possessions.

Spendthrift children finance most of the world's unsuccessful business ventures. And, unfortunately, the child's lack of understanding, technical ability, business judgment, and plain common sense cannot usually be corrected by even the most qualified advisers. Most professionals can tell fascinating stories about spendthrift children and their "lost causes." Every charming money hustler is a master at parting the spendthrift child from money. What is particularly frustrating is that the child usually has little or no confidence in the competent and trustworthy professionals who served the parents for many years.

In such cases, you can understand that in order to protect the spendthrift child from himself or herself, a parent must "bite the bullet," so to speak, and provide a trust prepared by an expert and reviewed by a financial institution. Let us emphasize that trusts for such children must be expertly prepared. The child's apparent disdain for material goods does not preclude a willingness to engage in litigation, which can be costly to the estate. In most cases, if there is only one trustee this should be a financial institution.

The problem of a spendthrift child may seem academic to you because at present you have a small estate. Consider, however, the combined assets from you and your spouse, life insurance proceeds, future inheritances, and other possible sources of capital and you may find the spendthrift child a reality in your life.

The Disabled Child

The disabled child may be a minor or an adult who, due to a mental or physical condition, requires special care. One of the parent's most difficult decisions in estate planning is accepting a pessimistic prognosis for a disabled child. Because most people are optimistic about the future, a realistic approach to the disabled child frequently requires a degree of understanding not needed for other problem persons. Thus, there is a natural tendency to treat this child in the same way as you would the other children. There is frequently a belief that new medical discoveries or present treatment will cause vast improvement in the child's mental or physical health. An estate planner must inquire into the ages and the physical and mental condition of all beneficiaries; and a determination must be made of the exact nature of the child's custodial problems and mental capacity. You, as a parent, will then have to consider the amount of the estate and the total divisible shares.

Although one spouse usually survives at least for a time to provide the services necessary to the child, you will still require the common disaster provision. For that reason the shares of your children become important. The first rule in dividing shares among children is to divide equally. For example, a testator dies without leaving a spouse. Two surviving children would each receive 50 percent of the estate. Three surviving children would each be entitled to one-third. Grandchildren of a predeceased child take *per stirpes*. In other words, if you had three children and one predeceased you leaving you two grandchildren, your estate would be divided into three whole shares. The two grandchildren would each receive one-half of the share to which their parent was entitled. Thus, "to my issue then surviving, *per stirpes*" means that each *level* of child existing at the testator's (grandparent's) death receives the share of its deceased parent. Without *per stirpes* the shares would be distributed *per capita*, and in the prior example each child and grandchild would receive one-quarter of the estate. Most estates provide for a *per stirpes* distribution.

Considering that the general rule is that each child is treated equally, the individual financial factors of the children should be examined. A child with a good position in business may always lose the job. Thus, that child's share should not be diminished. A child's spouse with independent wealth may always divorce your child. A child who is a successful professional may become disabled. For estate purposes, unless the evidence clearly indicates otherwise, you should treat all of your children equally, other than perhaps a disabled child.

It is obvious that a disabled child's interest should be held in trust. In general, one of the trustees should be a financial institution. If you are worried about the small amount that may be available for such a trust, you should be aware that a provision usually exists that permits termination, at the option of the financial institution, of a minimally funded trust. The question still remains as to what extent the disabled child is to share in your estate. If you have other adult children who have demonstrated sufficient moral qualities to assure you of a continued devotion to the disabled child after your death and that of your spouse, you should consider omitting the disabled child from your estate. If future social benefits are required for the child, the funds left to that child may have to be donated to an institution. In addition, a shortened life-span may result in additional probate costs and estate taxes before the child's share is passed to the other children. If your children are to share unequally in your will and if the disabled child does not have the legal capacity to execute a will, that child's share will be distributed by the rules of intestacy.

If you decide that the responsibility of providing for the disabled child should not be assumed by your other children, you must consider the corpus of the trust as either to be funded equally or disproportionately compared with your other children. Since in general children share equally in estates, you must have substantial reasons for treating the disabled child differently. Such reasons may include the cost of constant medical attention or the financial condition of your other children.

The trust for the disabled child is usually for the life of the child with the remainder to be divided among your issue *per stirpes* at the time of the child's death. The invasion powers of the trust would be based on ascertainable standards of health, welfare, and education. In general, the majority of the trustees should be independent. There is usually no objection to another adult child's serving as co-trustee providing there are two other trustees because of the possibility of conflict of interest with respect to the invasion powers. Thus, any withdrawals of principal affect the amount remaining in the trust for the future benefit of that trustee-child. In a common-disaster situation the trust should qualify for the Orphan's Exclusion.

The Child of a Former Marriage

A child of a former marriage should take a share from your estate unless your present spouse has legally adopted the child. If you are either the custodial or noncustodial parent, the child's share should be outright or in trust. If the child is a minor, innocent, spendthrift, or disabled, keep in mind the same considerations as for a child of your present marriage. Do not depend upon your present spouse to leave a share of your estate to a child of your former marriage. It is rare, subsequent to the death of a parent, for the child of a former marriage to be treated by a present spouse in a similar manner to the children of the present marriage. You may not believe the fairy tale, but estate planners all too often see the first part of "Cinderella" played out in real life. (Unfortunately, however, the prince rarely arrives to save the child from the stepmother.)

If you have a child of a former marriage and are remarried, discuss this problem privately with your attorney. Unless you are one hundred percent certain of the generosity and fair-mindedness of your present spouse, you should make special provision for the child of a former marriage, whether a minor or adult. If you die intestate, the child would share in two-thirds of your estate along with your other children. Using that portion for all of your children will give you a starting point in making an allocation for the benefit of that child.

The Aged Parent

An aged parent requiring financial assistance should be provided for by a trust or an annuity. A cash bequest without supervision is of little benefit. If supervision is required, the most efficient method is a trust. If the funds are available, an annuity provides a monthly income without requiring financial decisions. Because of the minimum taxable income requirements, the entire annuity in many instances may be received tax-free. If you wish to depend upon your spouse or children to support your aged parent, you must compute the income tax cost. You would also consider the after-tax value of the parent's personal exemption. Usually, the parent's receiving the income directly is the best tax posture.

The use of outright monetary payments to an aged parent also must take into consideration the forfeiture of funds if a prolonged institution stay might be required. If this is a foreseeable possibility and if funds are limited, financial dependency of the aged parent might be left to your spouse or children. You must carefully examine your own financial and family status before omitting from your will an aged parent who might require monetary assistance. It is rare that a cash bequest is made to an aged parent.

Another solution to the aged parent's financial needs is the short-term trust. The trust term must exceed 10 years from the date the property is transferred to the trust. A life estate satisfies the period, and the income is payable to the aged parent. Because of the zero bracket amount and personal exemption allowance, the parent usually pays no income tax. You lose the exemption on your return, but you also transfer the income used for the support to the parent. The trust may be either *inter vivos* or testamentary. The remainder interest would go to your spouse or children. A lifetime gift is subject to the gift tax.

Other Persons and Considerations

If there are other relatives and friends who are to be beneficiaries of your will, you must decide whether the legacies are to be outright or in trust. A trust may have more than one beneficiary, and the costs of administering a single trust with several beneficiaries are proportionately less than for a separate trust for each beneficiary. In the case of the single trust with several beneficiaries, the purposes of the trust and the powers invested in the trustees must be the same as for a single trust with a single beneficiary.

A token remembrance to a relative or friend should be by outright cash bequest. Grandchildren should be left some cash bequest even if parents are separately provided for. There is no better memorial to a deceased grandparent than the appreciation felt by a child on reaching majority and being presented with a bankbook left by the deceased grandparent.

Charitable bequests are usually satisfied by cash legacies. However, you may provide for a charity to share in the remainder interest of a trust. Charitable bequests are deductible from the taxable estate, and this includes the value of any remainder interest. Charitable bequests may also be made by lifetime transfers in trust. A percentage of the principal or a fixed amount may be paid to you and the remainder to charity. The remainder interest is valued first for income tax deduction purposes and later as an estate tax deduction. Before considering a charitable remainder trust, you should seek professional help.

Putting Your Estate in Order

You have been concerned with the needs of people and with how, technically, these needs are to be satisfied. The next step (or in many cases the first) is to determine the source of funds necessary to establish a meaningful plan. During your estate-planning period, you should devote a part of your energies to reorganizing your business affairs. Preparing a net worth statement is the beginning of the data-gathering process.

If you are a shareholder in a closely-held corporation, a buy-sell agreement is required. Otherwise, a fair price for your interest cannot be established, nor can a prompt liquidation of your interest take place. If you control the corporation, consider reorganizing the entity so that employees are given an opportunity to purchase your shares from future earnings or bank borrowings.

At your death your substantial interest in a corporation, partnership, or sole proprietorship must be liquidated unless there are persons capable of continuing the entity. In addition, the failure to provide a fixed buyout price by agreement may lead to extensive negotiations on that subject with the IRS.

Buying a business without money is an estate-planning technique. It permits capable employees without capital funds to acquire a successful business at the death of the owner or controlling stockholder. This procedure provides for an initial payment to be made to the estate from cash already accumulated in the corporation or from borrowings by the corporation if no cash is available. The balance of the payments is funded by future after-tax earnings or, if necessary, by borrowings. Legally, the corporation is buying the estate's share. This is called a "stock redemption." As part of the buy-sell agreement, the key employees are sold minor interests in the corporation for nominal amounts. By the corporation redeeming all of the estate's shares, the minor interest ends up owning all the outstanding shares. This method is widely used and has particular applicability in automobile dealerships as well as in other businesses requiring large capital investments with small liquidating value. A time span between an owner's death and new management can quickly erode a business's good will. That is why a buy-sell agreement is so important.

On the other hand, if you are an employee of a successful closely-held business, you should make every effort to be a part of a reorganization accompanied by a buy-sell agreement. Even if you die before the controlling shareholder, your estate will receive stock redemption proceeds. If your employer's controlling shareholder adopts a wait-and-see attitude on this subject, you may someday deal with strangers and have no leverage. Therefore, examine your own position carefully, and do not hesitate to prepare for a career change if the death of the controlling shareholder could be detrimental to you. The substantial advantage of a buy-sell agreement to your controlling shareholder nevertheless provides an excellent opportunity for your future benefit.

A buy-sell agreement is not a marriage, and a termination of employment of a minor employee-stockholder may be provided for by a formula that does not require detailed calculations or inventives. A simple formula is the terminated employee's share of capital stock and retained earnings as shown on the last federal corporation income tax return.

The entire area of redemptions and buy-sell agreements requires legal and tax assistance. You should have your own counsel to negotiate on your behalf, particularly if your bargaining position is weak.

Choosing An Executor

In general, the choosing of an executor for your estate should follow the following principles. Your spouse should be sole executor of your estate unless the spouse is a spendthrift or disabled. If your spouse is a spendthrift or disabled, you might omit the spouse and appoint a qualified individual or institution or both. On the other hand, if you foresee that the management of your estate may be prolonged or complicated by investments or business decisions, you should consider appointing co-executors to work jointly with your spouse. Do not appoint anyone without consulting your spouse. Adult children may not be qualified to be your spouse's co-executor. This may be the case where possible conflict of interest problems arise in estate administration. It is better to have an innocent spouse as sole executor than to appoint a co-executor who would be psychologically incompatible with your spouse.

If you appoint an attorney as an executor, you might ask for a letter setting forth the responsibilities to be covered by the executor's commission. Frequently, the attorney will include most of the "boiler-plate" legal work as part of the executor's duties if discussed during estate planning. Similarly, if you appoint your accountant executor, you could request that the preparation of the federal estate tax return and first fiduciary returns be included as part of the executor's fee.

Never appoint an executor without informing that individual or institution and receiving an acceptance. Your executor should know where the *original* (not a copy) of your will is located. If an institution is an executor, the original will should be delivered to its safekeeping.

Your will may be changed by codicil or by making a new will. (Destruction of your will or the lack of a will automatically subjects your estate to your state's laws of intestacy.) A codicil is executed similarly to a will. It only changes or adds to an existing will. A new will should be executed if the changes are substantial or if you are substituting new executors, trustees, or guardians. All persons named in wills and codicils must be notified by the probate court at the time the will is probated. If you have eliminated *anyone* from your will and you prefer that the person not know of the previous naming (e.g., "Uncle John" is no longer guardian, but you don't want to hurt his feelings), have a new will executed. It's mainly a typing job but can eliminate the problems codicils might cause.

Estate and Gift Taxes

In 1976, Congress substantially changed the estate and gift tax laws. Further charges were made in 1978. These were the first revisions in 35 years to affect all taxpayers. Under the changes the estate and gift tax rates were combined in a unified table. Previously the gift tax rates were approximately three-fourths of the estate tax rates; the new unified table reduces the advantage of making lifetime gifts of substantial property.

The gift tax law permits you to make annually a $3,000 gift to any person. If your spouse joins in the gift, the limit is raised to $6,000 per year. The annual exclusion only applies to gifts of a present interest. For example, an outright gift of $3,000 qualifies for the exclusion, whereas if a gift is made in trust only the value of the income *interest* is subject to the annual exclusion. Gifts in excess of $3,000 per year per person ($6,000 if your spouse joins in the gift) are subject to gift tax, and the rates are cumulative. Thus, you add each year's gifts to the prior gifts in computing the tax rates.

At death, lifetime taxable gifts after 1976 are added to your estate and a reduction in estate taxes is permitted for the gift taxes paid. In other words, the present advantage of making gifts is that the future appreciation and income of the property are transferred to the donee.

In general, if you are married and your gross estate does not exceed $250,000 ($125,000 if single), you do not have estate tax problems. However, even if you think you are substantially below these limits, do not skip the remainder of this chapter. The new "Fresh Start" rules (postponed until 1980) affect almost every estate, whether taxable or not. In addition, a feel of how the estate tax law operates is necessary because the methods of avoiding estate taxes will give you ideas for ownership of property. In addition, many states have their own estate tax laws and some states tax an estate that escapes the federal levy. Even though the rates may be small, a tax would be due. Unless your state's estate tax is equal to the federal credit for state death taxes, you should understand the workings of the federal law. Other reasons for learning about the federal law are (1) the possibility of property which you did not realize was includable for estate taxes; (2) the possibility of future inheritance; and

(3) substantial increase in your present net worth through perseverance and good fortune.

COMMUNITY PROPERTY STATES

In those states with community property laws, the precise rules for the inclusion of assets may vary. Property acquired during marriage while residing in a community property state is deemed owned 50% by each spouse. Only 50% of this property is subject to the marital deduction. After you move to a noncommunity property state, the asset still retains its original characteristic as community property.

ESTATE PLAN CHANGES

The 1976 estate tax changes cover the following:

1. Carryover basis (cost of property used in computing postmortem sales). The 1978 Act postpones the effect until 1980.
2. Marital deduction (increased portion of estate passing tax-free to surviving spouse)
3. Changes in inclusions, exclusions, and deductions
4. Limitation on valuation of farm and business property
5. Taxability of generation-skipping trusts (only affects the wealthy)
6. New administrative rules

Your *gross estate* consists of all property in which you had ownership rights. For example, cash, real estate, stocks and bonds are part of the gross estate. Insurance policies, and joint interest and continuing annuities are also includable in your gross estate. In addition, unusual assets such as powers of appointment (found in trusts) are property rights subject to estate tax. Gifts made within three years of death are also part of the gross estate.

All property is valued as of the date of your death. If the total of your property value has diminished after death, your executor may choose an alternate date to value the property. That date is six months from date of death.

After computing the gross estate, subtract funeral expenses, administration costs, and debts. The balance is your *adjusted estate*. The allowable marital deduction is then deducted to arrive at the *taxable estate*. The tax rates are applied to the taxable estate, resulting in the tentative tax.

Taxable gifts made after 1976 are added to the taxable estate, and the gift tax paid on these gifts reduces the tentative tax. The credits to be applied against this tentative tax are as follows:

YEAR	UNIFIED CREDIT	EQUIVALENT TO TAXABLE ESTATE
1978	$34,000	$134,000
1979	38,000	147,333
1980	42,500	161,563
1981 (and later)	47,000	175,625

If you possess rights in property, even though you don't benefit from those rights, you may own an asset includable in your estate. For example, your father's will left you the income from a trust. If, at your death, you can appoint by will the persons who will take the corpus of the trust, you are considered to own the value of the trust at your death.

Owning property with your spouse is called a "joint tenancy." If the property is real estate, the joint ownership with your spouse is referred to as "tenancy by the entirety." The consent of both tenants is required in order to dissolve a joint tenancy. A tenancy-in-common differs from a joint tenancy mainly because of the effect of death of a tenant. In a tenancy-in-common, the heirs of the deceased tenant are substituted. On the other hand, in a joint tenancy, at the death of a tenant, the tenancy dissolves and the surviving tenant owns the entire property. Between husband and wife, a joint tenancy is assumed unless a tenancy-in-common is specified. The presumption is the opposite where the tenants are not spouses. You are said to create a tenancy-in-common between non-spouses unless a joint tenancy is specified.

In estate planning, joint tenancies are often referred to as the "wills of the poor," but a joint tenancy creates estate tax problems. The IRS assumes that the consideration in a joint tenancy was furnished entirely by the deceased tenant. Thus, the surviving tenant must prove funds or other assets contributed to the purchase of the property. If the property has been owned for a long period of time, such proof may be difficult to obtain. Affidavits may be of some assistance, but in most cases proving that the deceased tenant furnished no funds (and, therefore that no value should be assigned to that interest) is a difficult task. In estate taxes there has been a great deal of effort expended on this problem, both by the IRS and in the courts. Except for the property that is your residence, you should avoid the use of a joint tenancy as a substitute for a will provision.

The 1976 changes in the estate and gift tax law permit you to elect to create a truly joint tenancy which applies to all property other than a joint bank account. Under these changes a gift tax return must be filed.

Real estate and personal property do not require an actuarial computation to create a qualified joint interest. This is done by straight computation of percent. If one spouse contributed nothing to the purchase of the real estate, 50% of the value would be the gift. You should consider the creation of this qualified joint interest by gift in order to avoid the controversy over the inclusion of the entire value of jointly owned property in the estate of the first to die. A family residence is a perfect asset to create the qualified joint interest.

GIFT TAX

An individual may make an annual gift of $3,000 or less to a donee without gift tax consequences. For married couples joining in the gift the limit to a single donee is $6,000 a year. To qualify for the exemption, the gift must be one of a present interest in property (i.e., cash or securities). Gifts in excess of the limits are subject to the gift tax. The estate and gift tax rates are unified for gifts after 1976. Therefore, for the year 1977 and thereafter taxable gifts are added to the estate and a credit is allowed for the gift tax paid. You may make a gift of up to $100,000 to your spouse without gift tax consequences. On the second $100,000 or any part thereof given to your spouse, you are only allowed the annual exclusion and must pay a gift tax. Gifts of over $200,000 to a spouse are subject to a 50% marital deduction.

Gift tax property is brought into the estate tax computations at the value of the property on the date of the gift. There is one exception: gifts in excess of $3,000 a year made within three years of death are includable at their value at death plus any gift taxes paid by the decedent. Life insurance policies, if given within the three-year period, are included at their face value.

As a general rule, a husband and wife should consent to gift-splitting (i.e., joining in a gift to a third party) even though only one spouse owns the property. This works particularly well where only one spouse has a small estate. There are instances where there should not be a consent, such as where both spouses have taxable estates and the difference in value between the estates is substantial. An estate tax computation should be made to determine whether the estate tax savings by not splitting the gifts is worth the additional gift taxes.

TAX RATES

The unified rates start at 18% for the first $10,000 of taxable gifts or taxable estate. At the $500,000 level the tax rate reaches 37%. The top rate is 70% for over $5 million.

MARITAL DEDUCTION

The marital deduction attempts to create a parity between states with community property and those which do not. There are 14 community property states. These are generally western states which had Spanish and French legal systems at the time of settlement.

The marital deduction permits up to a 50% deduction from the gross estate after expenses and debts. To qualify for the deduction, the surviving spouse must be left property or the power over property. In a will it is usual to limit the property bequeathed to a spouse to the amount of the marital deduction as finally allowed by the IRS. This is done either by fractional shares or by not mentioning the exact amount passing to the surviving spouse.

The marital deduction now provides for a minimum bequest that may be passed to a surviving spouse in the amount of $250,000. Thus, a formula in a will permitting the maximum marital deduction increases the amounts allowable in estates under $500,000 from 50% of the total to the maximum amount of $250,000. For example, a $400,000 estate is reduced to $150,000 ($400,000-$250,000) by this formula rather than $200,000 ($400,000 × 50%) if the 50% deduction were used. In some cases upon the death of both spouses, using the maximum marital deduction may cost more in estate taxes. This is a technical problem that has to be solved by an attorney.

ORPHAN'S EXCLUSION

An orphan (a child left without either surviving parent) is entitled to a deduction in the deceased parent's estate. The deduction is $5,000 times the child's age deducted from 21. For example, when his mother died following his father, John was 15 years old. Since John has no living parent, his mother's estate is entitled to a deduction of $30,000 or $5,000 times six (21 years less 15 years). If the orphan is 21 or older, no deduction is allowed to him or her.

RETIREMENT BENEFITS

Payment of a retirement benefit (employer-qualified plan, I.R.A., or HR-10) in a lump sum results in the inclusion of the retirement benefit in the taxable estate. On the other hand, if the I.R.A. payment is in the form of an annuity and not received by the executor, it is excludable from the estate tax. The HR-10 payment may be excluded if made over more than one year. If the recipient of a lump sum payout elects to be subject to ordinary income then the distribution may be excluded from estate tax. You should review any qualified retirement plans and change the payout provisions if they pose an estate tax problem. Thus, if you are married with the maximum marital deduction of $250,000 plus the unified credit and you have no taxable estate, you probably should retain the lump-sum payout for your surviving spouse's benefit.

RETAINED VOTING RIGHTS

If you have made a gift of stock and have retained the voting rights, for estate tax purposes you are considered to own that stock. This applies to transfers of stock after June 22, 1976 in 20% or more owned corporations.

SALES COMMISSIONS

Commissions and legal expenses paid on the sale of property during estate administration are deductible on the estate tax return as an administration expense or as an expense of sale on the fiduciary income tax return.

ADMINISTRATIVE AND OTHER MATTERS

Extended payment of estate taxes up to a period of 15 years at 4% interest is allowed if your adjusted gross estate includes a closely-held business. The requirement is that over 65% of the adjusted gross estate consists of the business interest. There are other provisions for extending payments of estate tax of up to a year where the percentage is 65% or less.

In the valuation of real property, a method may be employed basing the value on present use of the property and not best value. This means that farmland is not to be valued as if the land could be used for a shopping center. The value of such property cannot reduce the gross estate by more than $500,000. The qualifying conditions for this provision require professional assistance.

Where both spouses contribute either money or effort to a farm or closely held business, there is an estate tax exclusion for the surviving spouse's material participation in the business.

The payment of executor's commissions to a surviving spouse is rarely appropriate because the spouse would have to pay income taxes on the receipt of income, whereas the estate tax deduction allowing for a marital deduction is usually in a much lower bracket. Under these circumstances the executor executes a waiver of commissions.

CARRYOVER BASIS

Although the 1978 Act postponed carryover basis rules to 1980, you should be familiar with its operations. Before 1980, inherited property's gain or loss is determined by using as cost the estate tax value. The estate tax value is either the fair market value at death or at the executor's option of the value six months later. The rules of carryover basis determine how property sold subsequent to death is taxed. Since it is difficult to know the value of property (other than marketable securities) as of December 31, 1976, this appreciation is prorated over the periods before and after December 31, 1976. Generally, if property owned on December 31, 1976 is sold at a gain, the cost is the value on December 31, 1976. If the property is purchased after December 31, 1976, its cost and not date-of-death value is used to measure gain. Property sold at a loss uses the decedent's cost. (The above rules have been suspended for three years.) Household and personal property are allowed a date-of-death value of up to $10,000 for purposes of the carryover basis. This is to make matters easier for an executor.

For income tax purposes all assets received through an estate are entitled to long-term capital gains treatment. Until 1980, the income tax basis of estate assets will be their value for estate tax purposes. The post-1979 rules make basis computations complicated, and without adequate records they can become a very difficult problem. Computing your annual net worth will be of great assistance for the necessary carryover basis records after 1979. You should be alert to the real possibility that between now and 1980 the Congress will again do something about tax basis.

GENERATION-SKIPPING TRUSTS

In establishing trusts, wealthy people frequently provide for a life estate to child A, then the remainder at A's death to grandchild B. At A's death, no part of the corpus is taxable to his or her estate as long as A had no powers over the trust. This type of trust was referred to as a "generation-skipping trust" since the estate tax skipped from grandparent A to grandchild B. There is now a $250,000 exemption for a generation-skipping trust to each child. Trusts in excess of $250,000 must pay an equivalent estate tax on child A's death.

SOME ADDITIONAL POINTS

There are a number of highly technical rules which have not been discussed here. Only those matters which appear to have general application to your estate planning or were of general interest are covered in this chapter. The following additional items are also worth your attention:

1. If you own a tax shelter, many of the tax consequences at death are uncertain; so perhaps you should extricate yourself from the shelter during your lifetime. Before doing so you should consult a professional.

2. Your executor should be familiar with any outstanding Subchapter S elections (small business corporations). The executor should be familiar with your partnership agreements so that he or she knows the buyout provisions, tax elections, and what happens at your death.

3. The termination of your estate usually takes place after the IRS has accepted the federal estate tax return. In the final year, the beneficiaries are entitled to any net operating losses from businesses and capital loss carryovers.

4. If your estate contains U.S. Series "E" bonds, your executor has these choices: (1) include appreciation on your last income tax return; (2) include appreciation on your estate's first fiduciary income tax return; (3) report appreciation as bonds are redeemed; or (4) distribute bonds to beneficiaries for them to make a choice.

5. Income earned but uncollected by you at death is reported by your executor for both estate tax and income tax purposes. There is a deduction for the estate tax allowed on the fiduciary income tax return. Such income in respect of a decedent includes dividends declared before your death and payable thereafter. Interest on day-of-deposit-to-day-of-withdrawal savings accounts is also accruable for this purpose. Capital gains also may be income in respect to a decendent. There is a special rule for computing the capital gains deduction in this case.

6. Medical expenses paid within one year of death are treated either on your last income tax return as medical expenses or on your estate tax return as a debt.

PREPARATION OF THE FEDERAL
ESTATE TAX RETURN (FORM 706)

All estate planning requires the preparation of a tentative federal estate tax return (Form 706) as of now. The plan assumes the death of a person on a particular date. The tax and other consequences are computed for that date. (For your purposes, the net worth date should be satisfactory.) From the figures you assemble you should be able to decide on a reasonable course of financial action. You cannot work out the problems without the use of a pencil. Even if there is no federal estate tax, a state death tax may be due on your estate. In general, attempts should be made to equalize the estates of spouses. You will be alerted as to whether you are holding property in correct title when you have to decide who is to be taxed on its value.

In the example on the following pages an estate plan is to be prepared for Daniel and Louise Smith as of December 31, 1978. The computations have been made assuming that Daniel Smith predeceases his spouse since mortality tables indicate that females live longer than males.

UNIFIED ESTATE AND GIFT TAX RATES

The tax rates for the first $500,000 of gift value or taxable estate before credits are given below.

VALUE OF PROPERTY	TAX ON VALUE	RATE ON EXCESS
Under $10,000	$ –0–	18%
10,000	1,800	20
20,000	3,800	22
40,000	8,200	24
60,000	13,000	26
80,000	18,200	28
100,000	23,800	30
150,000	38,800	32
250,000	70,800	34
500,000	155,800	37

The state death tax credit applies to the taxable estate minus $60,000 (adjusted taxable estate). The credit for the bracket including a $500,000 estate follows:

ADJUSTED TAXABLE ESTATE	CREDIT ON FIRST COLUMN	RATE ON EXCESS
over $ 40,000	$ 0	.8%
90,000	400	1.6
140,000	1,200	2.4
240,000	3,600	3.2
440,000	10,000	4
640,000	18,000	4.8

Assuming a taxable estate of $550,000 and no taxable gifts after 1976, the estate tax for a decedent who died in 1978 is computed as follows:

1. Tentative tax on $550,000 is 37%
   of $50,000 plus $155,800 = $174,300
2. Unified credit in 1978 (see page 180) = $34,000
3. State death tax credit on $490,000
   ($550,000 less $60,000) is 4% of $50,000 plus $10,000 = $12,000
4. Estate tax on $550,000

   a) Tentative tax $174,300

   b) Less unified credit $34,000

   c) State death tax credit   12,000   46,000

   Estate Tax $128,300

OBSERVATIONS ON ESTATE PLAN

The Estate Plan for Daniel and Louise Smith is set up in a form similar to the federal estate tax return (Form 706). The plan assumes that Louise Smith survives her spouse Daniel. For financial reasons and without regard to estate taxes, the husband intends to leave his entire residuary estate outright to his wife. In the event of a common disaster, the wife is deemed to survive the husband, and provision is made to provide the maximum Orphan's Exclusion for the children.

The combined gross taxable estate is $155,200. This amount is considerably less than the threshold tax-problem estate of $250,000. However, a combination of two errors in estate planning could result in a federal estate tax of $32,900 on the wife's estate. Estate Plan #2 shows that the life insurance policies are owned by Mr. Smith, and Mrs. Smith's will fails to provide properly for the Orphan's Exclusion. These errors in planning would have resulted in a tax of $5,600 if the marital deduction clause limited the deduction to 50% instead of the maximum amount provided by law (see Estate Plan #3). Not having the insurance in the husband's name and not providing properly for the Orphan's Exclusion in a common disaster would have resulted in the Smiths' relatively small estates paying a tax of $32,900 plus a substantial state death tax.

Under each heading that follows, you will learn the factors considered in estimating values or positions taken in order to reach the final acceptable plan. The accuracy of the individual figures used in Estate Plan #1 is relatively immaterial because the marital deduction limitation combined with the low tax rates makes value a minor matter compared with the importance of understanding the concepts involved. For example, whether the Smiths' home is worth $10,000 more is insignificant, whereas the matter of which estate is taxed on the home's value demonstrates an important conceptual principle. For estate planning purposes, the figures have been rounded to the nearest $100.

The Smiths made no taxable gifts after September 8, 1976 which would affect the tentative estate tax or unified credit.

Cash

The cash balances were derived from the Proof of Cash workpaper. The figures also tie in with the Net Worth. For estate taxes, savings accounts paying interest to day of withdrawal require an adjustment for interest accrued from the last posting date to the date of death. Regular savings accounts only include the last posted interest date. The cash accounts, both checking and savings, are in individual names. The Smiths do not have joint accounts because of personal financial considerations, and probate problems. To establish who pays the life insurance premiums and other bills affecting ownership of property, they maintain separate accounts.

Due from Stockbroker

Amounts due from the stockbroker for unremitted cash transactions such as dividends collected or sales of securities are assets of the estate. Any margin account balances owing to the broker should be netted against the cash account balance. If there is a net margin balance, the difference is a debt of the estate. Unremitted dividends are income on the decedent's last tax return. However, dividends declared before death and payable after death are assets of the estate. These dividends are added to marketable securities and are referred to as "income in respect of a decedent." This means that the dividends are included both on the estate tax return and, when collected, on the fiduciary income tax return. A deduction is allowed on the fiduciary income tax return for the estate tax paid on the income. Similar treatment is required for interest on day-of-withdrawal savings accounts and on bonds from the last interest date to the date of death.

Marketable Securities

For estate tax purposes, marketable securities are includable at their mean prices on the date of death or six months thereafter. If a security is not traded on the exact date of death, there is a prorating to get its *mean* price, based on the last sale before death and the first sale thereafter. Dividends and interest due and unpaid are added to the security prices. U.S. Series "E" bonds are valued according to the monthly redemption table issued by the U.S. Treasury Department.

Mortgage Receivable

The mortgage receivable arose as part of the purchase price of land sold in a previous year. The unpaid balance of the mortgage is an asset of the estate. The estate tax value should be at face unless the collectability is doubtful or unless the length of time to maturity requires taking a discount. Before claiming a discount for the purposes of estate tax, arithmetic computations are required. Thus, if the marital deduction is involved, the discount reduces the estate tax by 50% of the top bracket. This must be measured against reporting as ordinary income the discount ratably over the period to maturity. The discount is a reduction based upon the use of the money. On the other hand, a deduction for doubtful collectability is based on risk factors. In general, therefore, mortgages receivable should be returned for estate tax at face value. Unpaid interest must be accrued in order to be taken as a deduction.

When the land covered by the mortgage was originally sold, Mr. Smith elected the installment basis for reporting the gain. An estate cannot continue the installment basis. On the last tax return of a decedent, the unrecognized gain for income tax purposes must be reported.

Loans Receivable

In general, loans receivable are shown at their face value. If the executor believes the loan to be uncollectable at the date of death, an income tax deduction should be claimed on the decedent's last income tax return. Returning on the estate tax return a loan at less than full value results in ordinary income to the estate or beneficiary when the loan repayments exceed the estate tax value. Because the income tax rates usually are far in excess of the estate tax rates, the loans are reflected at face value.

If the executor is uncertain as to the collectability of a loan, the fiduciary should begin proceedings immediately. This is done so that by the time the estate tax return is due (nine months from the date of death) the treatment of the loan will have been clarified.

Interest due and unpaid at the date of death is income with respect to a decedent and is an estate asset.

Prepaid Interest

Prepaid interest is of two types: (1) finance charges added to the loan to be written off or ratable over the period of repayment; and (2) interest paid in advance on a loan.

Finance charges added to a loan are not an asset of the estate. The liquidation of the debt gives rise to an interest deduction on the estate income tax return represented by the charge for the monthly unpaid balance included in the payments. For ease of computation, the estate might continue ratably to claim the finance charges.

Interest paid in advance subject to refund for repayment of the loan is an asset of the estate. A ratable portion of the interest may be claimed for estate income tax purposes.

Mr. Smith's prepaid interest is for finance charges added to the notes payable on the purchase of the automobiles. These finance charges would not be considered an asset of Mr. Smith's estate. The finance charges would be an estate income tax deduction when paid.

Individual and Employer Retirement Plans

The estate taxability of individual retirement, HR-10 (self-employment), and employer-qualified plans depends upon the method of payout. If a lump-sum payment is made (whether to the executor or another person), the entire payment is includable in the estate. There is an exception if the recipient agrees to ordinary income treatment. On the other hand, if payment is made in the form of an annuity the account is excludable from the taxable estate.

Depending upon the circumstances at Mr. Smith's death, his employer's pension committee would determine the method of payment. As the final tax of Estate Plan #1 shows, a decision to pay Louise Smith the employer plan account balance would not create any tax liability in either estate. There is $28,700 unabsorbed unified credit in Mrs. Smith's estate. At a tax rate falling within the 22% and 24% brackets, a $20,900 lump-sum payment would increase Mrs. Smith's tentative estate tax by about $4,800. (This is not a sufficient amount to result in a tax.) Similarly, the IRA payment in a lump sum at Louise's death would not create a taxable estate. Having your Estate Plan computations in front of you makes decisions fairly simple, but you have to know the rules.

The final decision for the payment of a retirement plan rests with the employer's pension committee. However, the committee usually consults with the beneficiaries so that the settlement option will be in the best interests of the family.

It is important that an *estate* not be a contingent beneficiary of plans (i.e., one spouse predeceases another and the payment is made to the survivor's estate) because in that case any annuity payment is includable for estate tax purposes. Therefore, the contingent beneficiary (the receiving party if no spouse survives) should be a child or children of the deceased. If the amount of the benefit exceeds $100,000, you should consider establishing an *inter vivos* trust to receive the benefits.

Life Insurance

In the Smiths' Estate Plan #1, the key tax decision was the ownership of $100,000 of life insurance on Mr. Smith's life. Mrs. Smith's ownership of the policies and her payment of the premiums from her own funds eliminated all estate taxes. The employer's group life policy of $50,000 was assigned to Louise at inception. You could argue that the marital deduction was oversubscribed in Mr. Smith's Estate Plan #1 and this made the ownership of the life insurance policies crucial to tax avoidance. Financial considerations dictate that Mrs. Smith should be the sole beneficiary. This unfortunately results in losing the entire unified credit in Mr. Smith's estate. The marital deduction interplay in estate planning is discussed in full on page 199.

To avoid a conflict with the IRS on the taxability of life insurance, you should make certain of the following:

1. The applicant for the policy is the owner.

2. The owner and the insured are different spouses.

3. No borrowings on the cash value are traceable to the insured.

4. Premiums are paid from the owner's personal funds.

5. The insured retains absolutely no rights to the policy.

Any gifts of life insurance policies, even where the terminal reserve value (approximate cash surrender value) is less than $3,000, should be reported on a gift tax return. This is known in tax parlance as "wearing suspenders and a belt at the same time." In other words, it is an evidentiary device, costing nothing, which establishes the facts. This is true even though the insurance company's records are the primary evidence.

In most states a group life insurance policy is allowable as a gift. Due to the nature of this insurance there is no cash value. An assignment to a spouse of the ownership requires no gift tax return because there is no value assignable to the policy.

National Service Life Insurance (G.I. or V.A.) is not assignable under present law. Therefore, all proceeds are includable in the insured estate. The social security and V.A. death benefits are refunds of funeral expenses, not assets of the estate.

The terminal reserve value of Mrs. Smith's two policies on Mr. Smith's life is includable as an asset of Mrs. Smith's estate. The face value of $100,000 plus unfundable premiums paid to the Smith children in the event of a common disaster escapes estate tax because of Mrs. Smith's ownership. You should make certain that after your spouse, your children or other persons are contingent beneficiaries of your life insurance.

Because in a common disaster the $100,000 would be paid directly to the guardian of the children, Mrs. Smith might consider an *inter vivos* trust to be funded by the proceeds in such a contingency. Then the secondary beneficiary would be this trust. (For discussion of *inter vivos* trusts see page 160.)

Automobiles

The Smiths' two automobiles were registered in Mr. Smith's name. They were financed by notes secured by chattel mortgages. The value of the automobiles was includable in the Estate Plan at a value of $300 over the amounts due on the notes. The automobiles costing over $11,200 were reduced by notes. This left an equity of $4,700 after deducting the $6,500 due on the notes. However, the fair market value of the automobiles was some $4,500 less than cost. Therefore the automobiles are carried at $300 over the notes. The figure is an estimate. For estate tax purposes, the automobile dealer's blue book showing the purchase prices of used automobiles is generally used for valuation purposes.

Furnishings

Furnishings are generally considered marital gifts to the wife. Records and source of funds may be used to establish a contrary position. If the values involved are considerable, the casualty insurance policy should indicate the ownership.

In the Smiths' home, the furnishings were purchased from retail stores. There were no valuable pieces to be separately considered. A value of approximately 50% of original cost was assigned to the furnishings, and this was included among Mrs. Smith's assets.

Appliances

For net worth purposes, appliances were carried as family assets. Therefore, in order to inventory all assets for the Estate Plan, the appliances were included, at about 50% of cost, as Louise Smith's property.

Household goods and personal effects of value not in excess of $10,000 are exempt from the carryover basis rules (see page 184). The maintaining of detailed records is important to establish ownership, and these records, are also invaluable for income tax purposes (e.g., casualty losses) and to establish a meaningful net worth computation.

Residence

Life insurance and the family residence are usually the key assets in estate planning for spouses. The ownership of these assets requires a decision based upon personal factors in addition to financial considerations. Changes in ownership require mutual consent. The general rule is to treat the marriage as a partnership with the goal being to equalize the equity of each partner. This not only saves federal and state death taxes but rests on sound philosophical grounds.

The family residence is the exception to the rule that property should be in separate names. If it is in both names, the residence property passes by law to the survivor. In the case of late second marriages, this rule may be modified. If the donating spouse is concerned about children of a prior marriage, a trust or other written agreement may provide for the life tenancy of the other spouse. To clearly establish joint contributions as well as joint ownership, you should (1) pay the contract deposit equally from separate funds, (2) ensure that the cash required at closing is clearly indicated on the statement as coming from each spouse, (3) make certain that the mortgage is in both names and (4) pay for all substantial improvements equally from separate funds.

The regular payments on the mortgage are support payments and do not enter into the problem of assigning ownership of the residence.

If you are unable to establish equal contributions to the family residence, you should consider electing the joint-interest provisions of the gift tax law (see page 181). By filing the necessary gift tax return and registering your deed (if necessary), you will have established to the satisfaction of the IRS the joint interest in the property. A jointly owned residence avoids probate, and this eliminates involvement of the other family members in the surviving spouse's immediate need for a place to live.

The fair market value of your residence is the price you could obtain if you were allowed a year in which to make the sale, the technical rule being "willing buyer and willing seller, neither under a compulsion to buy or to sell." The use of the one-year period avoids assigning an auction value or quick turnover price to the property. If you still have no "ball park" figure to use for the value of your house, you may use the prices of comparable residences in your neighborhood as as guide. You may also use the estimate of a local real estate agent who has an appraisal background.

The fair market value of your residence is reduced by any mortgage indebtedness in order to arrive at your equity. Since the mortgage is in the name of both you and your spouse, the amount of remaining mortgage reduces each spouse's share equally.

For estate tax purposes, the Smiths treated their home as owned equally. It was estimated to be worth $100,000. The mortgage at the year end was approximately $51,600. The equity was $48,400 divided equally.

You are permitted to make a $100,000 tax-free gift to your spouse. A family residence makes an excellent subject for this allowance. This joint interest always operates to avoid death taxes which may be costly even where no federal estate tax is due.

Vacation Home

Daniel Smith owns the vacation home. Since its purchase in 1973, the home has been an activity engaged in for a financial profit. For estate tax purposes, the vacation home is includable at fair market value less its mortgage. The fair market value is about $40,000. Reducing that amount by the mortgage of $23,800 allows an equity includable in the estate of $16,200.

Restricted Securities

Restricted securities are those which are not traded on the stock exchange. They may also include stock of a listed company which cannot be freely traded. Stock of a listed company which cannot be sold in the open market requires the services of an investment analyst to determine the discounted price. Restricted stock of the unlisted variety (i.e., stock of a closely-held corporation) may be extremely difficult to value.

A buy-sell agreement usually establishes an acceptable value. If the parties act independently and mutual benefit is inherent, the IRS generally will accept the value of a business as established by the agreement. On the other hand, without an agreed price, various factors such as goodwill and the death of a key executive may result in a wide variance between what an executor believes a business is worth and the IRS's view. The executor generally wants as low a value as possible and the IRS has the opposite objective. Many books have been written on this subject, including one devoted entirely to the Tax Court's approaches to this problem.

Mr. Smith's restricted stock is a minority position. One of his neighbors invented a widget. (The term "widget" is the "John Doe" of manufactured products.) Mr. Smith decided to invest $10,000 for a 20% interest in the corporation's stock. The corporation, Widget Manufacturing Corp., has not qualified as a Subchapter S Corporation. Therefore, no transactions affect the Smiths' income tax return. The stockholders have not entered into a buy-sell agreement, so no price between them can be established. The controlling shareholder and key executive told Mr. Smith that the corporation is still breaking even. There is no reason to believe the stock is worth more than what was originally paid for it. Thus, for the Estate Plan Mr. Smith used $10,000, the amount of his original investment.

If at the time of Mr.Smith's death there was no buy-sell agreement, his executor would probably negotiate a redemption by the corporation of the stock. In the event the stock appeared to be valuable at the time of death, the executor might either retain the stock or seek a third-party purchaser. An outside purchaser might be in a better position to offer a higher price than the corporation or its other shareholders. The decision of what to do with restricted stock not covered by a buy-sell agreement requires professional assistance.

Miscellaneous Assets

Miscellaneous assets consist of jewelry, personal effects, refunds due, insurance claims, security deposits, and items of usually an insubstantial amount not requiring a separate category.

Any property whether tangible or intangible in which you have an interest is includable in your gross estate unless specifically exempt by statute. The ownership of property as between spouses is determined by facts. Thus, jewelry insurance carried in the husband's name is evidence of his insurable interest. However, that fact would not be determinative of the wife's engagement ring. The insurance policy identifies family property. Custom, usage, and contributions determine estate tax ownership for estate tax purposes. This is particularly important for ownership of antiques and works of art. If the husband pays for a work of art with a value of not more than $6,000 and he desires his wife to have ownership, the bill of sale should indicate the wife as purchaser. The husband might write the wife a note indicating the cash gift. The insurance policy covering the work of art should be in the wife's name or in their joint names. Many times the intentional unwillingness of spouses to put anything in writing as to ownership operates later to mutual disadvantage. For example, the IRS's estate tax attorney usually contends that where there is doubt about ownership the property is to be included in the estate. If an appeal is necessary, a settlement generally requires some portion of the value to be taxed. Contrary to popular belief, rarely is a case on appeal even 60%–40% settled in the taxpayer's favor. A compromise costs money. Therefore, learn to avoid the conflict. The goal should be to equalize the estates as much as possible. Be specific and concrete on the ownership of the property.

Jewelry values are subject to obsolescence. Therefore, unless the insurance coverage appears within the price range, the executor should obtain new appraisals. The IRS requires appraisals to be attached to the estate tax return. If there is no sentimental value to a piece of jewelry in an estate, the jewelry should be sold. The sale price is the best indicator of value.

The carryover basis rules effective in 1980 exclude from its computations up to $10,000 of household goods and personal effects.

Mr. Smith's miscellaneous assets totalling $500 consist of an amount for his watch, cuff links, and clothing. The Smiths net worth statement did not adjust jewelry to fair market value because the amount involved was not deemed substantial. For Estate Plan # 1, Louise valued her jewelry and personal effects at $2,500. Again, unless the amounts are substantial, any differences will not materially affect the results.

For estate planning, little time should be spent in worrying about precise values. The first figure that comes to mind for value is probably within an acceptable range.

Gross Estate

The Smiths' gross estates are computed separately. The totals indicate that both gross estates are within the same area for planning purposes. Of the combined gross estate of about $155,200, the husband owns 55% and the wife owns 45%. These percentages are within an acceptable range of equalization for the amount of these estates.

The total gross estate determines whether an estate tax return should be filed. Thus, no estate tax return need be filed if the gross estate does not exceed the following amounts:

YEAR	RETURN REQUIRED IF GROSS ESTATE EXCEEDS
1978	$134,000
1979	147,000
1980	161,000
1981 and thereafter	175,000

For estate tax purposes, Mrs. Smith's estate includes the marital deduction claimed by Mr. Smith. However, the planning workpaper brings Mr. Smith's estate down to the marital deduction computation. This format clarifies how the marital deduction operates and also shows the total assets of each spouse independently. In other words, in a common disaster, Mrs. Smith's estate includes the asset "Due from Daniel Smith's Estate." The exact amount depends upon the provisions of the will. In the Smiths' case, the entire residuary estate of each spouse was left outright to the survivor.

Taxable gifts made after December 31, 1976 would be includable in your gross estate.

Funeral and Administrative Expenses

In estate planning, funeral and administrative expenses are usually estimated at about 5% of the gross estate.

Funeral expenses are subject to an allowance of a Social Security benefit and a Veteran's Administration burial payment. Some funeral directors will make application for the Social Security payment and reduce their bill accordingly. Payments for transporting the deceased, gratuities to clergymen, and food and transportation for mourners are includable funeral expenses

Administrative expenses include executors' commissions, attorney's fees, accounting expenses, and probate costs. Also included are all items of disbursements necessary to operate the estate from the death of the decedent until the closing of the estate by the final distribution to the residuary beneficiaries.

Executor's commissions vary according to the state and according to size of the estate. Special problems in managing real estate, for example, may cause a probate court to grant an additional executor's commission. If a financial institution is named as the executor, it usually has a fee schedule.

An attorney usually charges the equivalent of an executor's commission to represent an estate. An executor should require a retainer letter from the attorney setting forth the exact nature of the services and the amount to be paid. This is particularly helpful if the attorney is a family friend of long standing. The letter will prevent any unintentional misunderstandings as to what was to be done and for what charge at a later date.

Accountants are usually retained on a per diem arrangement, a specific amount per day for accountants of different levels of experience. The actual preparation of the federal estate tax return and its examination by the IRS is usually done by accountants. On the other hand, an attorney may be fully capable of preparing the return and dealing with the IRS representative. If there are problems of valuation and questions of ownership, the executor should speak freely to the attorney about engaging an experienced accountant.

The attorney representing an estate has an exceptionally high degree of professional responsibility since there are usually uninformed spouses and minor children involved. Therefore, if you are an executor, you should choose an attorney with whom you have rapport. Whatever the size of the estate, the executor must work closely with the attorney. Therefore, every attempt should be made to match the complexity of the estate with the experience level of the attorney.

Although the executor has various options as to whether certain administrative expenses are to be claimed as estate tax or income tax deductions, the estate planner in the first instance treats the expenses as reductions of the gross estate.

Debts

Debts of a decedent include all indebtedness at the time of death. A mortgage is usually shown as a reduction in value of the asset secured by it. Unpaid income and other taxes, interest due to date of death, credit cards, rent, telephone, guarantees, and any other obligations owing at the time of death are debts, and constitute reductions of the gross estate.

The decedent's share of income tax due after death is also a debt. Real estate taxes are due on the assessment date, not on the date shown on the real estate tax bill.

Rent due under a lease extending for a reasonable period (generally six months) after death is an allowable debt.

The debts shown for Mr. Smith are those shown on Mr. Smith's Net Worth. (See page 52.)

Adjusted Gross Estate and the Marital Deduction

The *adjusted gross estate* is the total value of the assets less funeral expenses, administrative costs, and allowable debts. The adjusted gross estate is not the net probate estate. The gross estate may include insurance, real estate, and other assets which by operation of law are not part of the probate estate. The adjusted gross estate measures the limitations for the marital deduction. The limitation is the greater of 50% of the adjusted gross estate or $250,000 if provided by will.

Mr. Smith elected the maximum marital deduction which oversubscribed his estate. His estate would be entitled to a $34,000 unified credit if he died in 1978. Since he has no taxable estate, the credit is of no use. Estate Plan #1 is said to oversubscribe the marital deduction. Because of the relatively small estate together with Mrs. Smith's financial needs, this formula is the only acceptable one for the Smiths.

If the marital deduction had been limited to 50% of Mr. Smith's gross estate and the insurance policies had been owned by Mr. Smith, no estate taxes would be due. However, Mrs. Smith's estate is fairly close to the unified credit. (See Estate Plan #3 on page 200.) There is a financial problem of limiting Mrs. Smith to less than the entire estate. In other words, what happens if Mr. Smith leaves his entire estate outright to Mrs. Smith and then uses the 50% maximum marital deduction clause in his will? This would be done so that Mr. Smith may use up his unified credit. In the Smith's Estate Plan #3 the federal estate tax cost of limiting the marital deduction to 50% would be $5,600 tax in Louise's estate. The safe posi-

Daniel and Louise Smith
Estate Plan #1
December 31, 1978

	Daniel	Louise	Total
Gross Taxable Estate (Fair Market Value)			
Cash	3900	8200	12100
Due from Stockbroker		1300	1300
Marketable Securities		15700	15700
Mortgage Receivable	8800		8800
Loans Receivable	2000	1200	3200
Prepaid Interest	—0—		—0—
Individual Retirement Plan		6700	6700
Employer Pension Plan	20900		20900
Life Insurance	—0—	1900	1900
Automobiles (Equity)	300		300
Furnishings		5400	5400
Appliances		1300	1300
Residence (Equity)	24200	24200	48400
Vacation Home (Equity)	16200		16200
Restricted Securities	10000		10000
Miscellaneous			
Jewelry, Personal Effects, & Misc.	500	2500	3000
Gross Taxable Estate	86800	68400	155200
Less, Funeral & Administration Expenses	4300	3400	
Debts	700	—0—	
Total	5000	3400	
Tentative Adjusted Gross Estate	81800	65000	
(Less) Add Maximum Marital Deduction	(81800)	81800	
(Less) Orphan's Deduction		(120000)	
Taxable Estate	—0—	26800	
Estate Tax			
Tentative Estate Tax	—0—	5300	
Less, Unified Credit	34000	34000	
State Death Tax Credit		—0—	
Federal Estate Tax	—0—	—0—	

	Daniel	Louise	Total
State Death Tax			
(New York Estate Tax)			
Federal Gross Estate			
(without Marital Deduction share)	86800	68400	155200
Less, Vacation Home Located			
outside state	16200 *		16200
State Gross Estate	70600	68400	139000
Funeral Expenses, Administration			
Expenses and Debts	5000	3400	
Tentative Adjusted Gross Estate	65600	65000	
(Less) Add Maximum Marital Deduction	(65600)	65600	
(Less) Orphan's Deduction		(120000)	
State Taxable Estate	-0-	10600	
Tax			
State Gross Estate Tax	-0-	212	
Less, General Credit	-0-	212	
State Estate Tax	-0-	-0-	

* state vacation home located may charge death tax.

	Daniel	Louise	Total
Plan #2			
(Life Insurance owned by Daniel and not qualified for orphans' deduction)			
Tentative Adjusted Gross Estate (per plan #1)	81 800	65 000	146 800
(Less,) Cash Value Life Insurance		(1900)	(1900)
Add, Life Insurance Proceeds	100 000		100 000
Tentative Adjusted Gross Estate	181 800	63 100	244 900
(Less,) Add Maximum Marital Deduction	(181 800)	181 800	-0-
(Less,) Orphans' Deduction		-0-	-0-
Taxable Estate	-0-	244 900	244 900
Estate Tax			
Tentative Estate Tax	-0-	69 200	
Less, Unified Credit		34 000	
State Death Credit		2 300	
Federal Estate Tax	-0-	32 900	32 900
Plan #3			
(Marital Deduction limited to 50% of Adjusted Gross Estate)			
Tentative Adjusted Gross Estate (per plan #2)	181 800	63 100	244 900
(Less,) Add Marital Deduction at 50% of Adjusted Gross Estate	(90 900)	90 900	-0-
(Less,) Orphans' Deduction		-0-	-0-
Taxable Estate	90 900	154 000	244 900
Estate Tax			
Tentative Estate Tax	21 300	40 100	
Less, Unified Credit	34 000	34 000	
State Death Credit		500	
Federal Estate Tax	-0-	5 600	5 600

202

tion is to provide for the $250,000 marital deduction. If you believe that using a formula which provides maximum absorption of the unified credit is important, you should seek professional assistance before varying the acceptable limitation structure.

Mrs. Smith, assuming she survives, has to account in her estate for Mr. Smith's marital deduction. Since that amount would be part of her gross estate, the heading "Adjusted Gross Estate" has been modified by the word "tentative" to avoid any misunderstandings.

Deductions from the adjusted gross estate are also allowed for charitable gifts whether outright or in trust. Gifts of income-producing property made during a lifetime with the remainder at death passing to a charity are an estate tax deduction.

In Mrs. Smith's estate, a limited deduction would be allowed for her orphaned children. (See page 182.) The Smiths have two children ages 8 and 10. The exclusion is computed:

	SON (8 YEARS)	DAUGHTER (10 YEARS)	TOTAL
Years to 21	13	11	24
Deduction allowed (24 × $5,000)			$120,000

The Orphan's Exclusion may be limited in the same way as the marital deduction.

Estate Tax

The tentative estate tax is computed using the unified gift and estate tax table. (See page 186.) A reduction is allowed for gift taxes paid after 1976.

Credits allowed against the tax include the unified credit and state death taxes. Foreign death taxes are also an allowable credit.

Mr. Smith has no tentative estate tax. Mrs. Smith's tentative estate tax is eliminated by the 1978 unified credit of $34,000. In addition, there would be an orphan's exclusion credit.

CONCLUSION

After examining the Smiths' Estate Plan #1, you will notice that the Smiths have first considered personal family needs. These needs, coincidentally, resulted in no federal or state estate taxes. With the Orphan's Exclusion and unified credit Mrs. Smith's estate showed no tax due. Before 1977, however, her estate would have been subject to tax.

Every item involved in estate planning requires a decision. The fact that there is no estate tax due does not mean that estate planning is simple. The "bottom line" in estate planning is not taxes, but people. The tax planning is relatively easy today unless the estate is in the millions-of-dollars category. Planning for people requires great talent and hard work.

7

LIFE INSURANCE

AS A GENERAL PROPOSITION, it is safe to say that almost no one has "enough" life insurance coverage. There are many intelligent, business-oriented individuals who have virtually no coverage, not because they don't think about such things or can't afford them, but because they do not believe in this kind of protection. Surveys have shown that certain types of highly creative and resourceful persons in business, the sciences, and the arts maintain only the most minimal coverage.

On the other hand, almost everyone has probably met the self-impor-tant person who does not wish to disclose his or her income, but who "subtly" lets you know his or her great worth by casually mentioning how much life insurance he or she carries. This individual may, without realizing it, be revealing that he or she does not understand very much about life insurance relative to his or her total financial picture. This per-son may, in fact, be outrageously overcommitted to insurance and may therefore be wasting money.

This chapter does not argue either for or against life insurance. It is nei-ther propaganda for the insurance companies nor does it prescribe hard and fast rules about coverage. (There is no fool-proof formula for know-ing how much coverage is "enough.") We are dealing here only with the *concepts* of insurance in order to show you how to relate these concepts to your and your family's needs. If you buy life insurance you do so main-ly in order to replace wages, provide for the liquidity of your estate, and pay debts. You may also consider life insurance as an investment or as enforced savings. You should make decisions regarding life insurance only after you have examined your own financial resources and have learned about the specific forms of coverage available. You should decide first what your needs are and then, how much you can afford. This is the only reliable method for selecting the right amount and kind of coverage for your life situation.

BASIC TERMS

Life insurance is a complicated subject, and the words we all use so casually, thinking that we know what we mean, demonstrate the problems. "Life" insurance, in fact, is a misnomer. We are really talking about "death" insurance, a payoff at death. The following is a basic glossary of terms that are used in discussing life insurance. Read the terms carefully and make sure that you understand them. Some of the words are so common that their "familiarity breeds contempt," with the result that we use the words incorrectly. Be careful. When you talk to an insurance professional, he or she may mean one thing by the words while you mean another. You are not buying what *you* mean by the words, but what the insurer means by them. Think of the following as the rock-bottom vocabulary for getting around in the world of insurance.

POLICY. A contract between two parties (insurer and owner) to pay a specific sum on the death of a third party (the insured). The owner and insured may or may not be the same party.

INSURER. The insurance company which undertakes to pay off at the death of a specific person.

INSURED. The party at whose death the policy matures.

OWNER. The policyholder who has power to change, surrender, and direct to whom the policy is to be paid on the death of the insured. The owner may be the insured, a member of the insured's family, a creditor, a trust, a business entity, or a charitable organization.

BENEFICIARY. The person who receives the payoff of the policy at the death of the insured. The beneficiary may be the owner or someone selected by the owner. A *primary beneficiary* is the first person eligible to receive the proceeds of the policy upon the death of the insured. If the primary beneficiary predeceases the insured, the *contingent* beneficiary receives the proceeds of the policy.

PREMIUM. A sum of money paid periodically to the insurer under the terms of the policy to effect the insurance coverage.

DIVIDEND. The annual participating amount, credited by the insurer to the owner, which reduces the premium cost. Dividends are not a contractual obligation. The amount depends on economic factors and on the experience of the insurer. The dividends may be left with the insurer, paid to the owner, used to purchase additional insurance or applied to reduce the premium. Dividends left on deposit with the insurer pay interest, which is taxable income.

CASH-SURRENDER VALUE. The amount the insurer agrees to pay before maturity (death) at the surrender of the policy. This value changes each year, and a schedule of cash-surrender values is included in the policy. Dividends left with the insurer or used to buy additional insurance are added to the cash value. This value is the investment aspect of the insurance policy. Some policies do not provide for a cash-surrender value.

LOAN VALUE. The amount which the insurer agrees to lend to owner. This is usually about 95% of the cash value, which stands as the collateral for the loan. The loan is usually renewable until the maturity of the policy. The interest charged is usually lower than commercial loan rates. (In most states the rate is about 8%.) The loan may be used for personal purposes or to pay premiums. Dividends may be used to purchase insurance to cover the loan so that the death benefit will equal the face value of the policy if the loan is still unpaid at the time of death.

SETTLEMENT OPTIONS. The choices given in the policy for methods of payout. Options include a lump-sum payment or various types of period payments. At the maturity of the policy a settlement option may be made by the beneficiary. Age and needs of the beneficiary determine the choice of settlement option.

PROCEEDS. The combination of amounts due the beneficiary under the provisions of the policy. Proceeds include the face amount of the policy, the refund of a portion of final-year premiums, less loan and unpaid premiums. Proceeds may also include dividends and interest from insured's death to date of payment.

PAID-UP VALUE. The amount at a given time which would be payable to the beneficiary at the death of the insured if no further premiums were paid on the policy.

INSURABLE INTEREST. The relationship required by law between the *owner* and the *insured*. Such required relationships include spouses, family members, creditors, and business associates. A *beneficiary* does not re quire an insurable interest. Friends do not have an insurable interest in each other. Thus, if you want a friend to be your beneficiary, you must be the owner of your policy, as well as being the insured. The theory behind insurable interest holds that if a policy could be purchased on the life of a stranger, a number of "premature" deaths might occur. If you have a question about the owner's insurable interest, you should check your own state law before the policy is drawn up.

INCIDENTS OF OWNERSHIP. The power of authority which may be possessed by a person over a policy. Possession of such a power determines includability of a policy for federal estate tax purposes.

WAIVER OF PREMIUM. The provision within a policy that requires no premiums to be paid during the insured's disability. Upon the termination of the disability, premium payments resume, but the premiums waived are not required to be repaid. (Waiver of premium is obviously an important policy provision.)

DOUBLE INDEMNITY. The provision for twice the face value of the policy to be paid to the beneficiary upon the accidental death of the insured. There is usually an extra premium cost for this provision.

Insurers generally provide life insurance coverage within the following types of policies.

TERM INSURANCE (1) is the cheapest form of individual life insurance; (2) is pure life insurance; (3) has no cash or loan value; (4) is usually the first kind of insurance purchased; (5) provides an instant estate; (6) refers to a specific period of coverage after which it terminates; (7) may include waiver of premium; (8) after five years or other period may permit renewal without a physical examination; (9) may be convertible at end of term to other kinds of insurance; (10) may diminish in face value over time (used for mortgage); and (11) insurer may pay dividends if a participating company is used.

ORDINARY, WHOLE LIFE, OR STRAIGHT LIFE INSURANCE (1) provides both life insurance and savings; (2) has cash and loan values (premiums are paid during insured's life); (3) may include waiver of premium; (4) financing arrangement may have tax advantages in interest deduction (minimum deposit); (5) may provide for limited payment period; and (6) has a single premium life used for tax-free accumulation of earnings as the savings factor.

ENDOWMENT INSURANCE (1) provides settlement options at maturity; (2) provides savings and life insurance; (3) provides retirement income; and (4) usually life insurance protection is declining term.

GROUP INSURANCE (1) provides coverage without physical examination; (2) is usually term insurance; (3) is for an employment, social, or professional group; (4) may be convertible; (5) may be tax-deductible for employer; and (6) in excess of $50,000, provides coverage taxable at rates favorable to the employee (the first $50,000 is a gift from employer).

FLIGHT OR ACCIDENT INSURANCE (1) pays off only at death by accident; (2) has term coverage; and (3) has low premiums, based on remoteness of aircraft death or other accidental death.

ANNUITY INSURANCE (1) provides periodic payment during life; (2) may cover two lives and may be guaranteed for a specific period; (3) may provide a refund at death; (4) is usually purchased for a single premium; (5) may start immediately or may be deferred; (6) usually has no cash or loan value; (7) may be written by an insurance company or by others; (8) may be included as a settlement option in an ordinary life policy; and (9) is available in qualified retirement plans.

For most kinds of insurance other than group life and annuities, the insurer must be satisfied that the insured's health meets its standards for the insured's age. The insurer may require bonus premiums to cover variations from the standard health condition. If the insured's health class is very substandard, the insurer may not be willing to write a policy of any kind. On the other hand, a different insurer may not be as conservative and might write the policy on an excess-premium basis.

Youth is an important factor in insurability. This is why term insurance, often convertible into ordinary life without a physical examination, is so popular with beginning wage earners.

MINIMUM-DEPOSIT INSURANCE is similar to term insurance in cost but has several advantages. Minimum-deposit is ordinary life insurance using the maximum borrowing power under the policy to finance the premium. The IRS allows the interest paid on the borrowings as a tax deduction provided you pay at least four annual premiums during the first seven years of the policy. This investment, of course, exceeds the outlay for term insurance. However, after the initial investment the cash payments reduced by the tax benefit of deductible interest are within the range of term insurance costs. The loan is covered by a one-year term policy, usually paid by dividends. In later years, the loans may be repaid and an annuity purchased at favorable rates. Minimum-deposit life insurance is very popular with young executives.

TERM INSURANCE VS ORDINARY LIFE

In setting up your insurance plan, you should first consider term insurance. It requires the least outlay of cash and is particularly valuable for the younger family. If you expect your annual earnings to increase by at least 25% over the next five years, you should probably be in the market for a five-year term convertible policy, which gives you the option of converting to more costly ordinary life after the fifth year. (Term insurance, because it is for a "term" or temporary, can be compared to "rented" protection, while ordinary life, as a permanent contract, is referred to as proprietary or "ownership" protection.)

If your career provides for slower increments, you might consider a 10-year term convertible policy. On the other hand, if your spouse is employable and if your earnings are relatively stable, you probably should stay with pure term. In all cases, a waiver of premium should be purchased. Since the disability risk is remote, the cost is small.

Because term insurance has no savings factor, the premiums are considerably lower than ordinary life. Adding five-year term to amount-renewable term raises the cost of term insurance slightly.

There is a theory which holds that if you can afford to purchase ordinary life, you should instead purchase term and invest the difference. In general, this has not held true over the last 15 years. After a number of years, the total cost of term plus savings is within the range of the cash value of an ordinary life policy. Leaving the premium difference in the savings bank probably would not increase the value substantially over the performance of most life insurance companies and in any case, your earnings would be taxable. You would also have to make a strong commitment to savings, which most people find difficult. Thus, those who can afford the choice should choose ordinary life. Term insurance premiums usually cost less than a third of ordinary life policy premiums, but this does not represent equity to the owner.

In deciding whether to choose term or ordinary life, decide on the amount of coverage you need and review the costs. Few young families have cash resources sufficient for all their insurance needs. You may elect reduced coverage in ordinary life because of the inherent savings factor.

Study your own situation and weigh personal and other probable factors before you choose.

GROUP INSURANCE

It is important for you to know whether your employer's group insurance is convertible to ordinary life if and when your employment terminates. The ordinary life available at that date is not cheaper than a private placement, but usually no proof of insurability is required, and this is a tremendous advantage to a person in a substandard risk class.

Typical rates for a group insurance policy are much lower than any form of term insurance because of the simple and economical administration of group plans. One professional group insurance plan has over four billion dollars of life insurance in force. This is a larger volume than 94% of the life insurance companies in the country. In this group, the rates are by age class, charging for the 35–44 age class 50¢ per month per $1,000 of coverage. That would be $180 for a $30,000 policy (50¢ × 30 × 12 = $180). Savings Bank Life Insurance (SBLI) charges $114 annually for a five-year-renewable term policy for the 35–44 age class. Both policies pay dividends. Last year the dividends on the first group policy were $72, making a net cost of $108. SBLI paid $8, reducing its net cost to $106. These are both very inexpensive policies. In the group policy, the age classification is re-determined each year with the groups in 10-year brackets. In effect, the group policy illustrated is a 10-year renewable term. In most states, group insurance may be assigned to your spouse.

NATIONAL SERVICE LIFE INSURANCE
(G.I. INSURANCE)

National Service Life Insurance was provided by the federal government to former armed services personnel. The veteran might elect term or limited-payment ordinary life insurance. Congress varied the coverage depending upon the period of service. Until the Vietnam conflict, the cost of the insurance was substantially less than with private insurers. However, insurance benefits for Vietnam veterans are more restricted. In any event, G.I. insurance is a good buy, and if you are eligible, you should seek maximum face-value coverage. The kind of insurance would then depend on your financial resources. Generally, the limited-payment life, even if a strain on your budget, is best suited for the under-35 age group. GI insurance cannot be assigned to your spouse or used as collateral.

SAVINGS BANK LIFE INSURANCE (SBLI)

Savings Bank Life Insurance (SBLI) was first offered in the early 1900s as an inexpensive approach to limited coverage. SBLI is sold directly or by mail to residents or workers within the state. The maximum coverage in New York is $30,000 face-value. Check with your savings bank for information about this insurance and its coverage.

SBLI premiums may be used as a yardstick for measuring similar policies. SBLI premiums are traditionally very low. However, if there are substantial differences in premiums you should require an insurer to explain them. The differences may be due to more extended coverage and higher limits.

Below is the annual premium currently charged for $30,000 face value policies issued at age 35. (Male and female rates are the same.)

POLICY	ANNUAL PREMIUM	WAIVER OF PREMIUM	TOTAL COST ($30,000 FACE VALUE)
5-year renewable term	$114	$5	$119
20-year decreasing term	108	3	111
25-year decreasing term	130	4	134
30-year decreasing term	156	5	161
Straight life	535	16	551
Life paid up at age 65	621	14	635
Endowment at age 65	770	17	787
20 payment life	784	10	794
20-year endowment	1,219	13	1,232

The above rates do not include provisions for dividends. Dividends reduce premium payments. Premiums can be paid monthly, quarterly, or annually.

SBLI rates for the two most popular kinds of policies indicate the savings in purchasing the maximum amount of insurance. Below are the premiums charged at age 35 for those policies:

POLICY	FACE VALUE			
	$5,000	$10,000	$20,000	$30,000
5-year renewable term	$23	$41	$76	$114
Straight life	93	181	357	535

If you purchased separate $5,000 term policies to reach the maximum, you would pay $138 annually ($23 × 6). The premium on a single $30,000 term policy is $114. You save 17% ($138 − $114 = $24 ÷ $138 = 17%). For straight life policies, the saving is 4% ($93 × 6 = $558 − $535 = $23 ÷ $558 = 4%). The difference in total premiums between the two face-value policies is approximately the same. The straight life premiums are more than four times the cost of a term policy.

The recent SBLI scale of dividends for policies (issued after January 1, 1972) indicates that for a $30,000 policy issued at age 35, the dividends were as follows:

POLICY	1ST YEAR	5TH YEAR	10TH YEAR	10-YEAR TOTAL
5-year renewable term	$8	$13	$—	$51*
20-year decreasing term	8	21	38	227
25-year decreasing term	8	22	39	236
30-year decreasing term	8	23	42	254
Straight life	18	66	151	813
Life paid-up at age 65	19	75	172	923
Endowment at age 65	21	93	210	1,116
20 payment life	21	94	214	1,134
20-year endowment	27	143	323	1,691

*five-year total.

On the basis of the above illustrative dividends, a $30,000 straight life policy issued at age 35 would cost the following in the 10th year:

Premium	$535
Waiver of premium	16
Total	$551
Minus illustrative dividend	151
Net cost	$400

The SBLI straight life policy results in the following costs and benefits, again using a $30,000 policy issued at age 35:

Annual premium	$535
Waiver of premium	16
Total outlay	$551
Premiums paid for 10 years	$5,510
Minus total dividends used to reduce premiums	813
Net cost	$4,697
Minus cash-surrender value after 10 years	4,800
Insurance cost for 10 years (figure in parentheses indicates a profit if policy surrendered)	($ 103)
Benefits at age 65	
Cash value	$15,870
Paid-up insurance	$22,680
Benefits at age 65 if dividends used to buy paid-up additions	
Cash value	$28,470
Paid-up insurance	$40,710

These examples are simple and do not give effect to the interest-adjusted index explained later.

You should now have an idea of the cost of insurance for a person age 35. Below are the current annual premiums (without waiver of premium) for $30,000 SBLI policies at other ages:

POLICY	AGES AND ANNUAL PREMIUM					
	25	30	40	45	50	55
5-year renewable term	$ 89	$ 96	$ 155	$ 224	$ 335	$ 509
20-year decreasing term	65	79	158	238	364	561
25-year decreasing term	72	93	192	290	443	
30-year decreasing term	83	110	232	350	528	
Straight life	374	444	653	807	1,009	1,278
Life paid-up at age 65	410	499	793	1,048	1,463	2,252
Endowment at age 65	501	614	992	1,326	1,877	2,953
20 payment life	604	686	904	1,049	1,230	1,465
20-year endowment	1,185	1,196	1,260	1,326	1,432	1,599

Use these rates carefully in comparing insurance costs. (If SBLI is not available to you, the rates may be academic.)

SETTLEMENT OPTIONS

Life insurance policies generally provide that at maturity your beneficiary is to receive a face amount plus dividends and earned premiums, reduced by loans and unpaid premiums.

For many people, a lump-sum payout is an invitation to unwarranted spending. For this reason, the insurer provides settlement options. This means that at the maturity of the policy (unless the owner has made an irrevocable choice previously) the beneficiary may elect a method of payout. Such settlement options include the following:

1. Interest payments: periodic interest payments are made while the principal is retained by the insurer. At a later date, a lump-sum payout or other option may be elected.

2. Fixed-period payment: a guaranteed payment over a definite period.

3. Fixed income: a specific income amount (including interest) is paid over a period of time until all funds have been paid out.

4. Life income: payment over the life of the beneficiary.

If the surviving spouse elects to receive insurance proceeds over a period of time, the interest included with the payment (up to $1,000) is excluded from income taxes. There is no income tax exclusion if the interest-only option is elected.

You should discuss settlement options with your spouse. Cash receipt requirements, a spouse's career, and the ages of the children are all factors in determining which settlement option should be elected. To permit even more flexibility in payout over the settlement options, you may use an insurance trust.

BENEFICIARY

As between spouses, the insured and the owner should be different. If the insured is the husband, the owner is usually the wife or vice versa. Ideally, the beneficiary and the owner should be the same. If a wife is the owner, the children should not be the beneficiaries; otherwise, the IRS contends that the wife at the death of the husband made a gift to the children. This gift is therefore subject to the gift tax. If the beneficiary is a spouse, the children or a trust can be named contingent beneficiaries.

If you own a policy and if your spouse is the beneficiary, you should consider assigning the policy to the ownership of your spouse. Since this assignment is subject to the gift tax if its value exceeds $6,000 (including the marital share), you could borrow against the policy to reduce its value. Subsequently, you could make gifts to your spouse within the annual limit of $6,000 and have the loan reduced. If you do not desire to reduce the value of the policy through loans, you might consider the $100,000 tax-free interspousal gift.

In most states, a group insurance policy may be assigned even though it has no value. Remember, if you assign a policy irrevocably, there is no way, without the consent of the owner, that the policy may be returned to you.

If you know that your estate will require funds to pay expenses or debts, make certain that your beneficiary will lend the money to the estate or buy some of its assets. A beneficiary who has not been carefully chosen in this respect may cause low prices to be received by the estate rather than the prices that could be realized through a slow liquidation. If you are in doubt concerning your beneficiary's ability or willingness to assist your estate by a purchase or loan (if this is necessary) you should establish an insurance trust. Remember, a legal obligation to pay is an incident of ownership.

Your estate ordinarily should not be the beneficiary of your policy. However, if you require liquidity and do not want to go the trust route, you may make the estate the beneficiary. In most states, insurance paid to parties other than your estate are not subject to the claims of your creditors. The insurance is *not* part of your probate estate.

POLICY PROVISIONS

Despite significant efforts by insurers to simplify the language of the insurance policy, the fact remains that the average policy provisions require detailed wording to spell out clearly each party's rights. If you have taken some trouble to understand the definitions and read the details of various kinds of policies, you should, in general, understand the policy provisions. Since the insurer prepares the policy provisions, in most states a dispute concerning unclear language is usually decided against the insurer. Before buying a policy, ask for a specimen of the *exact* policy and review the unclear language with the agent. If you are in doubt about the agent's interpretation, call your state insurance department for an explanation. If your state has strict regulations governing insurance companies, the wording of the provision should have been approved by the state agency. You should not hesitate to make a telephone call to the insurer's general counsel for an explanation of a policy provision. If you need further help you may also want to consult your own attorney.

It is rare that a large life insurance company and the parties involved in a policy cannot agree on a contract provision. Most provisions are termed "boiler-plate," which refers to a somewhat complicated clause designed, after many years of experience, to protect all parties from a future misunderstanding. Policy provisions are fairly uniform from insurer to insurer for the same kinds of policy because they are stipulated by state laws.

INSURANCE TRUST

An insurance trust is designed to solve the problem of having an owner other than the insured where there is no living beneficiary capable of investing or distributing the insurance proceeds.

The insurance trust is similar to an *inter vivos* trust used for a spendthrift spouse or child. It may be revocable or irrevocable. If revocable, the proceeds are includable in the donor's estate.

The insurance trust permits a more varied approach to handling the proceeds than the normal settlement options. For example, the trust may distribute income on the basis of individual need or tax status. This is known as a "spray trust" because the income and corpus may be distributed over a group (spouse and children), and in varying amounts. The "spray trust" gives the power to trustees other than interested parties both for practical and tax-saving reasons.

A settlement option to pay periodic amounts to specific individuals may not fit a family's needs. Your family has more flexibility using a trust, particularly if there will be substantial insurance proceeds. However, the cost of administration, together with finding proper trustees, should be measured against your personal targets. (You might reread the section on the spendthrift spouse in Chapter 6 to grasp the problem more clearly.)

The insurance trust is established during life by transferring the policy ownership to it. There is no annual gift-tax exclusion for this transfer. If desired, the trust may be for a short-term period (10 years and one day) after which the policy is returned to the donor.

The insurance trust permits invasion of the corpus for any beneficiary; and the trustee may be given wide discretion over corpus distributions. If a family group is involved, you may restrict the invasion powers to the

standards of health, welfare and education of the beneficiary or beneficiaries.

The trust may also provide for the remainder interest to go to
grandchildren, thus saving an estate tax at the death of a beneficiary.

The trustee generally has broad powers of investment and acts on behalf of persons not capable of handling their own financial affairs.

There is no income tax or estate tax savings in using a *revocable insurance trust*. If the trust is *irrevocable*, there may be an income tax savings
when combining the insurance with other income-producing assets. This
is a complicated problem, and if you consider doing it you should seek
professional help. Estate tax savings on an *irrevocable* trust are achieved
by removing the policy from your estate. If you do this, you cannot retain
any incidents of ownership in the policy and still make the transfer effective. You can set up an insurance trust in your will, but the usual method
is to establish the trust during your lifetime.

ANNUITIES

Purchasing a life insurance policy is really death-motivated. In other
words, what you are buying is a payoff at death, with, possibly, some incidental provisions. An annuity is motivated by life: its purchaser hopes to
beat the mortality tables for a while longer.

An annuity may be issued by an insurer or privately. It may be paid for
in periodic installments or purchased outright with a lump sum. A paid-up
life insurance policy may be settled as an annuity. An ordinary life policy
may provide for an annuity purchased at a specific age, such as 65. A
beneficiary may choose to receive an annuity under the settlement option.
The person receiving the annuity is called the *annuitant*.

An annuity payment may be fixed in amount or it may be variable as to
part of the payment. Payments may be periodic over the life of the annuitant with or without a refund provision. The policy may also pay for a
specific period ("period certain") even if the annuitant dies before the
end of that period. If you purchase an annuity with a 10-year certain provision and die before the 10th year, your beneficiary receives the periodic
payments up to the 10th year after payments commenced.

An annuity may be for two persons. This is called a *joint and survivor's
annuity* and is very popular in employers' retirement plans.

The annuity making the highest payment is the *straight annuity* with no
definite length of time (period certain) or refunds. An annuity may be deferred, that is, purchased now and received at a later date.

The fixed-payment annuity computation uses interest tables instead of the life insurance mortality tables. Inflation is a major objection to fixed-payment annuities. (This is why the variable factor was introduced.) Nevertheless, fixed-payment annuities are very popular with individuals of age 65 or older. They desire security and believe that by outliving the mortality table odds they will also be outliving the inflation depreciation of their annuity. Because of the limited years involved in an annuity, present rates of inflation probably should not be a material factor against purchasing a straight annuity.

The payment of an annuity contains two factors. One is the money you invested being returned and the second is the earnings factor. The tax effect of the payment is explained as follows:

1. Investment in contract: amount paid for annuity.
2. Expected return: mortality table computation usually supplied by issuer.
3. Annual annuity: periodic payments received over taxable year.
4. Divide the *investment in contract* by the *expected return* to get the *exclusion ratio.*
5. Multiply the *exclusion ratio* by the *annual annuity payment.*
6. Subtract #5 from #3 for *taxable income to be reported.*

The following is an example of the foregoing:

1. You paid in later years $50,000 for an annuity.
2. The expected return is $58,000 beginning at your age.
3. The annual annuity payment to you is $4,833.
4. Exclusion ratio: $\dfrac{\$50,000}{\$58,000}$ equals 86%
5. $4,833 times 86% equals $4,156, the amount excluded from tax annually.
6. $4,833 minus $4,156 equals $677, the amount taxable each year's payment to you.

If your life extended beyond the expected return, you would continue to report $677 each year as the taxable portion of the annuity.

A private annuity is an unsecured promise to make periodic payments based on mortality tables. You may wish to use a private annuity for family estate planning not involving an insurance company. The private annuity can also be a very important family financial tool where an aged parent owns valuable real estate and needs the rental income. You might well issue a private annuity to your parent in exchange for ownership of his or her property. If the expected return to you at your parent's death, discounted for present value, is less than the fair market value of the property, the difference is a taxable gift from your parent to you. The annual annuity is taxed to your parent, as follows:

1. Return of capital: nontaxable return of cost of property
2. Capital gain to extent of difference between fair market value and cost
3. Ordinary income for the balance

The computations are based on the annuitant's mortality rate. After the complete capital gain is reported, the balance is ordinary income. Usually at this time the aged parent's exemptions and other deductions reduce the tax bracket so that the taxable portion of the annuity is reported at a low tax bracket. The annuity cannot be secured by a mortgage, but must be an unsecured promise to pay. You own the real estate and all future appreciation goes to your account, but most important, the real estate is excludable from your parent's taxable estate. Your tax basis is the fair market value at the date of the transfer. The annuity is not part of the annuitant's taxable estate. Death terminates the annuity, and it has no value.

Since the private annuity can only be secured by a moral obligation on the part of the child to pay the parent, this intra-family tax-avoidance device should be used only where the parent does not expect to experience any psychological problem in transferring valuable property rights to the child. Since this arrangement puts the parent at the mercy of the child financially, it can have a devastating effect if there is any deterioration in the personal relationship between the two parties.

Retirement Plan Annuities

Annuities paid under a qualified retirement plan are excludable from estate taxes if paid to a party other than the estate. Even if the annuity is not paid by a qualified plan, it may escape estate taxes if the plan could have qualified with the IRS. Any part of the annuity paid for by the employee is includable in the estate. Only the employer's share is exempt from tax. A retirement plan annuity is subject to ordinary income tax rates.

INSURANCE RATES

The premium which you pay on an ordinary life insurance policy is based on four elements: (1) protection (the life insurance factor); (2) savings (cash value); (3) illustrative dividends (investment earnings); and (4) company retention (costs and profit).

There are two types of insurance companies: stock and mutual. To a policyholder, both companies are the same. Legally, a *stock* company is owned by its stockholders who receive dividends based on earnings of the company. (Stockholders are not required to be policyholders.) A *mutual* company is owned by the policyholders, and they participate in the earnings. In real life, both stock and mutual insurance companies issue earnings participating and nonparticipating policies. From your view, as long as the financial condition of the insurer is excellent, you should not be concerned with whether the insurer is a stock or a mutual company.

The Interest-Adjusted Method

To help you simplify judging insurance premium costs, many companies will supply you with an interest-adjusted index for a policy.

The interest-adjusted index for a policy reflects your cost each year per $1,000 of life insurance protection over the period used. It is the total of what you pay for a policy minus what you would receive on later surrender adjusted for an interest factor of usually 4% or 5%. Measuring competitive costs of insurance by the interest-adjusted method assists you in judging insurance values because the use of an interest factor helps you to compare policy costs among different insurers. The interest-adjusted index (also called the premium-outlay index) is not an infallible criterion, but in most cases it will be the one best suited to your needs. As an example, the interest-adjusted cost index for a particular $1,000 ordinary life insurance policy on a 35-year-old person is computed as follows:

5% RATE	10 YEARS	20 YEARS
1. Annual level premium	$20	$20
2. Accumulated premium for period at 5% interest	$264	$694
3. Subtract illustrative dividends for periods at 5% (if payable)	53	153
4. Balance	$211	$541

5. Subtract cash-surrender value at end of period	102	287
6. Net protection cost	$ 109	$ 254
7. Divisor (future value if $1 accumulated for the period at 5%)	13.206	34.719
8. Divide step 6 by step 7 (cost-adjusted for interest divided by future value of $1) for interest-adjusted cost index	8.25	7.32

The smaller the interest-adjusted index, the cheaper the cost of the insurance protection. Therefore, decide first the exact policy you want, then check various insurers' interest-adjusted cost indices at the same interest percentage. There are valid arguments for other bases of comparison, but the American Council of Life Insurance believes that the interest-adjusted cost index is the most suitable approach.

The interest-adjusted index for a policy does not consider death proceeds. The theory is that the lower the interest-adjusted cost index, using the same interest rate, the better insurance value you will receive for your money. Just because a company does not supply you with this index does not mean its rates are not competitive. Therefore, you should make your own calculations on a worksheet using computer printouts from different companies for the same policy.

You may also use the "retention method" for comparing rates. This combines the interest-adjusted cost index with a probability factor. Under this method, an insurer with a low-dollar company retention for the kind of policy you are purchasing is considered your best buy. Professor Joseph M. Belth of Indiana University in his book *Life Insurance, a Consumer's Handbook* uses this method for judging competitive values.

The interest-adjusted cost index and company retention figures may not be available to you. In addition, insurers may argue about judging a policy solely on the basis of these two methods. For these reasons, you should have a further yardstick by which to measure policies. Therefore, examples of premium ranges are given on the next few pages. Firstly, the SBLI (Savings Bank Life Insurance) premium rates are usually considered the low end, and an SBLI policy may be issued to only a maximum of $30,000 face value. However, you may not have SBLI available in your state, or you may require additional insurance above the SBLI limits. Given below is the premium information on a $100,000 whole life policy issued to a male, and the premium costs cover waiver of premium in case of disability. The company in the example has a reputation for low range. Lesser amounts of insurance may be computed by prorating. (A $50,000 policy premium is about 51% of a $100,000 policy.)

$100,000 WHOLE LIFE COVERAGE
(MALE, WITH WAIVER OF PREMIUM)

AGE AT ISSUE	AGE 25	AGE 35	AGE 45	AGE 55
One year's premium	$ 1,644	$ 2,248	$ 3,264	$ 5,015
Dividend	151	193	296	591
Guaranteed cash value	None	141	579	1,189
Ten years' premiums	16,440	22,480	32,640	50,150
Dividends (not guaranteed)	3,419	4,727	6,753	11,091
Premiums less dividends	13,021	17,753	25,887	39,059
Guaranteed cash value	12,652	17,191	22,611	28,993
Net payments less cash value	369	562	3,276	10,066
Interest-adjusted index (at 4%)				
(See page 221.)	3.16	4.37	7.43*	14.64*

*Excludes waiver of premium.

RESULTS AT AGE 65
(GROSS PREMIUM BASIS WITH DIVIDEND ADDITIONS)

Insurance benefits				
(policy and additions)	$233,000	$183,700	$144,400	$118,500
Guaranteed cash value	60,090	55,043	46,387	28,993
Total cash value				
(policy and additions)	153,200	113,600	77,500	41,900
Total premiums paid	65,760	67,440	65,280	50,150

Another insurer's whole life policy for a 35-year-old male issued in a state which allows 5% policy-loan rate is shown below:

Face value	$30,000	$50,000	$100,000
One year's premium	700	1,154	2,282

DIVIDENDS ALLOTTED AT END OF SECOND YEAR

Second year	$50	$84	$168
Third year	63	105	209
Fourth year	75	125	249
Fifth year	88	147	294

Note the following: (1) dividends left with company currently pay 6.25% interest; (2) guaranteed cash value for tenth year is $162 per $1,000; (3) loan value for tenth year is $154 per $1,000; (4) dividends are not guaranteed; (5) nonsmoker discount for male is $.89 per $1,000 and for female, $.62 per $1,000; (6) female discount is $1.00 per $1,000.

You will notice that the first company charges $2,248 for a 35-year-old male for one year's premium with a dividend of $193 on a $100,000 policy. The second insurer charges $2,282 with no dividends until the second year. The dividends of the second insurer start at the end of the second year and increase each year. On a gross-premium basis, policy #2 is 1.51% higher than policy #1 ($2,282 − $2,248 = $34; $34 ÷ $2,248 = .0151). This is not very significant when dealing with large amounts, and with two insurers which are considered to be in the low and high premium ranges. However, the total dividends not guaranteed for policy #1 at the end of 10 years are estimated to be $4,727. For policy #2 this total should be about $3,140. In other words, there is a 50% difference in dividends, making the cost of policy #1 more attractive.

	POLICY #1	POLICY #2
Ten years' premiums	$ 22,480	$22,820
Dividends (estimated)	4,727	3,140
Premiums less dividends	$17,753	$19,680
Percent increase		11%

The premium costs become significant at an 11% increase of policy #2 over policy #1. However, you would also compare 20-year premium factors to determine whether policy #1 continues to be your best buy. Since policy #2 did not offer an interest-adjusted index, that comparison could not be made without doing the calculations on page 221. It is important to reconcile the premium differences so you know what you are buying. The guaranteed cash value of policy #1 is $17,191 at the end of 10 years; for policy #2 it is $16,200. The difference here is 6.11%.

As you can see from the exercise, comparing $100,000 ordinary life policies is not easy unless you use some index. Remember, you will have to study your own requirements to make a decision. Differences in initial gross-premium costs alone are not the answer.

Below are further examples of *high-range* costs for different kinds of policies, assuming a face amount of $100,000 for a 35-year-old male:

	MINIMUM DEPOSIT	20 LIFE PAY-MENT	LIFE AT 65	20-YEAR ENDOW-MENT	ENDOW-MENT AT 65
One year's premium	$ 2,451	$ 3,386	$ 2,094	$ 4,560	$ 3,100
Net insurance protection during first year	101,225	101,693	101,047	102,280	102,801
Ten years' premiums	24,510	33,860	20,940	45,600	31,000
Dividends estimated	2,019[a]	5,594[b]	2,863[b]	8,472[b]	5,468[b]
Net premiums due	22,822	33,860	20,940	45,600	31,000
Cash value[d]		27,800	14,600	40,100	24,900
Total loan value	17,523				
Actual loan	13,442				
Equity paid-up value	4,081	51,524[c]	31,348[c]	53,296[c]	38,969[c]
Total cash payment (10 years)	11,844[e]	33,860	20,940	45,600	31,000
Net insurance protection	106,072	106,757	103,607	109,971	106,508

[a]Term insurance bought from part of dividends to provide maximum insurance protection.

[b]Accumulated to earn 6.25%, interest not guaranteed.

[c]Paid-up life insurance. No further premiums paid.

[d]Loan value about 95% of cash value.

[e]Premiums paid for four out of the first seven years.

The interest-adjusted cost index was not supplied by this insurer.

The following are illustrations of the *high-range* cost of five-year renewable term insurance for a 35-year-old male with waiver of premiums (40¢ per $1,000 discount for female):

Face value	$30,000	$50,000	$99,999
One year's premium	166	264	528
Dividends not guaranteed			
paid at end of second year*			
Second year	29	49	97
Third year	29	49	97
Fourth year	34	57	113
Fifth year	34	57	113

*Dividends left on deposit earn 6.25% interest, not guaranteed.

CHOOSING THE INSURER

There is no rule that says you must purchase your life insurance from the first company or individual who gives you a price quotation. You may have asked friends and associates for the name of an insurance agent. Any agent who is a C.L.U. (Chartered Life Underwriter) has passed a series of examinations designed to test life insurance knowledge.

If you don't know an agent you should answer an insurance company's newspaper advertisement or look under "Insurance" in the yellow pages of your telephone book. Or, call any life insurance company whose name is familiar. There are several thousand companies in the country, and you must make a beginning. You may visit the agent or, at your convenience, the agent will visit you. Some of the best insurance relationships have been created by a blind introduction. Insurers generally train their agents well, so despite what you might believe, the odds are in your favor that the individual who calls on you will be competent and well-qualified.

Before you meet with the agent, complete your workpaper (see pages 238 and 239) in order to give yourself an idea of how much insurance *you* believe you require. The agent will have other methods of determining your insurance needs. Listen to his or her determination of your needs and ask for a written workpaper documenting this determination. Study this workpaper against your own. You may decide to pick a coverage category higher than the one you originally believed you needed, but make up your own mind about the amount privately and do not be pressured into a decision. Before you meet with the agent, try to know enough about life insurance to understand most of the presentation. As the agent's presentation is made, write down your questions, leaving room on the page to fill in the answers later. Ask your questions *after* the agent has completed the presentation, and if a question has not been answered to your satisfaction, ask for a letter of clarification. Remember, you are a buyer in a buyer's market, so proceed slowly. It may be necessary to work with several agents until you find one who satisfies you professionally and personally.

After receiving the computer printouts from the agent of the insurance purchase recommended for you, compare premium rates. As we have shown, all insurers do not charge the same rates for the same policies. If you believe the agent is competent and you have decided on the kind of policy you need, check the rate first against SBLI rates, or compare the interest-adjusted index for the policy with those of similar policies offered by other companies.

You are under no obligation to purchase a policy unless you are *entirely satisfied* with the transaction. The higher price sometimes quoted by an insurer over another is supposedly due to so-called "service." Do not accept this as a valid reason for an extreme cost difference between two policies which are virtually the same. Most life insurance companies give excellent service and all pay off at maturity. You must be satisfied that the rate you are paying (including illustrative dividends) is *competitive* and reasonable.

Before signing, be absolutely certain of the financial strength of the insurer. If you are uncertain of the strictness of your state's insurance law, an excellent indication of the soundness of the insurer is its license to operate in New York. This state passed its first insurance law in the 1800s, and is considered to have the model statute. You can either write to the New York State Department of Insurance, Consumer Service, 2 World Trade Center, New York, N.Y. 10047, or call (212) 488-5642 as to whether an insurer does business in New York. If you write, enclose a postcard or a stamped, self-addressed envelope for a reply.

There are many financially sound insurers not licensed in New York. In that case, you will have to verify the strength of the insurer through *Best's Life Insurance Reports.* (Your library probably has a copy.) Do not be satisfied unless the insurer is strongly recommended by *Best's.* There are many insurers with similar names so be sure you know the exact name of the company. The insurance payoff is probably years away; therefore, you must establish today that your insurer is unqualifiedly capable of meeting its obligation to your family. *Never* compromise on the insurer's financial ability to pay. There is no government insurance agency similar to the Federal Deposit Insurance Corporation for your bank account to protect you.

SOCIAL SECURITY

Social security for a young family is life insurance with a single settlement option, a variable annuity. Since all persons insured by social security pay rates based on wage limitation regardless of age, the system does not involve actuarial computations (based on life expectancy). Your eligibility, premium rates, and benefits are determined by Congress. The Social Security Administration estimates that nine out of 10 American workers are covered by social security. In fact, social security is probably the most important part of your life insurance program. A 35-year-old individual who has had maximum coverage for the past eight years, would leave survivors benefits worth about $10,000 a year if he or she had two children. The value of these benefits is equivalent to a $100,000 life insurance policy with a single-settlement option of an annuity for a fixed period. The life insurance provided by survivor's benefits may be the most valuable financial resource of your family. A widow receives social security benefits until her younger child reaches age 22 if still in school, otherwise until the child reaches 18. She also will receive benefits for herself beginning at age 60. Social security also pays $255 toward funeral expenses. It provides disability payments and medical care costs (Medicare) for the aged and disabled. A husband may also receive social security if his deceased wife was insured.

FEDERAL TAXATION (ESTATE AND GIFT)

The proceeds of an insurance policy are includable in the insured's taxable estate unless (1) they are not payable to the estate, or (2) the insured is not the owner of the policy.

The first condition is rarely a problem. To prevent the application of this provision, the estate of the insured should not be named either as a primary or contingent beneficiary.

However, litigation in this area frequently arises over the question of policy ownership. In order for insurance proceeds not be taxed in an estate, the law requires the insured to have given up all incidents of ownership. This means simply that the insured gives up all and any power over the policy and its benefits. For example, if the insured has a written agreement with a beneficiary that part of the proceeds of the policy is to be used to pay debts and taxes, the insured is deemed to retain an incident of ownership. Therefore, the IRS argues, the entire proceeds of the insured's policy are includable in the taxable estate. There is an argument that only the amount actually used to meet the contract provision should be includable, but the insured's agreement provides for a retention of sufficient power to make the entire proceeds subject to tax.

Incidents of Ownership

The following is a list of six incidents of ownership, any one of which, if retained by an insured, will make the proceeds includable in the insured's estate (even though someone else is the owner of the policy):

1. Power to change beneficiary
2. Power to surrender or cancel policy
3. Power to assign or revoke an assignment of policy
4. Power to pledge policy or borrow against cash-surrender value
5. Power to choose a settlement option
6. A reversionary interest valued at more than 5% (actuarial computation which shows that policy has a ninety-five percent chance of never returning to insured's estate through death of beneficiaries— rarely applicable).

In small estates (less than $500,000 if married), the death of both spouses within a short interval could result in an estate tax if the proceeds of insurance policies were includable in the estates and if the surviving spouse's estate failed to qualify for the Orphans' Deduction. For this reason you should consider assigning your life insurance policies to your spouse.

Community Property

In community property states, the treatment of life insurance for estate taxe purposes varies. In general, a policy taken out while the insured and the insured's spouse were residents of a community-property state is deemed to be owned 50% by each. However, the entire proceeds of the policy would be included in the insured's estate if any one of the six incidents of ownership was retained by the insured. Of course, the proceeds would be subject to the marital deduction. The problem arises if the policy was not community property at inception. In some community property states, even if the insured retained incidents of ownership, the proceeds includable would be reduced by 50% of the proceeds paid from community property. If you reside in a community-property state, word the assignment of your policy to show surrender of all powers, including all community property rights.

CONTEMPLATION OF DEATH

In the days of the Roman Empire, anyone leaving on an extended trip usually disposed of property to family and friends as a gift *causa mortis* (because of death). The Justinian Code provided that such a disposition of property was conditional. If the voyager returned from the trip even years later, the property had to be returned to the donor. A *causa mortis* gift was a simple and effective estate-planning device. From this emerged the deathbed transfer of property in modern times to avoid estate taxes. This transfer was called a gift "in contemplation of death."

Until the passage of the 1976 Estate and Gift Tax Law, the contemplation-of-death rules were only presumptive. This meant that if within three years of death property was transferred by the decedent, the transfer was considered in contemplation of death and therefore subject to estate taxes *unless* the executors could show that the gift was not death-motivated. The courts were crowded with contemplation-of-death cases as a result of executors attempting to refute this presumption. In fact, whether or not the estate won or lost the contemplation-of-death issue, the interplay of estate and gift taxes made a deathbed gift an estate tax savings device. What happened was that the gift was included at its date-of-death value and the estate was reduced by the gift tax paid or owed. The estate also received a tax credit for the gift tax. (Fortunately for the IRS, most people were legally incapable of making any gifts by the time they were *in extremis.)*

In 1976 Congress changed the presumptive rules with the result that now all gifts made within three years of death are includable in an estate. The estate is increased for the gift tax and the unified rates are applied to it.

Prior to 1977, an insurance policy transferred within three years of death was presumed to be in contemplation of death, and the proceeds were includable in the decedent's estate. If only premiums were paid by the insured during the three-year period and no incidents of ownership were retained on a policy transferred earlier, the IRS agreed to include only the premiums paid by the insured during the three years before death.

Since 1976 the proceeds of a policy are included only if the gift has been made within the three-year period and if the value at the date of the gift exceeds the gift-tax annual exclusion ($3,000 for a present interest). However, a policy valued at $8,000 at the time of the gift would apparently require including 100% of the proceeds for estate tax purposes even though only $5,000 was subject to gift tax.

The old rules remain in effect through 1979 for decedents who made gifts prior to 1977 and who died after 1976. These same rules appear to apply to premiums paid by the insured. In other words, if the premiums do not exceed the annual exclusion, they are not includable in the insured's estate.

In order to avoid any problem, even where the premiums are less than the annual exclusion, the *owner* of the policy should make the premium payment. If your spouse is the owner of your policy, sufficient funds should be made available prior to the premium due date so that the record shows the payment was made by the spouse.

GIFT TAX

The transfer of a life insurance policy without adequate financial consideration may subject the policy's value to the gift tax. The taxable gift is the excess of the value of the policy over the $3,000 annual exclusion. The annual exclusion for life insurance does not apply to insurance placed in a trust.

The gift-tax value of a life insurance policy is not identical to its cash-surrender value. The worth of a policy is its interpolated reserve value. This includes cash-surrender value, dividends, the portion of unearned premiums reduced by loans, and unpaid premiums.

An interspousal tax-free gift of up to $100,000 is eligible to absorb the excess value of an insurance policy over $3,000. You also might consider borrowing against your policy and making cash gifts in later years in order to have your spouse repay the loans. Since one of the goals of estate planning is to equalize both spouse's estates, the transfer of the insurance policies is an effective means of carrying out part of this objective.

Do not make a gift of an insurance policy to your spouse and make your children the beneficiaries. This defeats the purpose of the gift, because the IRS's position is that at your death your spouse has made a gift of the proceeds to the children. A policy made the subject of a gift should make the new owner and beneficiary the same person. If you assign your insurance policy to your spouse, you may make your children the *contingent beneficiaries.* Review the use of insurance trusts.

ESOP AND RETIREMENT PLANS

An Employee Stock Ownership Plan (ESOP) or other qualified retirement plan is permitted to purchase life insurance for its participants. ESOP life insurance premiums are restricted to 25% of the money allocated to the employee. In a retirement plan approved by the IRS (qualified pension, profit-sharing, or retirement income plan), the life insurance premium limitation is generally 50% of the contributions made on behalf of a member of the plan.

Life insurance is an excellent investment for an ESOP and retirement plan. The $50,000 coverage limitation, while effective for plans, provides low-cost insurance in the excess ranges. The term insurance rates used by the IRS for the coverage in excess of $50,000 are much lower than group life insurance rates, and the premium on the excess coverage is treated as additional wages.

If your company has either an ESOP or some other qualified plan, you should speak to the trustees about either a group policy or an individual policy for your account. In plans computed according to actuarial tables, this may not be possible. However, a plan that is a money-purchase type (particularly favorable for small companies) should be able to buy a policy for you. This is an easy way to increase your estate without any out-of-pocket costs, and the policy can be used at your retirement to supply annuity benefits. Unfortunately, if your employer fails to make a contribution, your policy might lapse unless its cash-surrender value is sufficient to support several years' premium loans. This is in many cases a good gamble for you to take. In small companies, every effort is made to pay the employer's contribution since generally the controlling shareholders receive a favorable percentage of the total amount contributed.

TAX SHELTER

A tax shelter is a financial device that provides a deduction now (frequently in excess of the cash invested) in exchange for reporting the corresponding income at some later time. There may or may not be any real economic motive for a tax shelter other than the deferment of taxes. In other words, paying taxes later on income earned today is considered to justify making investments that have no economic "upside." (An "upside" means that the investor's earnings on the deal, before tax benefit, will be equal to a sound investment.)

When you consider that the investment income earned by the insurer on the premiums is not taxed to the policyholder, life insurance may be considered a tax shelter. Interest earned by the owner on dividends left with the insurer is taxable, however, because it is similar to having a savings account.

Where the policy is owned by a party other than the insured and escapes taxation, the tax-shelter aspects of life insurance become apparent (particularly at death).

A policy that is surrendered may result in a taxable transaction if the amount received by the owner exceeds the net cost of the policy.

INSURANCE AS A CHARITABLE CONTRIBUTION

Although the value of using a life insurance policy as a charitable contribution appears to be limited to larger estates, a donor may still receive tax benefits by using even a small policy. This approach should be considered by spouses without children who have a desire to help a specific religious organization or charity. (Incidentally, the first organization listed as a *bona fide* charity in the tax law is the government.)

The transfer of a policy during your life-time to a charity ranks as a charitable contribution on your income tax return. The value of that contribution is the interpolated reserve value of the policy (higher than its cash-surrender value) at the date of the gift. All future premiums which you pay on that policy are deductible as charitable contributions.

If a gift to a charity is made within three years of death, the proceeds are includable in the estate if the value exceeded the $3,000 annual exclusion at the date of the gift. In such a case the estate receives a deduction for a charitable contribution. The marital deduction, if available, is increased by the inclusion of the policy in the estate. Thus, the net effect of the donation within the three-year period may be favorable to the estate because it actually reduces the estate tax through an increased marital deduction. This is called a "deathbed contribution."

A trust may also be used for the donation of life insurance to charity. Great care is required, however, to make certain that the donor retains no incidents of ownership over the policy donated.

BUSINESS INTERESTS

Corporations and partnerships usually maintain insurance policies to fund the buyout of a deceased member's interest. In addition, insurance may be used to operate any business so that on the death of a key person time will be available to find new management talent.

There are many different plans which utilize life insurance for businesses. For example, the proceeds from a life insurance policy may be payable directly to a business. In other cases, the beneficiary may be the deceased business member's family. Or, the ownership of the policy may be split between the business and the insured, with, the business owning the cash-surrender value and the insured owning the proceeds. Insurance proceeds may represent the entire buyout price to be paid to a deceased stockholder's or partner's family.

If you are operating a business, life insurance can be a valuable asset. Study insurer pamphlets until you have a sufficient understanding of this subject, and then seek professional help. Your accountant and your lawyer should be consulted in all business insurance decisions.

STATE EXEMPTION LAWS

Many states exempt from death taxes a portion of life insurance ordinarily includable in the insured's estate. If the insured cannot or does not desire to transfer ownership of the policy, this exemption is important. Even though starting in 1977 the IRS raised the limits on the amount of your estate that escapes tax, many states still retain their old exemption laws. In view of this fact, the life insurance exemption is important. Usually the exemption must be reduced by the amount of the insurance proceeds claimed as a marital deduction. The impact of state death taxes should definitely be considered in planning ownership of your policies.

HOW MUCH INSURANCE?

After you have studied the life insurance definitions, the kinds of policies, the tax implications, and the role of social security survivor's benefits, the "bottom line" question remains: How much insurance do you require?

The answer to this question requires an analysis of four factors: (1) objective of life insurance, (2) net worth, (3) income, and (4) future needs.

Objective

Your objective is your immediate reason for seeking life insurance. If you desire liquidity in your estate to pay expenses and debts, the objective as well as the amount required may be substantially different from what would be needed to provide your surviving spouse with funds. The estate insurance needs may be disposed of by term insurance in an easily computed manner, whereas your spouse's needs require further analysis.

The usual objective of life insurance is to provide the family with funds either on a short-term or long-term basis. For the profile family, the Smiths, the objective is to allow the two children to complete their college education. The younger child is now eight; therefore, the program will cover the next 14 years. Mrs. Smith will be age 46 at that time and will not be eligible for widow's benefits until age 60. However, she is self-supporting and does not require immediate specific provision for her needs.

Net Worth

The amount of life insurance you require is directly related to your net worth and to the liquidity of your assets. Your residence, for example, may or may not be a liquid asset. When the spouse who provides the larger income dies, the first reaction is almost always to sell the home. This may be the wrong decision. The house should probably be the last asset to be liquidated. (You may purchase diminishing-term life insurance to pay off the mortgage on your home at your death.) If your need for life insurance as reflected in the formula on page 239 appears beyond your income today, rework the formula in various ways. If all else fails, your spouse may at your death have to consider selling the family residence and buying or renting a smaller home.

Income

Income, for life insurance purposes, is synonymous with cash receipts. Employer benefits, social security, spouse's earnings, and any and all sources of cash are included, whether taxable or not. Your income is measured on a present-value method so that the income extended over future periods may be reflected as a lump-sum amount.

Future Needs

Future needs requires annualizing the support requirements for the period of time required. Use your present cash flow to make the necessary adjustments for a deceased spouse. This requires a realistic appraisal of needs combined with a reserve for contingencies.

FORMULAS FOR COMPUTING YOUR NEEDS

The "yardstick formula" for judging your insurance needs is based on a multiplication factor applied to your age bracket and wages. This formula is a standard against which to measure your actual computations under a second, more detailed "present-value formula." If the actual computations are within a range (about 25%) of a formula based upon earnings, your results are acceptable. If the difference exceeds 25%, you must reexamine your computations. For example, if your actual figures show a need for $100,000 of insurance and the "yardstick" is $150,000 or $50,000 (each a difference of 50%), you should rework your actual formula. If the difference remains the same, ignore the "yardstick" and use the actual figures.

The yardstick formula to use is as follows:

AGE BRACKET	FACTOR
20–29	5
30–39	4
40–49	3
50–59	2

Thus, at age 25, a person earning annual gross wages of $15,000 under the formula requires $75,000 of life insurance ($15,000 × 5). A 35-year-old earning $15,000 per year requires $60,000 of insurance ($15,000 × 4). This is merely a starting point and a comparison device. You should *not* use this formula to make your final determination of life insurance.

The "present-value formula" appears to offer the most scientific way of evaluating insurance requirements. This formula starts by computing *cash resources* (including current life insurance) on a lump-sum basis. Items such as wages, interest, dividends, pensions, rents and social security survivors' benefits are included. Next, the *cash requirements* must be completed, including estate, funeral, and administration expenses, debts of the decedent, and annual cash disbursements for survivors' living expenses. If the home mortgage is to be liquidated, this fact must be considered. Also, a cash reserve for contingencies must be established. The difference between the cash resources and the cash needs is either a surplus or a deficiency. A cash deficiency is the amount of additional life insurance you require.

In working out the present-value formula, since certain items of *cash resources* (e.g., a spouse's salary) are expected to be received over a period of time, it is necessary to convert the money due in future years to today's value. Similarly, under *cash needs,* mortgage payments are made monthly and are expected to continue during future periods. These payments must also be reduced to today's monetary value (i.e., "present value"). For example, if your mortgage payments of $5,300 per year are to continue for the next 14 years, you would expect today's liability to be $74,200 ($5,300 x 14 years). However, since the money is paid out over the next 14 years, the total liability is said to have a present value of less than $74,200. The reason for this derives from the fact that the payments not currently due, if banked at interest, are earning money.

On the other hand, today's $5,300 may have a decline in purchasing power over the next 14 years due to inflation. The unknown interplay between the earnings on money and the inflation rate necessitates using an arbitrary percentage rate to determine what the value is today of having to receive or pay out money in future years. The higher the percentage rates used in these calculations, the lower the present value of money. Conversely, the lower the percentage rate, the higher the present value of money. The percentage rate chosen here is 4%. Over the 14-year period used, the spread between earnings and inflation *might* average 4% per annum. Since cash resources and cash requirements payable over future years are both affected, a difference in the percentage rate used would in most instances not substantially affect today's insurance requirements.

Your objectives and income today determine whether you should purchase either term insurance or ordinary life insurance. You should as a general rule buy an ordinary life policy. However, if your insurance needs are more than you can reasonably afford, term insurance is the answer. In any event, face the insurance deficit, whatever it maybe, and act promptly. You should recheck all of your financial data to make certain you have satisfied yourself about the reasons for any substantial differences in the actual formula as measured against the yardstick.

PREPARING THE INSURANCE WORKPAPER

Our profile family, the Smiths, consists of the husband 35, the wife 32, and two children, ages eight and 10. Both spouses are employed. Daniel Smith earns approximately $25,000 a year, and Louise Smith earns $10,000 a year. Their present life insurance coverage is included on their Net Worth Statement. The following workpapers develop the Smith's insurance needs.

		1	2	3	4

Formula #1 - Yardstick:

Age 35 - Multiple Factor — 4

Gross Wages × Factor = Yardstick

25000 × 4 = 100000

Formula #2 - Projected Future Needs:

Resources -

a. Based on 14 years (younger child reaches 22 years)

b. Present Value Factor at 4%
(savings interest less inflation)
$1 paid end of each year for 14 years
at 4%

Factor — 10.5631

	Annual	Present Value
Wages - gross wages (Louise)	10000	105600
Interest - Savings	500	5300
Dividends	500	5300
Pension Plan (lump sum)		20900
Proceeds Sale of Vacation Home (after Mtge.)		16200
Survivors Benefits - Social Security		100000
Loans Receivable		2000
Mortgage Receivable due in 2 years (plus interest)		9700
Proceeds Sale of Restricted Security		10000
Face Value - Current Life Insurance on Daniel's life		100000
New England Mutual Life Insurance Employer group - owned by Louise		50000
Total Resources (To Summary)		425000

238

			Annual	Present Value
			3	4
Cash Requirements:				
	Funeral and Administrative Expenses			4300
	Debts of Decedent			700
	Estate Tax – Federal and State			-0-
	Federal and State Income Taxes			-0-
	Income Tax Pension Plan Payout (Estimate 15%)			3100
	F.I.C.A. (Louise)		600	6300
	Housing:			
	Mortgage Servicing		5300	56000
	Real Estate Taxes		2000	21000
	Heat		800	8500
	Electric		800	8500
	Casualty Insurance		400	4200
	Telephone		400	4200
	Repairs		300	3200
	Food		3000	31700
	Clothing		1200	12700
	Child Care (5 years, factor 4.4518)		1300	5800
	College Education (chapter 14)		4700	49600
	Medical, Dental, & Health Insurance		1000	10600
	Individual Retirement Arrangement		1500	15800
	Auto (one car) – gas, oil, & repairs		600	6300
	– insurance		500	5300
	Automobile Purchases			
	3 bought over next 14 years			15000
	Recreation		1000	10600
	Cash Allowances		2500	26400
	Allowance–Mother		1200	12700
	Total Tentative Cash Requirements			322500
	Add. Reserve for Contingencies			
	(Estimated at 10% of Cash Requirements)			32300
	Total Cash Requirements			354800
Summary:				
	Cash Resources			425000
	Less, Cash Requirements			354800
	Balance (Current Excess Insurance)			(70200)

OBSERVATIONS ON INSURANCE NEEDS

The yardstick formula against which Daniel Smith is to measure his actual insurance needs resulted in a requirement for $100,000 face value of insurance. (His factor at age 35 is 4; his gross annual wage is $25,000; $25,000 × 4 = $100,000). This result must now be checked against the actual future needs of the Smith family assuming the following: (1) Daniel Smith dies at the end of the year; (2) Louise Smith continues to work; (3) protection is to cover the period until the younger child, now eight, completes college at 22; Louise Smith's financial needs from age 46 to age 60 (when her survivorship benefits commence) will be satisfied by her employment, by savings, and by substantially reduced living expenses (both children will have completed their educations).

In computing the estimated future needs, the figures for each item were derived from the annual cash flow, net worth, budget, and, in several instances, from estimated expenses. If you have not developed your workpapers in these areas, you can still work out your insurance needs by estimating key figures. If results are within range of the "yardstick," you are probably safe in using your conclusion for actual insurance needs.

There were a number of personal decisions to be made by the Smiths before doing the financial computations: The major ones were the continuation of Louise Smith's employment and not providing specifically for her from age 46 to 60 (the point at which her survivors' benefits begin). The financial needs of that 14-year period will be covered by Mrs. Smith's salary and savings, coupled with the proceeds from the sale of the residence, if necessary.

In a family discussion, the Smiths made the following additional decisions. (These, of course, would be subject to any necessary changes.)

1. Every effort will be made not to use present savings for future needs.

2. Marketable securities will be retained and dividends will be used for needs.

3. Pensions will be received as a lump-sum payment, since there is no estate tax problem.

4. The settlement option on pension life insurance and current life insurance will be a lump-sum payout.

5. The vacation home will be immediately sold. (The cash flow measured against the responsibility for maintaining the home in rental condition warrants the decision to sell.)

6. Restricted securities are to be sold, although this decision could change depending upon the subsequent financial condition of the issuing corporation. (This investment was in a neighbor's venture, and there would be no urgency in selling.) Provision has been made for a sale at cost.

Annuities were not chosen by Mrs. Smith because she felt that at her age the return from savings interest and other investments would exceed the insurance company's annuity contract at age 32. (The annuity settlement option is usually reserved for persons over age 55.)

For purposes of this profile the family residence would in the first instance be retained by Mrs. Smith. In computing needs, the last resource is the selling of the home and purchasing a smaller house. The personal trauma of moving, combined with the moving costs, almost automatically operates to negate any thought of selling. In the last analysis, decreasing-term insurance may provide for a rent-free home upon the death of the spouse earning the larger wage. If the retention of the family home is truly important to you, it can usually be somehow worked out.

Banks and mortgage companies often refinance mortgages, reducing the current monthly carrying charges by extending the due date, when this has been requested by a surviving spouse. In such a case, take a copy of your budget to the mortgagee, showing a need for a reduced monthly payment. A properly prepared budget will usually convince the company of your financial reliability.

Savings banks in New York have formed a Mortgage Appeals Board for reviewing rejected mortgage applications. Your state's savings bank may also have an appeals system. (Also, it is good business for mortgagees to view the payment obligations of single-parent families more leniently).

The income tax cost of the lump-sum distribution from Mr. Smith's pension plan was computed at a flat 15% rate. Part of this payout is subject to ordinary income taxes and part to capital gains. Employer contributions before 1974 are taxed at capital-gains rates. There is also a special 10-year averaging rule to reduce the tax impact of this distribution. In order to provide for the tax on the lump-sum payout, a reserve was set up sufficient to cover the federal and state tax liability. If there had been an Estate Tax problem, a lump-sum could still be paid and excluded from estate taxes provided that Mrs. Smith paid ordinary income taxes on its receipt.

The Smiths' education provision for their children required a separate workpaper since there would be two years during which both children would be in college at the same time. The present value of the educational needs is computed on the basis of an annuity. How this is done is explained in Chapter 14.

A reserve for contingencies of 10% of cash requirements was included to cover replacement of appliances in the home and other unforeseeable needs.

Based on the current actual needs for insurance, Mr. Smith has an excess of more than $70,000 in insurance. The "yardstick" of $100,000 in formula #1 was met with the current insurance coverage. The employer's group insurance policy is a bonus. If Mr. Smith terminates his employment, he has a choice of continuing the policy or surrendering it.

As a general rule, if you can afford the difference in rates, an ordinary policy (using the minimum deposit factor) is a better value in the long run than a term policy. This is true even if the figures at age 35 do not seem to confirm it. The results could be measured at age 65—if you could afford both policies. The difference at that age is minimal between ordinary and term taken out at age 35. However, if you live *beyond* age 65, the conversion is very expensive.

Mrs. Smith should be able to preserve her savings accounts, marketable securities, and part of the lump-sum payout of the life insurance policies until the time the children complete college. This leaves her with ample assets to supply her cash requirements until age 60, when she is entitled to survivors' benefits and from then to age 62 when she will begin to draw her own social security retirement benefits.

The life insurance value of Mr. Smith's social security survivors' benefits, combined with Mrs. Smith's earning power, will provide financial security in the event of Mr. Smith's premature death.

8

HEALTH AND CASUALTY INSURANCE

INSURANCE COMPANIES ARE IN BUSINESS to offer you financial protection against hazards for a price. These companies gamble according to carefully calculated tables that you will neither become so ill as to require great sums of money nor experience casualties. But if you do, you may receive far more than you ever paid for your coverage. The money comes not only from the price or premium you and the other clients paid but from the investment income from these premiums as well.

Insurance is now very big business. Casualty insurers, bowing to the pressures of competition, have experienced losses for many years in many of their underwriting lines, but the losses were offset by the favorable income from their investments. Insurers have come to realize that investment income is no longer to be considered separately from rate setting but must be viewed as integral to the process of insuring clients. The actual relationship between underwriting-based ratios and investment income is difficult to assess, and you really do not need to understand it. The insurance industry, however, is constantly examining its rate structures with the intent of determining the types of hazards to be covered and, in many areas, moving toward casualty packages.

Insurance companies are subject to two price structures. In some states, the insurer must obtain approval from the state insurance department before setting premium rates. In others, the insurance department of the state allows competitive pricing and approves or disapproves the premium afterward. A state may also permit a "hybrid" system allowing competitive pricing for specific lines and prior approval for others (usually automobile coverage).

Your conduct as the insured has a direct bearing on the premium rates. This is particularly true when investment income is not sufficient to cover the loss experience. In many lines of insurance, there is a strong competition operating to keep premiums relatively low. However, particularly in the automobile insurance business, there are major problems to be solved. These problems include large-scale discrimination by age and territory; the proper use of no-fault insurance; large settlements paid on personal injury claims; costly repair of automobiles and other property; over-regulation of the industry; and difficulty in obtaining insurance. These problems cost you money. The effect of inflation on insurance rates is minimal compared with the price tags of the major problems.

Health and casualty insurance are designed to cover major hazards. The overhead cost for processing a small claim is almost the same as for a large one. In insurance, loss-prone or accident-prone people are bad risks. The insurance companies quickly discover bad risks and do their best to rid themselves of "troublesome" clients. Generally, you have no right of appeal if an insurer refuses to renew your policy. (Some states have attempted to restrict the insurer's right to nonrenewal.) Your position is made worse by the fact that most casualty policies are written for one year. A three-year policy is considered an extended time period.

The fact that an insurer may appear to you to be a gigantic business enterprise does not mean that the company cannot move quickly to your disadvantage for its own protection. Trivial claims are not the purpose of insurance. Therefore, unless you have a substantial claim, you should be a self-insurer even within your policy limits. A self-insurer is one who bears the risks of a casualty loss without an independent insurer. In other words, a self-insurer is someone who has not taken out any insurance. The tax law permits $100 deductible for casualty losses. In the case of a relatively small loss for which you deducted a casualty loss, the IRS might argue that you should have filed an insurance claim and are therefore not entitled to the deduction. You, in turn, can argue that such a claim could result in the failure of the insurer to renew your policy.

If you find it impossible to secure a policy domestically, you may be required to find coverage abroad at higher rates. This happens sometimes in marine, aviation, and professional-liability insurance.

Insurance companies protect themselves against big disasters through reinsurance. An earthquake, a bridge collapse, an airplane crash, or a tunnel explosion would be too large a risk for one company. Therefore, the risk is laid off on other insurers. The most famous reinsurance group as well as a primary insurer for hard-to-place risks is Lloyds of London.

Lloyds is not a single company, but a group of insurers sharing individual risks. In its entire history no member of Lloyds has failed to meet a legitimate claim.

The financial condition of the casualty insurer, while of immediate concern to you, is not a long-range proposition as it would be for life insurance. There have been no large policyholder losses in recent years due to the financial collapse of a casualty company. (There has, in recent years, been a reorganization of one major automobile insurer, but the policyholders suffered no losses.) Generally, you would pick a casualty insurer for low premium rates and an efficient claims service.

Health and casualty insurance is purchased through a direct writer, insurance agent, or broker. The direct writer maintains his own staff to deal directly with you. One insurance agent may represent up to a dozen insurers. The agent is an independent businessman. Insurance brokers are found in urban areas; they deal with a large number of companies directly or through a company's agents. There are no general rules to follow in making a choice: the individual agent's reputation and the insurer's reputation are your paramount concern in deciding who will represent you. Geographical location should be of no importance since you can conduct your business by telephone and correspondence. Claim adjusters generally have no objection to meeting with you in a mutually convenient place.

The main purpose of this chapter is to discuss kinds of policies according to the hazards covered. The categories of policies discussed are ones you will most likely require. The cost of the premiums for some of these policies may be beyond your means. More important, some of them cover risks for which you may desire to be a self-insurer. In understanding the subject, the concepts of insurance are more important than the premiums. If you are uncertain about the hazards to be covered by a policy, request a specimen policy. Study it, outlining the hazards, dollar coverage, and, most important, the exclusions. Consider every possible risk you might encounter and be certain that the terms of your coverage are stated in clear, concise language. If you are uncertain of any item, do not hesitate to request written clarification of your coverage. Except in some areas such as automobile insurance, the insurance business is a buyer's market. It is your responsibility to avoid paying high premiums and buying overlapping coverages, especially in health insurance.

Representative premiums are usually presented with the specimen policy. Use these figures as a yardstick to help you develop a price range. You must seek competitive pricing for your age, territory, and risk classification. The hazard versus the premium tells a lot about a particular policy. The higher the deductible, usually the lower the premium. If you agree to be a self-insurer for a large deductible, your premium savings may be substantial in high-risk policies. On the other hand, for many hazards the cost of additional coverage adds only minimally to the premium. It is impossible for the average person to make an intelligent insurance decision by simply reading about a policy without working out the specifics on paper. For example, the high cost of jewelry insurance has made wealthy individuals extremely selective in insuring individual pieces. Thus, they usually insure very valuable gems and become self-insurers for the smaller pieces. Also, the self-insurer must be alert to the constant possibilities of theft and aware of the increased use of bank vaults and improved security devices for protection.

HEALTH INSURANCE

Health insurance provides payments for medical care, hospitalization, surgical benefits, home visits, supplemental income, and other expenses relating to your inability to work due to accident or illness. Some policies also include life insurance coverage.

The basic health-care package is Blue Cross and Blue Shield coverage or similar plans. There are over 90 million subscribers to the Blue Cross and Blue Shield plans. Blue Cross covers hospital costs and Blue Shield covers surgical-medical protection. Since in many states Blue Cross and Blue Shield are administered together, for the sake of convenience the basic health insurer will be referred to as "BC-BS." Because the Medicare program is administered in each state by a different private insurer you will have to check the name of your state's administrator of Medicare through your local social security office.

Many members of the medical profession are "participating" doctors who have agreed to accept BC-BS fee schedules in total payment of their bills. Establish this with your doctor prior to engaging his or her services.

In general, the costs of health-coverage plans are so high that many people cannot afford them, or at least cannot afford adequate coverage. A prolonged stay in a hospital can devastate a family's finances to such a degree that declaring personal bankruptcy is the only solution. This situation requires some sensible form of relief, and with the attention being given to health care by many concerned and intelligent people (insurers and consumer advocates among them) something is likely to develop within the next few years. Perhaps a national health insurance plan will prove to be the most constructive innovation.

Health insurance coverage is developed by hazard. Therefore, the order of policy discussion will in general follow the step-by-step insurance you should consider, based on your personal needs or cash flow. If you cover yourself with BC-BS and major medical insurance it is also probably a good idea to have an excess-liability policy for a catastrophic illness. In most cases, the order of your coverage follows the presentation with the exception of excess-liability insurance. This policy covers both medical, personal injury, and property damage. It is a low-premium policy (usually about $50 per year) and is almost a necessity in today's world. A typical excess medical policy provides 80% of the benefits after deducting $10,000 of medical expenses. The maximum benefit runs about $25,000. This is not major medical insurance and should usually be purchased *in addition to* major medical insurance. Because the prime coverage of an excess-liability policy is for personal injury claims, you will find the policy discussed in the casualty insurance section of this chapter. Unfortunately, many insurers are refusing to write excess medical policies at present because of high losses.

BLUE CROSS-BLUE SHIELD

Blue Cross-Blue Shield (BC-BS) provides basic hospital and surgical-medical insurance coverage for persons under 65 years of age. You may enroll on a direct payment basis or through a group plan. The group plan is cheaper to administer and its costs are correspondingly lower.

Since most people are covered by group plans, the coverage discussed here is specifically that offered by a "top of the line" BC-BS group contract. If your coverage is less than the profile plan, check the rate difference in your area and then consult your cash flow. If you can afford the additional cost, buy the best BC-BS policy available. The family plan covers both spouses and all children under age 19. If your employer pays for major medical, you may only require a minimum hospitalization policy and no surgical-medical coverage. If your employer supplies you with a major medical policy, you would start with that coverage and work back toward a basic-benefit policy only to the extent necessary to prevent a large gap in coverage.

The maximum-benefit BC-BS group plan available in most states generally provides the following: (1) hospitalization for 120 full-benefit days, with a semiprivate room in a member-hospital plus outpatient and home health care; (2) surgical-medical coverage for treatment by participating doctors, with allowances for most basic surgical-medical problems (including treatment by nonparticipating doctors). The cost of this combined plan is approximately $700 per year.

BC-BS is not major medical insurance. Its allowances are for surgical-medical problems and do not cover out-of-hospital illness. The allowances are insufficient to cover today's actual surgical-medical costs.

A family unit must establish its own priorities. Health insurance, as is indicated by the number of BC-BS subscribers, is a basic human need and is high on the priority list. However, there are personal needs which are of equal importance and which are difficult to measure precisely. Adequate life insurance, for example, is probably of greater importance than health insurance. In the event of a disastrous illness the options of public assistance or declaring personal bankrupty always exist. Life insurance, on the other hand, provides for a financial need for which there is only one substitute: public assistance. The bromide "I do what I can afford" is unrealistic if you examine your last year's actual expenditures. In most instances, reducing discretionary expenditures would go a long way toward providing necessary funds for some degree of life and health insurance coverage.

The maximum-benefits BC-BS policy is expensive. In most states premiums are set by insurance departments on a prior-approval basis. Thus, the loss experience has caused the constantly increasing premiums. This loss experience has a higher multiplying factor because the health-care industries' costs have risen higher than most other products and services in the consumer's price index.

To restate the order of coverage, you must first examine your budget and, on a conservative basis, allocate an approximate amount for health care. If your employer provides a health-care policy as a fringe benefit, your personal requirements are obviously lessened. Your first objective should be maximum BC-BS benefits. After that, if you have funds available, a major medical policy would be a wise investment.

If you are unhappy with a BC-BS decision on an allowance for services, do not hesitate to appeal to the BC-BS organization for a review. The review staff may grant you the added sums you claim are due.

MEDICARE

The federal government's program of health services for persons at least 65 years of age or disabled is similar to BC-BS plus medical care.

Medicare hospital insurance pays for most in-hospital services. After a $144 deductible, Medicare pays for 60 days of semiprivate hospitalization. For the next 30 days of hospitalization, Medicare has a $36-a-day deductible. There are 60 reserve days during a lifetime in the event a hospital stay exceeds 90 days. These 60 reserve days have a $72-a-day deductible. Each hospital stay starts a new benefit period with the exception of the reserve days.

Medicare medical insurance pays 80% of health care costs after a $60-per-year deductible. If in the last three months of a year you paid medical expenses, these payments may be carried over to the next year to meet the $60 deductible.

The Medicare carrier in your area (BC-BS or another private insurance company) determines "reasonable" charges each July 1 to arrive at the maximum benefits to be paid. A doctor or supplier may charge any amount, but Medicare will pay only "reasonable" charges. Prior to the performance of any service, a patient should ask the physician if the charges are fully covered by Medicare. If they are not covered, look elsewhere, if possible, before consenting to pay the difference. If the doctor or supplier accepts the assignment, Medicare pays them directly.

The Medicare hospital insurance coverage is automatic if you have social security credits. Medicare medical premiums are about $8 a month. The sign-up period is the first three months of each year.

The above is only an introduction to Medicare. For further information ask your Medicare carrier for the excellent free booklet *Your Medicare Handbook,* also available for 60¢ from the Superintendent of Documents, Washington, D.C. 20402.

MAJOR MEDICAL, ACCIDENT
AND HEALTH INSURANCE

Major medical or accident and health insurance covers you for substantial health expenses, but does not usually provide basic hospitalization and surgical benefits. Generally these policies are purchased as an addition to BC-BS to complete the average family's health insurance program. Major medical insurance provides benefits similar to those of accident and health insurance. Accident and sickness insurance usually provides a cash indemnity while you are unable to work.

In general, most major medical policies have a deductible factor for basic health care coverage. For example, the deductibles in a policy may be (1) covered by Blue Cross and Blue Shield ($100); (2) covered by Blue Cross only ($300); (3) covered by Blue Shield only ($800); (4) not covered by BC-BS ($1,000).

After satisfying the deductible, this policy provides a benefits percentage of 80% (50% for psychiatric hospitalization) for a lifetime maximum of $30,000. A life insurance policy is also provided in the amount of $4,000. Other policies offer greater benefits.

Some major medical policies provide (1) surgical allowances; (2) unlimited benefits; (3) total coverage after $2,000 of annual expenses ($5,000 for a family); and (4) life insurance at twice an individual's annual earnings (maximum $50,000).

Each year many major medical policies restore a portion of the used maximum lifetime benefits if you are insurable. Children are covered to age 23 if in school. (Some policies raise the age to 25 for a student.) Eligible medical expenses may include hospitalization (semiprivate room); physicians' charges for diagnosis, treatment, and surgery; registered nurses; and miscellaneous services, supplies, and drugs. Excluded medical expenses may include charges made by federal and state government hospitals, unless payment is required in absence of insurance; sickness or injury resulting from declared or undeclared war; routine checkups; and occupational injuries (these are covered by Workmen's Compensation).

A dental-benefit plan may also be included in a major medical policy. Such coverage is limited to a specific amount (in many policies, $1,000) each year, and a deductible is also provided. If extensive dental work is required, the dentist must usually have prior approval from the insurer. There are generally two classes of eligible dental charges involved. The first covers inlays, dentures, and bridgework, with reimbursement of up to 50%. The second covers routine examinations and fillings, extractions, root-canal therapy, and oral surgery, with reimbursement of up to 80%. Most dental policies exclude cosmetic and orthodontic treatment.

After age 65 the coverage of most major medical policies is substantially reduced due to Medicare, but persons covered by Medicare should seek supplemental coverage, particularly because of Medicare's limited allowance for nursing services.

Most group policies have a coordination clause between the policy and other benefits to prevent you from making a cash profit on your health-care costs. Therefore, make certain that you are paying for supplemental coverage and *not* for overlapping benefits. (The latter would be like paying for two policies in order to receive a single benefit.) This is important if you have an accident and sickness policy on a franchise (noncoordination) basis. Confirm in writing with your major medical carrier that you will receive total payment without any allocation to the franchise policy.

A major medical plan including the dental-care benefits and life insurance coverage costs about $500 per year. Thus, the maximum of BC-BS benefits and major medical for a family of four cost approximately $1,200 a year. An excess-medical-expense policy (which also includes personal injury and property damage) costs an additional $50 a year.

Accident and sickness (A&S) insurance overlaps both BC-BS and major medical. A&S insurance is generally obtained by those who cannot join a group plan and who require supplemental benefits.

For about $300 a year, at age 35 you can purchase the following coverage:

1. Accident indemnity: $30 a week for five years
2. Accidental death: $2,500
3. Sickness: $30 a week for two years
4. Hospitalization: $74 a day for 70 days and $50 a day for 295 days
5. Other hospital charges: $240
6. Surgical benefit: $600
7. Major medical: $20,000 (with deductible of $200)
8. Co-insurance: 75% up to $5,000; 80% of the next $5,000; 90% over $10,000; mental disorder out-of-hospital: 50%

This policy also provides that eligible expenses in excess of the applicable deductible amount must be incurred within two years immediately following the date the deductible amount has been exceeded.

There is usually no coordination of benefits in an A&S policy, and the insurer will be a primary carrier. In other words, no matter what other insurance you carry, the A&S insurer will usually pay what is required, based on your expenses. The difference between a primary and coordination provision is important. Before you purchase an A&S policy, make every attempt to compare costs between a primary and a coordinated policy. A primary policy, while overlapping a BC-BS, will in fact pick up costs beyond the BC-BS coverage. It reduces your out-of-pocket amount, whereas in a coordinated policy you would still have the out-of-pocket for the co-insurance factor.

DISABILITY INCOME

Disability-income insurance provides you with cash indemnity if sickness or injury prevents you from working. For this purpose, housework is considered employment.

For approximately $250 a year, a typical disability policy provides a 35-year-old individual with the following benefits:

1. Disability income $1,200 per month
   Accident: lifetime,
   Sickness: five years
2. Elimination period: 30 days
3. Hospitalization benefit: three months $600 per month
4. Supplemental hospital benefit: one year $20 per day

For approximately $100 per year, another insurer offers a 35-year-old individual the following coverage:

1. Disability income
   Accident: lifetime
   Sickness: two years $500 per month
2. Elimination period 90 days

If you can require the coverage and can afford it, the first policy is better value. (For two and one-half times the premium you receive almost five times the benefit.)

Disability income is not subject to income tax. The premiums for the disability-income portion of the policy are not for medical care. Therefore, they are not included in health-care premiums allowable for tax purposes as a medical-expense deduction. On the other hand, the hospitalization reimbursement portion of the premium is a health-care expenditure.

In most states, nonoccupational sickness or injury is covered by disability benefits. The premiums are paid by the employer and may or may not be subject to witholding from wages. Benefits are generally paid for 26 weeks at $100 a week. Self-employed individuals may purchase a disability coverage to be included with their employer's policy at a cost of about $100 per year.

Workmen's Compensation provides medical payments and disability income for occupational sickness or injury. This coverage is mandatory in most states and pays benefits until the employee is able to return to work.

If both of you and your spouse are gainfully employed, disability-income policies for each of you sufficient to cover your monthly mortgage-servicing costs or rent are usually adequate coverage. A benefit period for sickness of two years' duration would probably cover 90% of the cases. Accident benefits should be for lifetime coverage. The employee's disability-benefits policy also covers other household costs. If only one spouse is gainfully employed, the coverage should generally be twice the monthly mortgage-servicing costs or rent.

Social security also provides disability benefits, but the disability must be expected to last at least 12 months or result in death. The elimination period for persons over 22 is five months. The maximum disability family payment is in excess of $900 per month. This policy can count toward your disability-income needs. In most cases, therefore, if you are fully covered by social security, a disability-income policy covering your home maintenance will more than satisfy your total disability-income needs. The social security benefits continue as long as you are unable to work. A disabled person may collect social security benefits at age 50. If you are retired and are receiving social security benefits and become disabled, you may be eligible for higher monthly benefits.

Disability income is the lowest priority of health insurance, ranking behind BC-BS, major medical, and excess liability. The needs for health insurance coverage in priority order are hospitalization, surgical-medical, physicians and other medical care, major medical, and cash indemnity.

Your total health-care package should include coverage for each hazard, but there is still the question of how to allocate your cash resources. In general, you should maximize each step, starting with hospitalization and surgical-medical coverage. Thereafter comes coverage for major medical or accident and sickness. An excess-liability policy completes the health-care package. The cash needs of the family are supplied by disability income.

The approximate annual cost of this health-care package for a 35-year-old person, including medical care for spouse and children, is as follows:

COVERAGE	APPROXIMATE COST
1. Hospitalization: 120 days, full benefits	$500
2. Surgical-medical	200
3. Major medical: 80% co-insurance, maximum $30,000	500
4. Excess liability: extended to $65,000 by major medical coverage	50
5. Disability income: $500 per month for two years (accident: lifetime)	100
Total approximate annual cost	$1,350

This package obtains only when the individual is paying all the premiums. (See Daniel Smith's workpaper, page 261, where the employer pays for the major medical insurance.)

HOMEOWNERS MULTIPERIL INSURANCE

Your residence and its content should be insured by a homeowner's multiperil policy. The policy covers hazards affecting building structure, contents, and personal liability. Hazards to the structure and its contents covered by most multiperil policies include (1) fire and lightning; (2) explosion and smoke; (3) riot, vandalism, and malicious mischief; (4) windstorm and hail (*not* flood); (5) water damage from faulty plumbing or heating system; (6) freezing of plumbing or heating system; (7) vehicle or aircraft damage; and (8) collapse of building. Theft coverage includes (1) theft on and off the premises; (2) damage by thieves; and (3) hold-up or pickpocket. Personal-liability coverage includes (1) bodily-injury lawsuits; (2) property damage lawsuits; (3) sports accident lawsuits; and (4) liability for legal defense costs. In addition, a multiperil policy includes living expenses if your residence becomes uninhabitable, plus medical payments for injury to you.

A broad-named peril policy written for one year costing about $380 may cover the following:

	COVERAGE	AMOUNT
1.	(House and land valued at $74,000 plus garage at $6,000 equals $80,000.) Dwelling: full replacement value	$60,000
2.	Separate garage (appurtenant)	6,000
3.	Personal property: on premises (minimum)	24,000
4.	Personal property: off premises (in U.S. and Canada, including baggage)	2,400
5.	Additional living expense (residence uninhabitable)	12,000
6.	Liability (single occurrence)	300,000
7.	Guest medical payment (aggregate medical payment for one occurrence, $10,000)	250

8.	Deductible (except for cash, maximum $100 loss)	100

If the above deductible were increased to $250, this same policy would cost about $350 per year. It would be reduced to about $300 per year if written without the off-premises theft. You may be able to write your personal-property on-premises coverage on a replacement basis.

The building structure is rated by the territory and materials in order to determine the premium. There is no flood insurance, but the National Flood Insurance Corporation provides coverage for property in areas where floods are a hazard. (Ask your insurance representative for information.)

Many insurers do not cover your home's structure for full replacement value, so check your policy for complete information. As a guard against inflation, you should look for an insurer who will write a full-replacement-value policy for you with no co-insurance. If you fail to cover your house for its full value or cost, a partial-damage claim will be reduced accordingly. (You do not insure the land or foundation.)

It is possible to purchase separate policies covering your homeowner's risks. However, the multiperil policy is considered more economical, and it usually provides adequate coverage for virtually all hazards.

Jewelry, furs, works of art, silverware, and cameras are usually excluded from your homeowner's policy. For items such as these you would require a separate valuable-items policy.

AUTOMOBILE INSURANCE

In setting premium rates, automobile insurers consider such factors as age of the driver; place of residence; type of automobile; and purpose and extent of automobile use (business or pleasure, and mileage driven).

Many insurance carriers claim substantial automobile underwriting losses in various parts of the country. Therefore, policies are written on a very selective basis. One of the largest U.S. insurers will not issue a policy to a new driver. The company requires one year's experience in the high-premium assigned-risk pool before it will issue a policy. Consequently, your option may not be competitive rates but reduced coverage.

Consider as basic coverage $100,000/$300,000 for liability, $50,000 for personal injury, $100,000/$300,000 for uninsured motorists, with a comprehensive $50 deductible and maximum no-fault option. A practical approach to automobile insurance is to increase deductibles and reduce liability to the amount required by an excess-liability policy. Thus, in general, a $250-deductible collision policy including a $100,000/$300,000 liability with umbrella coverage of an excess-liability policy appears to be your proper approach to an automobile insurance policy. The increase of the collision deductible from $100 to $250 saves about $70 per year in premiums. A $1,000,000 excess-liability policy including medical benefits (if possible) to pick up losses over $100,000 costs about $50 a year.

On the other hand, raising the liability coverage for personal injuries to $1,000,000 costs an additional $35 for each automobile. The $15 extra for the umbrella policy is a good buy because you are also buying protection against liability lawsuits in other-than-automobile situations, and in many cases excess medical expense coverage.

If a car is more than three years old, consider eliminating collision and comprehensive fire and theft coverage. The swings range from $300 to $400 a year. A total wreck (which is remote) is co-insured by the IRS to the extent of your tax bracket less $100.

If you decide not to purchase an excess-liability policy, you should increase your liability insurance from $100,000/$300,000 to at least $300,000/$500,000.

A public adjuster may be employed to handle an extensive property damage claim, and the cost is between 10% and 15% of the cash recovery.

Whether you decide to settle an insurance claim quickly depends upon your personal experience. If you are certain of your values and of the amount of loss, and positive in your desire to settle, the insurer would be foolish not to settle quickly. (This excludes the question of physical damage to the person, which may or may not be permanent.) It makes no sense to waste time in a give-and-take situation. If you do not relate to the adjuster, request the insurer to provide a substitute adjuster *before* the settlement negotiations begin. When you are within a 75% range of what you believe is the bottom line, consider the effort and cost of obtaining the other 25%. (Experienced negotiators never *win*, they *settle* issues.) Your best approach is to treat the situation as if the adjuster were a personal interviewer and you a job-seeker. The impression you make may well influence his or her willingness to meet your terms. Be amiable but firm. If the situation becomes difficult, your broker and state insurance department may be of some help in settling matters between you and the insurer.

A minor accident should be settled between the parties without the involvement of the insurance companies. *Do not forget* to exchange general releases from all liabilities with all the other parties. Otherwise, if you fail to report an accident to your insurer within a reasonable time, your insurance protection for that accident is lost.

Price is not the prime consideration in choosing an insurer, unless you are lucky enough to live in a competitive area. Fast and equitable claim service is worth time and money. You should canvas your local service station and friends or neighbors to learn of someone who has had a recent automobile claim for opinions on claim service.

Unless you have no choice, do not purchase a policy from an insurer whose claims service is widely criticized. The argument by some insurers that their being tough keeps your premium down is not an alternative to fair treatment. The solution is for the insurer to eliminate questionable customers, and thereby assume that you, as an insured, are interested in only a proper and equitable settlement. (On the other hand, a minor accident is *not* the opportunity to reconstruct your automobile.)

The no-fault insurance provisions of many states cover liability for all but serious accidents. This is expected to have long-run favorable effects on premium rates. A typical policy for a medium-sized automobile in a suburban area covers the following:

COVERAGE	APPROXIMATE PREMIUM (1978)
1. Liability of $100,000 per person; $300,000 for the occurrence, and $50,000 property damage	$152
2. Uninsured motorist	4
3. Basic no-fault	46
4. Extended no-fault (out-of-state)	9
5. Comprehensive fire and theft ($50 deductible)	131
6. Collision ($250 deductible)	161
Total	$503
7. Excess-liability policy	50
Total annual premiums	$553

The annual cost of the policies without collision coverage is $392. By also excluding fire and theft coverage, the premium would be $261. As the age of the automobile increases, the need for collision protection is lessened. Therefore, ask yourself whether or not you can afford the risk of being a self-insurer.

If your car is destroyed in an accident, the insurance company does not pay you the original cost of the car. For a used car you receive a highly depreciated replacement cost which is usually somewhere between the wholesale and retail value at the time of the wreck. *The National Association of Automobile Dealers' Used Car Guide* may be of help to you in establishing value. The cost of replacing the wrecked automobile may be done using the techniques in Chapter 11, TANGIBLE PROPERTY.

VALUABLE-ITEMS POLICY

Your homeowner's multiperil insurance does not cover all risks involved with valuable personal property. The homeowner's policy may limit on-and-off premises loss to several thousand dollars and may cover only the United States and Canada. The policy may also severely restrict specific property most likely to be lost, such as jewelry. A valuable-items policy covers all casualities with limited conditions (for example, wear and tear) without territorial limits. The property covered includes jewelry; furs; cameras; musical instruments; silverware; golfer's equipment; postage stamps; rare coins; and works of art.

Premium rates are based primarily on the physical security of your neighborhood and of your place of residence. For example, the annual cost of insuring per $1,000 in an urban area may run: jewelry (2.8% per $1,000); furs (1.1%); cameras (1.5%).

The insurance covers the depreciated cash value of the article. There is an exclusion for loss caused by war or nuclear reaction. When a new policy is issued, always examine the schedule of insurance to make certain that you own the property referred to and that its cash value requires it to be covered. You should consider eliminating insurance for articles whose current cash value is less than $250. You can be a co-insurer with the IRS in the event of a loss. Remember, because of the high premium rates, there is a point of diminishing returns in insuring all items of jewelry. Therefore, examine your own cash flow and risk-taking attitude and be governed accordingly.

EXCESS-LIABILITY INSURANCE

A personal excess-liability policy including excess medical expense is frequently termed an "umbrella policy." This is generally accepted as low-cost disaster insurance. For an annual premium of $50 you receive the following basic coverage in excess of *retained limits:*

1. Your liability up to $1,000,000

2. Liability for an uninsured motorist up to $10,000 per accident

3. Medical expenses up to $25,000, subject to 80% co-insurance (unfortunately, in recent months many insurers have eliminated the excess medical expense provision).

The retained limit requires you to carry basic insurance for various cover risks. The excess-liability insurance pays losses over and above the portion of the risk which you covered through another policy or through self-insurance. The retained limits are as follows:

1. Automobile: $100,000/$300,000 bodily-injury liability (each person/ each occurrence) and $10,000 property damage for each occurrence

2. Homeowner's multiperil: $100,000 combined bodily-injury and damages liability for each occurrence

3. Medical expenses: $10,000 (maximum-benefit increase of $2 for every additional $1 by which the other coverage exceeds $10,000).

The insurer pays any losses up to the limit indicated in excess of the retained limits that you would be required to pay because of personal injury or property damage.

The uninsured-motorist provision pays you up to the specified amount ($10,000) if you are unable to collect from an uninsured motorist. The uninsured-motorist provision in your automobile policy usually satisfies the retained-limit requirement.

The excess-liability policy has broad-based coverage but also includes a number of conditions. For example, the policy, except for the uninsured-motorist provision, does not cover your property. The liability involving aircraft and watercraft is severely limited. The medical-benefit period continues for three years after your expenses for a single illness exceed the deductible and this period may be extended, provided you again meet the deductible-expense requirements. (You must incur the expenses within a consecutive 540 days.) The policy does not cover professional-liability (malpractice) insurance and officers' and directors' liability insurance.

MISCELLANEOUS CASUALTY INSURANCE

Some other casualty policies which you should have a general understanding of are professional-liability; travel; surety; marine and aviation; specific coverage; and federal government.

PROFESSIONAL-LIABILITY INSURANCE (including officers' and directors' liability insurance) protects the insured against suits for negligent conduct in carrying out a professional or business career. If you are a director of a cooperative or a condominium, you should make certain that you are insured by the corporation for officers' and directors' liability.

TRAVEL INSURANCE may cover lost baggage, cancelled flights, theft, sickness, accidents, bad weather, and almost any occurrence that might ruin your trip. Your present policy may cover some of these risks, such as off-premises theft of your baggage. For the risks it covers, the dollar-or-so cost for travel insurance seems nominal. However, the individual-trip cost may be far more expensive than other year-round coverage. Bad weather and cancelled flights appear to be risks for which most people are probably inclined to be self-insurers.

SURETY INSURANCE covers the faithful performance of a contract (the building of your house, for example) and employee fidelity bonds.

MARINE AND AVIATION INSURANCE covers watercraft and aircraft. This is a type of insurance that usually requires special services by an insurer to analyze various coverage possibilities.

under SPECIFIC COVERAGE, product liability, general liability, and fire are perils covered by business insurance policies. If you are self-employed, you must consider this coverage as a protection for yourself and the public.

the FEDERAL GOVERNMENT provides insurance in many areas in addition to social security, including deposit insurance (bank savings and checking accounts); crime insurance; flood insurance; and securities (investor-protection) insurance.

If you are unable to obtain insurance from a private company, ask the local office of the U.S. Housing and Urban Development Department if they offer the particular insurance you desire. If not, ask their representative what federal department may be the insurer for the risk you seek to cover.

INSURANCE WORKPAPER

The profile couple, Daniel and Louise Smith, prepared a workpaper reflecting their current insurance coverage. The schedule is written in pencil, and each time a policy or bill for insurance is received the workpaper is brought up to date. The policies are extracted so that limits of coverage are immediately available. In addition, the cash flow budget derives

				Annual Premium
1. Basic Coverage:				
Blue Cross				
Policy #	13433725 – W10 9/1/77			
Insured		Family		
Hospitalization – Full Benefit Days		21		
50% Benefit Days		180		
Surgical – Medical Plan		None		
Covered by Major Medical				
Children covered up to age		19		
Quarterly Premium		109		
Annual Premium (Withheld from Wages)				436
2. Major Medical:				
New England Mutual Life Insurance				
Policy #	GSP 21723			
Effective	10/1/76			
Insured		Family		
Life Insurance on Daniel Smith				
assigned to Louise Smith				
Beneficiary – Louise Smith				
Principal Sum		50000		
Medical – Cash Deductible per year				
Daniel		50		
Family		150		
Co-Insurance – Daniel (one Confinement)				
Expenses up to 2000		80%		
Over 2000		100%		
Family				
Expenses up to 5000		80%		
over 5000		100%		
Requires Basic Benefits Coverage				
Met by		Blue Cross		
Children covered up to Age				
Non-student		19		
Full Time Student		25		
Overall Limitation of Benefits		None		

			Annual Premium
Major Medical (continued)			
Surgical Allowances		By Schedule	
Pregnancy Expenses Covered		Yes	
Mental Illness			
Confinement Covered		Yes	
Period of Confinement Days			
Allowed per year		70	
Co-Insurance Difference			
Over Regular Hospital		None	
Charges Covered			
Hospital Room		Semi-private	
Surgical		By Schedule	
Physicians		Yes	
Nurses		Yes	
Supplies and Services		Yes	
No Coverage for			
Routine Examinations			
Dental Work Except			
if connected with			
Injury			
Coordination of Benefits with			
Other Policies		Yes	
Conversion Period After			
Termination of Employment			
Days		31	
Premium Paid by Employer			None

262

Daniel and Louise Smith
Schedule of Health Insurance
December 31, 1978

				1	2	3	4 Annual Premium
3.	Excess Liability:						
		Federal Insurance Co.			# 77944116		
		Period Covered			12/5/78 to 12/5/79		
	Medical- Insured					Family	
		Elimination Period				None	
		Deductible				10000	
		Maximum Benefit					
			Basic			25000	
		Extended by $2 for each					
		$1 of Major Medical over					
		25000					
			Major Medical has				
			no overall limitation			Not Applicable	
		Co-Insurance				80%	
		Benefit Period - Basic Days				540	
		Hospitalization - Room & Board					
			Cash Limitation per day			60	
		Convalescent Home					
			Days Limitation			30	
			Cash Limitation per Day			30	
		No Mental Illness Coverage					
			Except Hospital Confinement				
		Other- Personal Injury Liability to					
			Third Parties				
			Cash Limitation			1000000	
		Uninsured Motorist - Payable					
			to Smiths			10000	
		Retained Limits Covered By					
			Other Policies				
			Homeowners			100000	
			Automobiles			100000	
		Annual Premium					50

263

		1	2	3	4
					Annual Premium
4.	Disability Income				
	A. State (Non-occupational)				
	Elimination Period Days			7	
	Insured		Both Spouses		
	Cash Benefit per Week			105	
	Period of Benefits – Weeks			26	
	Annual Premium (Withheld from Wages)				
	Daniel Smith				15
	Louise Smith				15
	B. Social Security				
	Elimination Period – Months			5	
	Insured		Both Spouses		
	Cash Benefit per Month				
	Daniel			937	
	Louise			427	
	(Subject to Congressional increases)				
	Period Covered		Disability		
	Annual Premium included in				
	FICA Withheld from Wages				—
	C. Mutual of New York				
	Policy #	64X 3-11-42			
	Effective	11/4/78			
	Insured		Daniel		
	Elimination Period – Days			14	
	Cash Benefit per Month			500	
	Sickness Benefit Period				
	Months			24	
	Total Disability Benefit Period		Lifetime		
	Annual Premium				115

264

its input of insurance costs (other than life insurance) from this workpaper. Fringe-benefit insurance is also included in the workpaper.

OBSERVATIONS ON THE
HEALTH INSURANCE WORKPAPER

Assembling the proper health insurance package for your family is sometimes difficult because of the number of health insurance options available. It is also difficult because you are unable to measure precisely the hazards against which to insure.

In many instances, part or all of the package depends on the benevolence of your employer. Therefore, it is necessary to plan around existing insurance. If your employer pays for the major medical insurance, you then would pay for a basic benefit plan. In some instances the employer may pay for the entire health-care package.

Life insurance is usually included in major medical plans covered by a life insurance company. Since the policies generally provide for converting to term insurance without proof of insurability, you may consider the policy as part of your permanent life insurance plan.

Between jobs, if financially possible, you should continue the major medical plan financed by your previous employer until you have settled in a new position with company coverage.

The ownership of group life insurance included in the major medical plan in most states may be transferred to your spouse without gift tax consequences and the proceeds may be omitted from your estate.

The health insurance package for Daniel and Louise Smith includes the following:

1. Blue Cross paid by Mr. Smith by withholding quarterly from wages (no Blue Shield coverage)

2. Major medical financed by Mr. Smith's employer

3. Disability income:
   a) New York State disability benefits
   b) Social security disability
   c) Private insurance

4. Excess-liability insurance (of remote value)

Pregnancy and mental health provisions make an excellent yardstick in checking the adequacy of your coverage. For example, the Smiths' major medical plan provides for an $800 payment in the event of a delivery by cesarean section. This is an expensive surgical procedure and the allowance is generous. In addition, all expenses are paid for hospitalization due to mental illness or functional nervous disorders just as for other covered medical expenses. Check your group plan for these two medical items. The period allowed is 70 days per year. Many policies have 50% co-insurance for mental health problems.

The appendectomy allowance is another means of checking the surgical allowances against your area's average cost. Ask your physician for a general idea of what surgeons are charging for this operation. Mr. Smith's policy allows $200 (40 surgical units for the procedure at a $5 factor). If your physician's figure is about $250, your major medical policy is within reasonable range. You are responsible for the surgical cost in excess of the allowance. Many small-business employers usually adopt a self-insured medical care plan to cover the employee's co-insurance factor. You might suggest that your employer consult his or her tax adviser about the personal benefit for officers in this type of arrangement. At the same time, the company may fully or partially assist the other employees. The 1978 Revenue Act forbids discrimination among employees in medical reimbursement plans.

Do not hesitate to discuss with your employer's personnel department the possibility of updating the group plan. It is usually the officers who need the extended coverage, and often everyone involved is delighted to reexamine the company's group insurance. The cost of extending the benefits or of seeking a new insurer is subsidized by the federal and state (and in some cases, local) corporate income tax rates. Insurers are constantly developing new health insurance products. You might even be so bold as to make your own investigation by borrowing some friends' group plans or by writing directly to several insurers. You owe it to yourself to overcome the application of the bromide, "You are never insured for what ails you."

Immediately after accepting new employment, you should learn the provisions of your company's major medical plan. The plan's deductibles (both basic and cash), allowances, coverage, and maximum benefits determine the real value of this insurance to you. In other words, if your plan is inadequate, you must consider an excess-liability policy.

Daniel Smith's employer provides major medical insurance, and the policy is liberal in its allowances. The cash deductible is small. However, the plan requires basic hospitalization coverage. Mr. Smith chose the Blue Cross 21/180-day hospital plan at a cost of $436 a year. The 21/180-

day hospital contract was about $100 a year cheaper than a 120-day full-benefit plan. The 21/180-day plan pays full semiprivate rates for the first 21 days plus 50% of the hospital's charges for the next 180 days. This makes sense because the major medical policy co-insures to the extent of 80% of the first $2,000 of covered expense or $5,000 for the family. This means that the major medical policy pays for 80% of the first $2,000 of hospital charges over 50% for the 180 days and 100% of the cost over $2,000. Blue Cross has a 120-day full-benefit plan for $536 per year. The additional $100 premium covers only $450 ($50 for each deductible, plus 20% of $2,000) of Mr. Smith's cost for 99 days (120 minus 21). This is not a reasonable premium for the risk because of the major medical coverage. The major medical plan has a basic-benefits deductible which is Blue Cross or similar coverage. The major medical policy has surgical coverage and therefore, Blue Shield was unnecessary.

Mr. Smith's plan has two deductibles: (1) a basic-benefits deductible (Blue Cross) and (2) a cash deductible ($50 per year for him or $150 for the family). You will notice that Blue Cross covers children only until age 19. (The major medical policy extends the age to 25 if the child is a full-time student.) Therefore, to complete the family coverage, a child in college requires a Blue Cross policy after age 19.

The Smiths have included the medical-benefits coverage of their excess-liability policy under health-care coverage. However, it is remote that this policy will be of any help to the Smiths because of the generosity of the major medical plan. There appears to be no gap in coverage which the usual excess policy could pick up. This is overlapping coverage. Mr. Smith's excess-medical-benefits policy has a $10,000 deductible with a maximum benefit of $25,000. The maximum benefit is extended an additional $2 for each $1 of increased deductible over $10,000. It has a benefit period of 540 days. The policy limits hospitalization costs to $60 per day. Eligible expenses for miscellaneous hospital services and surgery are not limited. Since the major medical policy pays 100% of the cost in excess of $2,000, the Smiths have no present need for the excess-medical-benefits policy. Nevertheless, in the event of a termination of employment, this coverage might be of some assistance until another major medical policy could be secured. The excess-medical-expense provision was standard until recently in most excess-liability policies whose primary function is to insure you against personal-liability damage suits.

The disability-income portion of the health-care package has three elements: (1) state disability benefits for nonoccupational illness; (2) social security disability benefits; and (3) private insurance.

Both spouses are covered by *state disability benefits*. The coverage is limited to 26 weeks at $105 per week with a seven-day waiting period. The social security disability benefits commence, for persons 22 years or older, after a waiting period of five months. The work credit for persons 31 or older is for at least five years out of the 10 years prior to the date of the disability. For ages 24 through 30, the work credit required is 50% of the time between age 21 and the date of disability. Before age 24, the work credit is one and one-half years in the three-year period prior to the date of disability. A person disabled before age 22 does not require any work credits because the credit is based on a parent's earnings. Blind persons require a minimum of one and one-half years of credit including one-quarter year of work from 1950 or from age 21, whichever is more recent.

The *social security disability benefits* have a five-month elimination period. Persons disabled before the age of 22 do not have a waiting period. The benefits continue as long as you are unable to work. Disabled persons under 65 are eligible for Medicare if they have been receiving disability checks for at least two consecutive years. This includes disabled workers of any age, persons who became disabled before age 22, and disabled surviving spouses at least 50 years old.

Mr. Smith's *private insurance coverage* of $500 a month is to cover the mortgage payments on the house in the event of disability. The policy provides a 24-month sickness payout and a lifetime of coverage for total disability. Thus, between Mrs. Smith's earnings and the disability-income provisions, the Smiths should be able to meet their financial responsibilities in the event of Mr. Smith's disability. The Smiths have decided not to insure Mrs. Smith for disability since her illness, though disruptive to the family's finances, would not require a major change in the family's level of living. This assumes that a substantial portion of the health-care costs are paid by insurance. If both spouses contribute to the household equally or within a 40% to 60% range of each other, disability-income policies should be purchased for each person. Each of these policies might cover between 25% and 50% of the individual spouse's current gross earnings and be acceptable when considering the governmental benefits.

With the substantial increase in health-care costs over the past 10 years, insurers are attempting to restrict coverage as well as increase the policyholder's share of the co-insurance factor. For these reasons you must examine your policies for coverage gaps and overlapping coverages.

The gaps in coverage such as low surgical allowances or 25% co-insurance for a substantial part of the coverage require higher basic medical insurance, excess-liability coverage, or disability income to reduce your own risk. Having overlapping coverages means that you are paying two premiums for slightly more that one benefit. This comes about through the coordination-of-benefits provision in most health-care policies. Overlapping of benefits (coverages) is a particularly acute problem where there is not enough cash flow to protect against all hazards. The schedule of policies will show up problems of overlapping benefits, and in many instances your own risk would be relatively small if you cancelled the least desirable of these policies.

If you retire from a position, you have a limited period in which to convert your major medical policy to a senior care program. A new policy, however, will pick up the gaps in Medicare coverage, particularly for nursing services.

Although you build up your coverage as you choose different types of health policies, this rule applies only if you pay for the basic and major medical coverages. If your employer covers you for major medical, you can generally reduce the basic coverage to a minimum. This is particularly true if the major medical policy provides a liberal coverage.

OBSERVATIONS ON CASUALTY INSURANCE

The Smiths' casualty insurance consists of three policies: (1) homeowner's broad-named peril, (2) automobile, and (3) excess-liability.

The *homeowners broad-named peril policy* covers most risks in connection with fire and theft of the home and premises. It does not cover flood or nuclear explosion. Both of these hazards, the Smiths hope, are remote. The home is insured for the full value of its structure, a particularly important coverage in an inflationary period. The land and foundation are not insured since they are subject to little risk. The policy contains no co-insurance clause, and a loss would be paid in full except for a $250 deductible. This large deductible saves 10% a year on the premium.

The liability coverage is for protection against personal injury or damage to persons while on the Smiths' premises. The insurer here limits its risk to an occurrence, rather than to persons. If the damages exceed the coverage, the Smiths' excess-liability policy would cover such amount up to $1 million.

The unscheduled personal property coverage is part of the policy requirement although the Smiths' furnishings are below this amount, based upon their net worth. Since, however, the cost of replacement increases each year, the amount of the coverage would be a bargaining point in the Smiths' favor if a total loss occurred. The additonal living expenses are paid in the event the Smiths' home becomes uninhabitable and they are required to live elsewhere.

The off-premises loss coverage has no territorial limits. Therefore, on an overseas trip the Smiths do not require a baggage policy. Examine your policy for territorial limits and if you travel abroad, request extended coverage for off-premises losses. Airlines limit the amount they will pay for lost baggage, so that you would need the off-premises provision for adequate coverage.

The homeowner's policy costs vary in many parts of the country. Mortgagees require insurance to protect their equity in your home. Discuss with your insurance representative alternative homeowner's packages using the Smiths' coverage as a yardstick.

The Smiths' *automobile coverage* by a minimum policy is based on the age of the cars and the liabilities involved. The liability limit for personal injury is $100,000 per person and $300,000 for an occurrence. This coverage may be inadequate based on the number of personal injury legal judgments. The Smiths, however, carry an excess-liability policy which would pay for any personal-injury claims exceeding the automobile coverage up to $1 million. This policy requires at least $100,000/$300,000 coverage in your automobile policy.

If the automobile liability were increased to $500,000/$1,000,000, the annual cost for both cars would be an additional $70. The excess-liability policy is less expensive at $50.

The collision deductible is $250. This considerably reduces the premiums, and the Smiths are self-insurers to the extent of the deductible, sharing with the IRS only losses between $100 and $250. The uninsured-motorist provision permits the Smiths to receive payment for damages to themselves and their property in the event of an accident involving an uninsured motorist. They should consider increasing the uninsured-motorist coverage from $50,000 to $100,000/$300,000.

The extended no-fault provision pays the Smiths up to $100,000 for personal injuries, medical expenses, and property damage without the insurer's questioning who was responsible for the accident.

This automobile policy covers two late-model medium-sized vehicles which are used primarily for pleasure by persons of the Smiths' age, residing in a community within commuting range of a large city. If any of these factors vary, the premium rates change.

The *excess-liability policy* completes the casualty insurance coverage by insuring the Smiths against liability to others for personal injuries and property damage up to $1 million over the retained limits ($100,000 for

			1	2	3	4
						Annual Premium
1	Homeowners Broad Name Peril Policy					
3		Aetna Casualty & Surety		# 1SH 4944 456 PCA		
4		Period Covered		10/28/78 to 10/28/79		
6		Dwelling- Full Value				
7			No Co-Insurance		60000	
8		garage			6000	
9		Unscheduled Personal Property			24000	
10		Additional Living Expenses			12000	
11		Liability- Each Occupant			300000	
12		Medical Payments - Each Person			250	
13			Aggregate		10000	
14		Personal Property- Off Premises			2400	
16		Deductible Applied to All Losses			250	
17		(Maximum Currency Loss)				
18		After Deductible - 100)				
20		Annual Premium				346
22	Automobile Insurance					
23		Allstate Insurance Co.		# 00000		
24		Period Covered		11/2/78 to 11/2/79		
25		Both Automobiles Covered for				
26			Personal Injury Liability			
27			Per person		100000	
28			Occurance		300000	
29		Property Damage			50000	
30		Comprehensive Deductible			50	
31		Collision Deductible			250	
32		Uninsured Motorist			50000	
33		No-fault			100000	
35		Annual Premiums				
36		Ford Station Wagon			449	
37		Oldsmobile 88			503	
38		Total				952
39	Excess Liability Carried - See Health Insurance					

homeowers and $100,000/$300,000 for the automobiles). This policy also contains excess-medical-expense coverage which is superflous at present because of the extended coverage in the major medical. However, the cost of the excess-liability policy amounts to less than increasing the casualty insurance limits individually.

CONCLUSION

You should not permit the wide variety of health and casualty insurance packages to overwhelm you. Using a workpaper, develop alternative plans to determine which is best-suited to the needs of you and your family. You are the best judge of the extent to which you can be a self-insurer. Look carefully for gaps in your coverage. Make certain that the possible hazard is covered. Examine the cost of extended coverage against the reality of a possible loss. Remember that you do not buy insurance to make a profit, but to reduce your exposure to risk. Without a workpaper setting forth coverage and costs, you cannot make an intelligent decision. Also, you should consult with your insurance representative. He or she can offer invaluable assistance in informing you about different insurance packages; but you must make the final decisions based upon the facts you consider important.

Policies are usually issued annually, but the decisions you make after careful study do not have to be reanalyzed each year. Review the new policy to make certain that it reflects any changes in your needs.

It is a fact of life that in the event of a loss most individuals rarely have adequate insurance coverage. You can only try to do your best to buy coverage based on your own cash flow and on the well-reasoned comparison of the facts and figures of your daily, monthly, and yearly existence.

9
CREDIT

WE LIVE IN WHAT MIGHT EASILY BE CHARACTERIZED as "The Age of Credit." Private individuals and public institutions are all buying on time, and much of the money in our economy is made on money.

For many, credit is the attempt to realize hopes and dreams. For others, credit is a fact of life which, like gravity, is observed but probably not understood. For still others credit is a mystery like electricity—not to be fooled around with.

This chapter is intended to take at least the mystification out of credit. If you read and use this material attentively, you will know when you should ask for money, how much you should ask for, whom to ask, and how you should pay it back. Certain specific aspects of credit will be discussed in greater detail in the chapters on tangible and intangible properties, but this chapter in particular is intended to give you control over the basic *concept* of credit.

If you buy something and do not pay for it immediately, *credit* is the time in which the seller allows you to complete the payment. Since the seller has a right to his money as soon as you receive the goods or services, you compensate him for allowing you the convenience of a delay with an added payment of money called *interest*. In an earlier and simpler day, the town storekeeper may have allowed your grandfather credit on his request alone. Today, you must go into a bank to request credit in the form of a loan or a bank credit card. You may never see the same bank officer twice, and in any case, how is this bank which operates in 32 countries to verify your honesty? In other words, how do you *get* credit? If you have never had a loan before, will anyone give you credit if you don't have a credit history? There is a not-so-funny anecdote which tells of a young person requesting a credit card from a credit grantor. The grantor asks the applicant if he has ever had credit before and is told no. The kindly grantor then advises the youth to take out a one-year loan for $500, asking his trustworthy parents to co-sign the note. He is told that he should then deposit the $500 in a savings account without touching it, and after paying off the loan in six months, he should come back for a card. Unfortunately, this charade happens in the real world all the time.

ESTABLISHING A CREDIT RECORD

Let's assume that you are a college student or that you are just starting out on your first job. In either case, you have no credit rating as yet. If you need a telephone (as you no doubt will) one of the best ways to set up a credit record is to apply for a phone in your own name. You can either make a deposit with the telephone company or can have your parents or some other reliable person with a credit rating act as your guarantor. Once you have acquired the telephone, *pay the telephone bill promptly each month.* This will be a very strong factor in keeping the credit which you have acquired and in gaining new credit.

Another way to establish a credit record is to open a charge account in your name at a local store. Again, if you are a college student or are just beginning your job, ask your parents or some responsible adult to guarantee the account. Charge some items (only those you really need) and then pay the bills promptly. Some department stores will grant charge accounts to almost anyone who applies. Ask your friends or fellow workers for the names of these stores, and apply. Then, using these stores as a reference, build up the credit cards you require. Try not to incur any finance charges on *any* card until you have all the necessary cards.

The T&E (travel and entertainment) cards (American Express, Carte Blanche, and Diner's Club) have minimum income requirements for applicants. Before you apply for one of these cards, find out the minimum income requirement. T&E cards usually require a minimum salary of $10,000 a year against $8,000 per year generally needed to qualify for a bank credit card.

OVEREXTENDING CREDIT

In general, if over a period of 13 consecutive months you pay finance charges (other than for automobile or home improvement loans) *every* month, you are not using credit to your benefit.

Consumer-credit financing should not be used to purchase big-ticket items such as refrigerators and color television sets. The Annual Percentage Rate *(APR)* of 18% charged by most credit card grantors for the first $500 of credit is substantially higher than the 12% charged by banks over a 36-month period. If possible, finance appliances and furniture through bank loans. As a matter of both *principal* and *principle,* you should spend time to use bank financing for these items. You may charge them on your credit card, but refinance them within 25 days by using bank credit.

The credit card's real purpose is to provide working-capital loans to you. Businesses finance inventory building and accounts receivable through short-term working-capital loans. You should use your credit cards the same way. Most people have a serious cash flow problem at least one month out of the year. Analyze your last 12 months' credit card purchases and chart the highs and lows on a workpaper. Pick the three months when your purchases were the highest, and assume those months are your inventory build-up months. The total of the three months is your annual working-capital requirement. If the total were $500 and you pay 1/36 of this amount each month, you are probably paying $150 in finance charges at an *APR* of 18%. Liquidating this loan in 12 months costs you $33 at an *APR* of 12%, a savings of $117 in finance charges. Try this working-capital theory on your own figures. You will be amazed at the savings in finance charges you can make by using credit cards in this way. At the beginning, in order to rearrange your affairs, you must substantially reduce discretionary spending. In most families a four-to-six month austerity budget will realign the fiscal priorities on a more sensible basis.

If your installment obligations are causing you worry, counselling to correct your personal overextension of credit is available at a very modest charge. In fact, in some states, credit counsellors are not permitted to charge for services. If you cannot clean your credit slate one month in every 13 without refinancing, you should consider professional help.

The Consumers' Credit Counseling Service will help you establish a budget and, if necessary, will work out an extended payment arrangement with your creditors. (The Service will ask you to turn in your credit cards for a period of time.) Service offices are located in most large cities, and if you cannot find one, write to the National Foundation for Consumer Credit, 1819 H Street, Washington, D.C. 20006, requesting the address of the office nearest your home. An initial interview takes about two hours in order to develop the facts and problems.

Using a counselling service is an indication to your creditors that you are sincere about honoring debts. The counselling service rarely recommends consolidating your debts into one loan because experience has shown that after a consolidation loan most people will go out and incur further debt. The counselling approach is generally to ask your creditors to extend the time limit of your obligations, and you are required to operate a money management program.

If your debt should arise from a business loss or from a builder who discounted your note and then went bankrupt, you may have no choice other than to face bankruptcy. There are two types of personal bankruptcy. In the first type, the Federal Bankruptcy Court acts as your credit counsellor without discharging you from your debt. In the second, all your property (with limited exceptions, depending on state law) is sold to satisfy your creditors. You are then discharged from the unpaid debts, except for the last three years' income taxes. You cannot by law use this drastic type of bankruptcy more than once every six years. Gainfully employed persons discharged in bankruptcy find that within a few months of their discharge, most credit grantors will reissue their credit cards.

Under federal law collection agencies are not permitted to harass you for nonpayment of bills. If you request a collection agency to stop all contacts, the agency can then only collect the debt by a law suit in your local court. If you believe a credit charge is in error, you should write to the bill collector within 30 days of receiving the collector's notice. The collector is then required to obtain from your creditor a verified statement of your account. There are severe penalties levied on a bill collector for failing to follow this statute. (This law applies only to professional collectors and not to banks, department stores, and other credit grantors.)

You have a right to cancel most installment obligations within three business days. The seller must be notified in writing and return your deposit. This is called your *right of rescission.*

POINT-SCORING SYSTEM

The point-scoring system has been developed to judge your credit reliability. This is actually used in most cases to keep credit files on an equal-opportunity basis so that banks cannot arbitrarily turn you down for credit. For example, one of the highest individual point scores is given for having your own telephone. Another high value is placed on your other bank credit cards. Ages between 30 and 40 and over 50 are worth more points than under 30. Home ownership, other loans, occupation, years on job, and bank accounts are also scored. Your bank loan is based on your total score. The point system appears to be an additional "plus" if you have shown a debt stability in the past. A good point score under a particular bank's system probably would help you in a marginal situation if you have no adverse remarks in your credit file.

OVERDRAFT CHECKING

Overdraft checking allows a bank to pay checks in excess of your current balance. It is the same as a loan except that it is used only on demand. The same principle of being off the books at least one month in 13 applies to overdraft checking. The *APR* for both loans and overdraft checking is usually about 12% and is generally cheaper than credit card finance charges.

YARDSTICK FOR CONSUMER LOANS

Each area of the country charges different *APR*s and even within an area you can find bargains. One large consumer-loan-oriented bank currently charges the following rates for personal loans:

PERIOD OF INSTALLMENTS	APR
12	11.58%
24	12.59%
36	13.38%

Life insurance is not included in the above *APR*s. Check the above consumer loan bank in your area for "yardstick rates." If your own bank is within the range of the "yardstick rate," you will probably find your financial needs more quickly satisfied at your own bank. Most commercial banks aim to be full-service banks to their customers, and unless you have had some difficulty with the bank in the past, you should always consider using your own commercial bank first. If you do not maintain an account in a commercial bank, attempt to satisfy your loan requirements wherever the *APR* is competitive.

PASSBOOK BORROWING

Savings banks permit you to borrow against balances in your savings account. The bank holds your bank book as collateral and charges you an *APR* which is about 2% above what you collect in interest on your savings. This method of borrowing is based upon the belief that the savings would not otherwise be replaced.

This idea has merit, and if you suddenly need money and have a savings balance sufficient to cover the amount required, consider taking a passbook loan. This is worthwhile if you find it difficult to save systematically.

THE CREDIT BUREAU

The entire history of your dealings with creditors is recorded in your credit data file. You have a legal right to examine this file free or for a nominal charge if you believe your request for credit has under any circumstances been unreasonably denied.

If you believe, for example, that a problem you had a few years ago with a department store might jeopardize your credit position, request a copy of your own credit data before applying for a new loan. Ask your bank for the name and address of the local credit bureau, and write directly to them asking for an application for credit data. (The fee for a credit report is about $4.) The bureau will send you a form asking for your name, address, social security number, and addresses for the past five years and a check for the fee. The response takes about three weeks.

Study the information contained in your credit report. It covers your credit history, some of which may extend back almost 14 years. If there are any errors, there is space for your comments. If you challenge an entry, the creditor must verify the accuracy of your account within a relatively short period of time. If the creditor insists that his information is correct, your remarks will nevertheless be added to the data. The creditor who accepts your challenge and insists that the original entry is correct (even though you believe there is an error) should be reported either to your state consumer affairs office or to the local Federal Reserve Bank. Move quickly on this so as to put your credit file in order before requesting a new loan or other credit.

An error in your bill may bring into action the Federal Truth in Lending Act. You must notify the credit card company of the error *in writing*. (A telephone call does not preserve your rights.) You must write to the company within 60 days after you received the bill. If your account is paid automatically, you should notify the company within 16 days. The company has 30 days in which to acknowledge your letter. Within 90 days, you must receive a complete explanation of the bill. If the company claims that you are incorrect, you must notify the company within 10 days, in writing, that you are dissatisfied with its explanation. If you do this, the company is obligated to report your side of the story to the credit bureau.

Assuming that the problem is resolved in your favor, the company must notify the credit bureau to correct your credit file.

Even though one item on your bill may be in dispute, you are still required to pay the remaining open items. The company's failure to follow the rules prevents its collecting the first $50 of the disputed bill plus finance charges, even if it later turns out that you are incorrect.

In addition, if you purchased an item for more than $50 from a local merchant and you are dissatisfied with it, you are not required to pay if you attempted, in good faith, to return the item or gave the merchant a chance to correct the problem. You also have a right to rescind your contract with the merchant within three business days after the purchase.

If the credit card company is required to sue you, you are liable for the attorney's fees up to 20% of the amount due. In case of death, you are insured at no cost for the balance in your account. This credit life insurance is for persons under 66.

Two spouses are entitled to have credit card companies report information relating to their account in both names, but if they wish this done they must notify the company. (This is important in the event of a later termination of the marriage.) This allows both spouses access to credit sources without any problems.

To prevent being annoyed by a collection notice which you know is due to a creditor's error, you should consider paying the item in question if it is less than $25. Then, you should forward your statement along with a complete explanation of the error to the creditor. If you are correct your account will almost always reflect an adjustment within 30 days. Such correction should include adjustment of any and all finance charges. Your understanding approach to the credit card company's bookkeeping problems may work to your advantage at some later time, if and when a serious dispute arises. You will already have demonstrated to the company's satisfaction that you are not trying to take advantage of them.

If you move out of the area covered by your local credit bureau, you may have a problem in reestablishing credit quickly.

A copy of your credit file from the bureau covering your former residence can result in quick action on your new credit card applications. This is particularly important since the new area's credit bureau has no file on you and checking your name and former address may take a considerable length of time. If you are unable to learn the name of your present local credit bureau, write to TRW Credit Data, 20 Just Road, Fairfield, New Jersey 07006, enclosing a stamped, self-addressed envelope and ask for assistance.

TYPES OF CREDIT

You should obtain your maximum lines of credit in advance of need. For example, a credit card grantor may open your account with several hundred dollars' line of credit. (The average amount of a credit line is $800.) After six months, request an increase in this line even though you may not actually need it. Continue increasing your credit availability so that eventually you achieve the maximum line, which for most grantors is $2,500. This is a reserve that you can use in an emergency until more conventional financing can be arranged.

Types of credit and the *APR* ranges are listed below:

PERSONAL REQUIREMENT	PRIMARY CREDIT SOURCES	APPROXIMATE *APR* RANGE
Clothing and individual purchases under $100	Retail store or credit card	18% on first $500, 12% thereafter
Major appliances and furniture	Commercial bank	12%
Cash advances	Credit card, over-draft checking, or passbook loan	12%
Automobile	Dealer's credit or commercial bank	12%
Real estate	Savings bank, commercial bank, or other financial institutions	8%-10%
Home improvement	Commercial or savings bank	12%
Insurance (cash value)	Insurance company	5%-8%
Tuition	Commercial bank, specialized lenders, or U.S. Dept. of Health, Education and Welfare	7%-12%

A *credit union* is a source of borrowing which is competitive with commercial enterprises. A *finance company* is available if the risk of lending to you is deemed higher than commercial sources are willing to undertake. A finance company's *APR* may be two or more times higher than a commercial bank because of the high-risk nature of the loans it makes.

The following loan and credit calculation terms may help you understand the various options in the use of credit.

APR. The interest percentage charged by the seller expressed as the Annual Percentage Rate. The usual rate is 18% for the first $500 of credit and 12% thereafter.

%i. The periodic interest rate, the percentage charged each period based on the *APR*. The period rate is usually computed daily for credit cards and monthly for installment loans. The %i expressed in percentage is:

APR	%i PERIODIC DAILY RATE	%i PERIODIC MONTHLY RATE
18%	0.04931%	1.5%
12%	0.03287%	1%

The periodic rates are calculated by dividing the *APR* by the period. For example, if the *APR* is 18%, the periodic daily rate is 0.04931% (18 ÷ 365); the periodic monthly rate is 1.5% (18 ÷ 12).

N. The number of periods over which the period interest rate is to be computed. If you borrow $100 payable monthly for 12 months, the period or *N* equals 12. If your credit card company uses a daily periodic rate, *N* is the number of days a particular balance is carried in your account in calculating the interest to be charged.

PV. The present value of the money or credit extended. If you borrow $100 or are extended $100 credit, the *PV* is 100. *PV* is the same as the amount borrowed.

PMT. The payment required to be made periodically. If you borrow $100, payable monthly, and the *APR* is 18%, the *PMT* equals $9.17 per month. The formula is expressed:

$PV = 100$
$\%i = 1.5$ (128 ÷ 12 monthly payments)
$N = 12$

Using ordinary annuity tables, the *PMT* is $9.17

FV. The future value of the money borrowed or credit extended after adding the interest at the *APR*.

In the explanation of *PMT*, the monthly amount to be paid was $9.17 on a loan of $100 paying in one year with an *APR* of 18%. Therefore the total amount to be paid is $110.04 ($9.17 × 12 months). This total amount is the *FV*. Since the *PV* or original loan was $100, the interest paid for the use of the money was $10.04 ($110.04 − $100.00). Each monthly payment of $9.17 includes both interest and principal. The principal portion of the monthly payment is also called the *amortization* of the loan.

Understanding the six terms (*APR, %i, N, PV, PMT,* and *FV*) is essential to knowing how to borrow at the cheapest cost. In any question involving the extension of credit, the knowledge of three of the four variable factors (*%i N, PV,* and *PMT*) will enable you to compute the unknown. For example, *%i* is a function of *APR* and not actually a variable. Thus where the *APR* is 18% and payments are monthly, *%i* equals 1.5% (18 ÷ 12 = 1.5). *FV* is computed by multiplying *PMT* by *N. FV* is not a variable in credit problems. The remaining four factors, *%i, N, PV, and PMT*, are the variables you must work with in analyzing credit situations.

In working with credit costs, an inexpensive preprogrammed pocket calculator having the keys *N, %i, PMT, PV* and *FV* is invaluable. You will find this type of calculator indispensible in making investment decisions, but if you decide not to purchase one, your local Federal Reserve Bank can supply you with *APR* tables. In any event, the calculations in this chapter will deal with common enough situations to help you develop a feel for credit without an investment in a pocket calculator. (Incidentally, if you use the calculator for investment analysis, you may claim the cost as a deduction on your income tax return.)

Assuming a knowledge of any three variables, ordinary annuity tables programmed into the calculator will within seconds display the unknown variable. For example, assuming that you borrow $100 for 12 months and the *APR* is 18%, what is the monthly payment? If the *APR* is 12%, what is the monthly payment? The formulas are as follows:

APR	18%	12%
1. *%i*	1.5	1
2. *N*	12	12
3. *PV*	100	100
therefore		
4. *PMT*	$9.17	$8.88
and		
5. *FV (PMT × N)*	$110.04	$106.56
and		
6. Interest (*FV − PV*)	$10.04	$6.56

For the above facts, the difference between an *APR* of 18% and one of 12% is an annual increased interest cost of $3.48 where payments are made monthly. In terms of percentage difference (called delta percent and expressed as: $\Delta\%$) you are paying an additional 53% (3.48 ÷ 6.56). That is the percentage saved annually by borrowing at an *APR* of 12% rather than at 18%. On a $100 loan, the money difference may not appear to you to be significant, but on a percentage calculation, the difference may in the cost of borrowing at these two rates is substantial. In terms of savings, reducing the *APR* from 18% to 12% is a reduction in interest cost of almost 35% ($3.48 ÷ $10.04 = 35%). Again, increasing the *APR* from 12% to 18% is a 53% increase ($3.48 ÷ $6.56 = 53%).

To further illustrate the knowledge of three variables to find the fourth unknown, assume that you can afford maximum monthly payments of $50. If the *APR* is 12%, what is your borrowing limit for six months, 12 months, 18 months, 24 months, and 36 months? What is your borrowing limit if the *APR* is 18%?

	BORROWING CAPACITY		
MONTHLY PAYMENTS: $50	APR: 12%	APR: 18%	DIFFERENCE
6 months	$ 290	$ 285	$ 5
12 "	563	545	18
18 "	820	784	36
24 "	1,062	1,002	60
36 "	1,505	1,383	122

	INTEREST CHARGED $\Delta\%$		
6 months	$10	$15	50
12 "	37	55	49
18 "	80	116	45
24 "	138	198	44
36 "	295	417	41

The interest or finance charge is allowable as a deduction on your tax return if you itemize your deductions.

The above calculations illustrate the use of cash flow factors to determine your borrowing capacity (line of credit). The *APR* increase from 12% to 18% reduces your line of credit considerably when you reach the

36-month payment plan. The difference in your borrowings is $122, and the overall interest cost increases 41% (Δ%) if you are required to pay an *APR* of 18% rather than 12%. From these tables several observations can be made:

1. *APR* differences become significant on $50 monthly installment payments after 18 months.

2. The shorter the payout period, the less important the *APR* factor.

3. The time and effort in seeking alternative credit must be measured against the monthly payments and number of payments.

In retail installment contracts, the *APR* is stated in large print. The typical agreement allows you to pay *the greater of 1/36 of the balance or $5. (This includes the finance charge.)* Of course, if you pay the entire balance, you have no finance charges. However, some credit cards charge a maintenance fee of 50¢ per month if you are a prompt payer. The grantor's theory is that you should bear the cost of accounting for your purchases and the mailing of your statement even if you do not use your credit line.

The finance charges are computed daily at the rate of 0.04931% (*APR* = 18%) on a balance of $500 or less and at 0.03287% (*APR* = 12%) on balances in excess of $500. The minimum finance charge for a billing period is 50¢. If the balance subject to charges is less than $5, no finance charge will be required. The billing period is 25 days. This means that if you are billed on September 26, the payment must be received by the grantor by October 21.

This same credit card company allows cash advances at the daily rate of 0.03287% (*APR* = 12%). In addition, a 25¢-per-item charge is made. If you fail to make the 1/36 payment within 10 days of its due date you may be fined 4¢ per $1 of the installment due up to $5.

If you have sufficient funds in your savings account to purchase a big-ticket item but are not a systematic saver, you might become your own credit grantor. For example, you require $500 for a new appliance, and you withdraw the money from your savings account. You decide to repay yourself monthly, as if you were the lender. You can easily arrange to have your checking account debited each month and the money, including the current *APR* of 12%, credited to your savings account over a year.

The formula is:

$APR = 12\%$

$\%i = 1$

$PV = \$500$

$N = 12$

therefore

$PMT = \$44.43$ per month

You would round off the amount to $44 and request that this transfer of funds be made automatically each month to your savings account. Accordingly, at the end of 12 months your $500 would be intact, based upon current interest paid for savings accounts. On the other hand, if the amount withdrawn from savings is $300, the monthly repayments would be $26 ($300 \div 500 \times 44 = 26$).

If you decide to pay off an installment loan before maturity, the interest refunded to you is usually computed on a sliding-scale formula called the Rule of 78. This rule allows the lender to earn substantially all of the interest in the beginning periods. If interest were earned on a straight-line basis and you paid up a one-year installment loan in six months, you would expect to receive a refund of 50% of the interest. However, according to the way the Rule of 78 operates, your refund is 27%. Some lenders use the actuarial method of computing interest so that your prepayment in the early months results in a larger refund than under the Rule of 78. In any case, as you will see from the tables, generally you should not pay off an installment loan before maturity if more than 50% of the interest has been earned. The reason is that in the later periods you are using the lender's money at a relatively low *APR*.

The *78* in the rule is the total of adding 12 monthly installments over a period of one year:

$1 + 2 + 3 + 4 + 5 + 6 + 7 + 8 + 9 + 10 + 11 + 12 = 78.$

The figure 78 is the denominator of the fraction. The numerator is the remaining installments. Thus, under the Rule of 78 you would receive a refund of $84.62 of a $100 finance charge if you repaid the loan within the first month. The amount is computed as follows:

1. 12 (months to go) $\div$ 78 = 0.15384615%

2. $100 (finance charge) $\times$ 0.15384615% = $15.38 (interest earned by lender)

3. $100 - 15.38 = $84.62 (amount of interest unearned and refundable to you)

The tables of interest earned by the lender, based on a year's monthly installments with an interest charge of $100, follow:

MONTH	RULE OF 78 METHOD MONTHLY	CUMULATIVE	ACTUARIAL METHOD MONTHLY	CUMULATIVE
1	$ 15.38	$ 15.38	$ 15.11	$15.11
2	14.10	29.48	13.92	29.03
3	12.82	42.30	12.72	41.75
4	11.54	53.84	11.50	53.25
5	10.26	64.10	10.28	63.53
6	8.98	73.08	9.03	72.56
7	7.69	80.77	7.78	80.34
8	6.41	87.18	6.51	86.85
9	5.13	92.31	5.24	92.09
10	3.85	96.16	3.94	96.03
11	2.56	98.72	2.64	98.67
12	1.28	100.00	1.33	100.00
Totals	$100.00	$100.00	$100.00	$100.00

In the fourth month the lender has in both methods earned more than 50% of the interest. Therefore, unless some overriding personal factor makes it important for you to prepay the loan, you would continue payments after the fourth month. If you are going to prepay, do so before the lender has earned more than 50% of the interest.

If the installment loan is for more than 12 months, the Rule of 78 requires a different denominator:

PERIOD OF LOAN (MONTHS)	DEMONINATOR FOR PERIOD	FIRST MONTH'S NUMERATOR
12	78	12
18	171	18
24	300	24
36	666	36
48	1176	48

To illustrate a complete example, assume that you require $1,000 repayable in 36 months with an *APR* of 12%. What is: (1) the monthly payment, (2) the finance charge, and (3) the refundable interest after six months? The calculations are:

$PV = \$1,000$

$N = 36$

$APR = 12\%$

$\%i = 1\%$

therefore

$PMT = \$33.21$

$FV = \$1,195.56 (\$33.21 \times 36)$

$I = \$195.56 (\$1,195.56 - \$1,000)$

Rule of 78:

1. Remaining period after six months = 30
2. $36 + 35 + 34 + 33 + 32 + 31 + = 201$ Totals of first six months' numerators
3. $201 \div 666$ (see table) = 30.18% (interest earned after six months)
4. $195.56 (finance charge) $\times$ 30.18% = $59.02
5. $195.56 - $59.02 = $136.54 (refundable interest after six months).

Another approach to understanding how the balance declines in an installment loan using the figures in the example follows:

MONTHS PAID	BALANCE OF LOAN	PERCENT LOAN	TOTAL PAID	(PERCENT) UNPAID
0	$1,000	100%	$0	100%
6	857	86	199	83
12	706	71	399	67
18	545	55	598	50
24	374	37	797	33
36	0	0	1,196	0

After 12 months you have made 33% of the total payments required on the loan (100% − 67% = 33%). On the other hand, 29% of the loan balance has been paid (100% − 71% = 29%). The table above shows the amortization of an installment loan over a 36-month period. You will notice that the amortization (payments on principal) is considerably smaller in the earlier months against the percent of the total loan unpaid. After six months you have unpaid 83% of the total amount of the payments and yet the loan balance remaining is 86%. This is because the interest is chargeable on a declining balance. The amortization for the first six months shows these computations if

$$APR = 12\%, \%i = 1\%, PV = \$1,000, \text{ and } PMT = \$33.21:$$

MONTH	PAYMENT	INTEREST	PRINCIPAL	LOAN
0				$1,000.00
1	$ 33.21	$10.00	$ 23.21	976.79
2	33.21	9.77	23.44	953.35
3	33.21	9.53	23.68	929.67
4	33.21	9.30	23.91	905.76
5	33.21	9.06	24.15	881.61
6	33.21	8.82	24.39	857.22
Total	$199.26	$56.48	$142.78	

COMPUTING YOUR LINE OF CREDIT

The amount of money you have available for variable expenditures is called *discretionary income*. In other words, the amount of money you can choose to direct to voluntary expenditures such as vacation or entertainment, as opposed to a fixed expenditure such as a mortgage. The portion of your discretionary income used to pay installment debts is indicative of your immediate solvency.

A ratio of installment debt payment to discretionary income of 10% is considered no problem. A 25% ratio is about maximum. Over 25% requires an austerity campaign to build up cash reserves. Another yardstick is the simplistic approach of using 25% or your monthly gross salary (before deductions) as the maximum amount of installment debt to be paid monthly. The 25% gross salary test appears to be too liberal for most people, even though many banks use this percentage as an upper limit. Using the debt-to-salary ratio as a first test, you should do a more detailed analysis to develop your line of credit.

If your request for credit involves a borderline situation between a luxury and a necessity, the loan would more likely be approved for a necessity. However, unless you have a personal relationship with the lender, it is difficult to judge when you are on the borderline. This is why you should develop your own line of credit.

The period of the loan has a direct relationship to the ratios. For example, a $1,000 loan with an *APR* of 12% requires the following monthly repayment:

LENGTH OF LOAN (MONTHS)	MONTHLY PAYMENT	PERCENT
12	$88.85	100%
18	60.98	69
24	47.07	53
36	33.21	37
48	26.33	30

Extending a loan from 12 months to 24 months reduces the payments required to amortize by 47% ($47.07 ÷ $88.85 = 53%; 100% − 53% = 47%). This reduction may be significant in measuring your credit ratio.

Another approach is to compute the amount you can afford to pay for installment debt and stay within the 25% rule of monthly debt to discretionary income. Then, compute your borrowing capacity against different maturities. Let's assume that you can afford $100 a month. Your discretionary income is at least $400 before installment debt service. (Your real estate mortgage is not included in the discretionary income.) At an *APR* of 12%, you may borrow as follows:

REPAYMENT PERIOD (MONTHS)	LOAN CAPACITY	PERCENT
12	$1,126	100%
18	1,640	146
24	2,124	189
36	3,011	267
48	3,797	337

Interestingly, your borrowing capacity does not increase proportionately to the length of time you take to pay back the loan. Thus, 48 months, which is four times the period of 12 months, increases your borrowing capacity only 3.37 times, a reduction of almost 16%. The interest costs increase disproportionately as the loan maturity increases. If you were able to arrange to borrow $1,126 once a year, the four-year borrowing would be $4,504 ($1,126 × 4 = $4,504) against a 48-month loan of $3,797. This is a substantial cash difference of $707.

Knowing your borrowing ability at different maturities and *APR*s can assist you in determining your actual loan request. If you believe your loan requirement is $1,500 and if you can afford $50 per month at an *APR* of 12%, you should apply for a 36-month loan ($100 per month for 36 months equals $3,011; therefore $50 per month equals approximately $1,500 borrowed for the same period).

To coordinate your monthly bill-paying system with your loan requirements, you should request the lender to make each month's payment due on a specific date each month. For example, if you decide that your monthly bill-paying period is between the tenth and the fifteenth of each month, a lender should start your repayment date on the twentieth day of the following month.

In the business world as in private life, many people devote an enormous amount of time to "kiting" money. "Kiting" means issuing a check without sufficient funds in your checking account to cover it, and at the same time moving money into your checking account from another account to try to prevent the check you have written from "bouncing." Kiting rarely lasts over an extended period of time before the operation collapses. The solution is to devote your efforts to *underextending* credit, rather than to overextending it.

The Smiths have used the information from their Statement of Cash Flow to prepare a personal line of credit. They have not bothered with a point-scoring system. They prepared their Statement of Available Credit to determine whether they can afford to redo their kitchen within the next few years. The Smiths have no immediate need to make this decision; however, since finances play the major role in choosing which direction to follow, they began their decision-making process with the accompanying statement.

OBSERVATIONS ON STATEMENT OF AVAILABLE CREDIT

The bottom line of the Smiths' statement of available credit shows that they have *none*. Despite a substantial cash inflow, the fixed costs of running the household leave their discretionary cash below the minimum amount necessary to satisfy most lenders. A line of credit equal to 25% of discretionary cash is more than absorbed by the Smiths' installment obligations on two automobiles. Under the present facts, the Smiths cannot afford a new kitchen. In addition, with the mortgage receivable maturing at the end of 1980, they must plan either to pick up the substantial slack in their cash inflow or make drastic reductions in their cash outflow. The discretionary cash is currently being spent in such a manner as to leave nothing for savings.

Daniel and Louise Smith
Statement of Available Credit
December 31, 1978
Annualized

	1	2	3	4
Cash Inflow:				
Net Salary (H)			17400	
Net Salary (W)			8000	
Dividends			400	
Interest Income-Savings			700	
Interest Income-Other			1100	
Mortgage Receivable and Interest			5000	
Vacation Home Inflow		6700		
Outflow		5500	1200	
G.I. Pension			500	
Total Cash Inflow				34300
Cash Outflow (Fixed):				
Mortgage Servicing Residence			5300	
Real Estate Taxes			2000	
Heat, Light, & Water			1600	
Telephone			400	
Medical Expenses (Net)			400	
Income Taxes in Excess of Wtx.			-0-	
Food Stores			3900	
Auto Operations (Excludes Notes)			2000	
Child Care			1300	
Personal Insurance (Includes Interest)			1200	
Casualty Insurance			500	
Mother's Allowance			1200	
Total Outflow (Fixed)				19800
Discretionary Cash Available				14500
Line of Credit:				
Total Line of Credit (14500 x 25%)				3600
Less, Line Used				
Automobile Notes			3100	
Credit Cards (Average)			-0-	
Other			-0-	
Total Line of Credit Used				3100
Available Credit				500

While it is true that some lenders talk of a "yardstick" of 25% of *gross salary* for a line of credit (for the Smiths this would be almost $9,000: $35,000 × 25%), a detailed analysis of the Smiths' cash flow indicates that this is almost three times the credit line they can handle. The Smiths, at their present level of living, have $14,500 remaining for discretionary spending. Adding the following discretionary cash items (based on adjusting the 1978 cash flow for known items), will indicate dramatically the small amount of cash available for savings and contingencies:

ITEM	AMOUNT
Automobile notes	$3,100
Out-of-pocket cash	$3,000
Department stores	1,600
Individual retirement arrangement	1,500
Contributions	400
Vacation	400
Restaurants	400
Professional fees	200
Miscellaneous	400
Total	$11,000

With total discretionary cash of $14,500, the Smiths have $3,500 ($14,500-$11,000) left for savings and contingencies. This may seem a generous buffer, but as the analysis shows, it does not meet the criteria set up by most credit grantors. The Smiths must prepare now to plan reductions first in discretionary spending and secondly in fixed outflow. Each item must be studied for possible shifting of priorities. For example, the child care will be eliminated within the next several years as the younger child's school day is lengthened. Possible reduction in automobile usage by car pooling may have a substantial effect in reducing auto operations. Purchasing meats and canned goods in large quantities at sales prices may save 10% or more of food-store expenditures. Vacation costs can be sharply reduced by economical travel methods. But these are merely the tip of the financial iceberg.

Self-discipline is the most important personal factor when dealing with credit. Unless the Smiths, in a careful analysis of available credit, find that the figures are wrong, they must keep strict control of cash outflow for the next several years to prevent a cash squeeze. For each $1 increase in discretionary cash, 25¢ is added to their line of credit. Additionally, each $1 increase in salary is reduced by approximately 42¢ for effective federal and state taxes (top federal bracket, state bracket less value of state tax deduction on the federal tax return or $32\% + 15\% - 4.8\% = 42.2\%$).

CONCLUSION

Be persistent in seeking credit if you are gainfully employed and have no adverse comments in your credit file which you cannot satisfactorily explain. If there are adverse comments in your file, submit a polite letter of explanation. If you are refused a loan for a worthwhile purpose and according to your Statement of Available Credit you have not used your available line, challenge the loan officer's determination. Submit your protest in writing (along with the statement) to the senior lending officer of the lending organization for reconsideration. Do not antagonize the grantor in your request for an appeal. If you are unsuccessful, keep trying other lenders at the same *APR.* Your expenditure of energy should eventually be rewarded. Although a bank's primary responsibility is to its depositors, the bank should also satisfy worthwhile loan applications.

10

REAL ESTATE

REAL ESTATE CONSISTS OF LAND and the improvements to land in the form of buildings or other structures. Real estate is purchased and owned either for personal use or as an investment. Personal real estate would include your home and a vacation home, while investment real estate would include land which is unimproved (having no structures on it) or land which is improved (having structures on it). Investment or commercial real estate consists of properties held for the production of income, for use in trade or business, or for resale. Commercial real estate includes such typical improvements as warehouses, factories, offices, lofts, stores, shopping centers, restaurants, and theaters. Stores and shopping centers are commonly referred to as "taxpayers." A shopping center is a cluster of taxpayers operated under one management. One may also have as investment real estate a piece of land which currently produces no income, but which can eventually be sold at a profit. The various classifications of profit-oriented real estate permit different tax options for the owner.

Personal real estate may be converted into an investment and vice versa. Renting your vacation home for a period of time makes the property investment real estate for the portion of the year during which it is rented. Building a new home on vacant land which you hold for a period of time converts investment real estate into personal real estate.

Unimproved land is land in its raw state. (Fencing or other boundary markers are generally not considered improvements.) The construction of sewers, roads, electrical lines, and the filing of subdivision plans are considered improvements to land. A building on a piece of land is a substantial improvement. For tax purposes, mobile homes, cooperatives, and condominiums are classified as residential real estate. This is important for the applicability of the nonrecognition of gain sections of the tax law when you sell your residence. The Revenue Act of 1978 also makes this important for the exclusion of up to $100,000 of gain for persons 55 years and older.

Real estate held for investment differs from most other property in a number of important ways. Each piece is, by its very nature, unique and has strengths and weaknesses of its own. It may not be as readily convertible into cash as securities or certain other forms of property. (Vacant land in certain rapid-growth areas can increase substantially in value in a short period of time, but generally the value of land containing structures appreciates faster than unimproved properties.)

In some countries, owning real estate is considered the only safe investment. In the United States, perhaps because of the vast land area of the country, real estate is generally considered an alternative for capital. Real estate has a substantial advantage in the matter of leverage (borrowing to finance the purchase) in that improved real estate may be financed at up to 95% of its appraised value.

SELLING AT A GAIN OR LOSS

Gain or loss in all categories of real estate is measured by the difference between the adjusted basis (cost and improvements) and adjusted sales price (gross proceeds less expenses of sale). Loss on the sale of your personal residence is not deductible because it is a personal loss.

The problem in computing the gain or loss on the sale of real estate is in establishing the property's adjusted basis. There are several choices which the owner may make in order to increase or decrease this basis. One method of depreciation may reduce the basis faster than another. On raw land, you may elect to increase the adjusted basis by adding in the carrying charges rather than claim these as income tax deductions. (You would do this particularly if you were in a low tax bracket.)

In dealing with your personal residence, you should keep a schedule of all repairs costing over $100. You receive no tax benefit for these repairs, but if you sell your home, adding major repairs to your cost increases your tax basis. If you are uncertain as to the treatment of this item, consult a professional adviser in the year of sale (and *before* the sale).

Because the 1976 Estate and Gift Tax Law provides for a carryover basis on real estate at death (suspended until 1980), it is imperative that you establish the tax basis for your home. Even though your estate may not be subject to estate tax, a future sale of the home by your spouse could carry with it a carryover basis. The fair market value minus the mortgage is includable for estate tax purposes, while for income taxes your survivor uses the original cost plus improvements (adjusted basis) for measuring gain (unless Congress acts before the 1980 suspension period).

YOUR PERSONAL RESIDENCE

A mortgage is the security that the lender (mortgagee) holds on the real estate owned by you, the purchaser (mortgagor).

Lenders consider a mortgage on a personal residence the most stable loan that can be made. (This is based on the assumption that an individual's financial situation would have to be desperate before he or she would fail to maintain the payments on the home.)

If you elect to buy a home, the debt for the money is represented by the note you and your spouse signed at the time the mortgage loan was made. When there is a failure to pay the debt, the mortgagee sues. A judgment on the note is then enforced by commencing foreclosure proceedings against the property. In most states foreclosure on a first mortgage takes about a year. During that time the mortgagor may pay the debt and terminate the proceedings. In some states even after foreclosure, the mortgagor has the right of redemption. This means that for a specified period (usually six months) after foreclosure the mortgagor may pay the mortgage and reclaim the property.

Lenders are not in business for owning personal residences. If major illness, the loss of your job, or some other reasonable cause prevents you from meeting your monthly mortgage payments, arrange a meeting with the "workout" officer as soon as possible. These individuals are usually experts at helping to solve such problems.

Statistics indicate that an investment in a personal residence over the past 20 years has appreciated faster than inflation rates have risen. However, the fact that your residence is worth more today is not significant in investment terms unless you plan to reinvest the proceeds in a new residence. A personal residence is not an investment. It is not income-producing, and it is therefore erroneous to measure its value against investment assets unless you plan to sell it and reinvest the proceeds in a new residence or some other property. The payments on your mortgage are a form of savings, and the increase in your cash equity in your home would allow you, if you should sell it, to reinvest in a new home and keep some of the cash proceeds.

To understand how a mortgage operates as savings; you should follow the mathematics of a purchase, a sale, and, the subsequent reinvestment of the proceeds. Mortgage rates change constantly. The terms in this example are used only to illustrate the concept. (The mortgage department of your local savings bank will tell you about current mortgage rates.) Let's assume that 10 years ago you bought a home for $50,000. The mortgagee provided 80% or $40,000 at 7½% interest over 30 years with payments of $280 a month. You sell your house 10 years later for $65,000 and purchase a new one for that amount minus the expenses on the sale of the old home ($65,000-$3,000=$62,000). You again finance on the basis of an 80% mortgage in the amount of $49,600 ($62,000 x 80% = $49,600). As of this writing, you are likely to pay 8½% interest (and we hope again or some time in the not distant future) for 30 years, with a new monthly payment of $381. You have a choice of using the excess cash from the sale of the former home either to reduce the new mortgage or as savings. The accounting for the cash is as follows:

Sale of old residence	$65,000	
Minus commissions and expenses	3,000	
Adjusted sales price		$62,000
Mortgage assumed by buyer (first residence)	$40,000	
Minus 10 years' amortization	5,300	
Mortgage balance		34,700
Cash on closing (exclusive of adjustments)		$27,300
Purchase of new residence		$62,000
Minus tentative mortgage at 80% (see below)		$49,600
Cash required		$12,400
Cash received on old home		27,300
Excess cash		$14,900
New tentative mortgage of $381 per month or annually approximately		$ 4,575
Minus excess cash, reducing mortgage at 8½% for 30 years, in self-liquidating payments worth $115 per month or annually approximately		1,375
Net annual payment on new house		$3,200

If you used the excess cash of $14,900 to reduce the mortgage on the new house, your monthly payments would be $267 ($49,600 - $14,900 = $34,700, the mortgage at 8½% for 30 years). Your present monthly mortgage payments are $280. You have increased your cash flow by 4.6% or $156 a year.

On the other hand, if you could afford to meet the payments of $381 per month on a new mortgage of $49,600 (an increase of 36% or $1,215 per year), you could achieve a savings account of $14,900 at a rate of 7.75% (effective rate 8.17%). Interest compounded daily on these savings would be worth $157,337 at the end of 30 years. (Savings banks today will commit themselves to from seven to 10 years at the 7.75% rate.)

The increase in present values due to the similar rise in home replacement cash may act as a highly positive factor in your immediate personal financial picture. On the other hand, large-scale increases in home building, a slowdown in the inflation rate, change in the mortgage rates, and a stable home resale market may work to the disadvantage of your personal cash flow. Thus, the present unrealized gain on your house can be worth considerable sums to you on a compound interest basis. This theory is supported by the tax law which makes nonrecognition of gain *mandatory* when you reinvest the proceeds in a new principal residence. The law allows you to purchase the new residence within 18 months before or after the sale of your old residence. In addition, you are allowed to move into a newly constructed house within two years provided the construction was started during this 36-month period (18 months before and after). (The two-year rule does not extend to condominiums.) There is a new rule for changing jobs within the 18-month period or if you are abroad. To the extent that the proceeds on the sale of a principal residence are not reinvested, persons 55 or older may eliminate gain of up to $100,000.

If you fix up your home to make it saleable, these expenses are not part of the cost unless they are improvements. (See the chapter on COMPUTING YOUR NET WORTH for the discussion of improvements.) Regular painting is not an improvement but a maintenance item. However, these fixing-up expenses may be used to reduce the amount of money you need to spend to meet the nonrecognition-of-gain requirements. To meet these requirements, you must spend the net proceeds of the sale of your former home on a new house. The proceeds are reduced by sales commission, attorney's fees, closing costs and, for purposes of reinvestment only, fixing-up expenses. The fixing-up expenses must be incurred within 90 days before you enter into the sales contract and must be paid within 30 days after the closing of title (the date of sale to the new buyer).

BUYING YOUR OWN HOME

Although your choice of a home must satisfy both the emotional and practical needs of you and your spouse, you should follow a definite procedure in order to acquire the property at the lowest possible price. Use the following steps, revising the procedures to fit your own situation.

1. General Location

The first step in buying a home is to determine a general location.

If you have children, the quality of the area's schools is of paramount importance. Factors that you should consider in giving a school a good grading are: the number of children in the classroom; the student-teacher ratio for the school, the physical plant; the age of the textbooks and other equipment; the enthusiasm of the teachers and children; and the cordiality of the principal. Ask the principal for a comparison of the reading score of this school with those of other local schools. If this is unavailable, call the local board of education and ask for the information. If the entire area fails to maintain records of reading scores, you should reconsider moving into the area. This may sound extreme, but large numbers of intelligent, well-educated people devoted to their children's education have sold beautiful homes in lovely areas due to the inferior quality of the schools. Experience has shown that the first sign of a decline in home values occurs in areas where the schools fail in their primary mission. In our society, a major index of such a decline is a drop in the school's overall reading scores. Unless you can afford to educate your children in private schools, select a school which has reading scores that are at least equal to or better than those of the general area.

Ease in commuting is another extremely important factor in selecting a home location. You or your spouse may be commuting for a long time to come. Many former suburban "havens" have in recent years attracted office complexes and are now worse than "midtown" during the traffic rush hour. High-speed, air-conditioned trains or buses running on frequent schedules are an important consideration. Learn the full story, and be realistic about your ability to adjust to the schedules. (Perhaps you are really an urban person and should continue to be a renter.) And remember, even though you may think the suburbs are "good" for the children, they may actually suffer by having a commuter parent who has little time to spend with the family during the week.

The stability of the community is important. Drive around and see if there are a large number of "For Sale" signs. Buy the local newspaper on Thursday and Sunday and check the number of houses for sale in the area. An unusually large number may indicate an unstable community with uncertain furture property values. A large number of persons wanting to sell homes may also be an indication of rapidly rising real estate taxes in the area. If the tax rate has increased by only small increments over the past five years, the community would be considered stable.

2. Price: The Resale Home

In theory, the price at which you will purchase a residence is what you, as a willing buyer, and the seller, under no compulsion to sell, will exchange in money for the property. In fact, however, buyers and sellers of homes have time limitations. A seller frequently must dispose of a home quickly for financial and personal reasons.

In a geographical area where the maximum mortgage available from lenders on a single house is far below the 80% rule of thumb, a seller is at an extreme disadvantage in pricing a home. For example, a luxury residence being offered for sale at $175,000 may be sold six months later for $105,000 (a 40% reduction) due to a poor mortgage market. Thus, the first rule for judging the price on a resale house is to research your particular area. Ask yourself the following questions:

1. What is the Mortgage Market and its current terms (rate, length, and percentage allowed to appraised value)?
2. Might the seller's employer be willing to subsidize any part of the price?
3. Is the price within two and one-half times my annual income?
4. What mortgage and carrying charges would cover payments equaling 22% of my gross salary?

A house that is for sale because the owner has financial or marital difficulties can generally be bought at a bargain price, particularly if you can move quickly in closing the house and are not required to wait for cash until your present house is sold. Let's say, for example, that a house has been on the market for four or five months at $65,000. If the house meets your requirements, you should tell the real estate agent you could close within a month at a price of $48,750. (Pick an odd amount since the agent and the seller will think the figure is related to some serious financial calculation.) Actually $48,750 is 75% of the offering price, but you could use 74% or 76%. It is the concept you are working with here. Do nothing to antagonize the seller. Never mention that the asking price is too high. Do *not* take the agent into your confidence. Sit back and wait! After a month, if the house is still on the market, and if there is no reaction, you and your spouse should consider the next step. Ask the agent to ask the seller to state his minimum price. Whatever that price is, reduce it by at least 10% before you agree. This technique is special to home buying and has developed over the years to a point where no one appears ever to pay the asking price. You must realize that you may not get the house you want, especially if it is a particularly attractive one. You must then decide whether you *must* have a specific house or whether the features which make a particular house "irresistible" might not be readily found in a less expensive house which meets your needs.

If the seller accepts your offer, remember that you are bidding for the house only. Later, you may ask what furniture and equipment the seller would like to leave behind. Pay no more than about one-third of the retail price for carpeting, furniture, and equipment. In many instances, such items as carpeting are included in the mortgage through a complicated bit of financing law. Don't pay twice for what is already included in the mortgage just because the seller is "willing" to leave the material behind. Find out how old the carpet really is. Negotiate in this way on every item. If the seller knows that the house is really going to be purchased, the deal is not going to fall through for a few hundred or even a thousand dollars in furnishings. Don't feel compelled to take *anything* you don't want. As you are checking out such questions, you may also wish to inquire about insulation. In the ecology/energy crisis, insulation is a major question in the cost of a house. Its absence should allow you to bargain with the seller. Will the seller insulate so the cost is amortized with the mortgage? It's a good bargaining tool to ask to see 12-month fuel bills. If by chance you are looking at one of the famous "all-electric" houses, check out a year's utilities cost and think twice about the house.

The mortgage market in a particular location is important since not only does this affect your personal cash position, but also the number of buyers around. Mortgage money (at this writing) is generally easy to obtain in most areas. Check with a local savings bank *and* with a large urban savings bank to find out the state of the market: interest rate, lengths of mortgages, and mortgage-to-appraised-value percent. Make this a *personal* visit to speak with a lending or mortgage officer, unless your lawyer advises you that it would be better to have the broker or agent make the initial contact. If the 8½%, 30 years, 80% mortgage or one in a similar range is available, your discount percent over the asking price may not be as steep as 25%. There may be plenty of buyers with the 20% down payment or who put up less down payment and use some flexible finance method to meet the balance of the payment needed at closing.

If a seller's employer is a large corporation, this is likely to be an advantage to you. Such companies generally have the house appraised and as part of relocation expenses agree to make up the difference between the appraised value and the actual selling price. Since the seller's employer does not want to be in the house-owning business, a quick turnover is sometimes more important than the loss of money. If the seller's employer is a large company, use the 75% method.

The guideline for purchasing a resale home are (1) the ratio of the price to your salary, and (2) the ratio of your salary to the carrying charges. The first guideline says that the price should be about two and one-half times your gross annual salary. The second guideline is that your gross salary should be about four and one-half times the monthly carrying charges (principal, interest, real estate taxes, and insurance). Carrying charges are sometimes referred to as "PITI" (for principal, interest, taxes and insurance). Using a $25,000 gross annual salary, the parameters would be:

1. Price = $62,500 ($25,000 × 2.5);
2. Monthly payments =

    $463 ($463 × 4.5 = $2,084; $2,084×12 = $25,008).

As a result;

3. Mortgage at 80% of Step 1 = $50,000 ($62,500 × 80%).
4. Monthly payments on $50,000 mortgage at 8½% and 30 years = $384.
5. Salary to mortgage = 5.4 times.
6. Estimated maximum annual real estate taxes and insurance = $960.
7. Total monthly carrying charges = $464 ($38.40 + $1/12 × $960).
8. Salary to carrying charges = 4.5 times

If the real estate taxes and insurance costs are substantially above the $960 in the budget, the guideline price of the house would be reduced. For example, on a gross salary of $25,000 with total carrying charges of $5,560, the increase in the real estate tax and insurance reduces the guideline price as follows:

REAL ESTATE TAXES AND INSURANCE	MONTHLY MORTGAGE PAYMENT	MORTGAGE	GUIDELINE PRICE
$960	$384	$50,000	$62,500
1,200	363	47,200	59,000
1,500	338	44,000	55,000
1,800	313	40,700	50,900
2,000	296	39,500	49,400
2,400	263	34,200	42,800

The resolution of this dilemma is that the guidelines are used to set up *general* financial boundaries. On a $25,000 salary the price would be $62,500. However, real estate taxes play a dominant role in the size of the mortgage.

If you want to be more precise for your own guideline, prepare a statement of your line of credit. Eliminate the housing costs, and determine your cash discretionary income. Using 33⅓% of discretionary income as a base, reduce this balance by annual payments on automobile or other big-ticket items. If you constantly use retail credit, reduce this amount further by your revolving credit accounts' total annual balances. The remainder is your annual cash available for carrying charges. Now, ascertain the average real estate tax bill in the area. Figure your homeowner's insurance at between $250 and $300 annually. The remainder is the amount for annual mortgage payments that you can afford.

The guidelines are usually minimums. If the carrying charges for the home you intend to purchase run about 30% of your gross salary, your salary must increase by 36% over the next five years in order to avoid a chronic cash shortage. If you can't expect that high a salary increase, do not saddle yourself with such an expensive home unless you have carefully analyzed your cash flow.

After you have set your guideline price, the asking price that you should consider, based on an expected settlement price of about 75% of what the seller wants, is derived as follows:

GUIDELINE PRICE	ASKING PRICE
$20,000	$26,700
25,000	33,300
27,100	36,100
30,000	40,000

35,000	46,700
40,000	53,300
42,800	57,100
45,000	60,000
50,000	66,700
55,000	73,300
58,300	77,700

You are cautioned to use the information above only to *assist* you in your negotiations. In some cases, the asking price is already the "bottom line." (*Do not* rely on the real estate agent for this information.) You will have to use your "poker-table" experience to determine for yourself if the seller is bluffing.

A residence is an infrequent purchase and probably your most costly material possession. Make this purchase a rewarding experience.

3. Price: The New Home

Two people receive bargains when buying new homes in a development: the one who buys the first home and the one who buys the last. These odds are unfortunate. A developer generally operates a highly leveraged business, one in which a chronic cash shortage exists until the project is virtually complete. This has nothing whatever to do with honest value or personal integrity. The nature of the business is such that only financially shrewd individuals are successful developers. A successful developer offers more than his or her competitors, but for the same price. The first buyer is the developer's marketing tool. The last buyer represents the developer's profit.

To determine quality, there is a one-minute test that has been used with a high degree of accuracy. In the model home, examine the showerhead in the bathroom. If it is of top quality, what is behind the walls (electric, plumbing, and heating) is generally of the same quality. If it is a cheap showerhead, the chances are the rest of the construction meets the same minimal standards. Try this test in a hotel or motel bathroom and you will see that there is usually a direct relationship between the quality of the showerhead and the construction of the building.

The price set by the builder at the beginning of a project is fairly firm but you do have bargaining power for the extras. Therefore, if you can afford it, be sure, to do the following:

1. Bring the appliances up to top-of-the-line quality. Don't take chances with unknown brands. Use nationally known brands.

2. Order *plenty* of electrical outlets. This is one of the most important investments you can make. Study the plans carefully. Later changes in the location of outlets can be very costly.

3. Be certain that the house will have adequate electrical power: 100 amps is a minimum, but 200 amps is better.

4. Devote adequate time to deciding on the extras. Ask the developer for suggestions for extras and for upgrading the quality of the construction. (Every $1,000 in extras costs you $200 in the down payment and about an additional $6.00 on the monthly mortgage payment.)

Obviously, the reputation of the builder is of paramount importance. Ask for the location of one of his previous jobs, then drive around that area and look at the outsides of the homes. Do they look as if they have worn well? Strike up a conversation with one of the residents and find out casually what the houses are *really* like. Look around at the exteriors and compare them to the model you saw. If you can manage it, try to see the interior of one of the houses. (Realize that the developer paid a professional "contract" decorator many thousands of dollars to "do" the model house in "your" development.) If you hear a serious complaint about the homes in the older development, confront the builder with what you heard. If he replies with a careful analysis of a construction problem which was later corrected, you can probably accept the answer at face value. Beware of the evasive or general answer. Choosing a builder with a good reputation is the prime consideration in the purchase. The builder's actual financial resources are rarely important.

Never allow your cash deposit on the home to be held by anyone but an escrow agent (i.e., a lawyer or banker). Never sign anything other than a nonrecourse note for construction costs until the completed house is yours. *Nonrecourse* means that if you fail to pay, the lender cannot go after your personal assets. *Recourse* means that the debt can be satisfied out of any property that you may own. The federal bankruptcy courts are filled with home buyers who signed full recourse notes that were later discounted by builders. If a builder uses your funds to complete another job and goes broke, you, the buyer, are liable on a note without a house.

The guidelines of price to salary and salary to carrying charges apply also to the purchase of a new house.

4. The Real Estate Agent

The real estate agent is compensated only if the buyer and the seller close a deal unless, after contract, the seller refuses to close title. In most states the agent is entitled to a commission in such cases. The buyer also has a legal right either to specific performance (transfer of title) or to money damages.

Although the buyer approaches the agent, the agent in most instances works for the seller because the commission from the sale is paid by the seller. However, a reliable agent protects his or her local reputation by an intelligent consideration of the buyer's needs even though the buyer offers no remuneration.

The agent's function is to have available a good selection of homes in the general area within the price you are prepared to pay. The listing of homes in many communities is multiple. This means that every local agent has the same homes to sell. The initiating agent and the agent who actually makes the sale share the commission which runs about 6% of the selling price. If it is a very expensive home, the real estate agent may insist upon an exclusive listing for a 60-to-90 day period. Homes in this exclusive category are generally offered for sale through newspapers and magazines.

Most agents have strong persuasive powers, and therefore you should be wary of their enthusiasm. Ask questions and make no commitments. Do not confide your gross salary or even your guideline prices to the agent. The property listing should contain all the pertinent details about the house. Therefore, do not waste your time or the agent's looking at a house unless your basic needs are covered in that listing.

Telling the agent that you'll "think it over" is appropriate. Federal law allows you three days to rescind an installment contract with a creditor. This is considered a cooling-off period. Do the same for yourself in buying a home, even without any obligation. Thus, after seeing your "dream house," sit back for three days (including a weekend) and ponder the purchase of this house.

On one sheet of paper list the advantages and on another the disadvantages of the particular house. Together with your spouse concentrate on this, your most important (and possibly most costly) purchase. When you are both satisfied that you have a fairly objective view of the home and its relationship to your lives, then make the decision on the third day. If you are not positive that the move is right, *don't buy*!

If your decision is affirmative, engage a lawyer. Do this before notifying the agent of your decision to buy. Your lawyer may have valuable suggestions and knowledge to strengthen your bargaining position; and since the agent generally acts on behalf of the seller, you now need an intermediary to act on your behalf. Your dealing directly at this stage with the agent and the seller may create antagonisms which could act to your financial disadvantage.

5. Your Lawyer

There are several ways of finding the right lawyer, but by all means, find one for yourself. (Do not use one recommended by the real estate agent.) Although lawyers are now permitted to advertise, experienced real estate lawyers rarely use media advertising. Those lawyers who are interested and who are competent in real estate are usually members of the Section of Real Property of the American Bar Association or the local bar association. Similarly, a tax lawyer would be a member of the Section of Taxation. Visit the local bar association and ask for the ABA (American Bar Association) or local bar directory of section members. Copy down several names, then visit the county clerk's office and ask if they can tell you the names of the local lawyers who have recorded real estate deeds lately. This is one confirmation that a lawyer is active in real estate. You can also ask the mortgage officer if the lawyer is active. You might also ask some of your prospective neighbors if they have used any of the suggested lawyers on your list.

Your initial meeting with the lawyer should establish a personal relationship that may last for as long as you own your home. Therefore, you must make sure that the lawyer is competent and within your price range. Does he or she take telephone calls during the meeting? After all, it is your time, and unless it is important, most competent lawyers do not accept calls when they are interviewing prospective clients. This doesn't mean that you should refuse to hire a lawyer if he or she accepts calls during a meeting, but this factor may indicate overall performance.

The lawyer usually charges .5% to 1% of the selling price of the property to represent you. Ask how much the fee is at the first meeting, and if the fee varies from the standard rates, check with the mortgage banker or a recent purchaser of a home. Since lawyers are allowed to advertise fees, you can also check the local advertisements. Your lawyer's fee would probably be higher than an advertised fee because most established lawyers do not try to compete with advertised prices. However, if on your list of lawyers you find one who has advertised a reasonable fee for real estate closings, this is a positive factor in hiring that lawyer. Nevertheless, be sure to satisfy yourself that you and your lawyer will get along well.

Many real estate lawyers enjoy negotiating. Since they rarely go to court, they may consider it a challenge to "make a deal." But it is not up to the lawyer to make real estate "deals" (unless, possibly, in a multimillion-dollar operation). The lawyer's job is to protect the client's legal interests by seeing that the contracts back up the oral agreements reached. (Incidentally, the lawyer is entitled to charge you a fee for services even if the purchase falls through. So check his or her fee position before you sign a retainer.)

Every real estate lawyer develops techniques in handling a client's purchase. The lawyer may want to stay in the background and have you do the negotiations. You will have to trust his or her judgment as to how best to acquire the house at your price. If aspects of the negotiations are unclear, ask questions but do not attempt to second-guess your lawyer.

The time involved in price negotiations may require only a telephone call. The real estate agent presents your offering price to the seller, and if the price is accepted a conference is arranged later to cover (1) contract terms, (2) extras to be transferred, (3) inspection period, and (4) the closing date.

6. The Contract

The seller's lawyer usually prepares the sales contract. The contract is a memorandum of agreement enforceable by law which requires you to deliver a down payment (earnest money) and, at a future date, to pay the balance due in order to take title to the real estate. (The seller must deliver title to the house to you at the closing.) The contract generally provides for the professional inspection of the house, but the inspection may also take place before contract. If the house appears to be a particular bargain, the buyer should attempt to have the inspection completed prior to signing the contract.

The buyer usually makes the closing subject to the following conditions:

1. Systems (plumbing, heating, and electrical) have received professional approval.
2. Systems are in acceptable condition at time of closing.
3. Property is free of termites.

4. Mortgage financing has been established (specific amount and terms may be included).

5. Title to property has undergone verification and is in good order.

6. Furniture, fixtures, and appliances conveyed with the house. This may include tools, carpets, cabinetry, and all items easily removable from the premises which are to be conveyed to the buyer. Do not rely on the friendly verbal assurances of the seller.

7. Closing date has been set.

Time is generally not of the essence in a real estate contract. If the contract sets the closing date as December 10 and the seller has a cold, there is no penalty for postponing the closing until December 12. As long as the closing takes place within a reasonable time, there are no penalties. You can, however, *make* time of the essence by contract provision. Thus, a failure to convey the property on a specific date is either charged as money (rent) or the contract terminates. Unless there are substantial reasons for overriding the general rule, you should not make the exact day of closing important.

A failure on the part of the seller to close within a reasonable time (this may be 30 days or 60 days, depending on your state), permits the buyer to sue for either money damages or for specific performance. The buyer may force the seller to convey the house in exchange for the payment of money. This is *equity*. The money damages are the *legal remedy*.

Conversely, the seller has the right to money damages if the buyer fails to meet the closing date within a reasonable time. However, in some states the seller cannot force the buyer to accept title.

7. Inspection

The house you anticipate buying should be inspected by a professional engineer retained by you and recommended by either your lawyer or the mortgage banker. Never ask the real estate agent to suggest an engineer because it is in the agent's interests to have the house approved.

The engineer you select should not be "moonlighting" from another job unless you are certain that the engineer is insured for professional malpractice. A faulty inspection leaves you with no recourse but to sue the engineer; and if the engineer is a "moonlighter" without insurance your chances of recovery are almost nil.

Although unlikely, it is entirely possible that the engineer's report could be so full of warnings that the seller would be required to rebuild the house in order to satisfy the inspector. Unfortunately, some engineers frighten buyers away from sound and attractive homes by judging according to impossible "textbook" standards that have no relation to the real world. Therefore, you will have to rely upon your lawyer's judgment, along with your own, as to whether, after reading the complete report, the house is acceptable. A good engineer must protect his or her professional standing. Frequently, money is held in escrow for a period of time until a present defective condition has been corrected. The contract usually also provides for a written assurance that the house is termite-free.

8. Financing

Banks are in business first to protect their depositors' money and second, to lend money. A mortgage on residential real estate is the most worthy of secured loans. If you have trouble in getting a mortgage from one bank, try elsewhere. You might even call a bank in a distant city and ask a mortgage officer for available loan information. If you are worried about the property's being in a marginal area, many states have the Mortgage Appeals Board system. If you are turned down for a mortgage, the Mortgage Appeals Board makes every attempt to find a bank to take your mortgage. Published reports indicate that this new system, designed by savings banks, is functioning satisfactorily.

If you cannot raise the necessary down payment, there are companies which will guarantee a lender the spread between the necessary down payment and what you can afford. This raises your carrying charges and reduces the price you can reasonably afford to pay for a home. Nevertheless, a home is probably the best investment you will ever make. You may also be eligible for financial assistance from the government through the Federal Housing Administration or the Veterans' Administration.

The mortgagee is required to furnish you with a list of its closing costs at the time you apply for the mortgage or within three business days thereafter. Closing costs may increase considerably the amount of money required at closing, so find out these costs before applying for the mortgage. If all banks you apply to offer the same mortgage deal, look for a bank that offers the lowest closing cost.

Loan-origination charges paid at closing to the lender are known as "points." If it is usual to pay points in a geographic area, the cost is treated as additional interest and is deducted on your tax return in the year you pay it. On the other hand, if the points are paid for a title search or other services enumerated in the settlement agreement, they are part of the cost of your home and are not deductible as interest. Your lawyer or accountant can tell you if the points you pay can be treated as interest for tax purposes. The term *points* means percentage points charged to you. For example, a $40,000 mortgage costing one and one-half points means that you have to pay $600 for originating the mortgage ($40,000 × 1.5% = $600).

Commercial banks, credit unions, and insurance companies also place home mortgages, so don't confine yourself to savings banks and savings and loan associations. You can help keep the mortgage market competitive by shopping around for your mortgage. Usually you have a minimum time limit of 30 days from the time of contract to obtain a mortgage commitment.

The mortgagee requires you (the mortgagor) to pay for title insurance to the extent of the mortgage. If you are a worrier and have the money for the premium, you might purchase your own title insurance. You can also ask your lawyer to find out what title company is currently insuring the property and ask that company for a quotation. In some states your lawyer writes the title policy. Title insurance will cost you about .13% of the price of the house you are buying. The one-time premium will cost approximately $100.

9. The Closing

For most persons, a closing of the title to a house is a somewhat dramatic experience. The possibility of the deal falling through, possible hostility between the parties, and the nagging feeling that you may be doing the wrong thing in buying the house, are common to this situation. Always leave a full day for the closing, which could take one hour or four. There are no set rules, but don't allow anyone to rush you. Take your time and be satisfied.

The closing usually takes place at the offices of the seller's lawyer, but it can also be held at the offices of the lender, your lawyer, or the title company. Your job at the closing is to be calm and attentive. Sign the necessary documents according to your lawyer's instructions.

You should arrive at the closing with a certified check for the balance due, together with at least six blank checks for possible overages. (These include real estate taxes and other costs.) Even if your lawyer tells you the exact number of checks to bring you should still have some blank ones available. You are entitled to receive a *closing statement* a few days prior to the closing. Your lawyer will review this statement carefully and will answer any questions you have *before* the closing.

Your lawyer will give the lender a copy of the insurance binder. The binder indicates that as of the date of the closing the house is insured for fire and other perils. Later, after the title closes, the insurer will issue you your actual policy. In some cases the seller's insurance company may agree to assign the seller's present policy to you. A copy of this assignment is given you, and you are required to pay the seller the unearned premium on the policy at the closing.

If you are purchasing a house in a development, the house may not have been completed by the date of the closing. For example, the painting of certain rooms may not be finished, bathroom fixtures may not be in place, or many other items may not be finished to your satisfaction. The total value of the incomplete items may not be much in dollars compared to the cost of the house. Under such circumstances, the closing is not postponed, but a closing letter is exchanged between the builder and you indicating that within a specific period (usually 30 days) the uncompleted items will be corrected or installed. Your lawyer can provide either that (1) $1000 of the purchase price be kept in escrow, or (2) specify a money penalty for noncompliance by the specified date. (Leaving the money in escrow is the better solution.) If the work has not been done within the time specified, the escrow agent (usually your lawyer) will return the money to you, provided due notice has been given the seller.

In cases where the builder has an excellent reputation and the unfinished items are numerous, you may not want a closing letter. This might be the case if you are afraid you might inadvertently omit some important task from the letter. You might also want to eliminate the closing letter if you must close on a particular date because your old house is being sold at the same time.

If you are one of the first to purchase in the area, the lack of a closing letter, although risky from the legal point of view, can operate very favorably for you in terms of the extras you may receive. Many honest builders are so pleased at the trust implied by the absence of a closing letter that they have been known to take a personal interest in the buyer's home. Obviously, this is not something you can count on. The failure to receive a closing letter should occur only if you are absolutely certain of the builder's good reputation.

After the closing, your lawyer should send you a typewritten copy of the closing statement discussed earlier. If you have not received it within two weeks, call your lawyer and ask for it, because you will need it for tax purposes. The statement, containing the place, time of the closing, and the names of the persons present, will look somewhat like the following:

CLOSING STATEMENT
40 Sawmill Road
Tyler Hill, Pennsylvania
March 27, 1978

Purchase price		$62,500
Fire Insurance (12/4/77 to 3/27/78)		116
Oil		85
Real Estate Taxes Adjustment (1/1/78 to 3/27/78)		360
Total Credits		$63,061
Less, Contract payment	$6,250	
1st mortgage—Manhattan Savings Bank	50,000	
Water and sewer (12/1/77 to 3/27/78)	42	
Total debits		56,292
Cash at Closing Due to Seller		$6,769
Paid by certified check of buyer	$6,700	
Check of buyer	69	
Total	$6,769	

In addition, payments were made by the buyer at closing:

Security Title Company		$544
Covers: Title fee	$245	
Search	27	
Mortgage Tax	250	
Recording deed	11	
Recording mortgage	11	
Preparation of mortgage—legal		75
Title company closer (cash)		30
Legal		500

BUILDING YOUR OWN HOME

Building your own home requires infinite patience and the ability to accept incompetence and bureaucratic red tape as inescapable facts of life.

If you desire to literally build your home with your own hands, there is a growing and increasingly sophisticated selection of books available which cover everything from solar technology to the difficult politics of "the Code." For most families this will not be the most practical approach.

Unless you have undertaken technical studies or have had previous practical experience, you should not even undertake to act as your own general contractor. If you meet the requirements of experience and knowledge, you must still be able to devote most—if not all—of your time to overseeing construction. In most instances, the best approach is to retain a licensed architect for both exterior and interior design of a new house. If you decide to use both an architect and an interior decorator, be certain that they can agree on responsibilities and details. Many architects work with specific designers and can recommend capable ones. In the most sophisticated areas today, there is a considerable overlap between architecture and interior design, and many architects also function as interior designers.

After years of debate on the subject, the American Institute of Architects (AIA) recently changed its rules to allow member architects to also function as building contractors. Even if you do not use such a combination, it is worth the small extra amount to be certain that your architect inspects the construction work regularly to insure that all specified materials are actually used, and used properly. It is difficult to believe that a builder would construct a $100,000 house and not use rust-proof nails, for example, but this kind of thing happens frequently. Also, assume as a general rule of thumb that any price quoted by an architect or builder is only 75% of what the total will finally be.

If you engage an architect and/or a designer, you should certainly accept prudent suggestions, but you should not hand over *carte blanche* to these people. And remember that there is a profit motive involved in the building profession, so any increased costs should be justified. Anyone who has ever spent any time at a construction site can tell you about an AVO (Avoid Verbal Orders) book. If you discuss changes with your contractor or with any of the workers, note down in writing what was decided. Both of you should then initial the brief description. These are not intended to be exhaustive legal descriptions, so don't carry this to unusual lengths. It's a good idea to use local craftspeople and tradespeople for building, if possible. If they are in the area and are at all established, they are usually reliable and can provide high-quality work at good value.

Be absolutely certain that you sign notes for credit only against the property being built and never against yourself. This way you are protected if the builder goes bankrupt—a not-unheard-of occurrence. If any serious problems arise, let your real estate lawyer handle them.

SELLING YOUR HOME

The price you set for the sale of your home is directly related to the period of time available between your decision to sell and the date of closing. The longer the span of time, the higher the price you should ask. Be prudent, however, so as not to price yourself out of the market. A realistic price almost always produces the desired results.

You can arrive at a price by consulting reliable local real estate agents, neighbors, or by paying a real estate appraiser to give you a written appraisal. Real estate appraisers are generally members of the American Institute of Real Estate Appraisers, a reliable organization of professionals. The cost of the appraisal is an expense of the sale and is added to the tax basis of your house. Not only is an appraisal a great help to you in settling the price, but at the right moment it can be used to assure the "hot" buyer that the deal is a good one. The same appraisal can be submitted by the potential buyer to the lending institution with the mortgage application. Ask the appraiser for a fee schedule before engaging him or her.

Running ads in the newspaper is generally not a substitute for engaging a real estate agent to sell your home. However, you can try both if the agent doesn't demand an exclusive listing (as is often the case). The real estate agent can generally screen out the "sightseers" who will waste your time, and more important the real estate agent knows *how* to sell a house. A good agent knows what people look for in buying and can focus the attention of prospective buyers on the most positive aspects of your property. Trust the agent's judgment, but remember that you and you alone will have to decide on the final price you ask for your home. If there is a great discrepancy between your idea of price and the agent's, find out the basis of his or her calculations.

In selling a home, you should be wary of taking back a purchase-money mortgage from the buyer. Consider owning a second mortgage only when the mortgage market in your area makes it extremely difficult to sell the house. If you are taking back a purchase-money mortgage, always ask the buyer's permission to obtain credit data, and make certain the credit report is mailed *directly* to you.

The PM (purchase-money) mortgage should not be for a longer period than 10 years and should bear interest at least one and one-half to two points over the current mortgage rate. There are usury statutes limiting the rates which may be charged. A second mortgage should be self-liquidating and should be paid monthly. The legal costs and delay in enforcing your rights under a second mortgage should make you pause to think out the problem carefully before accepting it as a solution to a conventional sale.

If the buyer desires to assume your old mortgage, make certain that your mortgagee releases you from any and all liabilities at the closing.

Tax Considerations

If you sell your home and reinvest the entire proceeds in a new residence, for tax purposes, you have no capital gain recognized. The sale of your home without a reinvestment results in a gain recognized. If you receive up to 30% of the total amount of the sale in one year, and the balance in the next year or in subsequent years, the installment-sale election is available. This allows you to report the gain over the years during which the proceeds are collected. The calculations are explained in the chapter, COMPUTING YOUR NET WORTH. Remember that the risk of being a second mortgagee may not be worth the tax savings in an installment sale. The installment notes must bear interest of at least 6% per annum or the IRS will impute interest of 7% per annum.

The adjusted sale price of your home for reinvestment purposes is the gross sale price minus the expenses of the sale including commissions, legal fees, tax stamps, and appraisal fees. These costs are also used in figuring your gain. (Losses are not deductible on the sale of a personal residence.) In addition, if only for the purposes of determining how much money you must reinvest in a new residence, the fixing-up expenses also reduce the sale proceeds.

For tax purposes, show the sale of your house on Schedule D and indicate that there is no gain to be reported because you have reinvested the proceeds. IRS Form 2119 should also be attached to your return. If the sale is taxable because you are not reinvesting the proceeds, you would also use Form 2119. Otherwise, your return may be audited on the cross-check of deeds filed to tax returns. This IRS program attempts to verify sales data on residences by comparison with individual returns. Thus, if you show the sale and merely "net out" the proceeds, the IRS may audit your entire return in order to verify the figures on the sale. Therefore, either attach Form 2119 or show the sale price at gross, adding the expenses of the sale to your cost basis for this purpose. Persons 55 or older selling their personal residence may exclude up to $100,000 of the gain.

If the deduction for moving expenses applies to you the maximum expense of the sale allowed would be claimed as moving expenses and the balance would be claimed against the gain on the sale of the house. The reason for this is that an ordinary income tax deduction is worth more to you than a deduction from a capital gain.

As a checklist, the following items would increase your tax basis (or reduce the sale price): legal fees on purchase and sale (including lender's lawyers); appraisal fees; survey fees; title insurance; tax stamps; mortgage tax; recording fees; credit data; special tax assessments for improvements (but not maintenance charges); settlement costs (loan origination points that are not interest); and mortgage guarantee fees.

If you once claimed a casualty loss on your residence for tax purposes, you must decrease the basis for the loss claimed (in excess of the $100 deductible).

In the year of buying or selling a house, the interest and real estate tax adjustments are treated on your return as either an increase or decrease of deductions.

If your home is condemned for public purposes (involuntary conversion), you may either treat the gain as falling under the provisions of personal residence sales or involuntary conversions. Should your home be demolished to make way for a new highway, the taking of the property by the governmental unit is called a "condemnation." A condemnation is one form of involuntary conversion. A complete loss through fire or flood is also an involuntary conversion. A loss by condemnation is not a tax deduction, whereas a loss through fire, flood, or storm is deductible as a casualty loss. If you treat the gain as a condemnation, you have a longer time (three years rather than 18 months) to replace the property than if you made an outright sale.

Before closing the title, walk around your old home with a pad and pencil, writing down all visible improvements in every room. Then check this list against your bills to see if you have missed any improvements. Prepare a schedule of all the improvements, including any item that was not an ordinary repair. The first painting of the house or of a new room is classified as an improvement. If you do not have a bill, give the approximate date the work was done. You will also need the name of the person who did the work and the approximate cost. (See Chapter 2 for more details on improvements.)

Prepare your tax figures on the sale of a residence immediately after the closing. If you wait, you may fail to include basis items. Once you have the figures, you will later invariably recall some other improvements to be added to cost. If you wait until tax time you are likely to forget those expenditures. If the gain is to be reported on your tax return, you should consider selling some capital assets which have unrealized losses.

INVESTMENT IN LAND

Investing in raw or unimproved land is a venture for professionals. You should not purchase raw land as an investment unless you have patience, sufficient funds to carry the land without borrowings, and are in a joint venture with an experienced land investor. Land is considered inventory. Tax write-offs are limited to interest, taxes, insurance, and maintenance.

Raw land is purchased primarily for its appreciation potential. Therefore, to achieve the economic upside requires a minimum holding period of five years. Unless you are an experienced land investor, the opportunities to leverage (borrow against) raw land are extremely limited. If you *can* borrow in order to finance the purchase of land, the lender usually severely limits the amount at risk and requires personal guarantees.

The opportunities that occur for the average person who "relates to land" (this is a psychological factor) to make a profit are limited because of the competition offered by professional investors. Even raw land requires management: there are fences to be mended, grass to be cut, signs to be posted, and regular inspection trips.

Negotiating the purchase is easy; it is the sale that requires talent. Buyers of raw land from investors are usually "boot-strap" developers (i.e., with no funds). You are required to take back "paper" (notes in lieu of large cash payments). All of this is a professional undertaking.

You can make money in land if you are alone, but the chances of success are about the same as in roulette. The most favorable approach would be to invest with a small group of people. This form of organization is a *joint venture*. In general, a joint venture lasts for a shorter time than a partnership. It is like a partnership except that the purpose of the entity is to hold, maintain, and eventually resell the land. At least one member of the joint venture should be an experienced land investor or real estate broker. That person puts up a share of the money and in addition, runs the operation. It is usual to give an "edge" to the professional in the group by allowing his or her 20% cash investment to share 25% of the profits. Thus, if the land cost $20,000 and if there were four partners, the professional would receive a 25% interest in the profits (not capital) for investing $4,000 ($20,000 x 20%). The other three coventurers would pay $5,333 each for their 25% share. The $333 extra per nonprofessional investor is the immediate economic benefit given to the "pro" to induce the deal. The professional *must* come in with his or her share of the money, and the 5% gift of profits is a financial consideration only if the professional is the finder and manager. A change in the percentages depends on everyone's bargaining position. However, experience has shown that a four-person group generally works well and can carry large tracts of land where the opportunities for profit are greatest.

Large land areas have more value per acre to developers than small tracts. After five years, large tracts of valuable land appear to increase in value at a higher percent than similarly located small tracts. Usually the ultimate goal of land as an investment is to sell the land to a developer before subdivision. Subdividing land is costly. Although more profitable than selling off single tracts, subdividing can also have adverse tax consequences. A casual investor in raw land is taxed on the realized appreciation at capital gains rates. A subdivider (who breaks the tract into lots) is taxed at full, ordinary rates. (There is an exception that allows capital gains for *limited* annual sales of subdivided land.)

Some professionals have used the option method of land investment successfully. The land is rented from an owner who uses it for some purpose such as farming, an orchard, or cattle raising. The investors rent the land from the owner for 10 years with an option to buy it at a discounted price at the end of the tenth year. The land is then leased back to the owner at a nominal rent. The advantage to this transaction is that the payments to the owner may be claimed as rent expense. This is a sophisticated transaction and requires professional tax advice.

The carrying charges (interest, taxes, insurance, and maintenance) on land are usually claimed in most cases as a deduction on your tax return. Sometimes, however, if you are in a low tax bracket, you may wish to defer claiming the deduction. (You would seek to add the charges to the cost basis.) You may elect each year to capitalize these expenditures by a statement attached to your return. You may change your mind every year by choosing or not choosing to capitalize. However, in a partnership you would usually claim the deduction since at least one partner could use the tax benefit.

A *limited partnership* may be used in land investment. This means that everyone except the general partner (the professional) is limited in liability to the investment. However, the general partner usually wants an additional fee for serving alone. Since you should be adequately covered by liability insurance and the limited partnership is generally more costly to organize, a general partnership may be used for a land investment.

RESIDENTIAL REAL ESTATE AS A TAX SHELTER

Investing in residential real estate in the form of apartment building or low-income housing has substantial tax advantages. Most of the low-income housing built in the United States during the past 15 years has been financed as tax-incentive investments by individuals. The tax benefit is in the form of a tax deferment for a period of years created by accelerated depreciation allowances in early years which must be repaid in taxes at a later date.

The tax shelter in an investment partnership generally works as follows. (Remember that you receive little or no cash inflow each year on your investment.)

YEAR	CASH INVESTMENT	ANNUAL TAX LOSS	AFTER-TAX CUMULATIVE PROFIT AT 60% RATE
1	$100	$250	$ 50
2	100	170	52
3	100	150	42
4	—0—	80	90
5	—0—	70	132
6	—0—	60	168
7	—0—	50	198
8	—0—	40	222
9	—0—	20	234
10	—0—	10	240
CUMULATIVE 10-YEAR TOTALS :	$300	$900	$240

At the end of the tenth year in which you invested a total of $300 as a limited partner in the real estate, you have deducted $900 in tax losses and have received no cash return. If you are in the 60% tax bracket for each of the years, these losses reduced your tax by a total of $540 ($900 times 60%). After subtracting your $300 investment, you have made a "profit" of $240. If your bracket is 70%, the "profit" is $330. On the other hand, if your bracket is 40%, your "profit" would be only $60. Therefore, the first principle of tax shelters is to avoid them if your bracket is 50% or less.

The concept of profit is illusory, because at some time after the tenth year (usually at about the eighteenth) the investment results in a taxable profit and you have received no actual cash. In effect you are returning the tax losses to the government. By the end of the depreciation period (the twenty-fifth or thirtieth year) you will be monetarily even. The tax shelter is the annual tax deduction in excess of your cash outlay. This results because some of the costs incurred for interest and taxes during construction are paid through borrowings. In addition, depreciation in excess of payments on the loan result in a tax shelter. The key to the tax shelter in real estate is a tax write-off of about $3 for every $1 invested in the first 10 years.

Tax-shelter real estate investments require *independent* financial and tax advice. If you are not required to pay your adviser (whether or not you purchase the deal) and if the adviser receives a commission from the syndicator, the adviser is not independent. (Widows, widowers, and orphans should be careful of this non-cash-producing form of investment.)

Backing out of a tax-incentive deal is costly. You must recapture all of the excess deductions in one year. The greatest brains in the tax field are trying to find a safe trip out of tax shelters that have gone bad or have crossed over (tax profits and no cash). You must be totally convinced that your present use of tax money is paramount; otherwise, you are putting your money into a proposition that may have no economic upside. No one can predict whether after 10 years the mortgage market will improve so that your real estate venture will be able to refinance its mortgage and pay you some money. This does not mean that the tax benefits of deferment are not important, but you must weigh carefully your cash position against the tax benefits before making your decision.

Assuming that you paid the tax and put the $300 ($100 per year for three years) into a 10-year savings certificate, at the end of the tenth year you would have $609. After the tax paid on the interest at 60% you would be left with a profit of $124 and with no contingent liability in the future for taxes on cash not received. This compares with a 10-year tax profit of $240 which will eventually have to be repaid. At the end of the next 15 years the $609 in the savings bank becomes $1,979, and after 60% taxes your original $300 investment is worth $972. After 25 years in the usual tax shelter, your investment is worth zero. For example, in many low-income housing developments the tenants may purchase the project from the partnership at the end of a period (say 25 or 30 years) for $1 plus takeover of the mortgage. If long-term savings bank deposits continue to pay an 8.17% effective rate (7.75% regular rate), your after-tax profit in the

60% bracket is at least $672 ($972 minus the original investment of $300).

The previous discussion involved tax shelters on residential real estate, either apartment buildings or low-income housing. The tax figures for the two categories are fairly similar. In low-income housing you may turn over your investment without paying a tax. If you sell your partnership interest and reinvest the proceeds within a specified period, you do not have to pay a tax on your excess deductions over the cash outlay. In other forms of real estate, unless you exchange property, you must pay a tax when you transfer the property. Generally, gifts to trusts, charities, and individuals do not prevent the imposition of this tax.

There are other non-tax-incentive residential real estate deals that offer a small amount of tax shelter, pay out a cash flow, and have a possibility of realized profit after a period of time. These investments are usually undertaken by professionals, and if you can purchase a piece of a deal in which the general partner makes a substantial cash investment (and takes a finder's fee of 5% plus a yearly management fee of 5%), there is an excellent opportunity to make money. These investments yield profits of from 12% to 15% at the beginning, and if the geographic location remains favorable and taxes and the cost of other maintenance remain fairly stable, you may make 20% or more on your money. The big gain in these investments is the possibility of a "mortgaging out" in lieu of sale. This permits you to receive a cash payment on a refinancing of the mortgage without any tax consequences. The packagers of these investments do not advertise, since that would violate the "blue sky" laws of many states. You must actively seek out such deals through banks, accountants, and lawyers. (Most accountants have real estate clients who like to spread their risk by enlisting new participants.)

The cash flow for a conventional apartment house operation works as follows:

Cost of land and building:

Land	$60,000
Building	300,000
Total cost	$360,000
Mortgage (8½%, 30 years, 80% of value)	$288,000
Cash from investors	$72,000
Annual cash flow and taxable (loss) rent income	$50,000
Taxes, fuel, and other carrying charges excluding mortgage	14,800

Cash before mortgage servicing	$35,200
Mortgage servicing	26,600
Cash flow (12% return or $8,600 ÷ $72,000)	8,600
Add amortization for first year	2,200
Taxable income before depreciation	10,800
Depreciation, straight-line 25-year life ($300,000 × 4%)	12,000
Taxable (loss)	($1,200)

The above figures are intended to show you how cash flow and taxable income from real estate work. The tax shelter is the difference between the amortization on the mortgage and the depreciation for the first year ($12,000 minus $2,200). The tax shelter is reduced each year as amortization increases. The 30-year mortgage takes almost 23 years in order to reduce the loan to 50%. In other words, more than 75% of the 30-year mortgage period has gone by before the mortgage balance is reduced by 50%.

Used residential real estate may be depreciated at 125% of the straight-line rate if the useful life is 20 years or more. However, since the excess over straight-line depreciation is treated as a tax preference subject to a 15% excise tax, the election to accelerate depreciation should be carefully considered.

Under the current law, construction-period interest and taxes paid during 1978 on residential real estate must be capitalized and written off, 25% in 1978 and 25% in each year after the project is finished.

COMMERCIAL REAL ESTATE

Commercial real estate deals only with taxpayers (stores), factories, and office buildings. The tenants of commercial real estate usually are gainfully employed in a trade or business.

In addition to a different type of financing (businesses compared with individuals), the commercial real estate market is in a position to use a unique method of operation: the net lease. The tenant usually pays all expenses except the mortgage-servicing and fire insurance charges. The net lease is a substitute for outside financing. It also helps businesses use their capital more efficiently. Instead of having their capital "frozen in stone," businesses may lease their retail outlets, factories, or office buildings. These net-lease arrangements offer tax incentives for investors. The economic objective is to receive a payout on a future refinancing or sale of the property. The future cash payout is the business reason for the tax acceptability of these deals. In fact, after fees and other disproportionate divisions of refinancing and sales proceeds, the investments (after-tax profits) usually do not compare favorably with other types of low-risk ventures. However, from the tax-deferment point of view, a high-bracket taxpayer who actually employs the tax savings in other investments (e.g., municipal bonds) will show an economic profit on these prime net-lease investments.

The net-lease deal for a prime tenant (one having an excellent credit rating) works in the following way:

Cost of building		$1,000,000
(Land is usually not involved		
because there is no depreciation)		
Mortgage (8½%, 25 years, 95%)		950,000
Investor's equity		$ 50,000
Annual rent income (equals mortgage		
servicing plus 3% of cash invested)		
Mortgage servicing	$92,000	
Cash excess ($50,000 x 3%)	1,500	
Rent income		$ 93,500
Minus mortgage-servicing cost		92,000
Cash flow		$ 1,500
Add first year's mortgage amortization		11,600
Taxable profit before depreciation		$13,100
Minus depreciation ($1,000,000 x 4%)		40,000
Taxable (loss)		($26,900)

Thus, the investors on a total cash investment of $ 50,000 (made over a period of one year or more) can realize tax losses on a declining balance starting with $26,900. These losses will cross over and become taxable profits in the eighteenth year. The tax deferment, therefore, operates to provide tax losses for seventeen years on a total cash investment made in the early years. The investor gives these losses back to the IRS by reporting income over the remaining seven years of the mortgage. As you can see from this simple example, this benefits a high-bracket taxpayer with little cash available who wants to buy time in paying taxes. The big disadvantages are the lack of a measurable economic gain and being saddled with the future liability for taxes on an investment with little cash flow. The possibilities of a meaningful refinancing and a profitable sale after 25 years are usually remote. Many leases have renewal clauses which could encumber the property for periods in excess of 50 years. In the net-lease deal, tenants generally have excellent credit ratings. However, in the event of a foreclosure of the mortgage, the investors would be required to pay income taxes in one taxable year on recapturing all the prior years' deductions in excess of the original cash outlay.

As a general rule you should not invest in a net-lease package unless your tax bracket (federal and state) exceeds 60%. And then you should only invest sums sufficient to bring your bracket down to about 50%. Never "shelter out" below 50% because the economics are not favorable. Return is predicated on tax bracket, not on real estate value. In a net-lease investment you must in theory have the documents reviewed by an independent person. This is someone you will pay for consultation whether you buy a piece of the deal or not. If your lawyer or accountant is to receive a finder's fee from the sponsor (which is perfectly legal if this is disclosed to you), you should go to a professional adviser for an opinion. (The fee for an oral opinion is usually reasonable, but a written opinion is usually too expensive for a single investor.) Your independent adviser must review the offering memorandum, examine the illustrative figures, and study the legal opinion of the syndicator's attorneys. Since most of these investments are similar, an adviser should be able to sense the validity of the deal within a matter of hours. The adviser's opinion would stress all the possible tax problems (real and imaginary) that an IRS agent might raise in the event of an audit of the partnership. For this reason, the most constructive review that an adviser can furnish consists of a verification of the reputation of the packagers, of their past record for operational net leases, and of whether the current opinion of the syndication is that of known tax specialists.

In the conventional operation of commercial real estate, there are many firms which successfully own and manage factory buildings and taxpayers (stores). These firms are in business to attract the passive investor, offering cash returns through operations and possible future refinancing which exceed the earnings of no-risk ventures.

In many states it is unlawful for real estate operators to advertise for participants in a deal unless the deal is registered with the state's attorney general. For this reason you, as a passive investor, must *seek out* the operators. They will not come looking for you.

You may be able to approach one of these real estate entrepreneurs through accountants, lawyers, or mortgage lenders. You may even establish a contact through activities, but be cautious of a new or casual social contact who has "one last piece" of a real estate deal open for you. There are exceptions, of course, but make the exception to the rule bear an overwhelming burden of proof.

Some of the most successful real estate operators own and manage buildings in economically deprived areas. The buildings are well-maintained and are usually completely rented by small enterprises. In these cases, the risk for the investor is small because of the large number of tenants in diversified businesses. The cost of the building is substantially reduced because of its location. The mortgage market is nonexistent for these loft buildings, yet operators who specialize in this type of building can return 18% to 22% annually to an investor. Most of the problems of vandalism were solved years ago by sealing lower floor windows and by the use of other special protective devices. Thus, decent spaces at very cheap rentals can be profitable if the cash flow works out. Demand for such space can only expand. A 1978 tax law amendment allows the investment tax credit for improvements to nonresidential buildings over 20 years old. If you are a careful analyst, you may very well find cheap and unattractive properties that will be in demand in just another few years.

In deals of the type just described the operator usually puts up slightly less money for his or her share of the package (perhaps 15% to 20% of the cash required for 25% of the investment). Also, the operator usually receives 5% of the annual rent roll as a management fee. In addition, the operator or another broker receives the usual leasing commission for each new tenant. Be prepared to leave your money in any real estate deal of this kind for at least 10 years. Unfortunately, your interest is usually difficult to sell before that time unless you do so at a large discount.

Security deposits by a tenant are income in the year received unless the deposit is returnable at the end of the lease term. If the deposit may be used to cover the rent for the last few months of the lease, it is income in the year the money is placed on deposit. (The theory here is that the owner has received rent in advance.) In many states, rental security deposits must be deposited in separate interest-bearing accounts. The law requires any interest earned to be paid to the tenant annually or at the end of the lease. In any event, whether the money is paid annually or not, the tenant is responsible for the income taxes on the earnings.

"*Stops*" is a term used to denote rents adjusted for increases in real estate taxes, fuel, insurance, or other costs. Depending upon the market conditions, "stops" are used by landlords to regulate the cash flow. This is an attempt to convert conventional real estate operations into a "hybrid" net lease. If the real estate taxes on the building are increased above a certain base (usually the rate at the time the lease is signed), the tenant will pay a share of the increase. This is known as a "tax stop." Similarly, fuel and other "stops" work to increase the rent due to increases in costs. If the real estate market is competitive, the owner will have a hard time finding tenants who will sign clause leases containing "stop" clauses.

A payment to one tenant for the cancellation of that tenant's lease because another tenant requires the space is a *capitalized expenditure*. The owner amortizes the cancellation costs over the term of the new lease.

In commercial real estate, taxes and interest paid during a period of construction are written off over a period different from that for residential property. For 1978, the write-off period for commercial real estate is six years after the project is finished (the balance is amortized at a rate of 16⅔% per year).

ANALYSIS OF PROPOSED INVESTMENT

To understand the comparison between real estate and other investments, the following example reflects a 10-year projected cash flow for a proposed real estate investment:

Cash investment in 1978	$25,000
Estimated fair market value in 1988	35,000
Investment objective (annually)	15%
Projected cash flow 1979	$ 1,500
1980	2,000
1981	2,000
1982	3,500
1983	4,400
1984–1988 (per year)	4,500

The Smiths' investment objective of an annual return of 15% requires forecasting two factors: (1) the value of the property at the end of the investment period, and (2) the annual cash flow. Without some estimate within an error range of 25%, you cannot make a sound decision.

			Future Value (FV)	Periods (N)	Present Value (PV)
1) Cash Investment	25000				
2) Estimated Cash Value at end of 10th year	35000				
3) Periods Covered By Projection		10			
4) Investment Objective Earning Percentage (% i)		15			
Part I - Cash Flow Analysis					
December 31, 1978 - Cash Investment					(25000)
Cash Flow Projected					
1979			1500	1	1304
1980			2000	2	1512
1981			2000	3	1315
1982			3500	4	2001
1983			4400	5	2188
1984			4500	6	1945
1985			4500	7	1692
1986			4500	8	1471
1987			4500	9	1279
1988			4500	10	1112
Total Cash Flow			35900		
December 31, 1988 - Estimated Cash Value			35000	10	8651
Cash Flow (Deficiency)					(530)

**Part II – Measured Against
 Savings Account**

A. Investment in 10 year savings
 Account Paying 7.75% regular
 Interest (8.17% effective rate)

    25,000 invested is worth
    at end of 10th year   54847

B. Cash flow of real estate
 invested in regular savings
 account paying 5.25% interest
 (5.47% effective rate)

	No. of Annual Periods in Acct	Annual Cash Flow	End of 10th year Value
1979	9	1500	2422
1980	8	2000	3062
1981	7	2000	2903
1982	6	3500	4817
1983	5	4400	5742
1984	4	4500	5568
1985	3	4500	5279
1986	2	4500	5005
1987	1	4500	4746
1988	0	4500	4500
Subtotal			44044
Add, Fair Market Value of Real Estate			35000

Future Value of Cash Flow   79044

Real Estate Excess Return over Savings Account   24197

Average Annual Return over 10 years on 25000 Investment   12.20%

330

		1	2	3	4
1	Part III – Alternative Approach				
2	Annual Return on Cash Flow				
3					
4	Cash Investment				25000
5					
6	Present Value of Future Fair				
7	Market Value of Property				
8					
9	Real Estate – Future Cash Value			35000	
10					
11	Less, Present Value at 15% Compounded				
12	Annually				8651
13					
14	Present Value of Initial Investment				16349
15					
16	Total Cash Flow from Property			35900	
17					
18	Annual Cash Flow – Average over 10 years				3590
19					
20	Average Annual Percentage Return				
21	(Annuity Factor)				17.63%

Experienced real estate operators can do a cash flow analysis by instinct. However, lending institutions and mortals have to reduce the cash flow projections to present value. The accompanying workpaper provides an analysis of this investment.

OBSERVATIONS ON THE PROPOSED
REAL ESTATE INVESTMENT

Before any financial analysis is made of the property, the Smiths must determine (1) the acceptability of its physical condition, (2) the acceptability of its present location, and (3) the ability to maintain or improve occupancy rates.

After studying the broker's real estate fact sheet and investigating all costs and examining the leases, the Smiths projected a conservative 10-year cash flow. This projection was based on new rental expectations and on necessary repairs in the early years. The percentage return was required to exceed long-term savings bank rates. The objective annual rate used was 15%. In other words, what would be the present value of the future cash flow at 15%? Using $100 as the future value, the 15% formula provides present values as follows:

$100 FUTURE-VALUE TABLE AT 15%

YEAR	PRESENT VALUE	DISCOUNT % ON FUTURE VALUE
1	$ 86.96	13.04%
2	75.61	24.39
3	65.75	34.25
4	57.18	42.82
5	49.72	50.28
6	43.23	56.77
7	37.59	62.41
8	32.69	67.31
9	28.43	71.57
10	24.72	75.28
TOTAL	$501.88	

From the above table, $100 due at the end of 10 years is currently worth $24.72 at an earnings rate of 15%. The discount is above 75%.

The workpaper shows a $530 deficiency in meeting the objectives, but this is close enough to the objective for approving the acquisition. (A difference of up to 5% of the original investment is acceptable over the 10-year period.) This means that if the deficiency is $1,250 ($25,000 x 5%) or less you should study the figures again carefully, since any increase in cash flow or market value might easily eliminate the cash flow deficiency. If the property were projected to be worth $37,150 instead of $35,000 at the end of the tenth year there would be no deficiency.

Part II of the workpaper compares the property investment with a savings account on a 10-year basis. The Smiths projected a reinvestment of the cash flow at regular savings bank rates. The results show that the property returns 12.20% on an average annual basis for the 10-year period compared with 8.17% left to accumulate at the highest savings bank rate. This is in line with the risk to be taken in owning the property as compared with leaving the money on deposit in the savings account.

Part III of the workpaper is a simplified version of Part I, and not as precise. In Part III, the cash flow is averaged for the 10 years and is considered earned in equal portions at the end of each year. Where the differences are not substantial, as in this example, this presumption is valid. Using the same objective percentage of 15%, the future cash value (fair market value less mortgage at end of the tenth year) is discounted by compound interest. The table on page 331 shows that the present value of $35,900 at 15% for 10 years is $8,651 ($35,000 x 24.72%). The present value is then reduced by the original cash investment. The initial cash investment at present value is determined to be $16,349 ($25,000 - $8,651). Since the total cash return for the 10 years is $35,900 for purposes of this simple approach, the average return per year is $3,590 ($35,900 ÷ 10 years).

Using ordinary annuity tables, the average annual return is 17.63%. This, of course, exceeds the objective 15% return. Even reducing this percent return by the error in treating the cash flow as equally earned would not make enough difference to invalidate the conclusion.

In commercial and industrial real estate, many capital repairs can be legitimately classified ordinary repairs because of the nature of the occupancy. In addition, the mortgage amortization which reduces the cash flow improves the cash position. Therefore the expected $35,000 cash equity at the end of the tenth year is a conservative projection. Based on these facts this real estate investment has substantially met all the investment criteria established by the Smiths.

MORTGAGES

A mortgage differs from any other type of loan, particularly if the mortgage is made on a personal residence. The lender's philosophy holds that, excluding a catastrophe, the owner's equity in the property will be sufficient at all times to protect the mortgage debt. In other words, the mortgage loan is generally a prime low-risk loan. If the mortgagor has trouble meeting the mortgage payments, a workout of the loan is usually permitted before foreclosure.

Until the end of World War II, mortgages generally provided for fixed-interest payments and a payment of principal at the due date of the mortgage. The lender hoped to be paid the mortgage loan at the maturity date. The borrower prayed that a refinancing could be arranged. Obviously, there were many last-minute successes and failures on the due date of the mortgage. After World War II the self-amortizing mortgage became very popular, and today most mortgages are of this type. This means that regular payments are made to cover amortization (principal) and interest so that at the end of the mortgage term there is no balance owing.

A mortgage is actually a double instrument: it is a note and a mortgage. The note evidences the debt. The failure to pay the debt permits the lender to sue on the note. A legal judgment on the note provides the lender with the remedy of foreclosing on the mortgage. The mortgage is technically security for the debt.

The readiness of a lender to grant you a mortgage depends on the competitive market. Government money policies, savings, and institutional surpluses all interplay on the market. When the market is tight, you pay more and receive less.

Mortgage brokers are used by commercial borrowers to place mortgages. Their fees are mortgage expenses amortized over the life of the mortgage. A mortgage broker knows the market and the fee is easily made up by the points saved on obtaining the minimum carrying charges. Only experienced real estate operators should approach mortgage brokers since the latter rarely like to deal with "walk-in" business.

The terms of a self-amortizing mortgage revolve around (1) interest percent, (2) length of time, and (3) proportion of the loan to the appraised value of the property.

Commercial mortgages usually pay mortgage-servicing costs on a quarterly basis. Your home mortgage is generally paid monthly. For our example, the servicing costs will be computed monthly. The difference in costs for a $100,000, 25-year mortgage paid in monthly installments at different rates is shown below:

$100,000 Mortgage	7%	7½%	8%	8½%	9%
Monthly payment	$ 707	$ 739	$ 772	$ 805	$ 839
Delta percent (increase over 7%)	—	5%	9%	14%	19%
Total payments (25 years)	$212,100	$221,700	$231,600	$241,500	$251,700
Interest cost (25 years)	112,100	121,700	131,600	141,500	151,700
Excess over 7%	—	9,600	19,500	29,400	39,600
Average annual cost over 7%	—	384	780	1,176	1,584

You can interpolate this table for any mortgage loan. For example, a $50,000 loan would require a payment of $354 per month at 7% for 25 years ($707 x $50,000 ÷ $100,000 = $354).

The table shows that a change in rates of ½% costs about 5% more in carrying costs. On an average annual basis the difference between a rate of 7% and 7½% is not significant enough to present a substantial detriment to accepting the loan at the $100,000 level.

If you require a mortgage, first ascertain the competitive interest rate (percent) for your area on the type of property you intend to purchase.

The length of time the mortgage will run directly affects the amount of cash outgo for mortgage-servicing charges. Using the same $100,000 mortgage, the table below shows how extending the term of the mortgage affects the monthly payments:

$100,000 MORTGAGE
SELF-AMORTIZING YEARS TO MATURITY
MONTHLY PAYMENTS

	20 YEARS	25 YEARS	30 YEARS	35 YEARS	40 YEARS
7%	$775	$707	$665	$639	$621
7½%	806	739	699	674	658
8%	836	772	734	710	695
8½%	868	805	769	747	733
9%	900	839	805	784	771

From this table you learn that the monthly carrying costs of a $100,000 mortgage, with an interplay of different rates and maturities, may be almost identical. For example, using $775 as the appropriate monthly carrying cost, your five mortgage options are:

1. 7%   for 20 years ($775)
2. 8%   for 25 years ($772)
3. 8½%   for 30 years ($769)
4. 9%   for 35 years ($784)
5. 9%   for 40 years ($771)

The third element of the mortgage is the proportion the lender will advance against the appraised value of the property. For dwelling units the percentage is about 80%. Thus, if your house is appraised for $70,000 (not your purchase price), the mortgage will lend you $56,000. The higher the risk, the lower the borrowing percentage and the more cash you must invest in the property. Using an 8½% mortgage for 25 years, the following table shows how the monthly carrying charges vary as the percentage declines. (The appraised value of the property is $125,000, and the mortgage value at 80% is $100,000.)

80%	75%	70%	65%	60%
$100,000	$93,750	$87,500	$81,250	$75,000

Monthly carrying charge

$805	$755	$705	$654	$604

You will notice that there is a relationship between long-term interest rates on savings accounts and the mortgage market. Currently the 10-year savings bank interest rate is 8.17% (effective) and residential mortgages in many areas are costing about 8.50%. The spread of .33% covers the savings bank's overhead, profit, and risk. As mortgage rates increase, you can expect savings bank rates to also increase.

A mortgage can be obtained with a fixed quarterly amortization plus interest on the unpaid balance of the loan. The carrying costs of this mortgage decrease as the loan matures. This kind of mortgage does not require monthly payments and is usually reserved for large commercial projects.

"Balloon" mortgages are self-amortized over a longer period of time than the maturity of the loan. Thus, a 25-year amortization schedule might apply to a 10-year mortgage. At the end of the tenth year the borrower must pay off the "balloon" or refinance the mortgage. See below:

1. 25-year amortization schedule

2. Mortgage due in 10 years

3. Mortgage face: $100,000

4. Interest percent: 8½%

5. Monthly payments: $805

6. Therefore, amount paid off in 10 years: $18,230

7. "Balloon" at end of tenth year: $81,770

In the foregoing example it seems difficult to understand how at the end of 40% of the time period only 18% of the principal has been paid. The reason for this is that in the early years, the self-amortizing mortgage's interest factor is charged against a higher unpaid balance. Since the payments are constant (the same each month), the principal amount due reduces itself slowly over the first 40% period of the mortgage. Therefore 72% (18 years) of the period must pass before the mortgage will reach the 50% level.

In some states the legal interest payable on a mortgage is less than the going mortgage market rate. In these states the legal interest limit applies to mortages made to individuals only. Any above-limit mortgage interest is classified as "usury." Since the usury statute does not apply to corporations, mortgages at the higher interest rates are usually made to "dummy" corporations. Tax cases have held that the corporation serves a business purpose and have not permitted a pass-through of rent and expenses to an operating partnership. If you are involved with a mortgage held by a "dummy" corporation you should seek professional advice.

MEETING THE DOWN PAYMENT

There are a few alternate means of meeting the down payment requirements on real estate if you have sufficient income and a good credit rating. You should consider (1) a personal loan for extended maturity, (2) a Federal Housing Administration (FHA) loan, and (3) a G.I. mortgage. A $5,000 personal loan for a 36-month period at an *APR* (Annual Percentage Rate) of 12% costs $166 per month to amortize. (You can apply for a personal loan at your bank.) In many families, the older members contribute to the down payment on the home for a young couple if there is no loss of savings interest. A $1,000 savings account for five years at the current 8.17% effective long-term rates results in an account balance of $1,481 at the end of the fifth year. If you borrow $1,000 on those terms you would repay $20 a month for five years. (This assumes that the lender replaces the money in the bank each month.) This is compared with $22 a month on a bank's personal loan.

There are several new programs designed to help you meet a level mortgage payment during the early years of your mortgage by making smaller monthly payments. These flexible plans may or may not be available in your state, but they are certainly worth asking your real estate lawyer about.

The savings banks of many states have established mortgage appeal boards which review rejected applications. This is done to prevent "red lining" areas. "Red lining" refers to the inability of a credit-worthy individual to obtain mortgage loans because of the geographic location of the real estate. Do not hesitate to use the appeals system if it is available in your state. If your state does not have an appeals board and if you believe your mortgage was rejected without cause, write to the president of the bank or financial institution setting forth clearly and factually why you believe the mortgage should have been approved. (You might also send copies to the state banking department and your state legislator.) If you are so inclined, write to your newspaper as well. Many individuals in similar situations have done so with successful results.

To assist you in obtaining a mortgage, Congress has enacted legislation which guarantees a certain portion of the loan. If you are having a problem placing a mortgage on a residence and your state's savings banks do not have a mortgage appeals board, call the local Federal Housing Administration for information on its mortgage guarantee program. If you are a veteran, communicate with the Veterans Administration about GI mortgages.

There is a relatively new type of mortgage called a variable-rate mortgage. The interest is fixed for a period (generally five years) and then increases or decreases, depending on the interest rates available at that time. Because they are new to the market, the impact of these variable-rate mortgages has not been measured. Conventional mortgage bankers appear to believe these mortgages have limited application in today's market. However, they have been introduced by several large banks which have obviously based their decision on marketing research. If interest rates are lower five years hence, variable-rate mortgages could become popular. The up-and-down swings in interest rates are limited, and since one-half of a point is worth 5% of savings in carrying costs, the possible savings may be helpful. On the other hand, a fixed approach to mortgage payments may be what most people prefer to pay.

Meeting Terms

In obtaining a mortgage a mortgage application is made by the borrower. Within three business days the prospective lender must furnish a statement of settlement (closing) costs. If the mortgage is approved, the lender also issues a mortgage commitment letter. This letter is usually valid for 30 to 60 days. Once a lender has issued a commitment letter, it is rare that there is a problem in obtaining the mortgage.

The *prepayment clause* of a mortgage allows you to pay off or refinance the mortgage with another loan from the same or a different financial institution. Many mortgages permit prepayment after one year without penalty. A prepayment penalty during the first year may cost up to 3% of the unpaid balance. This is additional compensation to the lending institution for its overhead cost involved in making the loan.

SECOND MORTGAGE

A second mortgage is a subordinate lien on property. It takes second place to a first mortgage. In the event of foreclosure, the first mortgagee receives the proceeds of sale to apply against the unpaid portion of its loan. Thereafter, the second mortgagee's lien becomes operative.

In commercial real estate, a purchase-money second mortgage is used frequently to cover a portion of the purchase price remaining after subtracting the first mortgage and the cash downpayment. The purchase-money second mortgage may mature in from five to 10 years. It bears interest of two or more points above a conventional first mortgage. It may or may not be self-amortizing. The commercial purchase-money second mortgage's terms depend on how badly the seller wants to sell and how badly the buyer wants to buy.

Frequently, manufacturing businesses requiring additional capital and without bank services will use a second mortgage on their factory premises to obtain needed working capital. This is last-resort financing, and the discounts and interest charged for this type of commercial second mortgage are extremely costly. A Small Business Administration loan, if available, is preferable to resorting to a second mortgage on a factory building.

A second mortgage is used in commercial real estate to finance additions to property which are not extensive enough to warrant refinancing a relatively cheap first mortgage.

A homeowner who requires additional funds for extensions to or remodelling his or her home (or for other needs) enters the secondary mortgage market. Although the second mortgage is subordinate to the first mortgage, in many states the second mortgage is serviced by a legal device called a "second deed of trust." The second deed of trust permits the second mortgagee to accelerate foreclosure in a period substantially shorter than for regular mortgages. On the other hand, failure to pay the payments on a first mortgage may result in a workout period (interest only and no principal payments). Then, if the mortgagor cannot meet the financial goals set during the workout period, the foreclosure proceedings are commenced. The actual foreclosure of a first mortgage may take up to one year. On the other hand, foreclosing on a second deed of trust can be accomplished in a period of several months.

Be extremely cautious about using a second mortgage. Consider refinancing the first mortgage, particularly if the mortgage market in your area is favorable. If the additional funds are to be used for tuition, consider applying for the low-interest tuition loans which are available in most states.

The *APR* for a second mortgage costs about 13% for a period of 10 years. (A conventional mortgage at this writing is about 8½% for 30 years.) Before you apply for a second mortgage, you should ask a first mortgage lender and your accountant for their opinions.

INFLATION

Probably no single factor is more responsible for the high cost of real estate than the inflation of the last two decades. Many economists attribute the primary cause of inflation to the progressive income tax system. Tax-bracket percentages increase every $2,000 to $4,000 of income. The government's share of the income increases in pyramid fashion as wages increase to meet higher living costs. Inflation continues as the value of your money decreases, and for this reason most of the profits in real estate are illusory. In fact, with higher income taxes on gains including recapture of depreciation and minimum tax on preferences, there are good arguments that the tax on long-term real estate gains is partially confiscatory. And obviously Congress agreed in 1978 by reducing the taxable long-term gains percentage. In addition the tax law permits tax-free swaps of real estate, installment recognition of gain, deferment of gain on the sale of a residence, and $100,000 exclusion of gain on sales of residences by persons age 55 and over.

Nevertheless, the financial returns from real estate are superior to those from most other investments. These financial rewards in terms of cash flow and future appreciation of property are sufficient to overcome the lack of liquidity of a real estate investment. The time between a decision to sell real estate and the final closing date may be months.

To understand how inflation operates, assume that you purchased a property 15 years ago for $10,000. The annual inflation rate was then 6%. Today's value of your real estate, only to cover inflationary forces, is almost $24,000. In other words, the past 15 years' inflation is 2.4 times the original cost, and therefore a tax on this "gain" is illusory. You really have gained nothing. At a sale price of $24,000 you have merely received back your original cost adjusted for inflation. You have only to check social security wage limits to verify the accuracy of this statement. For 1979, the annual social security wage limitation is $22,900, in 1963, the wage limitation was $4,800. The increase in these limitations reflect an annual increase of 10%. Most of this increase was required to meet inflation, since social security limitations only reached the $4,800 level in 1958 after being in existence since the 1930's.

In view of the rate of inflation and the taxes on real estate, you should be reluctant to sell income-producing property. Instead, you might consider a tax-free exchange. Tax-free exchange of real estate is used extensively by professionals to upgrade their real estate holdings, and there are enough complications involved to require professional assistance. However, the economic benefits are important enough to merit your careful consideration. In many instances you can transfer a portion of the unrecognized profits to your children through the use of trusts.

REAL ESTATE TAXES

In many states, an equalization board makes certain that all real estate market values are determined by the same formula. This prevents the unjust allocation of real estate taxes and state funding to communities. Before real estate taxes are assessed, the property values of a tax area (city, town, village, county, or other unit less than a city) are appraised. This may be done by a local authority or by private assessors. The total fair market value of the property is reduced to a listed or assessed value. For the tax unit, all listed value must be the same percentage of fair market value. In many states, all listed value must be at fair market value. The next step taken by some units is called "the grand list." This is a percentage of the listed value to which the tax rate is applied. For example, the recent tax bill for a vacation home showed the tax computation as follows:

1. Appraised fair market value $15,000
2. Total listed value (50% of FMV)   7,500
3. Grand list (1% of listed value)   75
4. Real estate tax rate

Town tax	$1.19
School tax	5.05
Highway tax	.44
Total tax rate	6.68

5. Tax due (3 x 4)   501

In some areas, town and school taxes may be computed separately, using a different listed or assessed value.

The tax rate is determined by dividing the tax levy by the assessed valuation. This may be expressed as the tax rate per $1,000. If the total town tax levy is $1 million and the assessed value of real estate in the unit is $30 million, the tax rate per $1,000 is $33.33. If your home were listed or assessed at $9,000, real estate tax for the year would be $300 ($33.33 × 9).

If you purchase or sell real estate during the year, the real estate tax adjustments on the closing statement must be added or subtracted from taxes paid when you are computing your deduction for income taxes.

Improvements to your house increase your tax assessment. (Most interior improvements, however, go unnoticed.) Many homeowners defer making visible improvements until the entire tax unit in which they reside is reassessed for fear that an outlay for an improvement (such as an additional room) may substantially add to the tax bill.

Proceedings to redetermine your assessment are always available if you believe you have been unfairly handled by the assessors. Many real estate lawyers will appeal assessments for a small fee plus a contingency. That is to say, if they are successful in reducing your assessment, they receive a portion of the tax savings. (The contingency runs about 50% of your tax savings over the following two years.)

Before you move into an area you should consider the effect of the school population on your tax bill. If your children have finished school or if they will be finished shortly, an older area probably has a more stable school tax rate. (The school tax in new developments is likely to increase substantially as young couples begin to raise families.) An area planning industrial expansion presents a paradox. Inviting industry to the area provides jobs, and the industries pay taxes in the area. On the other hand, most jobs in industry attract married workers with children, so the educational plant will require expansion if there is any new influx of workers to the area. School taxes will then increase.

When buying a home in a new development, always verify independently the future real estate taxes with the local tax assessor. The builder cannot be relied upon to inform you of your correct future tax cost.

DEPRECIATION

Depreciation is a reduction of current income theoretically to reflect the loss in value of buildings, improvements, and other tangible property held for investment or business purposes over its useful life. For example, a building (excluding land) costs $100,000. Its useful life is estimated to be 20 years. The annual depreciation of this property would ordinarily be $5,000 ($100,000 ÷ 20 years = $5,000). This is *straight-line depreciation* because the charge-off is the same for each year of useful life.

There are accelerated methods of depreciation which result in a larger amount being charged to income in early years and declining each year. Generally, the depreciation charged is consistent with the tax law in effect at the time of acquisition or when the property went into service. The common declining-balance methods of depreciation are 200% (double) declining-balance, 150% declining-balance, and 125% declining-balance. *Declining-balance percent* refers to the ratio to straight-line depreciation. The various declining-balance methods are computed as follows for a property valued at $100,000 and whose straight-line depreciation allowance is $5,000 a year.

	200%	150%	125%
First year			
Cost	$100,000	$100,000	$100,000
Depreciation	10,000	7,500	6,250
Balance	$ 90,000	$ 92,500	$ 93,750
Second year			
Depreciation	9,000	6,937	5,859
Balance	$ 81,000	$ 85,563	$ 87,891
Third year			
Depreciation	8,100	6,418	5,493*
Balance	$ 72,900	$ 79,145	$ 82,398

Fifth year

Depreciation	6,561*	5,491*	4,828
Balance	$ 59,049	$ 67,719	$ 72,420

Tenth year

Depreciation	3,874	3,718	3,496
Balance	$ 34,868	$ 45,858	$ 52,448

Fifteenth year

Depreciation	2,288	2,518	2,532
Balance	$ 20,589	$ 31,055	$ 37,981

Twentieth year

Depreciation	1,351	1,705	1,834
Balance	$ 12,158	$ 21,030	$ 27,506
Depreciated cost	$ 87,842	$ 78,970	$ 72,494

*When accelerated depreciation is less than straight-line ($5,000 per year), you may automatically switch to the straight-line depreciation based on the undepreciated cost over the remaining life.

The method of depreciation chosen depends upon the type and condition of the property. You can always elect the straight-line method. The categories for declining-balance depreciation are below:

TYPE AND CONDITION	ACCELERATED METHOD
Residential property (new)	200%
Residential property (used, with useful life of at least 20 years)	125%
Other real estate (new)	150%
Other real estate (used)	None

There are special rules for depreciating capital expenditures made to rehabilitate substandard housing and historic buildings.

You may also use component-element depreciation. This method assigns various useful lives to each part of the interior and exterior of a building (e.g., the steel, elevators, walls, and so forth). An appraisal is usually made to determine the useful life of each component. The time and expense involved is usually not worth the effort unless large sums are involved. (This may be done in large apartment-house complexes.)

The useful life of the real estate is sometimes difficult to determine, even for a professional. One guide is the term of the mortgage. For example, if the only mortgage you can obtain is for a term of 15 years, you might consider electing a 15-year life. This is a short life for a building; however, a short life may be justified, particularly if the building is located in a decaying area. On the other hand, if the mortgage is for 30 years, you can still argue for a 20-year or 25-year life, depending upon the type of construction. This determination requires professional advice.

RECAPTURE OF DEPRECIATION

Property sold at a profit usually results in the taxation of the profit at the advantageous capital gains. On the other hand, to the extent that a portion of the gain includes excess depreciation, the gain is taxed at ordinary rates. *Excess depreciation* is the difference between the accelerated depreciation claimed up to the date of sale and the straight-line rate. The reduction of the capital gain by the portion of the depreciation deemed to be excessive is termed "recapture of depreciation." In other words, on the one hand you are allowed an additional deduction in the form of accelerated depreciation; on the other hand, when you sell the property at a profit you usually must recapture part of that profit as ordinary income. To remember all the recapture rules requires the "memory" of a computer. In general, real estate recapture rules apply differently to residential and nonresidential property. The years for which the depreciation was claimed and the period the property was held are also factors in determining the extent of the recapture. Recapture is limited to gain. If the property is held for 12 months or less, *all* depreciation is recaptured. For example, a building costs $100,000 (exclusive of land) in January, 1976. If its useful life is 20 years, the straight-line depreciation allowed would be $5,000 per year ($100,000÷20 years). However, if you were permitted to use accelerated depreciation, the 200% declining-balance depreciation would be $10,000 in 1976, $9,000 in 1977, and $8,100 in 1978 (see page 343).

The excess depreciation in each of the years would be as follows:

YEAR	STRAIGHT-LINE	200% DECLINING-BALANCE	EXCESS DEPRECIATION
1976	$5,000	$10,000	$5,000
1977	5,000	9,000	4,000
1978	5,000	8,100	3,100
Total excess depreciation for period			$12,100

The rules for recapturing this excess depreciation on residential rental property are extremely complicated. For further help, request IRS Publication 334, *Tax Guide for Small Business.*

IMPROVEMENTS

Your goals in accounting for improvements are different when dealing with your personal real estate as against investment property. Since tax deductions on your residence are limited to interest, real estate taxes, and casualty losses, your objective would be to increase the cost of your residence in order to reduce future gain. For investment or business real estate, your objective is to claim current deductions wherever possible.

In the first year of ownership of your home, most expenditures (e.g., painting, carpentry, landscaping, electrical work, and plumbing) may be considered improvements. After the first year, unless an expenditure increases the useful life of your residence, the amount is generally classified as a repair.

Because the new estate tax law (at present after 1979) requires your beneficiaries (even if your estate is not taxable) to use your basis (cost) for measuring gain or loss on a sale, you must maintain records showing dates, vendors' names, and amounts paid for all improvements.

SELLING REAL ESTATE

If in the year of sale you receive 30% or less of the selling price, you may elect to report the gain on the installment method. The balance of the sales price may be received over one or more additional years.

The installment method may be used on any sale of real estate where there is a gain other than the mandatory deferment in the case of a residence where there is a later reinvestment of proceeds. You report the gain on the sale over the period during which the proceeds are collected. You elect the installment sale by showing the computations on your tax return. (See COMPUTING YOUR NET WORTH, page 27, for a schedule showing how this gain is computed and reported for tax purposes.)

Under the tax law, notes paid in installments must bear interest of at least 6% per year. Otherwise, the IRS imputes 7% interest. This prevents making the entire sales price subject to capital gains rates. In other words, some portion of the deferred payments is interest and should be taxable at ordinary rates. The seller is required to receive interest on the unpaid debt.

Abandonment, foreclosure, and condemnation of real estate may trigger unfavorable tax consequences. Before becoming involved in any one of these proceedings, you should seek professional assistance. Timing is very important in dealing with these particular problems.

CASH FLOW WORKPAPER

Daniel and Louise Smith's operation of their vacation home as rental property serves as a guide to help you understand how to judge real estate as an investment. These workpapers are set up to measure the performance of an actual investment. The facts are as follows:

1. Property purchased December 15, 1973, fully furnished (land $7,500; building $25,000) $32,500

2. Original mortgage at 7½% for 25 years $26,000

3. Depreciation claimed annually on straight-line method over 25 years $1,000

4. Fair market value of property at 12/31/78 as per local comparable sales $40,000

There was no personal use of the real estate during the period of ownership. The visits were for inspection of the property prior to or following tenancy.

OBSERVATIONS ON CASH FLOW
AND NET INCOME OF VACATION HOME

The Smiths' vacation home is located in a resort area and was purchased as a real estate investment. The area is a year-holiday "playland," offering ski facilities in the winter and all sports at other times. The house is a three-bedroom chalet with oil heat and gas cooking facilities. The original purchase was made in the hopes of a cash return of approximately double

	1	2	3	4
	1974	1975	1976	1977
Rent Income	5500	5750	6100	6300
Expenditures:				
Real Estate Taxes	394	413	437	465
Repairs	378	287	387	125
Heat & Electric	754	785	793	840
Caretaker & Janitor	485	392	408	427
Gardening	412	210	203	231
Insurance	304	304	326	338
Advertising	268	254	215	197
Telephone	72	76	79	81
Supplies & Misc.	234	161	192	141
Inspection Trips	278	243	202	215
Total Expenditures Before Mortgage	3579	3125	3242	3060
Cash Flow before Mortgage	1921	2625	2858	3240
Less, Mortgage Servicing (Schedule)	2310	2311	2310	2311
Cash Flow for Year (Deficit)	(389)	314	548	929
Add Mortgage Principal Payments (Schedule)	371	399	430	463
Net Income (loss) before depreciation	(18)	713	978	1392
Less, depreciation	1000	1000	1000	1000
Net Income (loss) for year	(1018)	(287)	(22)	392
Tax Shelter (Difference between principal payments and depreciation)	629	601	570	537

Daniel and Louise Smith
Cash Flow and Net Income – Vacation Home
1974 through 1977

	1978
Rent Income	6700
Expenditures:	
Real Estate Taxes	486
Repairs	99
Heat & Electric	871
Caretaker - Janitor	472
Gardening	260
Insurance	346
Advertising	177
Telephone	84
Supplies & Misc.	146
Inspection Trips	237
Total Expenditures Before Mortgage	3178
Cash Flow Before Mortgage	3522
Less Mortgage Servicing (Schedule)	2310
Cash Flow for Year	1212
Add Mortgage Principal Payments (Schedule)	499
Net Income before depreciation	1711
Less, depreciation	1000
Net Income for Year	711
Tax Shelter (Difference between Principal payments and depreciation)	501

Daniel and Louise Smith

Analysis of Vacation Home Investment

December 31, 1978

	1	2	3	4
1. Did Investment return 15% per year?				
				Present Value
Cash Investment				
12/13/73 - Cost of Property		32500		
Less, Mortgage		26000		
Cash Paid for Property			6500	
Add Tax Adjustment at closing & other cash outlays			500	
Total Cash Investment - 1973				(7000)

Cash Flows (Deficit)

Year	Actual (see schedule)	Periods Owned	Present Value at 15%	
1974	(389)	1	(338)	
1975	314	2	237	
1976	548	3	360	
1977	929	4	531	
1978	1212	5	603	
Total Cash Flow	2614			1393

Cash Equity 12/31/78:

			Periods	
Fair Market Value		40000		
Less Mortgage (see schedule)		23837		
Cash Equity		16163	5	8036

| Net Present Value at 15% | | | | 2429 |

Answer: Yes, results are positive and, therefore, meet investment standards. (Actual over 21%).

	1	2	3	4
2(a) What was excess cash return over a savings account?				
(b) What was average return over years of ownership?				
(c) What is current cash flow return on original investment?				
(a) _Cash Invested at 7.75% Regular Rates (8.17% effective rate)_				
1973 – Future Value of Investment End of				
5th year– (invested	7000)		10367	
1974 – Future Value of Deficit End of				
5th year – (deficit	389)		533	
Future Value of Savings Account – 5th year				10900
Less, Cash Flow invested at 5.25% Regular				
Rate (5.47% effective rate)				
Year	Period	Cash Flow	Future Value	
1975	3	314	368	
1976	2	548	610	
1977	1	929	980	
1978	0	1212	1212	
Future Value of Cash Flow			3170	
Add, Cash Equity in Property			16163	
Future Value of Cash Return				19333
Excess Cash Return on Vacation Home				8433
(b) _Average Return_				
Cash Invested – Purchase		7000		
" " – 1974 Deficit		389		
Total Cash Invested			7389	
Future Value of Cash Return			19333	
Period owned – 5 years				
Average Annual Return (Compound interest)				21.21%
(c) _Current Cash Flow_				
Original Cash Investment			7000	
Current Cash Flow			1212	
Annual Return (Simple Interest)				17.31%

the then-current savings bank rate and an increase in value faster than the inflation rate.

Rentals are made for periods of not less than four weeks, with some tenants renting for an entire season. Tenants were originally obtained through advertisements in the Smiths' suburban newspaper as well as in the newspaper in the resort area. Each tenant supplies two personal references and makes a security deposit for damage claims of $200. If there are any damages, the bill is sent directly to the tenant for payment. The damage deposit check itself is returned to the tenant after the damages have been paid for. The Smiths usually inspect the home the day a tenant leaves. If this is not feasible, the caretaker makes the inspection and sends a report to the Smiths. The caretaker cleans the house, changes the linens, and prepares for each new tenant.

Each year, at the same time the income tax figures are being developed, the Smiths complete a statement of cash flow and net income for the vacation home. This record, which is different from the information required for tax purposes, shows the actual net cash inflow from the real estate. This cash inflow is then adjusted for mortgage principal payments (an addition), and depreciation (a subtraction) in order to arrive at the net income (or loss) for the year. The final net figure is the same as that reflected on the federal individual income tax return.

The figures for the past five years (1974 through 1978) are vital for the Smiths to understand their real estate investment. The wrong purchase terms and errors in operation will be clearly reflected by the figures. It is true many professionals in real estate know the figures on a piece of property so well that the accountants merely serve as a check on this knowledge. Nevertheless, these successful operators insist on verifying their mental accounting of the year's rents and expenses against the books of account. For example, in one case the fuel costs for the year were substantially higher than the operator estimated. A look at the bills showed that all were properly charged to the building. However, almost one-third of the bills lacked delivery signatures. In every case the operator himself had, at the time of paying the monthly fuel statement, received the back-up on delivery receipts. Being very busy, he had never realized that some of the delivery tickets were unsigned. Only when the fuel costs were compared with those from the prior year was it obvious that something was wrong. Fortunately, the operator had a sufficient number of open fuel bills at the time this "error" was discovered to offset the loss caused by the "phantom" deliveries.

The Smiths' investment objectives are not computed each year because it usually takes two to three years for the figures to begin to show constant trends. In addition, since an appraisal (usually done informally) is necessary to complete the picture, the study of the rate of return is sufficient on a five-year basis. This is true unless the figures begin to show negative trends such as constant reduction in the rent roll (income), or big-ticket items are replaced each year. A closer look more frequently than every five years should be made to decide whether or not to sell the property.

You must approach real estate with an investment objective. One approach is to require a risk-reward percentage. The Smiths decided that such a percentage should be 15%. If the total cash flow and appreciated value discounted on a compound-interest basis was somewhere around 15%, the Smiths would have reached their investment goal. Without an investment goal or a personal involvement in real estate, you should not consider a real estate investment. And unless you find the ownership of "bricks and mortar" satisfying in *more* than the financial sense, you will have difficulty in operating real estate.

The figures for cash flow, net income, and tax shelter all shown on the statement should be done each year. It is not necessary to rewrite the account titles every four years. If you use one sheet of four-column paper for your first four years and face this sheet with another sheet, drawing a line down the description column, you can use the open spread of two sheets of columnar paper for 10 years' figures. Unless you are a dealer, you should normally look to a minimum of a 10-year holding period before considering a sale or exchange.

Whether you develop your annual figures or transcribe them from an accountant's report, you must maintain your own annual *comparative* figures. These figures can also be used for a linear regression and for trend-line analyses (types of valuable statistical applications) discussed in the chapter, INTANGIBLE PROPERTY.

MORTGAGE AMORTIZATION SCHEDULE

Whenever you deal with mortgages, you must have an amortization schedule reflecting the allocation of each payment between interest and principal. The schedule shows the loan balance after the application of the last principal payment to the prior balance. This schedule is necessary to verify the correctness of the mortgagee's annual interest statement. Frequently, year-end payments are not posted by the mortgagee until the following year. Although the annual mortgage interest statement shows 12 payments, it may reflect a January payment from the prior year. Thus,

Daniel and Louise Smith
Amortization Schedule - Vacation Home Mortgage
Effective December 13, 1973

Rate - 7.50%, Term 25 years, 100 periods
Payment - $577.63 Quarterly
Loan - $26,000.00

	Payment No	Payment On Interest	Principal	Balance of Loan
1/15/74	1	487 50	90 13	25909 87
4/15/74	2	485 81	91 82	25818 05
7/15/74	3	484 09	93 54	25724 51
10/15/74	4	482 33	95 30	25629 21
Total 1974	2310 52	1939 73	370 79	
1/15/75	5	480 55	97 08	25532 13
4/15/75	6	478 73	98 90	25433 23
7/15/75	7	476 87	100 76	25332 47
10/15/75	8	474 98	102 65	25229 82
Total 1975	2310 52	1911 13	399 39	
1/15/76	9	473 06	104 57	25125 25
4/15/76	10	471 10	106 53	25018 72
7/15/76	11	469 10	108 53	24910 19
10/15/76	12	467 07	110 56	24799 63
Total 1976	2310 52	1880 33	430 19	
1/15/77	13	464 99	112 64	24686 99
4/15/77	14	462 88	114 75	24572 24
7/15/77	15	460 73	116 90	24455 34
10/15/77	16	458 54	119 09	24336 25
Total 1977	2310 52	1847 14	463 38	
1/15/78	17	456 30	121 33	24214 93
4/15/78	18	454 03	123 60	24091 33
7/15/78	19	451 71	125 92	23965 41
10/15/78	20	449 35	128 28	23837 13
Total 1978	2310 52	1811 39	499 13	

a current November payment would be the last one for the current year.

If you have mailed your payment check late each month and the mortgagee has posted it in the following month, use your records and not the mortgagee's for your tax return. Reduce the statement for last year's December interest payment posted in January and increase for this December's payment which was not posted in time. (Normally, you may obtain this information by calling the mortgagee and requesting to be supplied with the figures.)

TAX SHELTER

Mortgage payments reduce your cash inflow. The interest charge affects your income taxes. The principal payment increases your equity in the property. This is not a deduction. Instead of an amortization deduction, you are allowed a deduction for depreciation. The Smiths have chosen the simple straight-line depreciation, the useful life taken to coincide with the mortgage's length (25 years). The difference between the depreciation and the principal payments is the tax shelter. Each year the tax shelter is computed on the bottom of the cash flow statement. Multiplying the tax shelter by the Smiths' effective tax bracket (42% for 1978) results in an additional tax credit of $210. The cash flow exceeds the taxable income ($501 × 42% = $210). In the eighteenth year, this tax shelter will cross over and the Smiths will pay taxes on income in excess of the cash flow. Use of money for a deferment makes real estate so attractive as a tax shelter.

If the Smiths were to bank the tax savings for the first 18 years (the tax shelter cross-over point), the tax savings of $264 for the first year would be worth $1,085 at current savings bank rates. The $264 first-year tax saving is computed by multiplying the tax shelter of $629 by the Smiths' top tax bracket of 42%.

All of this is the result of depreciation allowed on both the cash invested and the mortgage. Land is excluded because it is not subject to depreciation. In cash terms, the Smiths invested $7,000 at the closing and the first year the depreciation was $1,000. This equalled 14% of the cash invested. If you add the tax loss and the negative cash flow, here is where the Smiths stood at December 31, 1974 and December 31, 1978:

Cash invested at closing	$7,000	
Add cash loss 1974	389	
Total cash loss		$7,389
Minus tax loss 1974	$1,018	
Times effective tax bracket	42%	
Minus tax savings		$428
Out-of-pocket cost 12/31/74		$6,961
Minus cash flows 1975–1978		3,003
Subtotal		$3,958
Add taxable income 1975–1978	$794	
Times effective tax bracket	42%	333
Out-of-pocket cash investment 12/31/78		$3,291

The above figures do not give effect, however, to two important elements of measurement: (1) the use of money, and (2) the future value of the property. In other words, standing alone, the fact that the Smiths are "into the deal" five years later for about $3,300 after taxes means nothing, except that it doesn't sound like much money as far as real estate is concerned. These figures are relative.

Real estate experts vary as to how they approach the concept of "worth." In the Smiths' case, the "yardsticks" are (1) an investment objective at the acquisition date viewed five years later; and (2) the results compared with leaving the money at long-term rates in a savings account.

INVESTMENT-RETURN OBJECTIVE

You have the benefit of hindsight when measuring investment-return objectives. The historic figures present the evidence on a factual basis. The Smiths have owned their property for five years and now they want to know what the "bottom line" is.

The investment-return objective is called the "risk-reward" factor. With savings accounts in their area of the country paying 8.17% effectively for long-term funds, an objective of about twice the savings bank rate (15%) appears to be an equitable "risk-reward" return.

The formula requires five years' information (from the date of acquisition) converted to the present value of money. In other words, what was the value on January 1, 1974 of $1 payable one to five years later at the rate of 15% per year? To make the example meaningful, $100 today is worth $100. Without the effect of inflation, $100 due a year from now is currently worth $86.96 at a 15% rate. The $86.96 is the present value of $100 due in one year.

Beginning with the $7,000 invested in December 1973, the cash flows for the years 1974 through 1978 are reduced to present value using the table on page 332. The final value is the property itself at present value. This is done by using an approximate fair market value. It is a guess based upon comparable sales of what the Smiths believe the property is worth. The mortgage at December 31, 1978 is subtracted from the fair market value. The result is the cash equity in the property. The present value of the cash equity is also added to the cash flows. The net results of subtracting the cash flow and cash equity from cash invested are a positive factor. Therefore, the investment objective of 15% has been achieved. A negative figure for the net present value would mean that the Smiths failed to meet their investment objective.

REAL ESTATE CASH FLOW VS SAVINGS ACCOUNT

Where investment objectives use hindsight or a present-value formula, the comparison of cash inflow with a savings account is a future-value problem. If the Smiths had left their money in the savings account, the compound interest at long-term rates for the 1973 purchase and the 1974 deficit would have resulted in a savings at December 31, 1978 of $10,900. On the other hand, the yearly cash inflow invested at regular savings rates at the end of five years would be worth almost $3,200. The $3,200 added to the cash value of the property (after deducting the mortgage) of about $16,200 results in a future value of the cash return of $19,300. This is over $8,400 more than the savings account balance at December 31, 1978 ($19,300 − $10,900). The $8,400 is the excess cash return.

The other computations refine the cash return on compound and simple interest bases. For the five years, the average annual return on a compound interest basis was over 21%. The 1978 cash flow on the original investment at simple interest exceeds 17% ($1,212 ÷ $7,000 = 17.31%).

The Smiths could have found the "bottom line" either through the investment objective (present-value) or cash-return (future-value) approach. Either example would have been sufficient to prove the point.

CONCLUSION

Unless you are a professional real estate operator, you cannot appreciate the "figures" until you have done them yourself. The examples for the Smiths should cover most real estate investments. Of course, you must make the final judgment about the risks involved in owning real estate. That is why for investment purposes, the strong suggestion is made for joint-venturing the ownership with an experienced operator. The "edge" this operator might require to put his or her money into the partnership is worth the reduction of the risk factor. There are many newspaper ads and books which tell you how to become a millionaire in a year or two through a few simple secrets of real estate investment; the prudent investor will realize that this is a tough game still best played by professionals.

11
TANGIBLE PROPERTY

TANGIBLE PROPERTY INCLUDES automobiles, refrigerators, television sets, and other material objects of a durable nature which have a useful life of three years or more. Certain household goods and clothing are excluded from this category either because their useful life is restricted or they are not "big ticket" items. This chapter will suggest when and where to buy what you need and will tell you how you can pay for these goods in a way that most effectively utilizes your cash flow.

There are certain background questions that you should ask yourself as you read. These questions should reflect your psychological and social needs as well as your purely material ones. For example, let's consider the purchase of a major appliance such as a stove. Before you run out to the first appliance sale you see listed, ask yourself some important preliminary questions.

Do you use a stove rarely or often? Does it simply take up space, or are you so passionate about cooking that your heart beats a little faster just looking at a stove? Do you use the oven often or never? Do you want a pilot light? (In this case, you may not care to consider the ecological dimension of the question, but every time you look at your gas bill, you may wonder why you need a pilot light.) Would it be worth the considerable extra cost to buy a professional restaurant-style stove?

Think about an automobile the same way. Do you really need a car? Suppose you live in the city and almost never leave the city except by bus, train, or plane. Would it make sense to use taxis and other forms of public transportation and rent a car for that occasional weekend in the country? Or would life be impossible without your own car?

We could go through dozens of questions about each piece of tangible property and not cover all the facts of your situation, so you should do this for yourself as the first step in thinking about major purchases. The slightest change in pattern could mean a major savings. First, try to see your needs clearly, then go ahead with the techniques described in the rest of this chapter.

AUTOMOBILES

Since automobiles account for the largest percentage in monetary value of any tangible property purchased by the average person, an understanding of the economics of purchasing is essential.

The beginning of the model year (the fall season) is the best time to buy an automobile for monetary and personal needs. The bargains at year-end clearances are more than offset by the lack of a difference in resale value and the inability to purchase the exact options you may really need.

Most successful dealers work on a unit profit per car. The dealer doesn't care whether you buy the $4,000 or the $7,000 model. Nor does the dealer really care whether you buy the all-inclusive option package or select individual items. The dealer wants to make x dollars per unit. At the beginning of the model year automobile manufacturers are anxious to move the new models out onto the streets. This is the time when you can get the most automobile for the least amount of money if you buy for your real needs.

Here are some important steps in buying: (1) never visit the dealer from whom you intend to purchase the automobile until you have researched the market and have all the facts and figures; (2) purchase a new-car guidebook to establish prices and options (buy the book that shows dealer's cost or work up all the costs yourself); (3) know your option package; and (4) prepare your own workpaper in order to be able to negotiate with the dealer.

Over 90% of the purchasers of automobiles know the exact model they desire. However, because few know their option package a tremendous amount of time is wasted negotiating with the dealer. The dealer makes his or her "extras" from the buyer who signs a contract, then before delivery, wants to change something such as an AM radio for an FM radio. This type of change costs you money.

Usually your local dealer is the best place to buy a new automobile. Unless the service department is known to be unsatisfactory, a difference of from $50 to $100 in price should not deter you from buying locally. The convenience of a nearby dealer usually more than offsets the slightly higher cost. While visiting other showrooms to ascertain models, options, and the financial aspects of your purchase, *do not become involved in negotiations where you have no intention of buying.* You will most certainly be the victim of what is called "low-balling." This is a practice used on "lookers" who, having no price with which to compare, think they are being offered a bargain. However, if the "looker" fails to make the deal immediately, that price is never available again. Automobile salespeople are tough negotiators and good performers. Don't waste their time if you are "just looking."

Before visiting your target dealer to make your actual purchase, make sure that you have worked out a price for the suitably equipped model you want. After you decide on the make and model, you are faced with the option package. In a medium-sized model, the dealer's cost of a typical option package runs about $1,000, which means the suggested retail price is about $1,300. If you upgrade or change any options *after* you sign the contract you can expect to pay almost retail for the difference. Compare your specific option needs with factory packages. You will usually find that the savings in a factory package are not comparable to selected options, but if the factory package approximates your needs, buy it. Except for air conditioning, automatic transmission, and power steering, the variations in the option packages make almost no difference in resale value. (Low mileage brings in more money at resale time.)

Don't worry about a new car which you buy in the fall and drive in rough winter weather. A spring cleaning and polishing will take off the street salt and other corrosives. There is little difference to be found in resale value between the first and last cars manufactured in a given model year.

The make of car you choose is a personal decision. Unless you are looking merely for transportation, buy an automobile from a manufacturer who you believe will be anxious to please a customer. One of the world's most luxurious automobiles has only limited acceptability among those who can afford it because of the manufacturer's failure to meet acceptable standards of service as set by medium-price competitors.

Price

Unless you are extremely limited in your cash resources, you should never base the purchase of an automobile on price alone. Reliability, service, styling, and convenience, are all important factors. Price may help you decide on the model, but it should rarely be the deciding factor in the make of automobile you purchase. Paying more for a car of substantially better quality and performance adds less than you might imagine to your total monthly payment. For example, at current financing rates, a $100 increase in the cost of an automobile means a monthly increase in payments of $3.36 on a 36-month loan and $2.67 on a 48-month basis. The $100 increase will cost you $21 more in interest for the 36-month loan and $28 more for the 48-month loan.

Assuming, therefore, that you have chosen the make, model and option package, the next step is to sit down with the dealer. Using your workpaper, determine a price which is acceptable to both parties. The dealer is working on a profit per unit of sales somewhere in the $350-to-$600 range. You will have to stand your ground to make the most satisfactory deal, but after your visit to other dealers you have at least one price to use for a yardstick. If you fail to convince your target dealer to accept your price, go to another dealer. The maximum you should pay your target dealer above the "yardstick" price is $100.

In general, a dealer's cost for the basic car is 80% of the suggested retail price. The option package costs the dealer about 77% of the suggested retail price. You will find that there is usually no markup on destination or delivery charges.

Financing

Currently, the credit affiliates of most automobile manufacturers offer as good a financing package as most commercial banks on the purchase of a new car. The *APR* (annual percentage rate), including life insurance, charged by one of the auto industry's "big three" is 12.83% for 36-month financing and 12.68% on a 48-month basis. The life insurance costs built into these rates for a $4,000 loan are $52.32 and $73.73. Use these rates as a guideline.

You may finance the entire purchase of a new car if your credit rating is satisfactory. You should already have computed your personal line of credit and you should stay sensibly within its limits. (Don't stretch it to the edge so that you have no further credit to fall back on.) Most buyers finance about 66⅔% of the cost of the car on either a 36-month or a 48-month basis. Here are the average costs of 24-month, 36-month, and 48-month financing on a $4,000 loan:

	24-MONTH FINANCING	36-MONTH FINANCING	48-MONTH FINANCING
APR	12.91%	12.83%	12.68%
Life insurance	$ 33.15	$ 52.32	$ 73.73
Finance charges	$ 564.53	$ 850.88	$1,140.51
Total payments	$4,597.68	$4,903.20	$5,214.24
Monthly payment	$ 191.57	$ 136.20	$ 108.63
Increase in insurance and finance charges	0%	51%	103%

If possible, always use the minimum-financing period in order to save money. It is true that a 48-month payment of $108.63 is 76% less than a 24-month payment of $191.57, but the increase in carrying the loan for double the period is 103%. The saving is $616.56 if you elect a 24-month payout over a 48-month payout. This is a savings of 13% on a loan of $4,000. The percentage differences are approximately the same for all amounts of financing, although charges increase as the loan increases.

The creditor's insurance offered with automobile financing increases the monthly financing charges:

NET LOAN OF $4,000

	24-MONTH FINANCING	36-MONTH FINANCING	48-MONTH FINANCING
Creditor life insurance	$33.15	$52.32	$73.73
Monthly cost	$ 1.38	$ 1.45	$ 1.54

The rates for this decreasing-term insurance are relatively inexpensive. If the owner dies during the payout period, the beneficiaries receive the automobile without any indebtedness. You should consider buying the creditor insurance as part of the financing package.

After the new models are introduced in the fall, many banks have special deals calling for a lower *APR*. By all means, time your auto purchase to coincide with these credit sales. The *APR* difference is your indication of the savings involved.

Used Cars

The new-car dealer is not really interested in your trading in an old car. A trade-in is, in most instances, wholesaled immediately to a used-car dealer. The dealer, in evaluating your used car, uses either the National Automobile Dealers' Association's *Official Used Car Guide*, published monthly, or a local auto price list, sometimes published weekly. There is very little financial maneuvering available to you in a trade-in. Unless time is of the essence or your old car is in poor operating condition, you should be able to make a much better financial deal by selling it privately.

When buying a used car, your first approach should be to look over the newspaper advertisements for a private seller. Many times you will find an excellent buy this way. Used-car dealers have, of course, a large selection, and that can save you time.

Never buy an automobile privately without a chattel mortgage search. If you live in a "title" state, all lien holders (lenders secured by the automobile) are indicated on the certificate of title. This is the transfer document of an automobile. If you live in a "non-title" state and are borrowing to finance the used car, your bank's loan department usually does a search. If your bank will not be searching for prior loans, you should make your own search. You will be personally liable to the bank whether or not there are prior liens on the car. Title searchers are listed in the telephone directory under "Abstractors" or "Titles Searched." The charges are usually about $20 for a search under the Uniform Commercial Code.

Whether you buy from a dealer or privately, have a responsible mechanic approve a used car before you purchase it. The mechanic will look for concealed accident damage and engine and transmission problems.

Servicing Your Automobile

If you have a problem with the structure or performance of your car which the dealer cannot—or will not—handle, notify the manufacturer at once. Arrange personally to meet the manufacturer's consumer representative at the dealer's premises. Prior to the meeting, you should prepare a complete written statement of the *facts*. If you are still unhappy with the representative's decision, write to the company's president. Enclose a copy of the statement of facts which were given to the consumer representative. But since the consumer representative has already indicated why the company cannot satisfy you, revise your statement of facts to cover those objections.

If you still do not achieve results and there is a small-claims court in your area, do not hesitate to sue the manufacturer. Do not threaten to sue, just go ahead and file a complaint. The manufacturer must use outside counsel at a minimum cost of $75 an hour. Unless you are really in the wrong, the chances are you will be able to negotiate a settlement.

There is a new program of which you should be aware. At this writing, the new program involves only General Motors and Ford, and in only a few areas of the country. If it is successful, it may well spread throughout the country. Under the program, customers with complaints regarding warranties or service from these companies have recourse to binding arbitration by a consumer appeal board. Ask around in your area about this program if you have a dispute you have been unable to settle through regular channels.

DURABLE GOODS

Durable goods such as major household appliances may be purchased by brand name or house name. Most of the nationally advertised brand-name appliances manufacture, under a different name, a line of appliances for the large chain stores. In fact, some national brand names may use the manufacturing facilities of a competitor for a similar product. For example, the Betamax home video cassette recorder (VCR) is made by the Sony Corporation. Sony also manufactures substantially all the parts for the Zenith VCR. The entire field of VCRs has cross-licensing and group manufacturing facilities. Brand names are marketing tools.

Always buy durable goods on the basis of the integrity of the manufacturer. Quality is a variable term. Thus, in a highly sophisticated electronic device, it is not unusual to have initial problems. In new models, the first assembly-line products may have "bugs" (problems or flaws). An inherent failure of quality refers to a manufacturing defect which becomes apparent only after a period of normal usage. A manufacturer should repair without charge any inherent failure of quality in its product, even if the problem arises after the termination of the warranty period. A well-known refrigerator's automatic icemaker on the first models operated for a six-month period before becoming defective. The manufacturer continued to replace icemakers for over two years although the normal warranty was for one year.

Local service managers come and go. Therefore, if you have a problem with a major appliance dealer, write directly to the company. If you are unhappy with the results, send a copy of your correspondence together with any additional comments to the Major Appliance Consumer Action Panel, 20 North Wacker Drive, Chicago, Illinois 60606. This panel has an excellent reputation for settling consumer complaints. If you are still unhappy, don't hesitate to use the local small-claims court to seek compensatory damages. You are a buyer in a buyer's market. Spread the word about your problem to your friends and neighbors. They will certainly hesitate to buy from that manufacturer. A former leading home-appliance manufacturer is no longer selling to consumers due to problems of quality and failure to service its product.

The following story illustrates how the local service department of a major appliance manufacturer can operate independently and mishandle consumer policy. A trash compactor, after a few years, failed to operate. A serviceman insisted on a $25 service charge merely to leave an estimate for a $130 repair. (A new compactor cost $225!) In other words, the local company decided to make a profit on *estimates*. Fortunately, the manufacturer, as part of its continual independent check on the efficiency of its service company, wrote directly to the purchaser. In the meantime the purchaser had bought a new compactor and would most certainly have chosen a different brand except for the space limitation. As soon as the manufacturer learned of the ridiculous situation of charging for estimates the service charge was refunded.

Major brands holding a leading position in the market do so through their integrity. If you have been satisfied over the years with a brand name, be careful of switching brands just because of styling changes. The next year's model of your present brand will usually be a further advance. If you expect integrity from a manufacturer you should return it with loyalty. It is not overstating the case to say that your loyalty is statistically vital to the success of any appliance manufacturer committed to product reliability.

Association of Home Appliance Manufacturers

The Association of Home Appliance Manufacturers has an excellent program for handling complaints from consumers who have exhausted all efforts with the maker. More important (and apparently little known) is their certification program for refrigerators and freezers. The Association will supply, for a small charge, their annual *Directory of Certified Refrigerators/Freezers*. The address is 20 North Wacker Drive, Chicago, Illinois 60606, [telephone (312) 236-2921].

The certification program guarantees to the public, by the presence of the AHAM certification seal, that the total refrigerated volume and total shelf area of a household refrigerator or freezer have been independently verified. Energy consumption is also independently verified. Since this certification "is open to all manufacturers, both members and non-members of AHAM, and to firms that market private brand models," you should look for the AHAM seal when purchasing any make. (All models manufactured by a participant must be rated.)

The Smiths' top-of-the-line refrigerator/freezer is a side-by-side automatic defrost. The AHAM Directory shows the following certified information about it:

REFRIGERATED VOLUME
CUBIC FEET

MODEL	FRESH FOOD	FREEZER	TOTAL	SQ. FEET SHELF AREA	ENERGY CON- SUMPTION KILOWATT- HOURS PER MONTH
G.E.—TFF24RV	14.93	8.57	23.5	27.2	161–177

Charts in the front of the AHAM Directory convert energy consumption for refrigerators and refrigerator/freezers, into costs at the rate of 4¢ per kilowatt-hour. The Smiths' model with a total refrigerated volume of 23.5 cubic feet costs between $5.50 and $8.50 a month to operate. This figure is not derived by multiplying 177 by 4¢ ($7.08), but by actual test methods. The Smiths' electric costs exceed 4¢ per kilowatt-hour. Based upon their latest electric bill, the maximum energy consumption for their model was about 10% of the entire household energy expense. The yearly cost is about $90. This model is one of the high electric users; on the other hand, the Smiths are very satisfied with its performance.

When you receive the AHAM Directory, compare the total refrigerated volume with the energy consumption of any model you are interested in purchasing. The model you like best with the least energy cost in your price range is the one to purchase.

Prices

The rules against compulsive buying are extremely important when buying big-ticket items. Durable goods or appliances are not only subject to periodic special sales, and discount houses flourish everywhere. Generally, you choose the make from past performance. If you are a house-brand purchaser, you can usually identify the manufacturer from the styling. House brands are acceptable if the model and price meet your needs.

You should study the current catalog of the brand name carefully. The next year's catalogs usually appear after Labor Day of the current year. Start with the top-of-the-line (most luxurious) appliance. This is the manufacturer's "dream" inasmuch as it gives you the best idea of the creative ability of the manufacturer in both styling and mechanics. If this is your choice, then make certain the measurements of the appliance fit your allotted space. Keep in mind, if you are financing the purchase at an *APR* of 12%, that each $100 of price costs you every month an additional amount:

PERIODS OF MONTHLY PAYMENTS

	12 MONTHS	18 MONTHS	24 MONTHS	36 MONTHS
$100 additional cost at *APR* of 12%	$8.88	$6.10	$4.71	$3.32

In order to determine which particular model satisfies your needs, use a four-column workpaper. On this paper, to the left list all the features of the top-of-the-line appliance. In alignment with each feature place an *X* in the first column to indicate all the features of the manufacturer's premier product, recording the discounted price at the bottom of the column. Heading the second column with another model which might also satisfy your needs; write an *X* next to its features. Do this for three or four possible choices. Study the workpaper and the prices to make your own determination as to whether the additional features of the top-of-the-line model are worth the price difference. Choose the appliance with the features you require at the price you wish to pay. (You cannot make a sound judgment without using the workpaper for comparison shopping.)

Are you satisfied that the additional features are worth the use of money required (based on a seven-year average life for an appliance)? If, on a seven-year life the additional total cost is $100 ($14.28 a year) you may consider this minimal. However, if you left the $100 on deposit, it would be worth $173 at the end of the seventh year. Thus, an extra $100 in appliance price costs you about $25 per year ($173÷7). If the appliance had a five-year life, the loss in money is $30 each year for the $100 additional cost. For a 10-year life the loss is $22 a year for the extra $100. (This is exclusive of financing costs.) If you believe the features in the top model meet your needs, and if the additional costs are within your cash flow, buy the model. But never make the decision without comparing models, features, and price differences.

If you want to compare brands and do not have catalogs available, you may purchase the *Consumer Reports Buying Guide*. The magazine *Consumer Reports* supplies helpful information on current major consumer products. It is felt that *Consumer Reports* tends towards the "spartan" life rather than the life of ease and comfort. You may sometimes disagree with its suggestions, but the magazine's integrity is indisputable.

Once you have decided on the make and model of the appliance you wish to buy, you have to negotiate the price. Discount stores generally have three prices: (1) the ticket price; (2) what the "other person" pays; and (3) what *you* pay. In the first instance, do not buy a brand-name appliance for more than 80% of the manufacturer's suggested retail price *unless you have absolutely no other choice*. The store (except for its house brands) is only a delivery system for the brand-name appliance. The manufacturer actually provides the service.

When you enter a discount store, always tell the first salesperson who approaches you that you are "just looking." (You *are* looking—in this case, for the salesperson who appears to have knowledge and seniority.) The ulterior motive is to save money. After you have spotted the "right" salesperson, wait your turn, then walk over to that person. State *quietly* but clearly the make and model you want to buy. Then, in an even lower, confidential tone, "What is your lowest price?" If the price is 85% or less of the already discounted ticket price, you should make the purchase immediately. If the selling price is not at least 85% of the already discounted ticket price (and after the salesperson has seen your workpaper), leave.

Go for a cup of coffee and ponder your next move. You have settled two of the three variables, the make and model. Only the price remains. You now have two choices: (1) return to the store for a second round of negotiations, or (2) move to another discount store and start again. If renegotiating works successfully just three out of 10 times, you are an adept buyer.

If you are buying a house-brand appliance, the ticket price is usually the final price. However, this price may be the same as "your price" at the discount store. Use the same workpaper to compare a house-brand appliance with the similar name brand. (The features may be slightly, but not significantly, different.)

Appliances may also be purchased with a credit card, but if they are to be financed over a period of time, you should refinance immediately at a bank. The difference in financing charges is substantial.

$500 APPLIANCE PURCHASED WITH
36-MONTH FINANCING

	18% APR CREDIT CARD	12% APR BANK
Monthly payments	$ 18.08	$16.61
Finance charges	$150.88	$97.96
Savings in finance charges	$0	$52.92
Delta percent savings in finance charges	0%	35%

REPLACING TANGIBLE PROPERTY: TIMING

Obsolescence is a state of change that makes a product out-of-date. In business, obsolescence is the prime reason for replacing machinery and other durable goods. Some degree of obsolescence occurs annually in almost every consumer product. At the consumer level, the prime reason for replacement is the cost of repair exceeding the replacement ratio. This means, simply, that if a repair is estimated to cost over 15% of the replacement cost of an appliance, you should consider buying a new appliance. For example, a five-year-old television set currently replaceable for $300 (discounted price) which requires $45 or more in repairs is a serious contender for a charitable gift and replacement with a new model. Of course, if you received only five years of use before a $45 repair bill was necessary, you might consider replacing the set with a different make. For normal usage, your minimum period before the repair-to-replacement ratio of a major appliance becomes operative should be five years and more likely seven years. This is based on the performance of top-of-the-line models in an average household. The first time you are faced with a repair bill over the 15% range, particularly if obsolescence is also a factor, you should replace the item.

Since most retailers have some inventory problems (space, cost, and lack of delivery), the only way to be sure of making an intelligent replacement choice is to examine the full range of models contained in the manufacturer's catalog. Write directly to the manufacturer of your favored make for its latest catalog.

If you subscribe to *Consumer Reports*, also check their evaluation of the appliance. Many criticisms cited in *Consumer Reports* are corrected in later production of the same model. However, you cannot be certain that the shortcomings have been corrected unless you are dealing with a well-known brand; and even then it is your responsibility to weigh the *Consumer Reports* findings against your own common sense. If the manufacturer does not have a catalog for your personal use, visit a retailer and ask to use their catalog on the premises. Do your workpaper either at home or at the store. A $300 purchase deserves 15 minutes of effort with a pencil and paper to determine whether it is worth buying.

The Warranty

Your appliance may come with a warranty card packed inside requesting you to mail it back (with *you* paying the postage) in order to "register" the item. Generally, this is a marketing research tool for the manufacturer. When a maker charges you $500 for an appliance and does not supply a postage-paid card, you should be of no assistance in answering various marketing questions. If you have to pay the postage, the warranty registration number is unimportant. In fact, the warranty is supported by your bill of sale, so don't be fooled by such statements as "Warranty void if not registered." Any manufacturer refusing a free repair within 30 days of purchase because you fail to mail back your card (at your expense) will not be in business long. Most manufacturers permit their service departments to use their own discretion in applying warranty standards, particularly when repairing top-of-the-line models.

The bill of sale for a major appliance is actually your proof of purchase. Keep the bill of sale in a separate folder. The warranty card is a unilateral commitment by the manufacturer as to what the company will do for you. Don't waste your time reading the warranty card unless after an extended period (two years or more) a defect occurs. In some cases a liberal warranty may extend your rights to free or discount repairs beyond the usual period. Since repair charges are so expensive, if you believe you have been unfairly treated, write to MACAP. (Page 365.)

Your chart of accounts provides an account for repairs. Review the specific repair charges for each appliance annually to determine if there is a continual problem with a particular manufacturer's products and whether the time has come to change brands.

Do not argue with a serviceman about service fees. Pay the bill and take up the problem with his employer. Beware of a manufacturer that wants to make its service department a "profit center." You will have trouble obtaining a fair deal on service calls.

Complaints

Some 30 years ago, a business-school professor assigned a student to compose a "paranoia-type" complaint letter to be sent to all major toothpaste manufacturers. The complaint stated that a hair had been found in a freshly opened tube of their toothpaste. Each week, replies were read in class. In most instances the manufacturer denied the possibility of a hair being found in that company's tube. Only one company wrote a letter expressing dismay that the hair might have been found in its product. This manufacturer declared that a full investigation was taking place, and hoped that the customer would allow the company time to make its own determination of the true facts. The company also stated that a replacement tube was being sent under separate cover. The letter thanked the customer for his or her helpfulness and hoped for continued loyalty.

Two weeks after the last response from the toothpaste manufacturers was received, the same student was required to write another letter to the companies apologizing for the complaint and stating that the hair had come from a hairbrush that had been accidentally placed beside the open tube by the writer's spouse, who then replaced the cap on the tube. The guilty spouse had "confessed" to this misdemeanor later. Most of the companies failed to respond to this letter and those which did evidenced no appreciation for being offered the solution. However, the same manufacturer who was investigating the problem wrote, thanking the customer, saying that the investigation could now, happily, be terminated. This company also sent another free tube of toothpaste for the courtesy of having been informed about what had happened. Today, its toothpaste is the largest selling brand in the country. A manufacturer's attitude that the customer is *almost* always right is the key to continued success.

If a manufacturer fails in its obligation to you, it is failing everyone. You owe a duty to yourself as well as to other consumers to pursue whatever complaint you may have in a deliberate fashion. Do not hesitate to tell your complaint to friends and associates. This is good for your mental attitude and it "blackballs" the unsatisfactory product. If your complaint involves a monetary amount of $50 or more, spend the time to use the small-claims court in your city. Your efforts will benefit all consumers.

NET-LEASE INVESTMENTS

Until the Tax Reform Act of 1976, there were alternative financing arrangements for airplanes, railroad "rolling" stock, computers, and other high-priced durable goods. The term describing this type of transaction is "net-lease." Formerly, the use of high leverage (borrowings) together with accelerated depreciation and the investment credit, made durable goods or tangible property a very popular tax shelter. Unfortunately, due to the intense competition among buyers to participate in these pre-1976 shelters, the economics other than tax deferment were not favorable compared with other risk-reward ventures. However, since the investor was not personally liable for the borrowings, the only substantial disadvantage was the early recapture of any tax benefits through a foreclosure.

Before 1976, many of these net-lease investments concerned marginal lessees to whom conventional financing would never have been available. These deals were generally bought by highly paid professionals and executives who considered the time and use of a tax dollar more important than the investment upside. The 1976 Tax Reform Act drastically changed this situation.

Because of the "at risk" rules, these tangible property investments are not flourishing currently. The "at risk" rules require you, the investor, to be *personally* liable on the borrowings for almost all types of property other than real estate. If someone tells you that a proposed deal is exempt from the "at risk" rules because of using third-party guarantees or U.S. Treasury Bonds, you should not invest without an IRS Ruling Letter or a clear, positive, and unequivocal written statement from a law firm that specializes in taxes. The IRS now has agents who are specialists in tax shelters, and the present form of the partnership return makes it easy to select tax-shelter transactions for audit.

Nevertheless, there are small private placements in growing businesses where an opportunity to invest in property combined with stock warrants may become available. The stock warrants allow you to purchase a specific number of shares in the company at a fixed price for a period of time. Since the warrant price is usually very low and the time period may be for periods extending up to five years, there is an opportunity, with warrants, to watch a small company grow before buying into it. These investment opportunities for leasing machinery and other tangible property to new businesses are highly speculative. Since any *bona fide* business presumably has many conventional sources of financing available, you must realize that you are taking risks if you become a lessor.

Generally, these investments can be found through an accountant, because accountants are usually aware of local business conditions and investment opportunities. The advisable approach is to make this kind of investment on a syndicate (joint venture) basis. Usually four to 10 persons are involved; and all investors put up equal shares, except for the finder who generally receives some "edge" over his or her cash investment. The group may either operate as a general or a limited partnership. Do not finance a tangible property acquisition on your own unless you yourself have professional experience. Your cash flow on these deals, aside from tax considerations, should be at least twice the savings-bank rate for long-term money. This is particularly true since there is usually no available market in which to resell your interest. On the other hand, if the deal is sold to you as a tax shelter, the cash flow is usually nominal. You must therefore be absolutely certain that the tenant (lessee) has an excellent business rating.

TANGIBLE PROPERTY: INTRINSIC OR ARTISTIC VALUE

Tangible property includes articles or collections having either artistic or intrinsic value, such as jewelry, paintings, antiques, rare books, coins, and stamps.

Within the last 10 years, these articles have generally risen in value far ahead of inflation. Their liquidity or cash potential has also greatly increased in recent years through auction houses, advertising media, and specific conventions. However, investment in articles of artistic or intrinsic value requires special knowledge, and a collector must rely on their increase in profitability through capital appreciation rather than on income.

You should measure this future value against that of a savings account. Thus, $1 invested today in a savings account will have a value in 10 years of 2.2 times its present worth excluding inflation. In collecting valuable items, you should expect at least to *triple* your investment within 10 years. Of course, if you collect for personal pleasure, you would not use a financial "yardstick" in evaluating worth.

AUTOMOBILE ACQUISITION

Daniel Smith acquired a new automobile in October, 1978. The Smiths made a better profit on their old automobile by selling it privately. The Smiths completed substantially all of their purchase workpaper before they set the final price for their new car with the dealer. The workpaper was prepared from the dealer's price list and from suggested options. The dealer's cost, of course, is no secret, and Mr. Smith was able to find out the exact cost of the basic automobile from a new-car guidebook. *Consumer Reports* publishes the cost factors for most automobiles in its annu-

		2 Suggested Retail Price *	3 Dealer's Cost *	4 Smiths' Cost *
	Date Delivered – 10/5/78			
	Model – Oldsmobile			
	Delta 88 Sedan (1979)			
1	Basic Automobile (Cost % = 79.8%)	5559	4437	
2				
3	Options:			
4	Window, S-Ray Tinted	76		
5	Molding, Door Edge	18		
6	Air Conditioning, 4 Seasons	581		
7	Axle, 2.56 Ratio			
8	fr 78×15, Tires W. wall (Radials)	94		
9	Convenience Group (Lights in glove			
10	comp't, trunk + hood)	34		
11	Molding, Body Side	48		
12	Window Defroster, Elec. Rear	94		
13	Mirror, Remote Control	16		
14	Engine, 260 V-8 2 bbl.	100		
15	Compaticolor, Carmine			
16	Tire Tax Adjustment			
17	Radio	96		
23	Total Options (Cost % = 77.0%)	1157	891	
24	Total	6716		5328
25	Add: Factory Delivery + Handling			13
26	Destination Charges			257
27	Total Manufacturers Charges			5598
28	Add: Dealer Preparation		–0–	
29	Dealer's Profit		402	402
30	Total Automobile			6000
31				
32	Add: Sales Tax (7%)			420
33	Total Cost of Automobile			6420
34	Less: Deposit		300	
35	Trade-in Allowance		–0–	300
36	Net Cost			6120
37	Less, Financing			4000
38	Cash Required at Delivery			2120
39	(* These prices, of course, are subject to change).			

al Auto Issue. The ratio of suggested retail price (sticker price or list price) to cost is called the *cost factor*. If the listed price is $5,000 and the car cost the dealer $4,000, the cost factor is .80 or 80% ($4,000 ÷ $5,000).

OBSERVATIONS ON THE AUTOMOBILE WORKPAPER

The Smiths' basic automobile cost the dealer approximately 80% of the sticker price, though this will vary somewhat according to the model. Federal law requires that the suggested retail price to be affixed by the manufacturer to a side window of every new car. (Thus the term "sticker price.") The options' cost ratio was 77%. The "Big Three" U.S. automobile manufacturers are somewhere within the cost factor of 80% for the basic car and of 77% for options. The differences between the makers are minimal.

In the Smiths' workpaper the actual percentage was available. If the 80% factor had been used for the cost factor, the difference in cost would have been an additional $10 (See page 375.)

The selected options were chosen from the dealer's "Specs Book" and the dealer's suggestions. The dealer's "Specs Book" contains, as you might imagine, all the specifications about the models offered. More importantly, all of the standard and available options are listed. The manufacturer's suggested retail prices are included. A fuel-economy guide to each model is included, and the engine transmission is shown in chart form. The standard accident-safety equipment is outlined in the "Specs Book," as is the theft-protection equipment. The book contains the answers to many of the questions you have about buying a particular model. This book is available either through the dealer or by writing to the manufacturer.

Most successful dealers are not interested in making a profit on your option package at the time you price your car. However, if you later change an option, the dealer will try to obtain as close to the list price on the new option as possible. Thus, it is important for you to prepare your list of options before you seriously negotiate for the automobile.

The option package you select is the key to proper buying. The Smiths left room on their workpaper for any additional options they might select when they discussed their ideas with the dealer, but most of their workpaper was complete before the serious negotiation started. (The Smiths already had their essential financial information, based on guidebooks and a visit to another dealer.)

The factory delivery, handling, and destination charges do not contain a profit factor. You are billed the amount that the dealer pays. The price-spread a dealer is seeking when selling an automobile includes the preparation ("prep") charge. A dealer who adds this charge separately should be required on negotiation to reduce the amount of his profit.

The Smiths' local dealer offered them the automobile for $6,000. (Please note this was the price at the time this chapter was written, far in advance of October, 1978.) This resulted in a gross profit for him of $402 or 6.7%, a very reasonable percentage when you consider the capital and labor involved in a dealership. (The competitiveness of the automobile industry is what keeps the dealer's profit margins relatively low.) The gross profit must be reduced by the dealer's general and administrative expenses before the net profit is realized. This is another reason why a dealer wants you to argue any "out-of-warranty" repairs directly with the manufacturer.

The Smiths ordered their new car just after the new models were shown to the public. The dealer was anxious to start the new-model year on an optimistic note. A quick turnover puts the new models on the streets immediately. We have already mentioned the "plus" factors of buying a new automobile early in the model year.

The sales tax paid on an automobile is a separately itemized deduction on your tax return. Use this in addition to the general sales-tax table for your purchases. The sales tax is deductible even if you finance your entire car. The transaction is treated as if you personally borrowed the money from the lender and paid the dealer for the total automobile, including the sales tax.

Your original deposit is deducted from the total cost of the automobile. If the Smiths had traded in their old car, the allowance would have been subtracted from the total amount due, but they sold their old automobile privately.

After deducting the deposit, the balance due on the Smiths' automobile was $6,120. The Smiths wanted to finance $4,000 of the cost. Local banks were charging an *APR* of 13.38% for a 36-month automobile loan. The manufacturer's credit affiliate was offering a financing of $4,000 at an *APR* of 12.83%. The *APR* included a $52.32 premium for decreasing-term life insurance. The difference in *APR*s is a savings over the three-year period of about $40. If you want to finance more than 67% of the cost of an automobile, your personal credit line will have to support the difference. A lender will increase your financing, depending on your credit rating.

The Smiths' financing charges for their automobile at an *APR* of 12.83% are $850.88 plus the life insurance premium of $52.32, making a total of $903.20. The monthly payments on the car are $136.20 ($4,000 + $903.20 = $4,903.20 ÷ 36 = $136.20).Since the financing charge added $903.20, the total automobile costs $7,323.20. In other words, the financing increased the cost by over 12%. Assuming that the Smiths left the $4,000 in the bank at current long-term rates and were able to pay the monthly installments from discretionary income, the following interesting financial results would occur;

Savings bank balance at 8.17% effective rate on $4,000 at the end of third year is worth	$5,063
Minus cash originally deposited	−4,000
Interest earned over 3 years	$1,063
Minus finance charges paid on car	−903
Net additional earnings by financing	$ 160

By using current cash flow for paying off the car, at the end of the third year the Smiths have an automobile worth about $2,700 and $5,063 in the bank. Of course, there are other factors to consider. If the Smiths were systematic savers, the results would work out differently. In other words, if the Smiths paid the $136.20 into a savings account each month at long-term rates, they would have $5,573 in the bank at the end of the third year plus an automobile worth about $2,700. Thus, they would be ahead by at least $500 by not financing the automobile. That is to say, $4,000 left on deposit, at a compound interest rate of 8.17% would be worth $5,063 at the end of the third year. On the other hand, $136.20 deposited in equal monthly installments would be worth $5,573 at the end of the third year. The difference is $510. Of course, if you don't have $4,000 in the bank, you must finance the car. The understanding of how free choices can affect your net worth carries over to all financial concepts.

CONCLUSION

Don't hesitate to take your pocket calculator with you when you buy an automobile. It is your best ally in working with a mass of numbers and options, and it will bring calm to a stormy negotiating session. All you have to do is to ask to be permitted to "work out the numbers." Playing with the keys of the calculator will usually restore the atmosphere of give-and-take to the bargaining session.

12

INTANGIBLE
PROPERTY

YOU CANNOT TOUCH OR FEEL INTANGIBLE PROPERTY. Money has no physical dimension. It is evidenced by a document (e.g., currency, savings bankbook, checks). Any personal investment asset lacking spatial dimensions is intangible property. Intangible property for investment purposes includes life insurance, bonds (federal, state, local and corporate), stocks, options, commodity futures, and mineral leases. Although a real-estate partnership interest is evidenced by an agreement, the underlying asset is real property and is therefore tangible.

Money is legal tender for the payment of money debts. The value of the money is determined by the value of the amount outstanding in relation to the quantity of goods and labor available to spend the money. Thus, money's value is supported by a country's industry and agriculture. Money is a medium of exchange issued by a sovereign government.

Article I, Section 8 of the U.S. Constitution provides that the Congress shall have power:

To coin Money, regulate the Value thereof; and of foreign Coin, and for the Standard of Weights and Measure.

In classical times, most money was gold or silver coin, its purity evidenced by the emperor's head or seal impressed upon its surface. At the beginning of the Republic, Congress issued gold and silver coins. When it also issued paper money, Congress had to promise to redeem it on demand with gold or silver. This promise was necessary because history teaches that governments debase money, thereby eroding savings and values. If you visit a museum with a fine collection of ancient gold coins, notice that gold coins of the same government and denomination became smaller as time passed.

The government's promise to redeem paper money with gold or silver was broken during the Civil War. The promise was restored and maintained until 1933 during the great depression. At that time, President Franklin D. Roosevelt, with the authority of Congress, determined that U.S. money would not be redeemable in gold. By Executive Order, the President gradually raised the price of gold from $20.67 an ounce to $35 an ounce. Only foreign central banks were permitted to obtain gold for U.S. money at the $35 price.

The right to redeem certain money in silver remained until the 1960s when President Lyndon B. Johnson and Congress terminated this redemption privilege. Even after President Johnson's action, the value of the U.S. dollar was still supported worldwide by the right of foreign central banks to exchange dollars for gold at the fixed $35 an ounce price. President Richard M. Nixon removed the last link of the dollar to gold or anything tangible. At this writing, gold sells for $182 per ounce on the London market.

With all this in mind, consider whether your paper money will become virtually valueless in the long run. If you think this, you must find alternative ways to protect your current savings from debasement.

Overseas, the value of U.S. money is influenced by many factors including trends in international trade and investment. The buying and selling of various countries' money by U.S. and foreign banks creates the "Foreign Exchange Market." The value of the dollar abroad is reflected in this market. The value of the dollar overseas increases with exports, decreasing inversely with imports. This is particularly true because of the large cost of imported oil. Large-scale foreign investments in this country help increase the value of our money.

Most governments use the private money market to raise money. The competitive market system is considered to be the most efficient way to borrow large sums at the least cost. Foreign and domestic governments use the market to finance projects and meet other short-term and long-term government needs. You normally participate in this market through bank accounts. A secondary market is maintained to allow corporations and individuals to purchase these government obligations. The primary market, or the first group, buys bonds from the issuing governmental body through syndicates or groups of investment bankers. The resale is termed the secondary market.

This chapter deals with intangible property as a form of investment or speculation. Such investment requires a relatively long-term holding period. It may result in both capital appreciation and income. A speculation is usually a short-term position with the opportunity for large profits (or large losses) for the amount of money invested. An investment is generally not so upward or downward in price movement as a speculation.

What one businessman may view as an investment, an older person living on a fixed income may consider to be speculation. The line between investment and speculation cannot be precise.

For your purposes, usual investments in intangible property include savings accounts, bonds, and stocks of non-speculative grade. Some everyday speculations in intangible property are speculative grade stocks, options, commodity futures, other future contracts and mineral leases. To know more about the recent history of different investment vehicles on some comparative basis and in order to appreciate the effect that inflation has on investment positions, you must look to averages with the benefit of hindsight. The following chart indicates the approximate present worth, as a result of inflation, of a $10,000 investment made about 10 years ago:

PRESENT WORTH OF $10,000 INVESTED IN 1967
(BEFORE TAXES)

INVESTMENT CHOICE	TODAY'S VALUE (INCLUDES EARNINGS MINUS INFLATION)
Savings account	$ 9,400
Bonds	10,400
Common Stocks	7,000
Home	11,800
Office building	12,000
Farm	15,600

The above is based on market averages and does not consider the ability to choose particular investments with a market strategy. Inflation eats away at real income. The consumer price index in the middle of 1978 is over 180 compared with 100 in 1967.

The chart shows clearly the depreciating value of money in an inflationary period. Without inflation, $10,000 deposited 10 years ago in a savings account at 6% interest *should* be worth $17,900 today, but inflationary forces have reduced the money value of the savings to $9,400, a decrease of over 47%. Inflation over a period of time has an astonishing effect on decreasing the value of money. Many economists now believe that our government tax policies are an affirmative factor in causing double-digit inflation.

Today's dollar measured 10 years from now (future value) ranges from a predicted high of 70¢ to a low of 50¢. Ordinarily at today's interest rates, $100 deposited in a savings account would be worth $219 in 10 years. With the inflation predicted, the future value of $100, *including* interest, would be $110 to $153, or a decrease of between 30% and 50% over noninflationary money.

Progressive tax rates slowly pyramid the bite taken by inflation by disproportionately reducing the take-home pay. At the $300-a-week wage level, a 5% increase leaves approximately 4.7% in take-home pay. The balance of .3% is paid over in withheld taxes to the Federal and State governments. The withholding-tax percentage, including social security at $300 a week with four withholding tax allowances, is about 21%.

Although a single 5% cost of living raise may not move a person into a higher bracket percentagewise, successive cost-of-living raises *reduce* the take-home pay by increasing the withholding tax rates in slow increments. The rate at which you pay taxes on an extra $1 of income is always higher than the average tax rate on all of your income. There are strong arguments in inflationary periods for reducing tax rates to give employees a chance to catch up on their savings. The results of inflation on persons of fixed income have been devastating.

The wealthy do not worry particularly about income except for tax purposes. Their first and usually only yardstick is capital performance, the difference in the market value of their net worth between the beginning and end of the year. If for any number of reasons there is an impairment of capital, the rich quickly move to realign investments. Following this, they examine their personal use of discretionary income. The wealthy do not seek to increase savings by reducing personal expenditures. It is the impairment of capital that is paramount in their minds. In order to keep up with inflation and general market conditions, the rich spend inordinate amounts of time reviewing investment opportunities. The children of the rich usually find this a boring waste of time. Thus the proverbial three-generation cycle from wealth back to shirtsleeves.

The vast majority of smalltown rich people make a semi-annual shopping trip to the "big city" to consult with their bankers, investment advisers, lawyers and accountants. They make this trek specifically to learn the new investment ideas and tax moves necessary to preserve and increase their capital.

The "luck" factor is always present in capital appreciation. But remember that a number of companies in today's "500" were not on the list 10 years ago. Although you may never reach the status of the "rich", emulating the industrious *attention* which they give to the care of money can only aid you in increasing your personal net worth.

The first source of capital is usually excess cash flow. As your initial goal, you must be able to save at least 15% of your annual take-home pay. If you have an IRA (Individual Retirement Arrangement) the annual contribution reduces the amount of your savings goal. That is the bottom line. If you think it is impossible to meet this goal, reread BUDGETING FOR THE FUTURE.

Savings give rise to capital formation. These funds are necessary to finance the long-term productivity gains required to maintain economic growth. You should share in this growth through capital appreciation. The securities markets, because of their erratic performance, have caused an individual decline in stock ownership. Nevertheless, stock ownership is the bridge between you and sharing the corporate productivity gains. The issue is investing today's resources (capital) in the economic future.

Your choices of investment of excess cash flow, other than in real estate or tangible property, lie within these categories: savings account, bonds (short-term U.S. Treasury, long-term U.S. Treasury, municipal, corporate), common stocks (non-speculative grade), speculative investments.

The investment funds are the resources remaining after providing for a cash reserve, life insurance, and health insurance. A rule of thumb for an immediate cash reserve requires about one-sixth (two months) of the prior year's cash outflow of fixed and discretionary expenditures. During the 60-day period for which the reserve may be needed, your investment assets may be liquidated to furnish your additional cash requirement. The cash reserve is held in a regular savings account and is not involved with investment positions. The rich rarely have savings accounts with more than token balances.

There are no fixed percentages for excess funds to be divided among investment possibilities. Instead, there are categories of investments which generally should not be in the portfolio of individuals falling within specific groups, either because the investment is of speculative grade and not appropriate for this group, or because the income and capital appreciation potential, which should be an objective of the group, is lacking in that investment. An "X" in a category of investment below means that the middle income group should normally avoid it.

			AGE GROUP	
	20-40	40-60	OVER 60 RETIRED	OVER 50 WIDOW (ER)
Savings				
Money Market Fund				
Bonds U.S.A.				
Exempt	X	X		
Corporate	X	X		
Convertible				
Stocks : Income	X	X		
Capital Growth			X	X
Leverage Real Estate			X	X
Mutual Funds				
Options	X	X	X	X
Precious Metals	X	X	X	X

The exact percentages to invest are totally flexible. A savings account, other than to hold a cash reserve, is not necessary in any group. If you have had no investment experience, wait until you have accumulated about $10,000 in excess savings before beginning your investment program. Part of the $10,000 may be held in a money-market fund which sometimes earns higher than a regular savings rate. The market fund is not insured. However, you are building an investment portfolio where "risk" and "luck" are an integral part of success.

An investment vehicle is a suggestion. You do not have to invest in all the available vehicles for your group. The open types are suggestions. You may restrict yourself to one or more types of investment. On the other hand, if you change age brackets, the rules do not require a liquidation of your position. The "X" refers to a situation less likely to meet investment objectives in a particular status or age. Your personality and specific inclinations and capabilities are important considerations. A professional age 35 with two children might decide to create for the children a short-term education trust holding income stocks. Ordinarily, income stocks are not the suggested type of investment for that age group. But study the chart, then move to specific needs. As there is no accounting for love, there are no rules to tell you where you must invest your excess funds. The chart is a guideline. Argue with it and make your own decisions.

The Financial Page

Unless you are prepared to spend at least one hour a week reviewing economic indicators, the savings account is your best course of action. Once you have learned your categories of investment, you must constantly consider switching within the group and possibilities outside the particular category. You require ongoing information in the investment world, even if you use investment advisers. Money matters are an ongoing subject.

The best daily source of information on financial, tax, and general newsworthy events is *The Wall Street Journal*. Once a week (usually Monday), there is a column entitled "Your Money Matters," on the last page of the *Journal*. Save this column for future reference. It tells you about current trends in investment, varied opinions, and practical advice. The weekly tax report appears on Wednesdays and is extremely informative. This newspaper includes all daily reports on financial markets and matters. Its feature articles give interesting views on little-known people and activities.

The business and investment magazines worth considering include: *Barron's, Business Week, Dun's Review, Forbes,* and *Fortune. Money* and *U.S. News & World Report* also have valuable current information on effective use of your money. Both *Newsweek* and *Time* cover economic trends and the business world.

For a beginner in the investment world, *Forbes* is probably the first choice. Reading *Forbes* is fun. The publisher is a man whose obvious love of the good life permeates the style of the magazine. The other magazines are written well but if you have had no investment experience, it may take you a longer time to train yourself to extract what you need. Sample all the magazines. Some are not sold on newsstands and in order to obtain a copy you may have to request one from a business acquaintance.

The Investment Adviser

"Running Money" is what the investment business is all about. An investment adviser's sole purpose is to make money with money. The criterion in running money is performance. The standard for running money is to exceed averages. No matter what the arguments are against averages, they are the yardstick. What Arbitron and Nielson ratings are to television, so the Dow, the Standard & Poor's (S&P) 500 and Moody's Aa bond yields are to the investment business.

The Dow is the Dow Jones stock average for 30 industrial stocks. The

Dow publishes other averages but its most popular index is the industrials. Critics say the Dow is overweighed by basic industries such as metals, chemicals and oils. The Standard & Poor's 500 appears in most instances to be the more appropriate stock market indicator. In most investment circles, a portfolio manager's performance is measured against the S & P 500.

The original Dow index was determined by adding all 30 stocks and dividing by 30. Because of stock splits (one share divided into more than one) and changes in makeup of the Dow industrial stocks, the current division is about 1.5. The S & P index base number is 10 for the period 1941-1943. Both the Dow and S & P 500 are available daily in the newspaper and on television.

Moody's publishes average corporate yields for rated utility and industrial bonds. The average yield for a particular group is a good indicator of the yield on a particular bond within the group.

The market price of bonds also fluctuates. When a new issue of bonds will yield 8.50%, a buyer will not be willing to pay the full face value for a bond issued in prior years paying only 7.50%. Because a bond must be paid off when it reaches maturity, it will not fluctuate in price by the full amount of its percentage change in yield. Depending on maturity, a 10-25 year bond will fluctuate by about one-half to two-thirds the percentage change in yield. When market conditions cause a drop in price from the issuance price, the interest paid remains constant so the yield automatically increases.

The chart of these stock and bond indices should be your basic yardstick in measuring your, or an adviser's, performance:

	STANDARD & POOR'S 500		DOW JONES INDUSTRIALS	
DATE	INDEX	ANNUAL % INCREASE (DECREASE) (1941–1943 = 10)	INDEX	ANNUAL % INCREASE (DECREASE)
12/31/72	117.50	—	1,020.02	—
12/31/73	97.55	(16.98)%	850.86	(16.58)%
12/31/74	68.56	(29.72)	616.24	(27.57)
12/31/75	90.19	31.55	852.41	38.32
12/31/76	107.46	19.15	1,004.65	17.86
12/31/77	95.10	(11.50)	831.17	(17.27)

Stocks also have yields (dividends) which may be used to measure total performance. For example, the yields on the stocks comprising the Dow Jones Industrials for the past four years were as follows:

YEAR	YIELD
1974	6.12%
1975	4.39
1976	4.12
1977	5.51

For your purposes, however, the index without the dividend yields will be sufficient for measuring performance.

Although bond prices fluctuate greatly, the usual yardstick in measuring a bond portfolio's performance is the average interest yield in the particular rated bond group. The Moody's corporate yields for Aa-rated bonds covering the average for the month of December were as follows:

MONTH OF DECEMBER	AVERAGE INTEREST YIELD Aa-RATED BONDS	ANNUAL % INCREASE (DECREASE)
1972	7.36	–
1973	7.92	7.61%
1974	9.20	16.16
1975	9.25	.54
1976	8.24	(10.92)
1977	8.50	3.16

You will notice in 1973 and 1974 as the stock averages suffered big declines, corporate bond yields increased. Similarly, as the stock averages continued to move upward in 1976, bond yields declined. Many knowledgeable people believe there is a correlation of stock prices to bond yields.

There are a number of other yardsticks for performance, such as The New York Stock Exchange Composite Index. For your purposes, however, the S & P 500 and the Dow will be sufficient performance guides.

A good rule holds that "an acceptable adviser must beat the market averages for the past five years." It is not necessary to have performed better in every year (that would be superior performance) but the overall performance must have exceeded the averages in the aggregate of the last five years. In any year of poor performance, the difference in percentages should certainly not have exceeded 25% of the S & P 500. In other words, starting with the year 1973, the above chart shows the movement of the stock averages. The portfolio is valued at December 31 of each year using the mean price (high and low for the day divided by two). The market value of the portfolio is adjusted for cash added or withdrawn during the year. The value of the portfolio at the end of the year is divided by the value at the beginning of the year. The result is the percentage that the new value bears to the old. In order to compute the delta percent or the percentage of change, subtract the number one from the answer.

For example, a portfolio was worth $10,000 on December 31, 1975 and $12,000 on December 31, 1976. The increase is 20% ($12,000 ÷ $10,000 = 1.200 − 1.0000 = .2000 or 20.00%). You achieve the same result using the delta percent key on a present-value calculator. During 1976 the S & P 500 increased by 19.15% and the Dow increased 17.86%. The portfolio outperformed these indices by .85 percentage points for the S & P and 2.14 percentage points for the Dow—a good achievement (20.00% − 19.15% = .85% and 20.00% − 17.86% = 2.14%).

There are two classes of individuals who assist you in purchasing and selling securities and other investments: the investment adviser and the investment counsel. There are no qualifications for calling yourself an investment adviser other than registering with the S.E.C. (Securities and Exchange Commission). Only someone who makes recommendations on an individual basis is permitted to use the term "investment counsel." A stockbroker cannot use the term investment counsel.

The minimum money (or security value) accepted by most investment counsels is $100,000. They are paid an annual fee, based upon the value of the fund, at approximately the following rates:

RATE OF FEE	VALUE OF PORTFOLIO	AMOUNT
$3/4\%$	First $500,000	$750
$6/10\%$	Next 500,000	3,000
$5/10\%$	Thereafter	

In general, the value of the portfolio measures performance. The counsel is not permitted a fee based on capital gains. There is a limited exception to this rule where the fee may be increased or decreased against some known standard such as the S & P 500 index. A few mutual funds use this kind of performance method of compensation.

In the securities business, the initials C.F.A. stand for Chartered Financial Analyst. The individual is required to pass a series of three examinations testing knowledge of the techniques involved with security analysis and portfolio management. A C.F.A. is required to have four years' experience in financial analysis. A college degree is required but may be waived by the examiners in certain circumstances. A C.F.A must subscribe to and conform with a code of ethics. The C.F.A. designation is not a license. In the investment field a C.F.A. may confine himself or herself to research and not handle portfolio management. An investment counsel with a C.F.A. is not a guarantee of superior portfolio performance. Excellent results could be achieved by a person without a C.F.A. certificate. The certificate, however, has the advantage of requiring minimum standards of knowledge for its holder. Performance is the first and only criterion for choosing investment counsel. Given several individuals with similar performance records, a C.F.A. designation should be meaningful in the final choice.

Assuming you meet the minimum money standards for retaining an investment counsel, you would request in writing representative portfolio performance records over the past five years assembled for persons with similar investment objectives. By SEC regulation it is a violation for an investment counsel to fail to supply *representative* portfolios. In fact, you are entitled after the first submission to examine *all* the counsel's portfolios. The names of the clients are omitted or blocked out. A portfolio manager who does not submit in writing the performance of *representative* portfolios with your investment objective should not be retained.

Since the cost of an investment counsel is tax deductible (unless municipal bonds are involved), common sense requires that an individual whose portfolio is $100,000 or more should retain investment counsel with a track record. The investment team may include not only an investment counsel to manage the portfolio, but a stockbroker to execute the orders for buying and selling of securities and a bank as custodian for the securities. The investment counsel may be the bank that is custodian of the securities. On the other hand, the securities may be in the custody of the brokerage firm.

A stockbroker may offer investment suggestions which you would submit to the investment counsel. If the brokerage firm is to be custodian of the securities, a written confirmation of the extent to which the firm is covered by insurance for security losses should be requested.

INVESTMENT TRUSTS

At the turn of the century, groups of rich people decided to pool some of their resources in trusts. They hired the most brilliant investment counsel to run their money. The original trusts continue today, mostly used for charitable purposes. The investment clubs of the 1960s were a much smaller version of such trusts except few of them employed investment counsel. Unfortunately, an extended downturn of the market in the late 60s saw the dissolution of many investment clubs. The basic idea is a sound one, and the mutual fund is a public version of these trusts.

If you do not meet the money standard for an investment counsel, you may invest in stocks and bonds on your own judgment with or without the help of a stockbroker. Before deciding whether you have the ability to perform for yourself, you must understand thoroughly the usual intangible property investment alternatives. Even if at this time the thought of your having any excess funds for investment is a "pipe dream," you should be an optimist and prepare yourself for that unexpected windfall. To continue this exercise, suppose you inherited $10,000 and decided to invest it. What would you do with the money? This chapter should help you understand your choices for investment.

SAVINGS ACCOUNT

You do not have to be an investment wizard to put all your excess money into savings accounts. If you choose the savings account as your sole investment vehicle, you still have to make two decisions: the type of bank and the terms.

Commercial and savings banks are insured up to $40,000 in separate accounts under the F.D.I.C. (Federal Deposit Insurance Corporation). Savings and loan associations, because they are permitted by law to invest a higher percentage of their assets in mortgages, are insured under a different program. There is a difference in coverage relating to the period of payout in the event of a bank's insolvency. The F.D.I.C. pays you in 30 days. The insurance for savings and loan associations may pay off over an extended period not in excess of 10 years. By law, commercial banks pay less interest than savings banks. Savings and loan associations pay the highest interest. The earning asset mix of the three types of banks makes interest vary. Government regulation sets the maximum interest rates for each class of bank.

Assuming you are seeking maximum protection of principal and immediate payout in the event of insolvency, you would choose either a commercial bank or a savings bank. However, the remoteness of a savings and loan association's failing and the possibility of a slower payout should rarely deter you from keeping your funds at an S & L. In any event, you must make a decision. Frequently your decision will be based on convenient location of the bank building, courtesy of employees and past relationship. Whatever bank you choose, you will rarely make a serious mistake.

The automatic transfer monthly from your checking account is a convenient method of savings. Holiday clubs are worthwhile savings devices to accomplish an objective. Some states require interest paid on holiday clubs. A holiday club is a big step forward for a chronic spender.

Some banks permit automatic transfers from regular savings accounts to long-term accounts for a minimum amount of $50. Banks are in business to make a profit; therefore, every device is attempted to make your savings easier. Mail deposits, advance interest, free checking, and gifts are some of the ways banks seek to overcome the difficulty many people have in saving money and to entice them to use their particular bank.

In many states there are six types of savings accounts available. The following chart indicates the current terms of the accounts. Usually, if one interest rate changes, all the rates will change. The chart shows the interest spread for different types of accounts. Effective rate is the interest rate divided by 360 days (not 365 days). Thus, 7.75% divided by 360 and compounded daily for 365 days results in an effective rate of 8.17%. You would receive an additional 11¢ interest annually per $100 of savings because of this difference.

| | COMMERCIAL BANK | | SAVINGS BANK | |
| | REGULAR | EFFECTIVE | REGULAR | EFFECTIVE |
TIME ON DEPOSIT	RATE	RATE	RATE	RATE
Regular	5.00%	5.13%	5.25%	5.47%
90-Day	5.50	5.65	5.75	6.00
1 to 2½ years	6.00	6.18	6.50	6.81
2½ to 4 years	6.50	6.72	6.75	7.08
4 to 6 years	7.25	7.63	7.50	7.90
6 to 10 years	7.50	7.90	7.75	8.17

Usually the periodic rate is the regular interest paid divided by the period, such as a daily rate being the regular rate divided by 365 days. On the other hand, the effective rate, which is in your favor, divides the year into 360 days and compounds it by the period. The above table shows the interest compounded daily.

In general, the minimum deposit for the 90-Day through four year accounts is $500. The accounts over four years accept $1,000 as a minimum deposit. You may add to the accounts but interest rates change if deposits are made within two years of maturity.

If you require money before maturity, interest forfeiture is considerable. A 90-Day account does not pay interest on withdrawals earlier than 90 days. An account other than a 90-Day account forfeits 90 days' interest and interest is paid at the regular rate on the money withdrawn. Because the bank makes long-term commitments on extended maturity accounts, the penalties for premature withdrawals are necessary. The forfeited interest is treated separately on your tax return.

To make a decision on terms of deposit requires you to have an investment objective. If the money is your cash reserve, you would use the regular account. Your maximum cash reserve generally should be one-sixth of your annual cash outflow. Since other investments may be liquidated or money withdrawn from extended maturity accounts, any excess in a cash reserve is an unnecessarily conservative investment decision.

Money saved for retirement purposes is usually held in the longest maturity account. Education or other specific purposes require shorter periods coinciding with the time the money is expected to be needed. At the maximum current rate of 7.75% (effective rate 8.17%) your money doubles every 3,220 days (8.82 years).

If you sincerely believe that you cannot manage investments by yourself or have no interest in investment advice, keep all your money in the bank. You may divide your savings between some or all of the six types of savings accounts. However, just because you were once "burned" by the stock market or by some other investment, don't foresake all opportunities for capital appreciation.

Investing in securities (bonds and stocks) requires decision-making and management. One of this chapter's aims is to present you with guidelines for managing a relatively modest portfolio ($10,000). This was done with the help of a C.F.A. who serves as investment counsel to a wealthy family. Before you commit yourself further to long-term savings accounts you should learn more about alternative investments.

Interestingly, the most vocal advocates of the "leave it all in the bank" investment theory are the speculative-grade stock buyers of the 1960s and early 1970s. They tried pure speculation with little knowledge and lost. Today they renew their certificates of deposit with the same enthusiasm with which they traded stocks years ago. In those days they were also against buying 5% loan interest insurance policies as a flexible investment capital source. Now most states allow the insurance company to charge 8%.

Most rich people have savings accounts on a modest scale, if at all. Their theory is that the banks should not make money with their money. Emergency cash is quickly available through loans and the sale of securities. Their excess cash is employed through investments in real estate, and tangible and intangible property. Real estate and tangible property can be excellent investments and, in addition, have tax-shelter incentives. Intangible property, except for tax-exempt bonds and mineral leases, has few tax-shelter possibilities. *However, capital appreciation is not taxed until the property is sold.*

BONDS

Bonds are certificates of indebtedness. Some entity agrees to pay interest for a period of time for the use of your (bondholder's) money. The bond is redeemable at a future time in a fixed amount (par or face value). Bonds usually pay interest twice a year. Bonds may be issued with a callable date. This means the issuer has the option of refunding all or part of the bonds outstanding before maturity at a price generally higher than par.

There are four types of bonds generally available: federal, municipal, foreign, and corporate.

When you purchase a bond you pay interest to the seller from the last interest date to the date of purchase. Bond interest paid on the basis of a 360-day year is called ordinary simple interest. For example, a $1,000 bond pays interest at 8% January 1 and July 1. You purchased the bond on February 18. The interest you would pay is $10.67 computed as follows: January 1 through February 18 equals 30 days for January and 18 days for February for a total of 48 days. You eliminate the first day and include the last day. The semi-annual period is 180 days (360 days ÷ 2). The semi-annual interest rate is 4% (8% ÷ 2). The semi-annual interest is $40 ($1,000 × 4%). The prorated purchase interest is $40 times 48 days divided by 180 days equals $10.67. If you sold the bond on February 18, you would collect the $10.67 interest.

Bonds are usually quoted in terms of a percentage of their face value. Normally they are available in face values of $1,000 or multiples. Thus, a $1,000 bond is priced at 10% of its selling price. An American Telephone & Telegraph Company bond is quoted in bond tables as follows:

BOND	CURRENT YIELD	SALES IN $1,000	HIGH	LOW	CLOSE	NET CHANGE
ATT7s01	7.8	120	90⅛	89⅞	89⅞	+⅛

This entry reflects a high grade (Aaa) bond paying 7% annual interest and due in 2001. The current yield of 7.8% is a combination of the interest currently paid and the discount price paid computed to maturity. Yield to maturity is the important earnings factor in a bond purchase.

Bonds are rated by independent firms such as Standard & Poors and Moody's. If the bonds are not in default (failure to pay interest, principal, or both) the ratings range from Aaa in descending order: Aa, A, Baa, Ba, and B. Some municipal bonds may be rated as low as Caa.

The price of a bond may vary considerably from its par or face value. Bonds are not always issued at par. The market price depends upon the riskiness of the bond, the interest rate, and the maturity date. All of these factors, together with money-market conditions, give rise to the market price. If the bond sells above par, it is selling at a premium. If it is below par, the bond is selling at a discount. In a period of declining purchasing power, the current price of bonds includes discounting for future inflation. This is reflected in the interest factor called "yield to maturity."

What you pay for a bond today has been measured by the market against alternative investment vehicles. In the future you can expect to receive par value when and if your bond is redeemed. Today's price reflects any possible risk of default and the market's expectation of the present value of the bond's future interest payments and the value.

The sales of the ATT issue on the market date were $120,000. Corporate bonds are usually issued in denominations of $1,000 so the sales for the day cover 120 bonds. The mean price for the day is 90: the high and low price divided by 2 (90⅛ + 89⅞) ÷ 2 or 90.125 + 89.875 = 180.000 ÷ 2 = 90. The last price of 89⅞ is the closing price and the net change of + ⅛ means the price of the bond has increased from the prior day's last price by $1.25 per $1,000. If you bought the bond at the mean price of 90 you would have paid $900 plus accrued interest and plus commission. The commission is paid because it is an already-issued corporate bond. The discount of 10% from par value reflects the fact that an ATT bond issued at this time would pay 8% interest or slightly more than 7%, which was the prevailing interest rate when ATT issued this bond.

Bonds are either coupon or registered. Coupon bonds are bearer instruments with coupons attached covering each interest payment. The coupons are deposited in your bank for collection like a check. The bank collects the funds on your behalf. The bonds are transferrable by delivery to a buyer. Unless a buyer knows you, you must supply proof of purchase. Although bearer bonds are transferrable by delivery, no one will pay money for one unless they are satisfied that the seller has good title. A stolen bond never gives the buyer good title. That is why proof of purchase must be retained.

A registered bond is issued in the name of the owner. Interest checks are mailed out twice a year. At redemption date a check for the face value amount of the bond is mailed to the owner.

FEDERAL OBLIGATIONS

Obligations of the United States are called government securities. They consist of bills, notes, and bonds.

Treasury bills are offered at a discount (less than face value). The interest is included in the reduced purchase price. They mature in a relatively short period of time——anywhere from 30 days to 52 weeks. There is always a current market for bills. Notes usually mature in periods ranging from one to ten years. Notes pay interest semiannually.

Obligations of the United States are taxable income for federal purposes. They are exempt from state and local income taxes, an important advantage they have over corporate bonds. In the numerical sequence of safe investments, they are ranked number one. Substantially all U.S. bonds (other than Series E and H) are held by financial institutions. There is fluctuation in the bond's market prices between issuance and maturity dates. The bonds are readily marketable and individual purchasers usually buy in excess of the maximum $40,000 insured savings account.

U.S. Treasury bills and notes can be bought directly through your local Federal Reserve Bank. Some U.S. issues reduce the usual minimum participation down to $5,000 to encourage small investors. You will find your local Federal Reserve Bank helpful in assisting you to purchase bills and notes according to their procedures. The Chicago Mercantile Exchange trades in Treasury Bill Options.

U. S. SERIES E BONDS

U. S. Series E Bonds were designed for the investment requirements of the vast majority of individuals. "E's" are sold at a discounted 75% of face value. They mature at different periods depending on date of issuance. Interest continues to accrue until the bonds are redeemed. Currently "E's" pay an average of 6% interest. The interest is deferred from tax unless you elect to report it currently. They are exempt from state and local taxation. "E's" currently come in face amounts of $25 to $10,000. They are available through payroll withholding and banks. Series E Bonds are perfect for specific objective savings (e.g., college tuition). "E's", like all U.S. obligations, are your prime safe investment.

For many years, the low interest return on "E's" made them an unpopular investment choice. Today, by shortening the maturity date, the bonds are excellent vehicles for middle-income families to save on a regular basis.

The interest return on "E's" differs depending upon the issuance date. For example, bonds issued prior to April 1, 1952 matured in 10 years. However, "E's" issued after December 1, 1973 mature in five years. Each month the redemption table changes. The tables are at banks.

Bonds continue to earn interest after maturity. Although a savings account for five years pays effective interest at 7.90%, it is subject to taxation on a current basis. At a 50% tax rate, the after-tax yield of a five-year savings account is 3.95%; at a 40% tax rate, the yield is 4.74%; and at a 30% tax rate, the yield is 5.53%. Thus, because of the ability to postpone indefinitely taxation on Series E Bonds, your earnings are in excess of current savings bank five-year interest rates.

Systematic "E" bond purchases, timed to mature with the need for tuition payments, may escape any taxation by registering the bonds in the child's name. You would file an income tax return for the child covering the first year of "E" bond purchases, electing to report the interest as earned. Since the child is entitled to a $750 exemption ($1,000 for 1979), no tax results unless the interest income exceeds the exemption allowance. The child is not entitled on the interest income to any allowance of the zero bracket amount. After the first year, there is no need to file a return unless the annual interest exceeds the exemption allowance. At the time the "E" bonds are redeemed to make tuition payments, the interest is all tax paid. The result is a totally safe investment with a higher return than if you kept the money in your own savings account. You could open a long-term savings account in the child's name and accomplish the same result. However, the minimum deposit allowed to open five-year savings accounts ranges from $500 to $1,000. In addition, if you require the money from the bank prematurely, you forfeit 90 days' interest on the money withdrawn and are paid at the regular bank rate.

To summarize: Series E Bonds permit tax deferment, a competitive investment return, marketability, ease of purchase, and safety of principal.

Another important feature of "E's" is the conversion into Series H Bonds without tax impact. H Bonds issued in face amounts of $500 to $10,000 mature in 10 years. They pay semi-annual interest (mailed to you) from six months after issuance, as follows:

PERIOD	INTEREST RATE
First check six months after issuance	4.2%
Next four and a half years	5.8
Remaining five years	6.5

The average interest for 10 years is 6%. When you trade in your "E's" for "H's," the original cost of the "E's" carries over to the "H's." This is stamped on the face of the "H" bond. For retirement purposes (when your tax bracket is generally lower than during your working years), the Series H Bond swap is an excellent move to increase current cash flow. The "H" bond interest coupons are mailed to you semi-annually, whereas an entire "E" bond must be redeemed and taxes paid usually on all prior years' interest.

You may purchase at cost (not face value) $10,000 of "E's" and "H's" annually. If you are a co-owner the amount doubles to $20,000 each year.

There are a number of Federal government agencies which issue bonds. Federal agency bonds usually yield slightly more than U.S. Treasury bonds of similar maturities because they are less marketable and are not for the most part direct obligations of the U.S. government. However, they are considered to be very high quality investment grade. U.S. bonds are used for holding tax dollars after a large capital gain. The bonds are held until the due date of the tax return and then sold. Wealthy people rarely hold these bonds for extended periods of time because the income is taxable and they have little capital appreciation factor.

MUNICIPAL TAX-EXEMPT BONDS

Municipal Bonds or "tax-exempts" are the most popular tax-avoidance device currently available. The interest paid on these obligations of state and local governments is exempt from federal income taxes. In most instances a state or local bond is also exempt from taxation in the same state as the issuing authority.

There are states that tax their own municipal bonds as well as those of other states.

The states that *tax* interest on their own bonds (there may be some exceptions for specific issues) are Colorado, Illinois, Iowa, Kansas, Oklahoma, and Wisconsin.

The states that *exempt* both their own and other states' bonds are Alaska, Connecticut, District of Columbia, Florida, Indiana, Louisiana, Nebraska, Nevada, New Mexico, South Dakota, Texas, Utah, Vermont, Washington, and Wyoming.

There is no central market place for municipal bonds similar to the New York or American Stock Exchanges. There is, however, a nationwide wire service available to bond dealers. Municipals are considered marketable securities because of the wire service and the excellent reputation of the bond-rating services.

Municipal bonds are sold without commission. The dealer earns the fee from the spread, that is the difference between the bid (low) and the ask (high) price. The spread is about two points. Thus, the dealer would earn $20 for each $1,000 bond sold. The exact spread depends on the day's market conditions and the dealer's inventory. Since municipal dealers maintain an inventory of bonds, prices for an exact issue may differ between dealers.

The municipal securities companies maintain inventories and are principals. They are called dealers and not brokers. Persons or entities trading stocks are generally called brokers since they act as agents for buyers and sellers. In syndicates or underwritings, a stockbroker may act as principal or dealer.

Municipals are usually sold in denominations of $5,000 although there are $1,000 face value bonds available. Transactions usually are done in $25,000 blocks. A sale for less than $25,000 face value is termed "an odd lot." This doesn't mean you cannot buy less than $25,000 face value of bonds, but that many dealers restrict their trading to that size lot. You pay, therefore, a slightly higher spread if you buy less than $25,000 or even $35,000 worth of bonds. It is like buying half a loaf of bread. The price is more expensive than for a whole loaf divided by two.

Most municipals are bearer bonds. That means they are transferrable by delivery of the certificate. You may purchase a registered bond at about a $20 discount per $1,000. A registered bond's ownership may only be validly transferred when entered on the books of the issuer. Bearer bonds have interest coupons attached. Registered bonds pay interest by mail to the registered owner. If you are holding a bond for a specific maturity, you can save money by buying a registered bond at a discount.

The transferability of ownership of tax-exempt bonds is not as free and easy as many people believe. The IRS may trace bond numbers and coupon cashing to ascertain the real owner of a bond. The rich usually engage a bank to act as custodian for their municipal portfolio. The bank collects the interest, tenders callable bonds and is responsible for the safekeeping of the bond certificates.

Municipal bonds, because of their tax-exempt quality, are held usually by the rich in the percentage range of 15% to 25% of their investment portfolio. These municipal portfolios are regularly upgraded by tax swaps. Thus, in a year in which a substantial capital gain is realized, municipals with unrealized tax losses are sold to offset part of the gain. Different issues of tax-exempts are purchased to replace the bonds sold.

The purchase of a particular type of municipal bond requires an investment objective. Persons of different ages and means buy different bonds. Bonds are rated by Moody's and Standard & Poor's. Their ratings depend upon the analysis of the security behind the bond and the ability of the issuer to pay interest. The rating of a bond is reflected in its market price. You may average a bond portfolio by owning bonds of different ratings. A chart of bond yields for different maturity dates indicates how the rating affects the return to the investor. This chart covered yields in the middle of 1977. The spread between interest rates on high-rated and low-rated bonds is not constant.

RATING	2 YEARS	5 YEARS	10 YEARS	15 YEARS	20 YEARS
Aaa	–	–	4.60%	5.10%	5.45%
Aa	3.40%	4.10%	4.65	5.15	–
A	3.60	4.21	4.76	5.31	5.64
Baa	3.92	4.66	5.24	5.66	5.96

At the same time as the above chart was prepared in the middle of 1977, New York City Bonds rated "Caa" yield to maturity as follows:

2 YEARS	3 YEARS	4 YEARS	5 YEARS	10 YEARS
7.50%	9.50%	8.50%	9.25%	9.35%

In other words, because of its financial crisis, New York City received the lowest bond rating. This reflected a yield to maturity (current interest plus present value of discount) in the five-year period table of 98.50% more than a Baa bond ($9.25\% \div 4.66\% = 1.9850 - 1.000 = .9850$ or 98.50%). The risk is reflected in the yield. In 1976 some New York City bonds were selling in the 50s ($500 per $1,000 bond) and in 1977 these issues rose in price to the 80s. Speculators made enormous capital gains on correctly predicting the market for these bonds. On every $1,000 bond bought an average of $300 profit was made in less than one year. A $1,000 New York City Bond bought at 50 equals a cost of $500; sold at 80 equals a sales price of $800; $800 − $500 = $300 profit.

Municipal bond dealers offer their inventory of bonds in a daily publication, *The Blue List of Current Municipal Offerings*. A typical entry on December 14, 1977 in the *Blue List* reads:

AMT. M	SECURITY	PURPOSE	RATE	MATURITY	YIELD/ PRICE	OFFERED BY
150	Puerto Rico—		5.80	1/1/99	7.50	Sterling
	WTR.RES.					Grace
	AU.EL.RV.					Munic.

These are Puerto Rico Water Resource Authority Electric Revenue Bonds.

A municipal bond dealer's calculator computes the exact price for these bonds at $82.15. A dealer purchasing the bonds generally receives a 75¢ concession. Therefore, another dealer would pay $814 for each $1,000 bond. You would pay about $840 for this bond.

The *Blue List* shows the bonds by states and indicates the ask prices (yield or price) at which the offering dealer will sell a particular bond issue. The amount column indicates the dollar value of the bonds offered. "M" is the symbol for thousands. Thus this dealer offers 150M or $150,000 of bonds. The purpose of this bond is obvious from its name. The coupon rate is 5.80%. The bond pays $58 a year or $29 semi-annually. The date 1/1/99 is the month, day, and year of maturity: January 1, 1999. The bond also pays interest twice a year on January 1 (maturity month and day) and six months later on July 1. On each interest date half of the $58 or $29 would be paid.

Yield to maturity contains two elements: (1) difference between present value and the future redemption price, plus (2) present value of all future interest payments.

Current yield is not to be confused with yield to maturity. The current yield is the annual interest divided by the cost of the bond. The approximate cost to you of the Puerto Rico Bond on the date quoted was $840 for a 5.80% coupon. The current yield is 6.90%. If you invest $840 for a $1,000 bond you receive $58.00 interest per year (two semi-annual payments of $29 each). Dividing $58 by $840 equals the current yield of 6.90%. At the same time, this bond, which matures on January 1, 1999, has a yield to maturity to a purchasing dealer of 7.50%. The computation was based on the discount price and coupon date on December 14, 1977 figured to a settlement date (usually five days later) carried forward to the redemption date January 1, 1999.

The par value is the amount that the issuer agrees to pay at maturity. The market price may be very different from par value. The yield to maturity is employed in the market place to determine price.

The difference between the discount price paid today on purchasing a bond and the redemption price is subject to capital gains tax. This gain is included in the year the bond is redeemed. If you sell a bond before maturity, any gain or loss is subject to tax. However, if you pay a premium for a bond ($101 rather than $98) you must amortize the premium over the remaining period to maturity. The premium is considered a reduction of the current coupon interest. For example, on January 2, 1978 you bought a $1,000 bond for a price of 103½. The coupon rate was 7%. The premium paid reflects the municipal bond market at the time of purchase. The $1,000 bond cost you $1,035. The bond matures 1/1/88 or 10 years later. The $35 premium is considered a reduction of your tax-exempt interest ratably over the 10 years or $3.50 per year. Thus, at maturity date, you have realized no loss on the redemption. If you sold the bond after five years, your tax basis is reduced by half of the $35, or $17.50. Your cost for measuring gain or loss becomes in the 5th year $1,017.50 ($1,035 — $17.50).

The offering price in the *Blue List* is the price at which the dealer is offering to sell the bond to another dealer less a small concession. You would pay about $20 more than the ask price. You may look over a daily *Blue List* for bond offerings and check the ratings in either Moody's or Standard & Poor's. The Puerto Rico Water Resource Bond quoted previously was A rated by the bond services.

Municipal bonds may be called by the issuer for early retirement. A sinking fund is provided to retire a portion of the issue. Revenue bonds such as water resources, turnpikes, and airports may be callable. The market place does not currently find favor with a call feature of less than 10 years after issuance. No one would be interested in buying this bond. If your bond is callable, you usually receive a premium over the face value for the call feature. The market price reflects the call for this feature element.

The distribution of municipals in this country reflects the belief in their safety factor. Almost half the bonds outstanding are owned by commercial banks. Banks usually average the yield on their portfolios by staggering the maturity dates.

The extent to which the tax-exempt feature of municipal bonds is material to your investment decision depends upon your federal tax bracket. The following chart compares the after-tax return of long-term savings bank rates and corporate bond yields for different marginal tax brackets:

1978 JOINT TAXABLE INCOME	1978 FEDERAL TAX BRACKET	8.17% SAVINGS BANK AFTER-TAX RETURN	7.50% TAXABLE BOND AFTER-TAX RETURN
$ 7,200	19%	6.62%	6.08%
11,200	22%	6.37%	5.85%
15,200	25%	6.13%	5.63%
19,200	28%	5.88%	5.40%
27,200	36%	5.22%	4.80%
35,200	42%	4.73%	4.35%
47,200	50%	4.08%	3.75%

The table shows that a married couple with a taxable income of $19,200 is in the 28% tax bracket. In that bracket the after-tax return on long-term savings is 5.88% (100%-28% = 72% after-tax dollar remaining; 8.17% effective rate × 72% after-tax dollar = 5.88% the after-tax interest rate). The after-tax return on a 7.50% corporate bond at the 28% tax bracket is 5.40% (100%-28% = 72%; 7.50% × 72% = 5.40%).

On the other hand, a 6% tax-exempt bond has an equivalent return of taxable interest paying 8.33% at the marginal tax rate of 28% (100% − 28% = 72% after taxes; 6% ÷ 72% = 8.33%). Thus, at the 28% bracket a 6% tax-exempt bond produces more after-tax income than either a savings bank account at 8.17% or a corporate bond at 7.50%.

There is an increasing value of tax-exempts as an income producer in the higher brackets. At the 50% tax-bracket, the maximum tax rate for personal service income (i.e. salary, pensions), a 6% tax-exempt bond is worth 12% taxable interest. At the 50% bracket, your net return on a savings account paying 8.17% is 4.08% or half the effective rate paid.

Municipal Bonds are usually general obligations (G.O.) of the taxing authority. These bonds are not subject to any limitations on the governmental unit's ability to collect additional taxes in order to refund the bonds. The full faith and credit provisions of the United States Constitution as well as state constitutions as interpreted by the courts have prevented issuing authorities from later changing bond covenants. Once issued, a municipal bond is a binding contract. This principle was upheld by the New York Court of Appeals during the financial crisis of New York City.

It is extremely remote that a state's police power will operate against you as a bondholder. Even in the depression of the 1930s, the defaults in paying interest on municipals was mostly temporary. Realizing that New York City's financial crisis in the 1970s would have an adverse effect on the entire municipal market, the greatest brains in banking, business, and municipal financing prepared a format to save the city from bankruptcy. Unfortunately, the city was the victim of inaccurate bookkeeping and excessive generosity. The first order of business was to "do the city's books" in understandable fashion. The lesson is that you can't deal with the facts without proper information.

The Federal Bankruptcy Act does permit municiplities which default on their obligations to file under Chapter IX. The law requires 66% of the bondholders to agree to a settlement or deferment of payment.

In addition to general obligation bonds, municipalities issue revenue bonds. These bonds depend upon the income of a specific project to pay the carrying charges. Revenue bonds include turnpike authority, bridges, airports, water resources, power, hospitals, housing, sports complexes, and industrial revenue. These bonds generally are *not* guaranteed by the municipality. You are required to look to the revenues of the specific issuers to satisfy the bond indebtedness. Revenue bonds are very popular because it is easier for the financial analyst to understand the economics (the amounts available to pay these bonds). It is often difficult to understand the complicated finanical dealings of the issuing municipalities in handling G.O. bonds. Although a revenue bond is not a general obligation, it is remote that a state legislature will not vote funds to help the issuing agency meet a temporary cash shortage. This is called a moral obligation. However, if the bond is used for industrial development, it is doubtful whether moral obligation exists. When buying an industrial bond, look to the guarantor (the business enterprise).

Housing bonds may be guaranteed by the federal, state, or local governments. When you purchase this type of bond, your dealer can supply you with a prospectus or letter stating the guarantee. The safer the bond, the less the yield to maturity.

Several new programs insure municipal bondholders against default. There are two private companies that have set up insurance plans. AMBAC (American Municipal Bond Assurance Corporation) and MBIA (Municipal Bond Insurance Association) are the insurers. Policies are issued to the municipality for your protection. Standard & Poor's rates a bond Aaa if it is insured with MBIA and Aa if insured by AMBAC. Moody's gives no weight to the insurance.

A large corporate or individual municipal bond portfolio may be insured by the MGIC Investment Corp. (the parent company of AMBAC). A bond dealer can arrange the insurance. The insurance is valuable if the bond ratings in the portfolio are varied. This is very much like title insurance on a house. It helps worriers to sleep better. Since most portfolios are upgraded regularly, you do not find insurance in most substantial municipal bond portfolios.

The tax-exempt status of municipal bonds is supported by the U.S. Constitution and legislation. The exemption from state income tax of U.S. Treasury bonds is also derived from the Constitution.

YIELD TO MATURITY

In order to understand how the market works in municipal bond offerings, you should understand the arithmetical computations necessary to determine yield to maturity when the price of the bond is known.

The yield to maturity is the price criterion for buying a tax-exempt bond. The *Blue List* issue of December 14, 1977 reflected Puerto Rico bond's (see page 400) yield to maturity as 7.50%. This was the yield to a purchasing dealer without a price concession. Assume you paid $840 for this bond at the settlement date. What is your yield to maturity?

The formula involves the present value of the future interest payments added to the present value of the redemption price. A bond dealer has a calculator designed to key in the factors. In the case of the Puerto Rico bond, your yield to maturity would be 7.30% assuming a settlement date on January 2, 1978.

The yield to maturity percentage of 7.30% results in the present value of the redemption price of $1,000 computed to January 1, 1999 to be worth $222. Adding to this figure, the present value of all interest coupons at the same 7.30% rate results in a value of $618. The combined total of $840 is what you would pay settlement date of January 2, 1978.

MUNICIPALS AND INVESTMENT OBJECTIVES

The choices in municipals revolve around ratings, yield to maturity, coupon rates, and maturity dates. If your state exempts from tax only its obligation, you would consider first your state's bonds. In general, obligations of Puerto Rico are exempt from both U.S. and state income taxes.

The purpose and recommended purchase may be summarized:

PURPOSE	MUNICIPAL BOND POSSIBILITIES
1. College tuition— 10 years from now.	Maturity date in 10 years and each year thereafter; A or better rated; high yield to maturity; capital gains to child.
2. Professional individual for future retirement income.	Staggered maturity dates through age 80, A or better rated; high coupon rate.
3. Self-employed with fluctuating income.	Short-term maturities; Aaa bonds.
4. 35-year-old employee	Maturity dates immaterial; high yields; low coupon rate; Baa rated or better.
5. Retired—spouse, no heirs and substantial pension.	Long maturities; high coupon rate; A or better rated.
6. Retired—heirs and limited pension.	Maturities to age 85; Aaa rated; high coupon rate.
7. Profit Sharing Plan Distribution Reinvestment (no tax-free rollover)	Staggered maturities; Aa rated or better; high coupon rate.

MUNICIPAL BOND FUND

It may be that you would like to participate in the municipal-bond market but are undecided about the bonds to buy or your capital is extremely limited. In that case you should consider purchasing units in a municipal bond fund. The units usually sell in $1,000 denominations.

These funds are generally of two types: closed-end investment trust and open-end fund.

In the closed-end fund you pay about $35 per $1,000 unit to buy into the fund. Thus if the fund is paying 6¼% yield to maturity, your return is about 6%. In these funds, no more bonds are purchased after the fund is established. The proceeds of any bonds sold at the direction of the fund's management or called by the issuing authority are distributed to the investors. The closed-end funds pay no management fees. There are provisions for repurchasing units on the basis of the fair market value of the fund. There is no fee for repurchase. You may purchase units in an already established fund by paying a fee. Bonds that are subject to tax in your state may be included in the fund. The funds provide a good return and at the same time avoid your involvement with the complexity of bond dealings. The $1,000 unit price is an incentive for small investors. You should examine the inventory of bonds before you buy to see if they meet with your investment objectives. Some critics are not happy with the quality of these portfolios. You can judge if the fund merits your attention by comparing the bonds you should be buying with the fund's portfolio.

The open-end fund pays its management an annual fee of about ½% to 1%. On a return of 6%, you receive about 5½%. There is a secondary market for you to buy and sell these closed-end funds. There is generally no attempt to provide maximum current income. An open-end fund buys and sells its own shares on a regular basis. You can easily check the performance of a particular open-end fund against *The Bond Buyers* list of 20 representative long-term municipals' average yields as follows:

20-BOND INDEX — MUNICIPALS

1st Week of January	Average Yields to Maturity
1970	6.61%
1971	5.74
1972	5.03
1973	5.08
1974	5.18
1975	7.08
1976	7.13
1977	5.78
1978	6.36

INTEREST TO CARRY TAX-EXEMPTS

You cannot borrow money to buy municipals and deduct the interest from your federal taxes. If you mortgage your house for the purpose of buying municipals, the interest paid on the mortgage is not an allowable tax deduction according to the IRS and several courts.

CORPORATE BONDS

Corporate bonds are taxable. A chart of the yield to maturity is below:

	CORPORATE AAA (DECEMBER 31, YEAR-END YIELD)	CORPORATE AA (MONTH OF DECEMBER AVERAGE YIELD)
1973	7.50%	7.92%
1974	8.41	9.20
1975	8.40	9.25
1976	7.82	8.24
1977	8.35	8.50

When your income-tax bracket is low, corporate bonds are an excellent investment to increase current yield (coupon rate) in excess of municipal bonds.

Some corporate bonds have a convertible feature which permits you to exchange the bond for the issuer's common stock at a specific price. This is a risk-reward factor which allows you to share in the corporation's anticipated future capital appreciation.

The bonds of many corporations are listed on the New York Stock Exchange. The American Stock Exchange also lists bonds. Newspapers report current yields on these bonds (interest coupon divided by cost).

STOCKS

Owning a share in American business through common stock ownership has had its downside over the past 12 years. Nevertheless, in this country most great fortunes are based on common-stock values. Stocks fall into two classes: preferred and common. Preferred means that the second-class or common shares of a particular issuing corporation are subordinate in some fashion to the preferred shares. The preference may be in dividends or liquidation distributions, and is usually in both.

You usually refer to "shares of stock" as the ownership of certificates of common stock in a particular quantity. However, in practice, the terms "shares" and "stock" are synonyms.

One of the great tax advantages of owning stock is that when it does appreciate in value, you may select the year to pay the income tax on the gain. Only a sale, taxable exchange, or redemption makes the gain taxable. Unrealized capital appreciation itself is not subject to tax. On the other hand, interest income from savings banks and corporate bonds must be reported in the year credited or payable.

Bonds are corporate obligations. A bondholder is a creditor. Stocks are an ownership. Stockholders are proprietors.

A corporation, which goes "public", usually has its shares first sold O-T-C (over-the-counter). O-T-C shares are not listed on a stock exchange. However, they are quoted in the daily "Pink Sheets" (The National Daily Quotation Service). This service provides a listing of all the brokers offering particular stocks for sale. In many instances proposed bid (low) and ask (high) prices are stated. If you desire to buy an O-T-C stock, your broker consults the *Pink Sheets* and calls the offering brokers for a price. Active O-T-C stocks (two or more brokers are willing to offer 100 shares at a price) may be listed on the computer service operated by NASDAQ (National Association of Security Dealers' Active Quotations). This permits brokers to buy and to sell the most active O-T-C stocks using computer terminals located in their offices. You can read from the computer display the names of all the brokers making a market in the particular stock and the bid and ask prices. The O-T-C market is often volatile in price. Unless you are very experienced in the ways of the stock market, exercise great caution in buying O-T-C stocks. Tipsters abound in giving information on so-called undervalued O-T-C stocks that are described as future Xerox's. As the expression goes, a fool and his money are soon parted. On the other hand, the tipster may be correct since future winners begin in the O-T-C market. But most novice investors should be careful in dealing in the O-T-C market.

If a company grows and meets certain minimum listing standards, it may apply for a listing on the American Stock Exchange (AMEX) or the New York Stock Exchange (NYSE).

The NYSE's minimum current listing requirements are:

1.	Number of round-lot stockholders (100 shares or more)	2,000
2.	Number of shares in public hands	1,000,000
3.	Market value of shares in the public hands	$16,000,000
4.	Net tangible assets	$16,000,000
5.	Current earnings before income taxes	$2,500,000
6.	Earnings in each of the two prior years	$2,000,000

There are about 1,550 corporations listed on the NYSE.

Negotiated commission rates are charged by brokers for buying and selling stocks. Brokers are free to set whatever rate of commission the traffic will bear. Below is a table of full commissions. Some brokers may offer you substantial discounts from this table. Active traders pay a fraction of these rates.

TABLE OF FULL-RATE BROKERAGE COMMISSIONS
(In effect April 30, 1975)

NUMBER OF SHARES

STOCK'S MARKET PRICE	50	100	200	250	300	400	500
$10	$14	$27	$55	$69	$74	$90	$107
15	18	35	67	84	89	124	149
20	21	42	77	96	117	146	177
25	25	49	87	109	134	169	205
30	27	54	109	136	150	191	233
35	30	59	120	150	167	214	260
40	32	64	132	165	184	236	288
50	36	72	154	193	218	280	325

One of the major securities firms currently charges three different rates: For example, for a purchase or sale of 100 shares of stock selling for $30 per share, the commission plans are:

1. Retail commission $63
2. Individual discount service (advance payment on securities deposited) $51
3. Sharebuilder $47

NOTE:

Fixed commission on April 30, 1975 by this firm $57

Full rate commission per foregoing chart $54

Both the NYSE and AMEX regulate the exchange trading and their own members. The function of a central market place is to permit buyers and sellers to operate in a competitive atmosphere. Specialists are appointed by the Exchanges to keep a "book" on a specific stock. The book prevents volatile price changes in the stock which would affect the orderliness of the market. In theory, the market at any moment should reflect all known information and expectations of buyers and sellers.

The Securities and Exchange Commission (S.E.C.) is planning to consolidate all securities market activities through electronic buying and selling. There will be changes in the future, but how effective they will be no one can be certain. For example, the S.E.C. forced negotiated commissions as of May 1, 1975. This has not necessarily resulted in lower prices to you as an individual but has caused a decline in the number of brokers finding institutional business profitable.

PICKING THE STOCK

Unless your portfolio is at the $100,000 level, the masters of investment counselling will not be personally available to you. You can, of course, choose to invest through mutual funds. If *you* want to be responsible for your portfolio, you must be prepared to keep detailed records and constantly study economic trends and market conditions. The time to buy and the time to sell is crucial no matter what stock you acquire.

If you buy stocks for investment, you buy them through a cash account. This means you will own the stock outright. You will not borrow money from the broker to buy the stock. Currently you may buy stocks on 50% margin. In that case the broker lends you 50% of the money towards the purchase price of the stock. The broker charges you interest on the money while holding your stock as collateral. You are initially required to put up 50% margin. If the stock falls sufficiently in value, the broker makes a margin call. If you fail to respond to a margin call, the stock is sold. The broker remits to you the net proceeds after deducting the margin loan and interest. Buying stocks on margin is a speculative play for professional traders. In this section you will be dealing with stock as an investment. These stocks are purchased for cash. Your stocks may remain in the broker's custody or the certificates may be delivered over to you. If you plan to buy and sell frequently, you may leave the certificates with the broker. Your account is insured for at least $50,000. Some brokers have obtained additional insurance.

MARKET PRINCIPLES

There are many theories of stock-market operations for the average investor, and many valid theories found in recommended books in picking specific stocks. The most practical theory will not function unless you have the temperament to buy stocks. You must believe that capital appreciation and income are attainable in the market. The extent of gains and income depend on the type of stock. To function profitably in stocks the results must be more rewarding over the long period than other investments. The stock market works on averages. You must beat the averages. Nevertheless, you do not require the mental agility of a Mississippi riverboat gambler to be a stock investor.

Although stocks are marketable, no one uses them as a depository for cash reserves. You buy stocks from savings, gifts, or an inheritance to build up your net worth and at the same time to earn income (dividends) on your money. Individual stock losses are not important. It is the value of the entire portfolio which measures performance. Staying power is paramount in the market. In a period of great bargains in stocks, many of those once burned in stocks refuse to recognize that wounds heal and you learn how to keep away from fire.

To deny the stock market as a favorite investment is to doubt the American dream. In Europe, the average person rarely considers stocks as a sound investment. Real estate is the favorite place to invest excess money. The difference in the attitude of the average working person here and abroad toward their economic systems is reflected in the chosen investment vehicle. Most Americans deeply believe in a system of profit-oriented enterprises. The important point is that your choice of stocks as an investment vehicle requires a particular economic philosophy.

"Realize your losses and stay with your profits" is a theory put forward by many. Some successful investors "cull" their stocks the way a dairy farmer culls a herd, selling off the non-producers. Over an eight-year period the dairy farmer develops a herd which is more valuable than its separate cows. The whole is worth more than the sum of the parts.

There are over 3,000 listed stocks from which you can choose. Any number of combinations will result in a good portfolio. The yardstick against which to measure performance is the Standard & Poor's 500 and Dow Jones Industrial Indices. If you beat the indices, your portfolio has performed well. On the other hand, a failure to beat the indices requires you to rework your portfolio carefully. Determine if your industry choices are still sound. There are people who argue against indices as a measure of performance, but since the S & P 500 and Dow are widely used, you should accept them as your yardstick until you feel you have become too sophisticated to use them.

A little over 10 years ago, the Dow Index was at 800. Based upon buying-power changes over the last 10 years, the Dow in early 1978 should have been at 1500. Unfortunately, the Dow on December 31, 1977 closed at 831.17.

The stock market index preferred by investment counsel appears to be the Standard & Poor's 500 index. This index of 500 stocks has more broad-base trend movement than the Dow Jones 30 Industrial Average. So-called "index funds" attempt to duplicate the performance of the S & P 500 by buying stocks comprising a substantial percentage of the value of that index. This is called "indexing the market."

Other factors enter into stock market attitudes towards a stock. Corporate directors and officers may have virtually all their personal fortune invested in their own company's stock. In such cases, they are usually seeking to improve earnings per share so as to make their stock an attractive investment. Their continued purchase of the corporation's stock is another good indication of optimism.

A corporation's stock market position is important when it seeks additional capital through an underwriting. Unless the stock exchange performance is favorable, an underwriting for additional capital may not be possible. The underwriter sells this new stock directly to the public or financial institutions, whereas the exchange sells already issued and outstanding stock among investors. The exchange is considered a bridge for creating a market for future capital needs.

The market price of a stock reflects the consensus of all known public information and is discounted for all forecasted future earnings. The consensus varies widely from year to year. It cannot be correct because it is impossible to predict the future with accuracy. There are, therefore, stocks whose future earnings are greatly undervalued as well as ones that are overvalued. The threshhold question, then, is how to find some of the undervalued stocks while trying to avoid the overvalued ones.

If inflation continues to prevail at 5% to 7% per year, a gradually rising market price of a particular stock needs to yield that much more in long-term results. In general, stocks with future growth possibilities cannot be categorized. Good investments may be found in many industries.

The financial page of your newspaper contains the market indicators on a day-by-day basis. If your interest is that of an investor, a quarterly look at your portfolio (unless something dramatic takes place) should be sufficient to keep you abreast of market developments. When you buy a stock, make a note of the Dow and S & P 500 at that date.

To understand how stock is bought or sold, learn to read the stock tables. For example, on December 31, 1977, the following listing was found in the financial pages of your newspaper (this listing covered the NYSE prices of the prior day):

YEARLY				YLD.	PE	SALES				
HIGH	LOW	STOCK	DIV.	%	RATIO	100'S	HIGH	LOW	LAST	CHG.
71	58¼	Mobil	4.20	6.6	7	859	64⅜	63	63⅝	−¾

This is the listing for Mobil Corp., the major oil company which owns Montgomery Ward and other companies.

During 1977 (excluding December 30), Mobil sold for as high as $71 a share and as low as $58.25. If you were buying, you would also pay a brokerage commission. Most trading prices refer to market price. The buying and selling commission is mentally added at about one point ($100 per 100 shares).

"Div." is the annual dividend currently paid in the amount of $4.20. This is the regular annual dividend payable quarterly based on the last dividend declared. The board of directors votes the dividends. The board is elected by the stockholders to formulate corporate policies. The board appoints officers to carry out these policies.

"Yld.%" is the dividend divided by the closing price. Mobil's yield percentage was 6.60%. The current annual dividend of $4.20 divided by $63.63 equals the yield % of the closing price of 6.60%. The yield is the important measurement in purchasing income stocks.

"PE Ratio" is the price-earnings ratio. This formula takes Mobil's latest 12-month earnings and divides it into the closing price. The ratio here is seven times. That means that you are paying approximately seven years' of Mobil's current earnings to buy a share of stock. Mobil earned a little more than $9 per share in its latest 12-month earnings (63⅝ which is $63.625 ÷ 7 = $9.09). For the calendar year 1976, Mobil actually earned $9.08 per share. For the latest 12 months (four quarters ending December 31, 1977), Mobil earned $9.49 per share.

The price-earnings ratio is a very important indicator in choosing a stock. The lower the PE ratio, the more interesting the stock may become as an investment.

"Sales 100's" shows that 85,900 shares changed hands on that day. The volume figure includes trades on regional stock exchanges where Mobil is listed as well as the NYSE.

"High", "Low", and "Last" show the highest price of the day, lowest price of the day and last price at the close of the market. The change of down ¾ (or 75¢)is the decrease from the previous day's closing price to the December 30, 1977 closing price.

The mean price of Mobil on this day was $63^1/_{16}$ ($64^3/_8 + 63 \div 2$ or 64.375 + 63.00 = 127.375 $\div$ 2 = 63.6875 or $63^1/_{16}$).

These statistics are important when dealing with industry comparisons. For example, in the list of the top 50 largest industrial corporations (rated by sales volume), there were 16 oil companies. In other words, 32% of the largest 50 industrials were energy-related entities. A table of the yield percentage and PE ratios at the close of the stock market on December 30, 1977 indicates:

STOCK	YIELD PERCENTAGE	PRICE EARNINGS RATIO	12/30/77 CLOSING PRICE
Amerada Hess	2.9%	5 times	$27^3/_4$
Ashland Oil	6.6	5	$30^1/_2$
Atlantic Richfield	3.9	9	$51^3/_8$
Cities Service	5.6	7	$53^3/_8$
Continental Oil	4.7	8	30
Exxon	6.2	9	$48^1/_8$
Gulf Oil	7.1	7	$26^3/_4$
Mobil	6.6	7	$63^5/_8$
Occidental Petroleum	5.4	8	$23^1/_4$
Phillips Petroleum	3.3	9	$30^5/_8$
Shell Oil	4.8	7	$33^1/_2$
Standard Oil of California	6.2	7	$38^7/_8$
Standard Oil (Indiana)	5.3	8	$49^1/_2$
Sun	5.9	6	$42^5/_8$
Tenneco	6.5	7	$30^3/_4$
Union Oil	4.2	6	$52^7/_8$

If you believe that all future expectations of a stock have been discounted in the market place and fuels are the growth stock of the future, you could make a choice based only on this table. A professional investment counsel would also consider such factors as domestic and international oil reserves owned, financial strength, dividend record, earnings record over a period of years, and outside business interests.

There is much to study before you can make a truly valid selection. If you are not in a position to afford an investment counsel, you may use a stockbroker. Once you have decided that as a group energy companies represent the industry of your interest, your broker (based upon the research available) may help you make the specific choice.

To make this exercise more meaningful, examine today's Yld % and PE ratios for the oils. Insert these figures in the table. That will give you an idea of how the market works on these yardsticks. If the mean prices rose, you would have made a profit. The entire price increase is called capital appreciation. If these stocks did not perform, remember that your money in the savings bank earns 5.25% regular interest against the dividends earned within this group. Dividends are not guaranteed.

Within this group of stocks, there are arguments as to whether certain companies may fall within the definition of an oil company. For example, Tenneco is primarily a natural gas line company, and it has large manufacturing interests. It has a fair portion of income from oil production, and it has therefore been included. There are between 25 and 30 industry classifications for the 500 largest industrial corporations. In addition, there are insurance companies and financial institutions.

The analysis and information available to you about stocks is enormous. The following are just a few of the excellent books available to increase your knowledge in picking a particular stock:

How to Buy Stocks by Louis Engel
The Art of Low Risk Investment by Michael G. Zahorchak
Stock Market Strategy by Richard A. Crowell
The Only Investment Guide You'll Ever Need by Andrew Tobias.

In addition, Standard & Poor's publishes *The Stock Guide*. The year-end edition is of particular value. *Moody's Handbook of Common Stocks* contains valuable information for over 1,000 stocks. The *Stock Guide* lists most public companies but with only summary information. The cost of these books is tax deductible.

If you have decided to be your own investment counsel, there are five cardinal rules to follow:

1. If they are not directly involved in the stock market on a full-time basis, forget your neighbors and associates as a source of advice, unless you know from past experience that their advice has been exceptionally fine.

2. Maintain a quarterly performance chart on all your holdings.

3. Read financial news regularly.

4. Try not to follow the crowd when most people think a stock is going

to advance. Their buying has already raised its price excessively. When everyone has heard about a company's troubles, investigate the possibility of its stock's being a bargain.

5. Be bullish when things look bad and cautious when things look good!

These last two rules have been the keys to many successful investments. The future looked bleak during the great depression and when the Germans captured Paris and when President Kennedy had just been reported shot, yet these moments were among the best possible times to have bought stocks.

DIVIDEND TRENDS

The mathematics function of linear regression is easily computed on an inexpensive present value calculator. This function may be used to project future dividends based on known historical data.

This does not mean that conditions of an unexpected nature will not alter the future event. You will learn, however, the prime candidates for increased dividend payments. A trend line produces certain graphic charts which are reflected in the calculator memory.

Many very successful investors believe their dividend trend analysis is a "follow the crowd" procedure and, therefore avoid it. But if you are looking for increased income, you may find it to be of some assistance. It can be useful for making projections concerning very large companies. Be certain that conditions have not greatly changed from those of the past, otherwise the forecasting is invalid.

Mobil Corporation paid the following dividends for the years 1967 through 1976:

YEAR	DIVIDEND PER SHARE	YEAR	DIVIDEND PER SHARE
1967	$1.85	1972	$2.65
1968	2.05	1973	2.80
1969	2.25	1974	3.20
1970	2.40	1975	3.40
1971	2.55	1976	3.50

From this information you can develop a trend-line analysis to answer these questions:

1. What dividend could be expected in 1977?
2. When will the annual dividend reach $5.00?

A trend-line computation based upon the historical data of Mobil over the past 10 years results in:

1. 1977 projected dividends of $3.68.
2. $5.00 dividend in 1984.

In fact, the 1977 dividend was actually $3.90, a difference of 6% ($3.90 ÷ $3.68 = 1.06 − 1.00 = 6%). Adding the actual 1977 dividend to the historical data, the trend-line analysis indicates that the 1978 dividend should be $3.94 and the $5.00 dividend would be reached in 1983. Test the accuracy of the Mobil historical data trend-line predicting a 1978 dividend of $3.94 against the actual 1978 dividend unknown at this writing. If the present quarterly dividend rate continues, the actual 1978 dividend should be $4.20.

There are other types of analysis for forecasting that use linear regression to input financial data to a specific company. These permit a present-value calculator to predict when two points on a vertical and horizontal axis may intercept. For practical financial problems you must first make the determination that the information is valid. Thus, if you think there is a relationship in a certain company's sales to earnings per share you might set out a problem as follows:

YEAR	SALES	EARNINGS PER SHARE
1973	$185 million	$2.32
1974	193	2.60
1975	201	2.87
1976	210	2.93
1977	225	3.60

The shares outstanding must be constant during the period or the earnings adjusted so that the data are correctly related to each year.

QUESTIONS:

1. What will the earnings be when the sales reach $250 million?
2. What will be the sales when the earnings reach $4.00 per share?
3. What is the incremental earnings per $1 million of sales?

Using the linear-regression mode of the calculator, the data entry for the two sets of known facts forecasts that:

1. At sales of $250 million, the earnings per share will be $4.29.
2. Earnings of $4 per share will be reached when the sales are $240 million.
3. Each $1 million of sales increases the earnings by .03¢.

Other questions emerge from these facts:

1. In what year will sales reach $250 million?
2. In what year will earnings of $4 per share be achieved?

Using the same analysis as in dividend forecasting, the answers are:

1. Sales will reach $250 million in 1979.
2. Earnings will be $4 per share in 1981.

There is another type of linear regression which you may find valuable, particularly in analyzing a blue chip company's data. Compare the earnings of every third year of the past 15 years, then forecast the earnings for a future year and in what year the earnings would reach a specific amount. If the company pays a dividend based on paying out a percentage of earnings, you may forecast future dividends from this data.

For example, blue chip A shows the following earnings per share over the past 15 years at three-year intervals:

YEAR	EARNINGS PER SHARE
1965	$1.80
1968	2.37
1971	3.51
1974	4.10
1977	5.23

After looking at this steady growth pattern, you believe that blue chip A currently returning a yield percentage of 6.3% is a good investment at a price earnings ratio of nine (stock is selling at $50). You want to know:

1. What should be the earnings per share nine years from the last figure (1986)?
2. When will the earnings reach $7 per share?

According to a curve based on natural logarithms, a present-value calculator forecasts:

1. 1986 earnings per share of $12.12.
2. $7 earnings per share in 1980.

If this is correct, then in three years the dividends should be $4.20. At $50 the company pays 6.3%, or $3.15 per share. They are paying out 60% of earnings ($5.23 × 60% = $3.15 and $7.00 × 60% = $4.20 dividend for 1980). At a $50 price, currently the stock will yield 8.4%. Therefore, if the historical data are correct and no economic downturn intervenes, the income portion of the stock investment has beaten the currently-projected inflation rate of between 5% to 7% per year.

On the capital appreciation side of the investment, the stock is forecasted to sell at $60. (Assuming a 7% yield and payout of a $4.20 dividend in 1980, the price would be $4.20 ÷ 7% = $60.) You would have had capital appreciation of 20%.

The three examples of forecasting, dividend trends, sales to earnings, and earnings trends are simplistic approaches to stock buying for income and appreciation. These techniques are just the tip of the iceberg to the sophisticated approaches of asset management. You may want to examine a particular favorite stock because you like the company's goods, public image, management or for many other reasons.

After you have made an industry choice, calculated your linear regressions and picked the particular stock, ask the stockbroker what his firm's research people think. If they disagree with your choice, ask for their fact sheet on the stock. Compare and discuss. You will learn quickly to be your own money manager.

Merrill Lynch maintains what they call a "QRQ" system for about 1,000 stocks. It contains a wealth of information on when to buy and sell a particular stock. A Merrill Lynch office will give you samples of the output on your stocks without any obligation.

You can't control waves, but you can ride with them. If you have large profits in a stock and the market becomes unstable (stocks continue to drop in price over a period) there is nothing wrong with taking profits and investing your money in short-term paper (U.S. Treasury bills or high-grade corporate commercial paper). This is an approach sophisticated investors use while awaiting the bargains. The close of 1977 saw many stocks at bargain prices. No one was certain at that time whether the market had bottomed out. Investors at the beginning of 1978 were extremely cautious about making purchases of stocks.

The bull is an optimist, the bear, the pessimistic hibernator. A short seller (one who sells stock borrowed from the broker and purchases later) is a bear. The bear believes stocks will continue to drop in price. A believer in improved future conditions is bullish. You may be bullish and be a short-term bear. You would keep your position liquid until you believed there were indications of the beginning of a bull market.

You may follow a company's past performance by using the *Fortune* and *Forbes* annual listings of the 500 leading industrial corporations. Learn where a particular stock stands in relation to a series of market and industry indicators. You may find that new ideas come to you for additional investment opportunities from these listings.

Every time there is a new market trend, a previously unknown investment counsellor announces his or her particular method for success. Such announcements should be regarded with caution. If you believe their approach was a fair and responsible one, ask them for complete reprints of their advice going back at least 10 years. (Usually the first issue published each year is representative.) Only if they have been substantially correct in the past, do they deserve any credence.

MUTUAL FUNDS

Stock brokerage firms offer a wide variety of vehicles in which to invest your money. If you want to move beyond the savings bank account to the next level of intangible property investment, ask yourself whether you personally have the diligence to supervise your investments and, more important, whether you have the capital to be employed in investments. You will need staying power for record-keeping, study, discussions, and decisions. You will experience frustration as well as achievement. You have constantly to be measuring your performance against yardsticks. If you have the staying power, you may choose to be an investor.

If your capital for investment purposes is between $10,000 and $100,000, you may use a broker to help you select investments. Do not pick your broker because he is your friend. Find out how his or her advice is regarded by the most successful people you know. Find out how successful the broker has been, not just in generating commissions for the firm but in making profits for clients over a period of years. Look for a conservative, respected person who knows a great deal about many stocks and many industries. If your broker receives his advice on what to do from others, including his or her firm, it is unlikely the broker will be above average in performance.

The floor amount for investing in a portfolio is $10,000. Your purchases should be in companies with long profit records and reasonable dividends. You should not change more than 15% of your holdings in a single year. Overtrading in time generally leads to large losses. With less than $10,000 in capital, you should reconsider the market place and leave your invest- ment money in a savings account, high-grade municipals or corporate bonds. You may differ and work with considerably less money in the mar- ket. The $10,000 floor appears, however, from experience based on stock prices, to be a basic sum for diversification. If your capital exceeds $100,000 you should retain investment counsel.

A person with $100,000 to invest may not have the staying power but may be able to use investment counsel effectively. Staying power is really a prime requisite for the $10,000 to $100,000 group. Within this group a lack of staying power but a desire to invest is solved by mutual funds.

Mutual funds specialize in the many areas of investment opportunity including municipal bonds, corporate bonds, income stock, growth stocks, growth and income stocks, capital appreciation stocks (often same as growth), bank and insurance stocks, gold shares, foreign stocks, and over-the-counter shares.

There are always new and different funds coming to the market place. However, the 10 classifications above are sufficient for your use.

There are three principal types of funds: closed end, open end (no load or no commission) and open end (load or commission paid on purchase).

A no-load fund charges you no commissions to buy or withdraw. Fund managers are compensated by management fees usually based on asset values. The closed-end fund means the total capital has been issued. You buy into the fund by buying outstanding shares in the open market. An open-end fund is bought directly from the fund.

The method of a particular fund's purchase or operations plan is impor- tant even if you are a long-term investor. For a load fund, the initial buy- in price differential may cost 7% premium on the money invested and take nearly two years to recoup.

The closed-end fund is bought and sold on the stock market, usually at a meaningful discount from net asset value. Since you benefit from the in- come on the entire portfolio but may have bought in for a 15% discount, you are in position of obtaining the professional management for free. In addition, the income earned by the fund in this discount will also offset within about two years the brokerage cost of buying and selling the fund.

An open-end no-load fund is purchased for net asset value. Such a fund increases in size but not in per-share value as more people invest.

In reality, it is performance you are buying so the kind of fund you choose is less important than the performance of the fund's management.

After reviewing the list of the 10 available classifications, return to page 384 and study the chart of persons and investment opportunities for your category. This chart gives general principles of investments to be avoided by different ages and occupations. If you are satisfied that the chart accurately describes the investments you should avoid, make a list of the investments remaining in your age category and occupation. You may then relate these choices to one or more mutual funds.

There may or may not be a difference between "growth" or "capital appreciation" funds, depending upon the management of the fund. Understand that funds with such labels do not aim for high current income.

Option funds have not been listed since some option-share funds are speculative. These funds buy and sell puts and calls. However, there are conservative option funds that have a portfolio of stocks and sell calls using the proceeds to increase income and reduce risk.

Some fund managements permit you, for a nominal fee, to switch funds within the management group. This conversion factor has become an advantage and should be considered when buying a particular fund.

Assuming that you are in your mid-30's and would like to divide your money between growth and income funds, the growth percentage would be about 75% of the investment and the income factor about 25%. You then have a choice of separate funds or a combined fund. What is important is the past performance of the fund you buy. You can obtain from the financial press or from the funds themselves the performance figures for the past 10 years of all the funds in the classifications you have chosen. The S & P 500 index is the yardstick for comparison.

For example, in 1977, five growth funds increased their net asset values from just over 20% to almost 44%. If the same funds performed well in the prior four years, they would be prime candidates for your consideration. *Forbes* and *Barron's* regularly publish mutual fund performances.

There are over 600 mutual funds available for people who don't want to work at investments. Choose first by classification, then refine your choice by the fund's performance record. A fund that has failed to perform satisfactorily is no bargain. It is a prime candidate for a tax swap.

SPECULATIONS

For the purpose of this section, a speculation is a high-risk investment made with the hope of an abnormally high return. An unlisted stock in the

O-T-C (over-the-counter) market for your purposes representing less than 10% of an investment portfolio may be an acceptable speculation. It is a "flyer" for increasing performance. Speculations permit large profit and loss potential for a relatively small capital investment. Options and the futures market fit within this definition. Hedging, straddles, and arbitrage are also part of this package. Unless you have risk capital of $50,000 and a substantial net worth, you do not belong in speculations.

There are "systems" involving these speculations which claim to "guarantee" a 15% return without risk. Unfortunately over a five-year performance period, the only ones who generally made money were the brokers. The option and future markets are for professionals with substantial capital. There is money to be made but not by limited capital investors.

OPTIONS

Because there is a clearing house for open contracts, the option market exchange has become popular in recent years. The developer of the clearing house was the Chicago Board Options Exchange (CBOE). The AMEX and other exchanges have option trading. The exchange supplies a central market place for those who want to buy or sell options on a particular listed stock. The prices are reported daily in the financial pages.

A call writer receives money for a contract permitting someone to buy a stock from the writer for a limited time at a particular price. This is a call option. The price to be paid is the strike price. An option may expire in three, six or nine months. The call writer believes that the stock will not rise substantially during the option period. The buyer of the call thinks the opposite. If the stock price begins to rise to the point at which the buyer may exercise the call, the option seller has three choices:

1. Buy back the call and realize a capital loss.

2. Buy the stock (if not owned) and protect the downside risk.

3. Do nothing and wait for the buyer to exercise the option.

A person owning the stock and selling calls is dealing in covered options. A naked option means that the seller has an unlimited risk if the market price of the stock rises rapidly during the option period.

A "put" permits the purchaser to sell stock at a specific price for a period of time. The option unit is a 100-share lot of the stock. The put buyer has the right to "put" the stock to the put writer at a strike price. There are currently about 25 put option stocks. This compares with several hundred call option stocks. The put writer, who may also own the underlying stock, believes the stock will rise. On the other hand, the call writer who may also own the specific stock believes the stock will move sideways or decrease. The call seller (writer) and put buyer are bears (pessimists). The call buyer and put seller (writer) are bulls.

The underlying stocks for option trading have a large market following and are usually blue chips. Here is how the call option operates:

1. Dow Chemical stock is selling at 26⅛ on December 21, 1977 ($26.125 + commission). The strike price is $25.
2. A call option is 3⅛ ($312.50 per 100 shares). The option expires July 29, 1978.
3. A call writer (seller) receives $287.50 on a 100 share-call option ($312.50 less a minimum commission of $25).
4. The buyer pays $337.50 for the option ($312.50 + minimum commission of $25). The option cost per share is 3⅜ ($337.50 ÷ 100).

Dow's stock action during the seven-month period to July 29, 1978 may be:

1. Increase above 28⅜ (strike price of 25+ 3⅜, the option cost per share).
2. Trade between 25 and 28⅜.
3. Decrease below 25.

In the first case, if the stock increases above 28⅜, the buyer will exercise the option. The seller will lose money. The $287.50 received by the seller reduces the stock's cost. The buyer's cost of $337.50 increases the purchase price of the stock. The buyer may also have sold the option at the new high price before the expiration date rather than exercising it. If the seller has not closed out the option, the seller is required to purchase the stock (if not already owned) for delivery to the buyer.

In the second case where the stock trades between 25 and 28⅜, the buyer will exercise the option even though he will lose money. As long as the stock trades above 25 it pays the buyer to exercise to recoup some of the option cost. The seller makes money. Options have a continuous market. They are usually held by speculators who buy and sell frequently. The seller may also have closed out the option by repurchasing it for probably more than $287.50.

In the third case, where the stock sells below 25, the buyer will not exercise the option. The buyer will have lost the entire investment. The seller makes money on the option. However, if the seller owns the stock, the profit on the option will offset some or all of the loss of the stock's market value.

Most options are sold by large investors, institutions or individuals who already own the stocks. These options are known as covered options since the downside risk to the seller is not unlimited. The seller does not have to go out in the market and buy the stock if the buyer exercises these options. The seller already owns the stock.

Many knowledgeable Wall Street investors believe that in the long run the buyers of options lose money the way customers do at a casino. The sellers of options, like the casino owners, normally make profits, as do the brokers.

The current commission rates on option trading are based on the purchase or sale price of the contract. Generally, the minimum commission is $25 for a trade. A $100 to $2,499 contract costs 1.3% of the value plus $12. A $2,500 to $4,777 contract costs .9% of the value plus $22.

The commission for the 10 contracts of Dow at 3⅛ on these rates would be:

1. Cost of contracts excluding commission:
   a) $3.125 × 100 shares = $312.50
   b) $312.50 × 10 contracts = $3,125.00

2. Commissions:
   $3,125 × .9% = $28.13
   Unit Charge =   22.00
      Total Commission $50.13

The seller (call writer) receives $3,074.87 ($3,125.00 − $50.13). The buyer pays $3,175.13 ($3,125.00 + $50.13).

In a declining market, call premiums will be low and put premiums will be high. Premiums reflect current expectations about future stock prices.

COMMODITIES

Headlines reading "Soybeans Soar on India Sale Rumor" and "Bigger Cocoa Crop and Lower Prices" caption typical commodity-futures financial stories. Someone will make a "killing" and someone else will be "murdered" in the commodity world for being on the right or wrong side.

The soybean story tells about the large exporter who was supposedly buying soybean products for sale to India, resulting in the prices of beans and oil futures reaching new heights on the Chicago Board of Trade. Thus, feast, famine, technical adjustments, weather, negative influences, positive influences, bread prices, government action, and innumerable other factors caused a rise and fall in the commodity futures markets.

Commodities are a speculative vehicle for those with the 50/500 minimum financial standard ($50,000 risk capital and $500,000 net worth excluding home and life insurance). People buy commodity futures because of the low margin requirements. A stock margin account requires 50% of value. Commodities require about 10% margin. In volatile markets, you can make (or lose) faster than any other legitimate money play, as Adam Smith explains superbly in *Super Money*.

Commodity trading plays a very important role in economic life. The high risks in commodities are the reason the exchanges were designed. The baker could know his wheat costs months in advance by buying a wheat futures contract. Today it is rare that anyone takes delivery of the wheat under the futures contract. Rather, the wheat is bought in the open market and the futures contract is sold for gain or for loss. If the price of wheat rises, the gain on the futures contract reduces the increased cost of wheat. If the wheat drops in price, the loss on the futures is added to the open market price of the wheat. This is called "hedging" raw materials.

Because of the financial excitement in the commodity-futures market place, the successful traders are treated with unusual deference in the financial world. "Resourceful," "astute," "lucky," are some adjectives applied to long-time traders. It is a "feel-it-in-the-guts" speculation.

Unlike stocks and bonds, which are long-term property interests, each buyer long (owning) a commodity contract must be balanced by someone selling (short) the same contract. There is no net property interest involved. The short may be a producer or grower or a speculator. The long may be a user or may also be a speculator.

For example, a miller may be short wheat in amount equal to part of the flour being processed. A grower may be short some part of the expected crop. On the contrary, a manufacturer who has contracted to deliver a given amount of wire in the future could be long a quantity of copper. The long and short interests in a commodity future are always precisely equal. In the long run, few speculators have profited from commodity trading.

Each night all the commodity exchange members balance out their transactions against one another through a clearing house. If the total value of the open contracts rose from the inventory of the previous day, the member prepares a cash draft on the exchange clearinghouse. If the total value is lower, the member sends its check to the clearinghouse. Thus, at the close of each day, all of the outstanding contracts have been balanced. The exchange members call for margin money from clients whose contracts have been reduced below the percentage currently allowed (about 10%). If the price increases, there is no credit to the account but the customer may withdraw the change (value times margin percentage less cost times margin percentage).

Commodity futures trading is done in most agricultural products and metals. The possible difference between the price at the time for protection and the product requirement date creates the commodity futures market. There is also a futures market for U.S. Government obligations (Treasury Bills and Ginnie Mae certificates) and foreign exchange.

STRADDLE

The straddle is a trading mechanism used by sophisticated investors, traders, and speculators. Put and call options with the same strike price and expiration date are a straddle. In addition, buying and selling the same commodity future for different months' delivery is also a straddle.

If you own the underlying stock, you may have a covered straddle position by selling puts and calls. Since there are about 25 stocks for which there is a put option market, one of any of these issues may be used to write a covered straddle.

In the ideal situation in a covered straddle, the underlying stock moves sideways (usually within two points of the stock striking price). Thus the put and call options are worthless. The straddle writer's goal is to increase the yield in stock ownership by a straddle position in a stock which the owner believes will not move in price (low price volatility). Traders write naked straddles, i.e., an uncovered position. The underlying stock is not owned. This is a very risky business.

In the commodity field, the straddle has been used to defer income taxes. By buying and selling futures contracts for delivering in different months of the following year, the holder has an option to close out the loss contract at the year-end. This offsets other capital gains. The other contract with a profit is closed the next year. The IRS has ruled that straddles in the commodity market cannot be used for the primary purpose of reducing other current capital gains. Silver futures have been a favorite commodity for this play since prices are volatile and yet there is no significant difference between delivery dates. Thus a substantial loss may be generated at the end of one year and a large gain the following year. The straddle for tax deferment has come under very close scrutiny by the IRS.

ARBITRAGE

Arbitrage is the process of taking advantage of inefficiencies in the market. For example, Royal Dutch Petroleum is traded on many stock exchanges throughout the world and in many currencies. Because of constant fluctuations in stock prices and currency exchange rates, it is sometimes possible to buy Royal Dutch on one exchange and simultaneously sell it on another. The profit is realized without bearing any risk.

Another frequent arbitrage situation involves mergers. If Company X is taking over Company Y and giving a single share (selling at $40) for each share of Company Y stock selling at $38, there is a profit to be realized by buying Y stock and selling X stock.

Risk arbitrage occurs when the takeover price is uncertain. This movement can generate large profits (or large losses). In 1977 the big risk arbitrage movement was in Carborundum Corp. An arbitrageur, believing that a bidding was about to break out for the acquisition of Carborundum, bought a substantial stock position (on margin and borrowed funds) in that company. During the fall of 1977, one company (Eaton Corp.) announced a takeover bid for Carborundum at $47. Carborundum (the target company) was then selling around $30. The arbitrageur, believing the final price would be more than $47, began to buy stock in the target entity.

In the middle of November, Kennecott Copper Corp. offered $66 per share which was accepted. The closing took place on December 30, 1977. The takeover bid (despite court action by some unhappy Kennecott shareholders) was successful. The arbitrageur profited from the difference between the $66 takeover price and the market price in the fall of 1977. Assuming an average cost to the arbitrageur of $47 per share, the profit of $19 per share or 40% is fantastic for a three-month position. If a new bidder for Carborundum had failed to materialize, the price might still have remained firm. The arbitrageur then would have been out the interest cost of the money borrowed to support the position. There is always the risk that the price will plummet after a failed takeover bid. This happened in 1977 when a target company, Gerber Products Company, successfully opposed a takeover bid by Anderson Clayton & Co.

Arbitrage is for the sophisticated and requires professional guidance.

THE SHORT SALE

For tax purposes a sale of stock does not take place until delivery of the shares. The trade date (stock sold) and settlement date (stock certificate delivered or money exchanged) have important tax and legal distinctions. Nevertheless, your holding period (more than one year for long-term gains) is measured by the trade date. The timing of a loss is the tax year of the trade date. A gain takes place in the tax year of the settlement of the sale. These seemingly inconsistent statements are the law.

In the ordinary course of trading, the last day of the year for taking gains is five days before December 31. The date changes each year. Losses may be realized until the last trading day of the year. If you must take a tax profit in a particular year, after the normal settlement date your broker may arrange a cash settlement before the year end.

A market investor believes in the long run that stocks will rise. In the short run, if a person believes the market will fall, that person may take a short position by means of a short sale. You may also use a short sale to defer taxes on stocks you presently own. In a short sale, someone lends the short seller the stock to deliver to a buyer. In "short against the box," the short seller owns the stock. However, the usual short sale is covered by stock borrowed from the broker.

The short seller owes cash dividends payable on the stock to the lender. Stock dividends, rights, and stock splits are also the liability of the short seller.

The proceeds of the short sale are held in the brokerage account as part collateral for the borrowed stock. The broker will need an additional 50% margin for protection. If the stock shorted rises, the broker may request additional collateral. The short seller awaits the market decrease to repurchase the stock. The delivery of the purchased stock to cover the short closes out the short transaction for tax purposes.

There are special tax rules if you hold the shares of stock in a corporation and then go short in the same stock. Holding periods are adjusted which may result in short-term gains or long-term losses because of your prior position. Professional tax help is required if you sell short a stock you own in order to defer reporting a gain until a subsequent year.

FLAT BONDS

Some corporations are delinquent in paying bond interest on income bonds. These are bonds which pay interest only if the issuer has a specific amount of earnings. These bonds sell "flat." You pay no accrued interest when you buy flat bonds. If you purchase a bond flat and it later pays interest earned in periods prior to your purchase date, the interest received reduces your cost. It is not income. If you sell the bond, you have a larger gain. If you have a large capital loss and do not wish to have a carryover to future years, you might ask a broker to find you a flat bond which has made an announcement of paying a prior period's interest in the future. You can then buy and sell the bonds and absorb your capital loss.

OIL AND GAS

The senior vice-president of the petroleum division of a major bank (himself a recognized petroleum engineer) said, "The number of public oil programs which have ever made any real money for investors may be counted on the fingers of one hand. And there has been only one bonanza!" Therefore, in general, you are contributing towards the welfare of a promoter when you buy a public oil program. In addition, you may be providing the funds to prove up someone else's land. Like all statements of principle, there are exceptions. The exceptions cover a small fraction of the offerings.

The simplified mathematics of public oil and gas tax shelter programs for someone in the 60% marginal tax bracket operates as follows:

1. $50,000 is invested in the oil or gas program.

2. The taxpayer claims a $50,000 intangible drilling-cost deduction on his or her tax return. Instead of paying the IRS the tax on $50,000 or $30,000 ($50,000 × 60%), the taxpayer pays $50,000 to the program. At this stage, the person is out the $20,000 that would have been left if the tax had been paid. Thus, the program was paid $50,000, the individual's taxes were reduced by $30,000, and the individual has $20,000 of his or her own money in the deal. If the taxes had been paid, the individual would have had the $20,000 amount left for savings.

3. The program is drilled. If any prospect results in a commercial well, there is a 15% minimum tax payable on its drilling costs. No minimum tax is due in this example to the extent that the drilling costs of the successful wells were less than $10,000, which today is the basic minimum tax-preference allowance. The program's petroleum engineers report after three years that the present value of future oil or gas production is appraised at a specific amount. The taxpayer donates the program unit to a public charity, claiming this specific amount as a charitable deduction for tax purposes. This reduces the year's tax by the marginal tax bracket of 60% times the specific amount.

4. The appraisal is the key to the program's success. In order for the taxpayer to break even, the appraisal on a present-value basis must be in excess of $50,000. This is after considering that the intangible drilling costs on the successful wells are reportable as taxable income in the year of the gift. Mathematical computation assumes inflation to be 6.5% per year. At the end of the third year, the $20,000 must be worth $24,159 (6.5% compounded annually for three years). Therefore, the net out-of-pocket profit must be at least $4,000 in order to break even. The tax on an assumed $10,000 cost of successful wells at the 60% bracket is $6,000. The tax benefit of the donation must equal $30,000 ($20,000 + $6,000 = $26,000 + inflation of $4,000). To achieve a tax benefit of $30,000, the value of the gift must be $50,000 ($30,000 ÷ by 60%). To summarize:

YEAR	ACTIVITY	TAX WRITE-OFF	(OUT-OF-POCKET) CASH PROFIT AFTER TAXES (60% TAX BRACKET)
1	Cash invested	$50,000	($20,000)
3	Charitable Gift	50,000	30,000
	Intangible drilling costs on commercial wells: income	(10,000)	(6,000)

Gain (inflation at 6.5% reduces real gain to zero) $ 4,000

5. Experts claim that with few exceptions, publicly held oil and gas programs have failed to return one dollar for each dollar invested over as long a period as 15 years. In view of the history of these programs, the chances of a valid appraisal reaching a break-even point after three years are remote.

The above shows you how difficult it is to profit from a typical oil and gas tax shelter. The appraisal is subject to close examination by IRS petroleum engineers. Some of the best engineers in the country work for the IRS, including one who was a former reservoir engineer for Aramco in Saudi Arabia. The IRS knows if the oil is "there" so you may have a dispute over appraisal values.

On the other hand, you can make money in oil if you have $200,000 a year or more to spend and commit yourself to a five-year-one million dollar program. You can participate in industry-type deals: "thirds for a quarter." For each 33⅓% of the cost of drilling a well that you pay, you have a 25% participation in the working interest. The working interest usually is about 80¢ of a revenue dollar. The other 20% goes to the land owner, geologist, and landsman. You only pay "thirds for a quarter" until casing point. This is the point at which the well is believed to be successful and a pipe is to be set in the hole. After casing point (just before the setting of pipe) everyone who has a working interest must pay his own share of costs and lease operating expenses. In the "thirds for a quarter" deal, the operator receives a free quarter interest in the drilling for putting the prospect together. Included in the original drilling costs is about a 35% profit to the operator which reimburses them for prior cost outlays.

Everyone knows that oil drilling is a high-risk business. Only an average of one out of 10 exploration drillings result in a commercial well. By spreading out the prospects, the probability of total loss decreases.

People outside the oil business are said to know nothing about wildcatting (looking for oil in virgin territory). Instead, these outsiders do development drilling without the real profitable opportunity (other than taxes) that is possible in exploration drilling.

The oil business moves fast. You know usually within 30 days after the rig moves on site if the oil or gas is there in the ground. Everyone in oil country knows one another. Oil people are robust, friendly folk who operate with the minds of cunning foxes. They don't like to be questioned by the investors about every move. In order to be in the oil business, persons residing outside the oil country require a person to act as an agent. That individual should be a person of good reputation who will act for the investor. The person is either a geologist or engineer, who may be found through the special industries department of a large bank. These oil and gas professionals screen prospects and manage oil properties. If an independent expert does not carefully review the prospects, the chances of success are extremely limited.

Another type of drilling deal is the turnkey deal. An operator agrees to drill a well to a predetermined depth at a fixed price. If the contracts are signed and the money is paid in 1978, you may claim the tax deduction in 1978 although the turnkey well may not be drilled until 1979.

Oil is a popular risk investment because substantially all the drilling expenses are a tax writeoff (intangible drilling costs). The casing point pipe and certain other expenditures are capitalized. The tangible costs are subject to a 10% investment credit and accelerated depreciation.

Oil and gas revenues may be reduced by 22% depletion tax allowance. This means a person in the 70% or top marginal tax bracket pays about 55% on oil income ($1 − 22¢ = 78¢ × 70% = 54.6¢). If you have a commercial well, the IRS claims a minimum tax (15%) on substantially all intangible drilling costs for this well. This is an excise tax which reduces the incentive to individuals for oil and gas exploration.

Geothermal energy also has many of the attributes of oil and gas exploration. Geothermal experts believe a large-scale program of development could result in 20 years in 15% of the electrical energy of the country being generated geothermally. Congress has appropriated large sums of money for assisting geothermal development.

Most "on shore" United States oil and gas drilling is done by independent operators. The major oil companies, prefer to drill abroad and offshore.

Occasionally there are excellent opportunities available for individuals with personal financial reserves to make profits in industry-type oil and gas deals.

LOUISE SMITH'S INVESTMENT PORTFOLIO

In the fall of 1973, Daniel and Louise Smith believed that the moment had arrived when they should begin to share in the growth of American business. They decided to enter the stock market. Louise had saved $10,000. The Smiths decided to purchase a mixed portfolio of stocks with the prime objective of capital growth with income a secondary consideration.

The "Stock Trends" column in *Forbes* magazine dated October 1, 1973 by Myron Simons (the director of research in a well-known securities firm) indicated that the time had come to invest in stocks. This column, entitled "The Turn is Near" stated "A major buying opportunity exists." The author recommended the following stocks according to industry classification:

SEPTEMBER 25, 1973

	DIVD. ($)	YIELD %	PE RATIO	CLOSE ($)
AUTOMOBILES				
Ford	3.20	5	5	60⅛
General Motors	4.55	6.9	7	66¼
CHEMICAL				
Dow	1.00	1.7	23	58¼
DuPont	5.45	3	17	176¾
Monsanto	2.00	3	12	66

FOOD

General Mills	1.08	1.7	21	63¾

NONFERROUS METALS

Alcoa	1.94	2.6	14	73¼

OIL

Exxon	3.95	4.3	11	91½
Texaco	1.72	5.3	8	32⅝

PAPER

St. Regis	1.60	3.4	12	47½
International Paper	1.50	3.2	15	46¾

RETAIL

Sears Roebuck	1.60	1.7	23	96⅞
J. C. Penney	1.12	1.4	26	79⅜

STEEL

Bethlehem	1.40	4.3	8	32¾

In addition, for personal reasons, Daniel asked Louise to add to her list:

Macmillan, Inc.	.15	1.8	7	8⅜

A controversy existed at that time between the believers and nonbelievers in the stock market. The believers contended in 1973 that the "buy" signals were apparent. In the long run only a managed stock portfolio could produce growth to combat the inflationary forces eroding capital. The nonbelievers argued that the stock market, after their experiences of the late 1960s, was too speculative. High bank and bond interest rates would for the foreseeable future prevent capital growth.

At the close of 1973, the Standard & Poor's 500 index was 97.55 and at the same time the Dow Jones Industrials stood at 850.86. At the close of 1977 (four years later), the S & P 500 was 95.10 and the Dow was 831.17.

Declines for the four years of these indices were:

	PERCENTAGE POINTS (DECREASE) 12/31/73 TO 12/31/77	% CHANGE
S & P 500	(2.45)	2.51%
Dow	(19.69)	2.31%

Using the S & P 500 as a yardstick, the following table of an investment illustrates the results from a $10,000 investment in the stock market on January 1, 1974:

COMMENCE-MENT DATE	INVESTMENT	PERIOD IN YEARS	INCOME EARNED*	CAPITAL (DECREASE)	12/31/77 VALUE
1/1/74	$10,000	4	$1,835	($251)	$11,584

*Assumed yield for this purpose of 5% based upon the average of Standard & Poor yearly beginning and ending index.

A deposit in a savings account on January 1, 1974 for four years would have been worth $13,149 before taxes at December 31, 1977. This is based on the four-year regular rate at January 1, 1973 of 6.75% (7.08% effective).

The comparison of total return of a stock market investment indexed to the S & P 500 and a savings bank account over the past four years reflects the following:

12/31/77 VALUES

INVESTMENT 1/1/74 OF	SAVINGS ACCOUNT	STOCK MARKET	(DECREASE)	% (DECREASE) IN CAPITAL
$10,000	$13,149	$11,584	($1,565)	(11.90%)

On the basis of this table, the overall return loss in stocks was almost 12% over the past four years compared with the safe savings-bank investment. Interestingly, the continued debate over the worthiness of the stock market for individual investments shows large numbers of these disbelievers are employed in the professions: lawyers, accountants, physicians, dentists, and engineers.

After the Smiths read Mr. Simons' article in the October 1, 1973 issue of *Forbes* Magazine they began to set up the portfolio on September 26, 1973.

A chartered financial analyst (C.F.A.) with an excellent portfolio performance record volunteered to assist in the development of stock investments. At the beginning he was restricted to Mr. Simons' stock choices. However, the C.F.A. did suggest two new industries after eliminating four from Mr. Simons' list. The C.F.A. had no discretionary powers. He made recommendations in future years after year-end tax selling. Those suggestions were followed. At the end of 1977 only one stock on Mr. Simons' original list remained in the portfolio.

In fairness to the C.F.A., he operated with minimum capital ($10,000) and was substantially restricted at the beginning through 1974 year-end tax selling to Mr. Simons' recommended stocks.

With the foregoing background, you should appreciate the Smiths' problems in entering the stock market with limited capital and a choice of some 3,000 listed stocks and countless unlisted ones.

After studying the facts sheets of Mr. Simons' recommended companies in *Moody's Handbook of Common Stocks* and agreeing with Mr. Simons that the time was right for stock buying, the Smiths arranged to meet with a college friend, Mr. George Winter (a pseudonym), C.F.A., a security analyst on Wall Street. Winter, after hearing the investment objectives of the Smiths and studying the listing from *Forbes* magazine, eliminated from the list the the chemical, food, nonferrous metals, and retail industries. He raised objection to Macmillan as a stock purchase. However, for Mr. Smith's sentimental reasons, Winter allowed this stock to remain in the purchase group. Winter's advice was as follows:

Automobiles: Toss-up between Ford and GM. He preferred Ford.

Oil: Either Exxon or Texaco was acceptable. He preferred Texaco.

Paper: Liked St. Regis.

Steel: Approved Bethlehem.

In addition, Winter suggested two other industry groups: for conglomerate: Textron Convertible Preferred and for home building: U.S. Gypsum.

LOUISE SMITH'S OPENING PORTFOLIO FOR 1974
(BOUGHT SEPTEMBER 26, 1973)

NO. SHARES	SECURITY	DIV.	YIELD %	PE RATIO	PRICE PER SHARE	TOTAL COST
50	Bethlehem Steel	1.40	4.3	8	33⅜	$ 1,704
25	Ford Motor	3.20	5	5	60¾	1,551
100	Macmillan	.15	1.8	7	8¾	901
25	St. Regis Paper	1.60	3.4	12	47¾	1,222
50	Texaco	1.72	5.3	8	33⅜	1,704
60	Textron 1.40					
	Conv. Pfd.	1.40	5.5	10	26⅜	1,616
75	U.S. Gypsum	1.60	7.4	8	21⅞	1,675
	Total Original Investment					$10,373

A transcript of Louise Smith's purchase and sales from September 26, 1973 through December 31, 1977, follows:

DATE	DESCRIPTION OF TRANSACTION	DEBIT	CREDIT
9/26/73	Original Portfolio Acquired	$10,373	
12/27/74	tax selling: Sold 25 Ford		$ 815
	Sold 50 Texaco		983
	Sold 100 Macmillan		297
	SUBSTITUTIONS:		
	Bought 25 Mobil	916	
	Bought 50 National Distillers	702	
	Bought 100 Kaiser Industries	455	
11/25/75	Bought 75 U.S. Gypsum (for tax swap)	1,314	
12/3/75	Sold 60 Textron Pfd.		$1,249
12/29/75	Sold 75 U.S. Gypsum (9/26/73 Lot)		1,196
5/12/77	Sold 100 Kaiser Industries		1,819
11/23/77	Bought 300 Financial General Bankshares Class A	2,679	
12/28/77	Sold 50 Bethlehem Steel		1,008
	Totals	$16,439	$7,367
	Less Debit Totals		16,439
	Balance		$9,072
	losses sustained	$3,603	
	profits realized	1,364	
	Net loss sustained		$2,239
	Balance of Cost 12/31/77 (see below)		$6,833

Don't let the mass of statistical information frighten you from grasping the market concepts. Read the figures as words. Look at whole groups of numbers and not the individual dollars or percentages. In all of this data you are dealing with four concepts:

1. Position (inventory of stocks) reflecting unrealized gains and losses.
2. Gains and losses realized on sales of stock.
3. Dividend (income on stocks).
4. Performance Measurements.

Louise Smith's basis of securities owned and mean prices at December 31, 1977 were as follows:

NO. SHARES	SECURITY	DATE BOUGHT	TAX COST	12/30/77 MEAN PRICE
300	Financial General Bankshares Class A	11/23/77	$2,679	$2,981
25	Mobil	12/27/74	916	1,592
50	National Distillers	12/27/74	702	1,041
37	St. Regis Paper (12 shares 1973 stock dividend)	9/26/73	1,222	1,131
75	U.S. Gypsum	11/25/75	1,314	1,655
	Totals	12/31/77	$6,833	$8,400

The previous financial information together with the dividends received are the basic data required to prepare the accompanying workpapers.

OBSERVATIONS ON STOCK PORTFOLIO

The "bottom line" of the Smiths' adventure in stocks shows that a savings account would have outperformed the stocks over a four-year period. The calculations are as follows:

SAVINGS ACCOUNT:

1. 1973—4 to 7-year regular rate 7% (effective rate 7.35%)

2. $10,373 on deposit 9/26/73 to 12/31/77, 1,557 days

3. Day-of-deposit interest value at 12/31/77 $14,040

STOCK INVESTMENT:

Fair market 12/31/71 (includes cash) $9,748

Total Dividends:

1973	$119	
1974-1977	2,041	
		2,160

Total Capital & Income at
12/31/77   11,908

Difference in Return $2,132

No. of Shares	Security & Cost	Fair Market Value			
		12/31/74	12/31/75	12/31/76	12/31/77
50	Bethlehem Steel (9/26/73 for 1,704)	1231	1644	2019	
37	St. Regis Paper (9/26/73 for 1,222; 12 shares split 12/12/73)	708	1262	1429	1131
60	Textron 1.40 Con. Pfd (9/26/76 for 1,616)	930			
75	U.S. Gypsum (9/26/73 for 1,675; Tax Swap 11/25/75 for 1,314)	1036	1246	1978	1655
25	Mobil (12/27/74 for 916)	903	1181	1625	1592
50	National Distillers (12/27/74 for 702)	704	812	1256	1041
100	Kaiser Industries (12/27/74 for 455)	460	850	1500	
300	Financial General Bankshares - Class A (11/23/77 for 2,679) (See page 00)				2981
	Cash Balance		1196	1196 *	1348 *
	Total Fair Market Value	5972	8191	11003	9748
	Less, Tax Cost	8290	7509	7509	8181
	Unrealized gain or (loss)	(2318)	682	3494	1567

* In chapter 2, used these balances for beginning and end of 1978.

No. of Shares	Security	Date Acquired	Date Sold	Net Sales Proceeds	Cost	Gain or (Loss)
25	Ford Motor	9/26/73	12/27/74	815	1551	(736)
50	Texaco	9/26/73	12/27/74	983	1704	(721)
100	Macmillan	9/26/73	12/27/74	297	901	(604)
	Totals Through 12/31/74			2095	4156	(2061)
60	Textron 1.40 C. Pfd	9/26/73	12/3/75	1249	1616	(367)
75	US Gypsum (Tax Swap)	9/26/73	12/29/75	1196	1675	(479)
	1975 Total			2445	3291	(846)
	Cumulative Totals 1/1/74 - 12/31/75			4540	7447	(2907)
100	Kaiser Industries	12/27/74	5/12/77 *	1819	455	1364
50	Bethlehem Steel	9/26/73	12/28/77 *	1008	1704	(696)
	1977 Total			2827	2159	668
	Cumulative Totals 1/1/74 - 12/31/77			7367	9606	(2239)

* In chapter 5, tax planning used these
dates as 1978 transactions.

440

No. of Shares	Security	1974	1975	1976	1977
50	Bethlehem Steel	115	138	100	75
25	Ford Motor (sold 12/27/74)	80			
100	Macmillan (sold 12/27/74)	24	6		
25	St. Regis Paper	46	53	57	61
12	" " " split 12/12/73				
50	Texaco (sold 12/27/74)	105			
60	Textron 1.40 Con. Pfd	84	84		
75	U.S. Gypsum (Tax Swap 11/25/75)	120	120	120	120
25	Mobil (bought 12/27/74)		85	88	98
50	National Distillers (bought 12/27/74)		60	70	80
100	Kaiser Industries (bought 12/27/74)		26	26	
300	Financial General Bankshares Class A (bought 11/23/77)				
	Totals	574	572	461	434

Note: 1973 Dividends
from 9/26/73 to 12/31/73
were 119

	1974	1975	1976	1977
Capital Appreciation **(Depreciation):**				
Market Value – Beginning	10373 *	5972	8191	11003
Market Value – End	5972	8191	11003	9748
Increase (Decrease)	(4401)	2219	2812	(1255)
% Increase (Decrease) in Portfolio	(42.43%) *	37.16%	34.33%	(11.41%)
% Increase (Decrease) Standard & Poor's 500	(37.00%) *	31.55%	19.15%	(11.50%)
% Increase (Decrease) Dow Jones Industrials	(34.12%) *	38.32%	17.86%	(17.27%)
Income:				
Average Cost of Securities (Beginning + End ÷ 2)	9332 *	7900	7509	8193
Dividends Received	574	572	461	434
Yield Percentage	6.15%	7.24%	6.14%	5.30%
Yields on Dow Jones Industrials	6.12%	4.39%	4.12%	5.51%

* Used stock purchase date   9/26/73
       Standard & Poor's 500   108.83
       Dow Jones Industrials   935.43

442

The percentage decrease over a safe savings bank investment in the four-year period is 15.19%. Between September 26, 1973 (the date the portfolio was acquired) and December 31, 1973, the Standard & Poor's 500 declined 10.36% (108.83 to 97.55). A delay in purchasing the stocks until the end of 1973 may well have reduced the difference in total return. This demonstrates the great importance of timing in the market place.

If the Smiths had entered the market a year later, at December 31, 1974, when the S & P 500 was 68.56 and the Dow was 616.24, there would have been a complete turnaround in results. The stock market believers would have been victorious. Unfortunately, you cannot rewrite actual financial history in the stock market.

The position workpaper reflects the costs and fair market values of all securities held at the end of each year. The market price is the high and low for the last day of the year divided by 2. This is called the mean price. The mean price multiplied by the number of shares in position gives you the fair market value. (See page 439.)

The total fair market value of the position is compared with the tax cost of those securities. The result is the unrealized gain or loss in the position. The individual stock gains or losses may be determined by subtracting the cost (shown below the stock name) from the fair market value. Usually in November and December loss selling for losses is done to take advantage of the tax law and at the same time to upgrade the quality of the portfolio.

Capital gains are accumulated for both taxes and statistical purposes. The tax cost at the beginning of a period plus the securities purchased minus the cost of securities sold equals the tax cost at the end of the period. (See page 440.)

	1974	1975	1976	1977
Tax Cost—beginning of yr.	$10,373	$8,290	$7,509	$7,509
Add Purchases	2,073	1,314		2,679
Cash Balance		1,196*		1,348
Total	$12,446	$10,800	$7,509	$11,536
Minus Cost of securities sold	4,156	3,291		2,159
Cash Balance Reinvested				1,196*
Tax Cost End of Year	$8,290	$7,509	$7,509	$8,181

Note: *In order to keep the beginning account intact, the 1975 excess sales proceeds distributed to Louise Smith were reinvested in the market in 1977.

The dividend income workpaper shows the payment trends for all the stocks. This workpaper proves each year to the cash inflow and Forms 1099 filed with the IRS. (See page 441.)

Bethlehem Steel, which reported record earnings in 1974 and a down-trend in 1975 and 1976, in 1977 charged off for statement purposes one of the largest losses in the history of American business. That loss of almost $1 billion decreased the stock value by almost 40% by the end of December, 1977 over the price paid for the stock in 1973. The value dropped by 50% during 1977 alone. The 1978 quarterly dividend trend for Bethlehem is a decrease of 50% of the prior first quarter dividend. Thus from 50¢ a share quarterly, the dividend looks to be 25¢ a share or $1 for the year as against $2 in 1976. Based on hindsight, Bethlehem was a good sell at the end of 1976. However, at the 1977 year-end stock price and the rise in steel prices, the Smiths decided to sell Bethlehem for a tax loss.

Financial General Bankshares, Inc. is a corporation which owns a number of commercial banks primarily in the District of Columbia and Maryland region. Its two classes of common shares are listed on the AMEX. Class A common shares sell at a discount over the regular common shares. On November 23, 1977, Louise Smith reinvested the proceeds on the sale of Kaiser Industries in 300 shares of Financial General Bankshares Class A at 8¾. This purchase which cost $2,679 was made on the recommendation of the C.F.A.

The Class A shares were not quoted in the AMEX stock table on December 30, 1977. Therefore, the mean of the regular common was reduced by the discount of the prior day as follows:

	HIGH	LOW	MEAN
December 29, 1977			
Regular	11½	11⅜	
Class A	10⅛	10⅛	
Spread	1⅜	1²/₈	(Higher)
			1.3750
December 30, 1977			
Regular	11⅜	11¼	$11.3125
Class A	Not quoted		
Minus discount for Class A (above)			1.3750
Mean price per share for Class A			$9.9375
No. of shares			300
Fair Market Value December 31, 1977			$2,981

Another acceptable method of valuating these shares uses the price on the last closing date. In this case, the mean price would be 10⅛ (December 29, 1977) instead of $9^{15}/_{16}$ ($9.9375).

The portfolio performance workpaper is the bottom line. Even if statistically the portfolio failed to beat a savings account over the four-year period, there is always "next year" for the bull. In fact, the minimum period for stock market performance with the investment objectives sought by the Smiths is five years. The year-end 1978 should be very interesting to compare with 1977 low prices. (See page 442.)

Performance is measured by the value of the securities at the beginning and end of the period. In the Smiths' case, the calendar year is used. For computing the percentage change, the beginning value is the divisor. For 1976, the 34.33% is computed by the delta percentage key of a present-value calculator. A two-figure input gives the answer. On a regular calculator the computations are more time-consuming: $11,003 \div$ $8,191 = 1.3433 - 1.0000 = .3433$ or 34.33%.

In every year except one, the portfolio beat the Standard & Poor 500. It lost to the Dow Jones in two out of four years (in 1975 by 1.16%). In 1976 the portfolio performance was spectacular. It beat the S & P 500 by 79.27% and the Dow by 92.22%. In the very weak price year 1977, the portfolio's performance was almost identical to the S & P 500 (11.41% as against 11.50%, both decreases). It was better than the Dow by 33.93%.

The dividend yields paid more than a regular savings account in every year except 1977. The yield of 5.30% for 1977 was .17% less than the 5.47% effective rate on a regular savings account. The dividend yields for the Smiths' account for the four years have been satisfactory. The portfolio yields exceeded the dividend yields of the Dow Jones Industrials in every year except 1977. The total dividend yield for the four years was 24.83% compared with the Dow's total yield of 20.14%.

The Smiths' original objective was a long-term investment policy based on a limited investment of $10,000. As the years go by, the stock holdings will change. They hope that at the time they need the stocks for the children's education or their own retirement, the capital appreciation and income will show a considerably better return than the money left in safer investments.

The Smiths' portfolio cannot be used as an index for your needs. You have over 3,000 listed stocks from which to choose. If you are bullish you should consider buying quality stocks for investment.

Another exercise in stock history is to review the state of the market with respect to the stocks rejected by the Smiths for their original portfolio. The following table presents the historic financial facts of the stocks suggested by the *Forbes* article:

	CLOSING PRICE 9/26/73	CLOSING PRICE 12/31/77	% CHANGE INCREASE (decrease)
Alcoa*	47⁄8	465⁄8	(4.60%)
Dow*	291⁄8	263⁄4	(8.15)
DuPont	1763⁄4	1203⁄8	(31.90)
Exxon*	453⁄4	481⁄8	5.19
General Mills*	317⁄8	303⁄8	(4.71)
General Motors	661⁄4	627⁄8	(5.09)
International Paper	463⁄4	433⁄4	(6.42)
Monsanto	66	575⁄8	(12.69)
J.C. Penney	793⁄8	351⁄2	(55.28)
Sears Roebuck	487⁄16	28	(42.19)
Total % Change			(165.84%)
Average % Change (Total % Change ÷ 10)			(16.59%)
Standard & Poor's 500 Index	108.83	95.10	(12.62%)
Percentage Point Difference (Decrease)			(3.97)

*Reduced for stock splits from September 26, 1973 through December 31, 1977.

Simons' rejected choices of September 26, 1973 in total delta percentages compared with the close of 1977 showed a decrease of 16.59%. The Standard & Poor's 500 over the same period declined 12.62%. Using the S & P as a base, the stocks eliminated by the C.F.A. from the original portfolio underperformed the market by 3.97 percentage points, as the above table indicates.

Louise Smith's portfolio from September 26, 1973 until December 31, 1977 declined 6.03% in capital value ($9,748 ÷ $10,373 = .9397 − 1.000 = .0603 or 6.03%). A table would show:

% DECLINE IN VALUE

SEPTEMBER 26, 1973 TO DECEMBER 31, 1977

	REJECTED STOCKS	LOUISE SMITH'S PORTFOLIO	S & P 500
% (DECREASE)	(16.59%)	(6.03%)	(12.62%)

In summary, the 1973 decision to reject stocks in the chemical and retail industries was a sound one. But food, metals, and motors stocks outperformed the portfolio. Louise Smith's portfolio did better than the S & P 500 by 6.59 percentage points over the more than four-year period.

At the end of 1977, Thomas Wilson, the Director of Research for Standard & Poor's, in an interview in a *U.S. News & World Report* issue dedicated to the investment outlook for 1978 said: "Thus, the stock market should be able to finish next year on a higher plane than it started. But I don't think it will be straight up all the way—too many uncertainties remain. . . . I think there are quality stocks that are bargains at present prices. Much depends on the time horizons and the kind of money involved." Some of the stocks for long-term holding recommended by Mr. Wilson's firm at the close of 1977 were:

SECURITY	CLOSING PRICE 12/31/77	PRICE AT DATE OF YOUR READING*	% CHANGE INCREASE (DECREASE)
IBM	273½		
Aetna Life & Casualty	36⅝		
Abbott Laboratories	56½		
International Telephone	31¾		
Standard Oil of Ohio	70⅞		
Southern Natural Resources	34		
Panhandle Eastern Pipe, Inc.	46⅞		
General Motors	62⅞		
Ford	45¾	_____	_____
Total % Change	XX	XX	%
Average % Change (Total % Change ÷ 9)	XX	XX	%
Minus S & P 500 Index	95.10		%
Percentage point difference increase (decrease)			

*If between December 31, 1977 and the date of your reading there have been any stock splits or stock dividends, you must adjust the December 31, 1977 price. You can tell if there has been a change in the last 12 months from the stock guide. Thus, if a 2-for-1 split has taken place after December 31, 1977, you would divide the 12/31/77 price by 2; if a 3-to-2 split, you would divide the December 31, 1977 price by 1.5. A 4% stock dividend requires you to divide the December 31, 1977 price by 1.04.

Although these stocks were suggested for long-term holding, it is a good exercise for you to monitor Mr. Wilson's stock list on a short-term basis. Using the S & P 500 as a yardstick, price the stocks at the closing price published on the date that you are reading this section. Compute the percentage of change.

For example, IBM's closing price at December 31, 1977 was 273½. Assume at the date of your reading the price is 280⅝. The percentage change increase is 2.61% (280.625 ÷ 273.50 = 1.0261 − 1.0000 = .0261 or 2.61%). If the price were 240⅞, the percentage change decrease is 11.93%, expressed as "(11.93%)" in parentheses. (A 4-for-1 stock split would reduce the 12/31/77 price by the divisor 4 or 68⅜.)

If Mr. Wilson's recommended list percentage change has beaten the percentage change of the S & P 500, he is a winner in the short term. It can be argued that this is too simplistic an approach. But until some other performance measurements are available for the average individual, the S & P 500 and Dow Jones Industrials indices will continue to be the yardsticks.

There is a rule in business: you cannot know another person's worth unless you are in possession of the facts. Similarly, do not allow the financial triumphs and tragedies of others to deter you from making your own objective investment decisions. Knowledgeable people believe that a well-managed portfolio is not gambling in the sense of a lottery or horse race. There is a risk-reward ratio and the long-term prognosis is favorable. If this were not the case as 1978 begins, pension plans, trusts and well-informed individuals would not be holding, waiting for a "stabilized" market to start buying quality stocks.

13
LEASING VERSUS PURCHASING

WHETHER TO LEASE OR TO BUY is a question which crops up quite often in individual and corporate business. The solution to the problem of leasing versus purchasing requires a determination of the amount of money which would make leasing costs and ownership costs equal.

The decision in many leasing/purchasing situations is so obvious as to require only common sense. A two-week vacation trip to a foreign country where there is a need for an automobile usually calls for a car rental. On the other hand, extending the trip to a number of months may require you to consider an alternative such as buying a car and then selling it before returning home. Or, you may decide to ship the car home. Here the answer to the leasing/purchasing question is not so obvious.

Suppose you discover in the late spring or early summer that your four-year-old automobile needs extensive repairs. The new model-year starts after Labor Day. Do you repair the old car? Do you buy a used car, sell it after Labor Day, and immediately buy a new one? Do you lease an automobile for two or three months? Can you arrange for a car on loan from the dealer? Do you buy a current year's model? Do you do nothing and use alternative transportation until after Labor Day? Except for doing nothing, each question is relevant to the leasing/purchasing decision.

To illustrate the simplistic approach to the various options, let us suppose you are planning a two-month auto tour of Europe. You cannot intelligently choose leasing or ownership in this situation without an economic study of the time-value of money.

If you arrange the European car rental or ownership before leaving on your trip you will be dealing in U.S. dollars. In general, the U.S. dollar abroad weakens in the summer due to foreign travel by Americans. So, as a general rule, it pays to make financial arrangements in dollars well before you leave. The foreign exchange rate doesn't affect the equation since both sides would be increased or decreased almost proportionately. The facts of the study are as follows:

1. Leasing costs are $20 per day plus 10¢ per kilometer. Collision insurance is $1.50 per day. The leasing costs include liability insurance. Gasoline is not a factor since under both leasing and ownership you would pay for fuel. Conversely, the two months' maintenance costs would be borne by both the lessor and the seller. The sales tax on leasing has been included in the costs.

2. Ownership of the automobile will cost you $5,500. You plan to sell the car before returning home. The dealer will repurchase the car after two months for $4,000. Your insurance coverage for collision and liability costs $150.

3. Your projected tour will cover 3,500 kilometers.
   On a straight-cost basis, the results are as follows.

1. Leasing: Basic daily rental charge	
(60 days at $20 per day)	$1,200
Mileage (3,500 kilometers	
at 10¢ per mile)	350
Insurance (60 days at $1.50 per day)	90
Total leasing cost	$1,640
2. Purchasing: Cost	$5,500
Insurance	150
	$5,650
Minus salvage (resale price)	− 4,000
Net cost of purchase	$1,650
Cost of leasing	$1,640
Cost of purchasing	1,650
Savings on leasing	$ 10

In the above case either decision would seem to be correct. The same would hold true if you rented a car with no mileage charge for $210 a week including collision insurance. At a total cost of $1,680 for leasing (eight weeks at $210 per week), the spread is $30 in favor of purchasing. However, this does not take into account the two months' savings bank interest you would lose on the $5,500 required for the car purchase. (The interest income lost would be about $70.) If you were required to borrow the money the cost would be over $100. Given these facts, the decision based on the time-value of money, is clearly in favor of leasing. This is the financial answer. Other considerations such as a desire to ship an automobile home after the trip may weigh in favor of a purchase. There are foreign laws, licenses, and taxes to comply with, so investigate the situation carefully.

The financial problem of personal leasing/purchasing involves the economics of using property such as automobiles, real estate, television sets, or any other tangible asset you may require. In general, leasing costs more than ownership. The lessor (owner) may be in a position to buy or to build the property at a substantially lower price than a lessee or buyer. The lessor may also be in a position to borrow money at a cheaper rate than the lessee. Many leasing companies are substantial financial institutions with prime-rate borrowing potential. This means they are charged a lower interest rate by banks.

As an owner, you have full control over the property you buy. You can improve or sell the property whenever you choose. As an owner, you avoid the fixed term of a lease and you avoid increases in rental payments after the initial lease term has ended. There are also certain tax advantages to ownership, such as fast-depreciation writeoffs. The 10% investment-tax credit on the value of tangible property may not always be available to the lessee in a lease arrangement. And even if the lessee is allowed to receive this tax credit, there are strict tax law requirements to be met.

When you own a home, your real estate taxes are a deduction on your income tax return. These taxes are not deductible if you lease your residence. The interest expense on your mortgage is a tax deduction if you are an owner. A renter (lessee) of a personal residence has none of these income tax advantages.

However, if a leased time or property is used in business, the lease rentals are a deduction. There are certain types of leases that are considered purchases under the tax law. (These leases pose special problems which are beyond the scope of this chapter.)

THE OPERATIONAL LEASE (TEMPORARY NEEDS)

If the use of property is only a temporary requirement, leasing is usually the best choice. A typical example is the rental of an automobile at an airport for a few days. For lodging requirements during a temporary work assignment, you would either stay in a hotel or motel or enter a short-term apartment lease.

An *operational lease* is practical in a short-term or temporary need for the use of property. It is used where it would be totally uneconomical to consider a purchase or a long-term arrangement. This type of lease has nothing to do with the time-value of money. (The other types of leases, including a financial lease, do require a study of the time-value of money.)

TIME LEASES (THE FINANCIAL LEASE)

An alternative to ownership of property is the *time lease*. This lease extends the initial lease period to coincide with the useful life of the property. A truck with an economic life estimated at seven years and which is leased for exactly seven years is subject to a time lease. At the end of the time lease, the lessee is given the choice of (1) buying the property for its salvage value, (2) returning the property to the lessor, (3) renewing the lease at a lower rental; or (4) leasing a new piece of property as a replacement.

This type of lease is a "payout" or financial lease, since it returns to the lessor the cost of the property plus a profit through a straight financing arrangement.

The same lease for less than the economic life of the property may be considered an operational lease to the leasing company and a financial lease to the lessee. In this case you, as a lessee, do not care particularly how the lessor classifies a less-than-economic-life lease. You are interested in the actual cost of leasing versus purchasing over more than a temporary period. When in doubt, treat the lease as a financial one and prepare an economic study.

LEASING COMPANIES

Leasing companies justify their services by maintaining that you have the use of the property without purchasing it, thus conserving your business's working capital (cash, receivables, and inventory minus current debt). In a period of inflation a long-term lease does save money because the future rental payments are made with cheaper dollars. This preserves today's accumulated capital. Future costs and revenues are more nearly matched with the same currency value through a leasing program. Usually leasing companies are involved with tangible property costing at least $5,000, covering a lease period of 18 months or more.

PERSONAL LEASING NEEDS

In your personal life, you may find that leasing equals ownership at a particular money cost not only in the obvious automobile or residence situation, but also in considering landscaping equipment or any other property item where maintenance and labor may be part of the lease arrangement. People do not generally lease refrigerators, television sets, or furniture over long periods. If these are needed on a short-term basis, an operational lease can be arranged. The purchase of "big-ticket" durable items through credit card financing or bank loans almost automatically makes leasing uneconomical.

The question of leasing/purchasing becomes one of finance when the lessor has the ability to buy or build the property more cheaply than you can. An economic study should be made to arrive at the correct decision.

OPTIONS IN USING PROPERTY

You usually have four options in the use of property: (1) outright purchase, (2) installment purchase, (3) a loan, and (4) leasing. Immediately eliminate the option where the possibility is obviously negative. For example, if you don't have the cash to buy the item you would eliminate the first alternative. If you have borrowed your maximum line at the bank, you would eliminate a loan if your dealer doesn't have the facilities for an installment purchase, so that alternative is also eliminated. Therefore you have no choice but the fourth alternative.

Normally you can usually meet two of the four alternatives in any given situation. Revolving credit plans or credit card purchases of "big-ticket" items are really installment purchases. Bank loans and installment purchases may have similar monetary results, although bank charges are generally less than retail installment-purchase carrying costs. In any event, in making your economic study you assume that more than one alternative applies unless the nature of the property itself prevents this conclusion. For example, currently you can only *rent* a postage meter. Thus, your option is restricted to leasing.

An installment purchase requires that between 10% and 30% of the purchase price be paid immediately, with the balance to be paid over a period shorter than the economic life of the property. The seller receives interest for the use of the money and usually retains a lien on the property or conditional ownership until all installments have been paid. A loan financed through a bank or other credit facility permits the purchase of the property.

Before you consider leasing as an alternative to owning property, ask yourself three critical questions:

1. Why should the transaction be a lease?
2. Why with this particular lessor?
3. Why lease now rather than later?

TIME-VALUE OF MONEY

Time-value relates to savings accounts, bonds, loans, annuities, and all the future and present uses of money. *Interest* is generally the term used for the price factor in the time-value. In order to make the leasing/purchasing decision it is necessary to understand the concept of time-value.

The time-value of money is usually expressed as a line with a beginning point and an end point:

Beginning   End

The line is divided into sections, or time periods:

Beginning   End

The time periods may be numbered:

0   1   2   3   4   5
Beginning   End

Numbered time periods are assigned the symbol N (for Number). The beginning is Present and the end is Future:

0   1   2   3   4   5
Present   Future

If today (Present) you deposited $100 in the bank for five periods, what would the amount be worth at that future date? The answer depends on two facts: (1) the periodic interest rate, and (2) whether the interest is simple or compound. Assume the interest rate for each period is 10%. The actual length of the period is unimportant at this stage, but to help visualize the problem, N equals one year. Thus, 10% per year is the periodic interest rate.

Simple interest means that the interest is applied only once to the initial amount.

In this problem:

Present value   = $100 ($P$ for principal)
Periodic interest   =   10% (r for rate)
Periods   =   5 (t for periods)

The formula is, therefore, P times r times t equals interest, which is usually expressed as *Prt*.

The answer is determined:

I (interest) = Prt
$I = \$100 \times 10\% \times 5$ periods
$I = 100 \times .10 \times 5$
$I = 50$

The interest is, therefore, $50.

In time-value of money studies, simple interest is not used. The interest factor considers that interest earned in each period is entitled to have interest earned on itself for the next period. Thus, the future value is the present value multiplied by a rate applied to each period's interest on an *accumulated* basis. The time period is no longer represented by the letter t, but by the letter N.

Starting with $100 deposited the first year, the computations are:

PERIOD (N)	PRINCIPAL AND INTEREST (P + I)	RATE (r)	INTEREST EARNED (I)
0	$100.00	10%	$ 0
1 (YEAR)	100.00	10	10.00
2	110.00	10	11.00
3	121.00	10	12.10
4	133.10	10	13.31
5	146.41	10	14.64
END OF 5TH PERIOD	$161.05		$61.05

This is compound interest, which is the key concept in the leasing/purchasing formula. The formula is expressed: the future value of $100 due in five years at 10% interest per annum compounded annually is $161.05.

It may also be expressed as: the present value of $161.05 due in five years at 10% compounded annually is $100.

These two formulas are expressed as:

F/P = future worth of a present amount

or

$161.05 = future worth of $100 placed at 10% annual interest for five years

P/F = present worth of a future amount

or

$100 = present worth of $161.05 due in five years at 10% annual interest

The present-value and future-value concepts relate to tangible property considered subject to the lease. The rate is the crucial factor in the formulas. The arguments as to the correct rate to use will be discussed later.

The third concept in the leasing/purchasing financial formula is the annuity. An *annuity* may be any series of equal payments made over the same time periods, such as (1) rental payments, (2) installment payment of loan, (3) mortgage payments, (4) insurance premiums, and (5) social security checks. If the payments are made at the end of the period, the annuity is an *ordinary annuity* (e.g., a mortgage payment or installment loan payment). If the payment is due at the beginning of the period, it is called an *annuity due* (e.g., rent, insurance premiums, or social security checks). In leasing calculations, the payments are considered an ordinary annuity.

Let's assume the bank loans you $1,000 due in five years. Payment is to be made in five equal installments at 10% interest. A 10% ordinary annuity table indicates the factor is .26380. Therefore, the annual loan repayment would be $263.80 ($1,000 × .26380).

To prove this at the rate of 10% the table shows the following:

PERIOD (N)	TOTAL PAYMENT	INTEREST (I)	PRINCIPAL (P)	BALANCE OF LOAN
0				$1,000.00
1 (year)	$263.80	$100.00	$163.80	836.20
2	263.80	83.62	180.18	656.02
3	263.80	65.60	198.20	457.82
4	263.80	45.78	218.02	239.80
5	263.80	24.00	239.80	–0–
Total interest or time-value of money		$319.00		

The $263.80 paid annually is the annuity from the present amount of $1,000 at 10% for five years. This is expressed as A/P = $263.80. The present worth of an annuity of $263.80 for five years at 10% is $1,000. The symbol for this is P/A (present value of annuity). The five payments totalling $1,319 ($263.80 × 5) are expressed as F/A (future worth of an annuity).

SYMBOL	DEFINITION	EXAMPLE
F/P	future worth of a present amount	$161.05 is the future worth of $100 deposited now at 10% interest p.a. (per annum) for five years.
P/F	present worth of a future amount	$100 is the present worth of $161.05 due at the end of five years at 10% p.a.
F/A	future worth of an annuity	$1,319 is the future worth of a $263.80 annual annuity for five years at 10% p.a.
A/F	annuity for a future amount	$263.80 is the annual annuity at 10% p.a. for five years to accumulate $1,319.
P/A	present worth of an annuity	$1,000 is the present worth of $263.80 annual annuity for five years at 10% p.a.
A/P	annuity from a present amount	$263.80 is the annual annuity payment on $1,000 advanced now, repayable in five years at 10% p.a.

Returning to the last trend line of the time-value of money example:

```
        0   1   2   3   4   5
        ├───┼───┼───┼───┼───┤
Present                           Future
```

you can now apply the formulas to the trend line.

The single-underlined figure is the known amount and the double-underlined figure is the answer.

1. *F/P* (future worth of a present amount)

YEARS

0	1	2	3	4	5
$1,000			$r = 10\%$		$1,610.51

2. *P/F* (present worth of a future amount)

YEARS

0	1	2	3	4	5
$620.92			$r = 10\%$		$1,000

3. *F/A* (future worth of an annuity)

YEARS

0	1	2	3	4	5
0	$100	$100	$100	$100	$100
			$r = 10\%$		$610.51

4. *A/F* (annuity from a future amount)

YEARS

0	1	2	3	4	5
$r = 10\%$			$163.80		$1,000

5. *P/A* (present worth of an annuity).

YEARS

0	1	2	3	4	5
$100	$100	$100	$100	$100	
$379.08			$r = 10\%$		

6. *A/P* (annuity from a present amount)

YEARS

0	1	2	3	4	5
$1,000			$r = 10\%$		
			$263.80		

When you deal with amounts at the beginning or the end of the period, you are involved with a problem in compound interest. If the amounts are in connection with regular payments, it is an annuity situation.

A present-value calculator or annuity-compounding table shows the factors for 10% annually for five years, as follows:

	(1) F/P	(2) P/F	(3) F/A	(4) A/F	(5) P/A	(6) A/P
Factor	1.611	.6209	6.105	.16380	3.791	.26380
Multipler (from examples)	$1,000	$1,000	$100	$1,000	$100	$1,000
Answer	$1,611	$620.90	$610.50	$163.80	$379.10	$263.80

These are basically the principles of compounding. It is not necessary to learn these formulas since later tables in this chapter will cover most of your leasing/purchasing situations.

FORMULA FOR LEASING VERSUS PURCHASING

The formula for leasing versus purchasing assumes that (1) cost will be borrowed at current interest rates; and (2) lease payments and purchase costs are equal at a particular interest rate. The purpose of this equation is to determine the rate. The equation is: lease=cost. Cost equals the original purchase price minus salvage. *Salvage* is another word for resale or trade-in value. The formula then becomes:

lease payments = purchase price minus salvage
or
lease payments plus salvage = purchase price
$$LP + S = PP$$

Without complicating the problem with service costs and other variables, and to give you the overall picture, the following example shows how the formula operates. Let's say you want to buy a car for $6,000. You can either pay cash or borrow the entire amount. A leasing company offers you a 36-month lease on the same car for $135 per month. If you buy the car, at the end of 36 months (based on current trade-ins for three-year-old cars), the resale value should be about $2,800. The lessor offers no purchase agreement. It is a closed-end lease. (An open-end lease permits you to purchase the automobile at a fixed price when the lease comes to an end.)

LEASE-COST

With these facts, you set out the following formula:

the present value of monthly payments of $135 for 36 months

plus

the present value of the $2,800 salvage worth of the car in three years

equals

the $6,000 cost of the car at what interest rate?

Since the banks charge about 11% for a 36-month loan, you start with 11% as the possible factor:

the present value of a $135 per month annuity for three years at 11%

plus

the present value of $2,800 salvage at
11% compounded monthly (same as annuity)

equals

what purchase price?

ANNUITY FACTORS

The annuity factors of 11% for three years compounded monthly are:

P/A = 30.5449
P/F =   .7200

therefore

30.5449 × $135	= $4,124
.7200 × $2,800	= 2,016
Purchase price at 11%	= $6,140

Since you are looking for an interest factor (time-value of money) to bring the purchase price down to $6,000, you increase the interest factor to 12%:

P/A = 30.1075
P/F =   .6989

30.1075 × $135	= $4,065
.6989 × $2,800	= 1,957
Purchase price at 12%	= $6,022

The interest factor is then higher than 12%. If you wanted to be precise, you would use 13% and interpolate as follows:

$P/A = 29.6789$
$P/F = .6785$

therefore

29.6789 × $135	= $4,007
.6785 × $2,800	= 1,900
Purchase price at 13%	= $5,907

interpolated

$$\frac{(\$6,022 - \$6,000)}{(\$6,022 - \$5,907)} \times 1\% =$$

becomes

$$\frac{22}{115} \times 1\% = .1913\%$$

The exact rate is 12% + .1913% or 12.19%.

All factors being equal, if you can borrow from the bank at less than 12.19%, you should not lease the car. On the other hand, if you can borrow only at a higher rate than 12.19%, you should lease.

Using this same example, suppose the resale value of the car increased $500 or decreased $500. The results would be the following:

COMPARATIVE SALVAGE VALUES OF AUTOMOBILE

Salvage values:	$2,800	$2,300	$3,300
11%: Lease payments (P/A)	$4,124	$4,124	$4,124
Salvage (P/F)	2,016	1,656	2,376
Purchase price	$6,140	$5,780	$6,500
12%: Lease payments (P/A)	$4,065	$4,065	$4,065
Salvage (P/F)	1,957	1,608	2,306
Purchase price	$6,022	$5,673	$6,371
13%: Lease payments (P/A)	$4,007	$4,007	$4,007
Salvage (P/F)	1,900	1,561	2,239
Purchase price	$5,907	$5,568	$6,246

The salvage value factors are:

$$11\% = .7200$$
$$12\% = .6989$$
$$13\% = .6785$$

If the automobile's salvage is $2,300 at the end of the 36th month, the present value at 11% compounded monthly is $1,656 ($2,300 × .7200).

On a short-term lease period (under seven years) the impact of the salvage estimate is substantial. That is why you will find that for short-term automobile leases the bank and lease payments may be a fraction apart. Nevertheless, since you are using some savings bank money for a down-payment, ownership is generally cheaper. There are exceptions when, because the leasing company pays less for the automobile, the insurance rates under a leasing agreement are cheaper and maintenance may be included in the leasing deal. The insurance premiums become an annuity as does your estimate of annual repair costs. All these factors complicate the formula, but they are necessary to a proper decision.

Be sure that you have learned the basic theory before moving on to the more complicated problems. For example, a lessor charges $240 per month for an automobile on a 36-month basis. The rental payments include maintenance and insurance. At the end of the 36-month lease term you may purchase the automobile for $2,200. If you bought the same car for $6,000, you would withdraw $1,000 from a regular savings account and borrow $5,000 from the bank at an *APR* of 11.40%. The bank includes life insurance in the 11.40% rate. Which is your better deal? First, set up the problem in three columns, based on what you know and don't know:

LEASING VS. PURCHASING

COSTS	LEASE	PURCHASE
Payments	$240 per month	$6,000
Period	36 months	36 months
Purchase price at end of lease	$2,200	not applicable
Insurance (casualty)	included	?
Insurance (life)	?	included
Maintenance	included	?
Salvage value	not applicable	?
Financing savings, 5.25%	not applicable	$1,000
Bank loan, 11.40%	not applicable	$5,000

The open question in leasing is the cost of the life insurance premiums. You have a choice of either reducing the bank rates for the life insurance premiums or adding your premium cost to the lease payments. The life insurance cost in the bank rate is $61.47 for the 36 months. Assuming that you would use life insurance as a factor, you would then add the insurance to the other lease costs. This completes the lease-payments side of the equation.

On the purchase side, you require (1) the cost of casualty insurance, (2) the maintenance, and (3) the salvage value at the end of three years.

The *casualty insurance* which you would buy on the retail market would cost you $500 per year for the three years, or $41.67 per month. Don't worry about the inflationary forces at the level of 6% or less. If you wanted to be precise, you could adjust the insurance costs for estimated inflation each year. On the other hand, the insurance rates might go down. It is not an important factor.

Maintenance is very difficult to estimate. If in the third year of ownership the transmission fails, you would have a major repair problem. However, estimating normal repairs for each of the three years, you could assume the total repair bill for the period would be $450, broken down as $100 for the first year ($8.33 per month), $150 for the second year ($12.50 per month), and $200 the third year ($16.67 per month).

The *salvage value* of the automobile may be estimated by using the current *Official Used Car Guide* obtainable from any dealer. You can also estimate the salvage value by using 80% of the advertised price for a car of similar make and model. The average trade-in value (what the dealer would allow you) for a three-year-old similar car, is $2,700.

The formula becomes:

leasing payments of $240 per month for 36 months plus life insurance premiums of $61.47 plus purchase cost of $2,200 at the end of 36 months

equals

purchase price of $6,000 plus casualty insurance premium of $41.67 per month for 36 months plus maintenance charges of $450 minus savage value of $2,700.

The question is: At what interest rate do both sides of the equation become equal? The question may also be stated as:

At what interest rate does the leasing payment plus life insurance, minus the purchase cost from lessor, minus casualty insurance, minus maintenance charges, plus salvage value equal the purchase price?

In mathematical terms, at what interest rate does

1. the present value of a $240 per month annuity for 36 months (lease payments)

plus

2. the present value of $61.47 payable equally over 36 months (life insurance)

minus

3. the present value of $2,200 at the end of 36 months (purchase price)

minus

4. the present value of $41.67 per month for 36 months (casualty insurance)

minus

5. the present value of maintenance payments payable at $8.33 per month in the first year; $12.50 per month in the second year; and $16.67 per month in the third year

plus

6. the present value of $2,700 at the end of the 36 months (salvage value)

equal

7. $6,000 (purchase price of automobile)?

Since the bank is charging 11.40%, start the leasing percentage at the next full rate of 12%:

FACTORS

1. Present value of monthly lease payments of $240 for 36 months at 12% *(P/A)* $7,226

2. Present value of life in - surance premiums of $1.71 per month over 36 months at 12% *(P/A)* $51

3. Present value of $2,200 purchase price at end of 36 months *(P/F)* $1,538

4. Present value of casualty
   insurance payable $41.67 per
   month over 36 months *(P/A)* $1,255

5. Present value of maintenance costs:

   a) First year
   $100 ÷ 12 months = $8.33 per month
   Present value of $8.33 per month *(P/A)* = $94

   b) Second year
   $150 ÷ 12 months = $12.50 per month
   P/A: 24 months = $265
   P/A: 12 months = __141__
   P/A: beginning = $124

   c) Third year
   $200 ÷ 12 months = $16.67 per month
   P/A: 36 months = $502
   P/A: 24 months = __354__
   P/A: beginning = $148
       Present value of maintenance *(P/A)* $366

6. Present value of $2,700
   salvage value at end of 36
   months $1,887

Therefore, at 12%:

		LEASE EQUALS PURCHASE	
		ADD	DEDUCT
1.	Lease payments (*P/A* of $240 per month)	$7,226	
2.	Life insurance (*P/A* of $1.71 per month)	51	
3.	Purchase price at end of lease (*P/F* of $2,200)		$1,538
4.	Casualty insurance (*P/A* of $41.67 per month)		1,255
5.	Maintenance (*P/A* of $450 in total)		366
6.	Salvage value (*P/F* of $2,700)	1,887	
	Totals	$9,164	$3,159
	Less	3,159	
	Purchase price at 12%	$6,005	

To save time, the lease payments were adjusted to bring the total price to about $6,000 so that no additional computations were necessary.

Since the purchase cost equals 12% and you could finance the car for a maximum of 11.40%, the financing deal is better. However, if one of the variables is wrong, such as estimated maintenance over the three years, the results would be different.

If the car was used for business, ownership allows you up to the 10% investment tax credit. Usually in a short-term lease the lessor does not pass the investment credit through to the lessee. Accelerated depreciation methods are also available when you own the automobile and use it for business purposes.

Even though you are considering using $1,000 of your savings bank money to finance the car, you assume in the equation that the entire cost is to come from outside or debt sources. In otherwords, if in fact you only borrowed part of the money at 11.40% and the balance was withdrawn from savings at a 5.25% rate, your borrowing cost is less than 11.40%. A borrowing is comparable to the lease payments. To make the equation more meaningful, the purchase price is assumed to be entirely borrowed.

There may be other reasons for leasing the automobile which are not apparent from the figures, such as difficulty in financing the entire car, limited insurance coverage (or coverage available only at high cost), responsibility for maintenance shifted to lessor, or the ability to update your automobile more frequently through a closed-end lease.

STUDIES OF LEASING VS. PURCHASING

Businesses conduct detailed analyses of leasing versus purchasing. These economic studies are grouped into three categories, referred to here as the financing-rate method, the cost method, and the capital cost method.

The *financing-rate method* equates the interest percentage between the lease payment and the cost of owning the property. (This is what you did in working out the previous automobile problems.) If the financing rate determined in the equation is less than the bank or borrowing rate, then leasing is acceptable (all other factors being equal). The advantage of the financing-rate formula is its easy use, enabling you to determine immediately in a situation whether leasing is less economical than ownership.

The more complicated *cost method* computes all the tax advantages of ownership as opposed to leasing. This method is frequently used for a more accurate understanding of the overall costs when the financing rate and the borrowing rate are almost the same.

The *capital cost method* is also complicated and employs more factors than either the financing-rate method or the cost method. However, for alternative property uses and different financing methods, this is effective. For your purposes, the financing-rate method used in this chapter will be the most acceptable for everyday problems.

The leasing/purchasing question is answered by using a six-step analysis. (Set out the problem on columnar paper.) The six steps are: (1) get a clear understanding of what you want to know, (2) set down the alternative methods of solving the problem, (3) write out a description of the facts to be used, (4) know the appropriate formulas to be applied to the facts, (5) work out your conclusions based on the relevant formulas and other factors, and (6) choose the final conclusion of your best alternative.

In business, there are also choices other than the alternative of a lease versus a purchase. The types of leases vary considerably, from net leases (for the use of property only) to leases which include insurance, maintenance, local taxes, and renewal and purchase terms.

In solving the time-value of money, you will require a *table of factors* in which the known figure multiplied by the factor supplies the unknown. Since automobiles generally have a useful life of about 48 months and banks presently grant 48-month financing, a table of 48-month factors at the same rates is shown here. You will also find this table meaningful for business, since the 10% investment tax credit is allowed for tangible assets having a useful life of seven years. All of the factors at interest rates charged currently (10%, 12%, and 14%) are presented in the table. (The tabulations are based on end-of-month payments since this is the usual choice for most individuals.)

MONTHLY COMPOUNDING AT EFFECTIVE RATE-PER-YEAR
FACTOR APPLICABLE TO END-OF-MONTH AMOUNTS

	4 YEARS (48 MONTHS)			7 YEARS (84 MONTHS)		
	10%	12%	14%	10%	12%	14%
Future worth of a present amount (F/P)	1.4894	1.6122	1.7450	2.0080	2.3067	2.6494
Present worth of a future amount (P/F)	0.6714	0.6203	0.5731	0.4980	0.4335	0.3774
Future worth of an annuity (F/A)	58.7225	61.2226	63.8577	120.9504	130.6723	141.3758

Annuity from a future amount (A/F)	0.0170	0.0163	0.0157	0.0083	0.0077	0.0071
Present worth of an annuity (P/A)	39.4282	37.9740	36.5945	60.2367	56.6485	53.3618
Annuity from a present amount (A/P)	0.0254	0.0263	0.0273	0.0166	0.0177	0.0187

To give you an idea of how this table operates, we have calculated the first column of factors at 10%.

**MONTHLY COMPOUNDING AT 10% EFFECTIVE
RATE PER YEAR (48-MONTHS FACTOR APPLICABLE TO
END-OF-MONTH AMOUNTS)**

	GIVEN AMOUNT OF ANNUITY PAYMENT	FACTOR (FROM TABLE)	ANSWER
1. Future worth of a present amount (F/P)	$1,000	1.4894	$1,489
2. Present worth of future amount (P/F)	1,000	0.6714	671
3. Future worth of an annuity (F/A)	100	58.7225	5,872
4. Annuity from a future amount (A/F)	1,000	0.0170	17
5. Present worth of an annuity (P/A)	100	39.4282	3,943
6. Annuity from a present amount (A/P)	1,000	0.0254	25

ASSETS: BUSINESS USE

The computations for the leasing or purchase of business property (assets) are too complex for inclusion here. However, you should be aware that the factors for figuring the cost of business property differ considerably from those which apply to personal property. Business property can almost always be purchased on an installment arrangement whereas personal property frequently cannot. Business assets are also eligible for a tax allowance for depreciation and for the investment tax credit.

ASSETS: PERSONAL USE

The long-term savings bank interest rate of about 8% is an acceptable "yardstick" for personal assets. The time-value (P/F) of $1 at 8% due at the end of each of 10 years is given in the following table.

PRESENT VALUE FACTORS (COMPOUNDED YEARLY)

YEAR	P/F FACTOR AT 8%	YEAR	P/F FACTOR AT 8%
1	.9259	6	.6302
2	.8573	7	.5835
3	.7938	8	.5403
4	.7350	9	.5002
5	.6806	10	.4632

Present-value factors compounded monthly are more accurate when dealing with individual choices, particularly since payments are usually made monthly. However, the small factor difference between yearly compounding and monthly compounding of .27% at 1 year, 1.38% at 5 years, and 2.74% at 10 years is not significant when dealing with the same difference in all equations. You will find that for your purposes annual compounding will be easier to work with in the alternative computations.

For personal assets like the family automobile, tax savings remain a factor because the interest and sales tax are allowable tax deductions. However, for personal use there would be no depreciation or investment tax credit allowed.

USE OF THE LEASING/PURCHASING EQUATION

Whenever the cost of an asset exceeds $500, there are alternative financing arrangements available.

The use of the formulas given earlier may be applied to unusual situations such as the temporary need for expensive medical equipment. Let's assume that a dependent requires the use of a diathermy machine for an indefinite period of time. Let's also assume that the machine leases for $50 per month but that you could purchase it for $1,500. An outright purchase permits a medical deduction on your tax return of $1,500 (assuming the other medical expenses exceed the 3% limitation). At a 40% tax bracket, the $1,500 machine costs you $900. The machine is actually needed for 18 months. At the end of that time, let's say that you donate it to a charity, which appraises it for $1,200. The $1,200 contribution saves you $480 in taxes. Therefore, your out-of-pocket cost of the machine is now $420 ($900 − $480) against a net rental cost after taxes of $540 ($50 × 18 months = $900 × 60% = $540). Thus, owning the machine for 18 months is $120 cheaper than leasing it on an out-of-pocket basis.

If you require the machine for more than 18 months, the savings increase by $30 per month after taxes less the depreciating after-tax value of the machine as a contribution. In the rental situation, in order to qualify for any tax benefit you must have other medical expenses of at least the 3% limitation. These facts do not give any weight to the time-value of money or the cost of borrowing to pay for the machine. This is a perfect example of using the present-value alternative formulas at the 8% rate to make the decision.

Other everyday examples of using time-value formulas include (1) buying a lawnmower and garden tools to do your own landscaping vs. hiring someone for a monthly fee to do the entire job (don't forget to include the value of your own services); or (2) buying a vacation condominium and leasing it during the year vs. renting a condominium when you require a vacation home.

In solving these problems, use the approximate 8% savings bank interest rate paid on long-term borrowing.

THE SMITHS' AUTOMOBILE ALTERNATIVES

During the past summer, the Smiths realized that the four-year-old family automobile had reached the crossover point. This is the time when the cost of repairs and the age of the car indicate that a new car is required. Before making the leasing/purchasing choice, the Smiths decided to wait until after Labor Day when the new auto models are displayed. Their old car was to be sold privately.

The alternative plans for acquiring the new car were:

1. An outright purchase, using funds from their savings account.
2. Partial financing, paying approximately one-third down and financing the balance at the lowest rates over a 36-month period.

3. Leasing through a 26-month, closed-end lease including maintenance and insurance.

4. Leasing through a 36-month open-end lease including insurance
   and purchase option.

The Smiths decided to apply the time-value-of-money principle to the
above options, although there were other choices available (e.g., 48-
month partial financing, complete financing, and various leasing plans).

The facts on which the Smiths based their economic study included the
following:

1. Automobile has a useful life of four years.

2. Salvage value is computed from the *Official Used Car Guide.*

3. Partial financing is based on one-third (33⅓%) cash down payment
   plus sales tax, with balance payable over three years at current interest rates.

4. Closed-end, 26-month lease includes sales tax on payments for automobile and maintenance, with no sales tax on the insurance portion of the payment.

5. Open-end, 36-month lease includes sales tax on the automobile
   rental portion of the lease.

6. Computations are based on end-of-year compounding consistently
   applied.

7. The current savings bank four-year term money rate is effectively
   8.17% per annum. Therefore, 8% has been adopted as the time-value-of-money factor for the study.

The objective of the Smiths' economic study was to determine which of
the four methods of acquiring a new car was the least expensive. Since
the alternatives are not equal in time periods or in coverage, a separate
workpaper brings the costs to a comparative level. The first step was to
compute the present value of the cash flow based on each of the four
plans. Then the adjustments were made to properly compare the different
methods. The workpaper shows how each equation is computed for the
decision-making process in the use of a personal automobile.

Since the useful life of the new automobile was estimated to be four
years, all computations, in order to be comparative, would be placed on
an equal economic footing of four years. The time-value of money, therefore, was based on a four-year period at the appropriate rate. Outright

purchase is considered to incur a debt. In other words, what would the Smiths pay to borrow all the money? Since business use of the car is not a factor here, the interest rate is that applied to the money the Smiths would borrow from themselves. The current four-year effective savings bank rate is 8.17% per year. Therefore, the nearest whole rate for this purpose is 8%.

The Smiths' choice of payout for partial financing of 36 months rather than 48 months was a cash flow decision. They felt the family budget could handle a 36-month rather than a 48-month payout with the additional finance charges.

The first objective of an economic study is to convert to present value all future cash flow at a time-value rate. The alternatives are presented according to the terms of the arrangements on an annual basis for ease of computation. (Over the four-year period, the difference in using monthly or annual computation is insignificant.) Later, the individual plans are converted by adjustment to comparative costs. The "bottom line" then become the basis for the final decision.

The equation for the workpaper is:

cash outlay (purchase cost, loan payments, or annual payments minus salvage) minus

tax savings

equals

cash flow.

then:

cash flow

times

time-value of money

equals

present value of money.

Since items specifically allowed as deductions on the Smiths' tax return are included in the cash outlay, these amounts must be segregated as deductibles. These include sales tax on the purchase and interest on the loan. If the automobile was used for business, depreciation and the investment tax credit would also be shown on the workpaper. Sales tax on the purchase of an automobile may be claimed separately for income taxes even though you use the general sales tax table in computing your deduction.

The sales tax payable on rentals was not a deductible item for the Smiths since they used the general sales tax table which includes an allowance for this taxable purchase. If you claim sales tax on your return as an exact tabulation of your taxable purchases, then the sales tax on the rental is treated as a deductible item.

The Smiths' effective income tax rate combining federal and state taxes is 42%. To that extent, the deductibles reduce the cash outflow. Therefore, cash outlay minus tax savings equals cash outflow. The final figure is set in brackets to reflect an outlay of cash. Since salvage value is cash inflow, it is shown without brackets. The amounts in the cash flow column are the cash outlay reduced by the amounts in the tax savings column. The year's cash flow is multiplied by the present value factor of 8% (the percentage the Smiths would have earned had they left the money in the savings bank over the period of time involved).

On the straight purchase deal, the immediate cash outlay must be reduced by the present value of the salvage or trade-in allowance. According to a current *Official Used Car Guide*, a four-year-old automobile of the make and model the Smiths preferred is worth approximately $2,000. (You may also use as the salvage value 80% of the newspaper-advertised price for a four-year-old automobile of similar make and model.)

Excluding inflationary factors, $2,000 in the future is worth $1,470 in the bank today. In other words, $1,470 compounded annually at 8% is worth $2,000 at the end of four years. Therefore, the present cost of the cash purchase is the purchase price less the tax savings on the sales tax less the present value of the future trade-in price. The table for 8% compounding annually shows a present value factor of .7350 for end-of-year payments. Applying that factor to $2,000 gives the present value of the salvage as $1,470 ($2,000 × .7350).

You can, of course, use monthly rather than annual compounding factors for a slightly more accurate comparative cost. This is particularly true since loan installments and rentals are paid monthly. However, the end results of the annual vs. monthly method do not differ from one another significantly, and for this study the annual computations are easier to manage. The workpapers for the automobile alternatives set out the present value of the cash flow for a purchase, partial financing, 26-month lease (including maintenance and insurance) and a 36-month lease (including insurance and an option to purchase). The purchase requires the present value of the cash flow, which is the cash outlay, to be reduced by the present value of what the salvage value is expected to be in four years. The work papers follow on pages 474 and 475.

Full year		Cash Outlay (Purchase cost, Annual Payments Annual Rentals)	Deductibles (Sales Tax + Interest)	Tax Savings (42%)	Cash Flow	Present Value of Cash Flow 8%
	1. Purchase:					
0	Cash	6,420	420	176	(6244)	(6244)
4	Salvage	(2000)			2000	1470
	Totals	4,420	420	176	(4244)	(4774)
	2. Partial Financing:					
0	Cash	2420	420	176	(2244)	(2244)
1	Loan	1,634	412	173	(1461)	(1353)
2	Loan	1,634	288	121	(1513)	(1297)
3	Loan	1,634	151	63	(1571)	(1247)
4	Salvage	(2,000)			2000	1470
	Totals	5,322	1271	533	(4789)	(4671)
	3. 26 Month Lease (Maintenance + Insurance):					
0					0	0
1	Rental	3281			(3281)	(3038)
2	Rental	3281			(3281)	(2813)
3	Rental	547			(547)	(434)
	Totals	7109			(7109)	(6285)
	4. 36-Month Lease (Insurance + Purchase):					
0					0	0
1	Rental	2613			(2613)	(2419)
2	Rental	2613			(2613)	(2240)
3	Rental	2613			(2613)	(2074)
	Purchase	2175			(2111)	(1676)
4	Salvage	(2000)	152	64	2000	1470
	Totals	8014	152	64	(7950)	(6939)

		1 Purchase	2 Partial Financing	3 Closed End 26-Month Lease	4 Open End 36-Month Lease
1	Tentative —				
2	Comparative Costs				
3	(Present value of				
4	Cash Flow)	4774	4671	6285	6939
5					
6	Adjustments for Comparison:				
7					
8	1) Insurance - Life				
9	Included in financing at				
10	52.32 for 3 years				
11	Payable monthly or				
12	17.44 per year (P/A)		(45)		
13					
14	2) Insurance - Casualty				
15	Included in leasing —				
16	Add to Purchase and				
17	Partial Financing				
18	$500 per year				
19	Assume paid at beginning				
20	of each year (P/F):				
21	0 year = 500				
22	1 " = 463				
23	2 " = 397	1360	1360		
24					
25	3) Maintenance				
26	$300 per year in closed				
27	end lease plus 6.2%				
28	sales tax = 319 (P/F):				
29	1 year = 295				
30	2 " = 273				
31	3 " (2 mo.) 42			(610)	
32					
33	4) Closed End Lease - Estimate				
34	value of auto at 26th				
35	month less scrap at 48th				
36	month				
37	Cost 26th month = 3000 (P/F)			(2yrs) 2572	
38	salvage 48th " = 2000 (P/F)			(1470)	
39	Comparative Costs	6134	5986	6777	6939
40					
41					
42					

OBSERVATIONS ON
AUTOMOBILE ALTERNATIVES

The workpaper figures for the second alternative show that the annual loan repayments are $1,634. Actually, this is the monthly schedule for a 36-month loan, annualized. The interest is correct but it excludes life insurance spread over the three-year period. This computation was done by an amortization schedule as follows:

Loan	$4,000
Total finance charges	851
Total repayment	$4,851
Payments on an annual basis ($4,851÷3 years)	1,617

(Life insurance of $17 per year is excluded for this computation. The workpaper shows a cash outlay per year of $1,634, which includes life insurance.)

Annual percentage rate

N = 3 years

PMT = $1,617

PV = $4,000

Therefore, APR equals 10.30%
(The 10.30% is taken either from a present value calculator or from the annuity table).

The division of loan payments into interest and principal is called an amortization schedule. The schedule for the $4,000 loan follows.

	YEAR	PAYMENT	INTEREST	PRINCIPAL	LOAN BALANCE
1. Loan Balance	0				$4,000
2. Interest first year at 10.30% on $4,000	1		$412		
3. Subtract interest from payment: $1,617 __412__		$1,617		$1,205	

4. Loan balance end of first year: $4,000 1,205				2,795
5. Interest second year at 10.30% on $2,795	2		288	
6. Subtract interest from payment: $1,617 288		1,617		1,329
7. Loan balance end of second year: $2,795 1,329				1,466
8. Interest on third year at 10.30% on $1,466	3		151	
9. Subtract interest from payment: $1,617 151		1,617		1,466
10. Loan balance end of 3rd year: $1,466 1,466				-0-
Totals		$4,851	$851	$4,000	-0-

In partial financing, the tax-deductible items are the sales tax on the purchase price and the interest charges on the loan.

The tax saving is the deductible sales tax and interest times the effective tax rate. For the first year of loan repayments, the tax saving is $173 ($412 × 42%). The cash outflow for the first year is $1,461 (cash outlay for loan payments of $1,634 less $173 tax saving). The present value of this cash outflow at 8% is $1,353 ($1,461 × .9259). Thus, $1,353 is the 8% time-value of the $1,461.

In the fourth year of partial financing, there are no loan repayments under the 36-month borrowing plan. There is a cash inflow item of the salvage value of the automobile. This is the same figure as in the purchase option. The trade-in or salvage value is reduced to present value in a similar manner.

Alternatives # 1 and # 2, outright purchase and partial financing, show present value totals of $4,774 and $4,671 respectively, with a difference of $103 in favor of the partial financing. However, the figures at this stage of the study are not really comparable. The adjustment needed to make them relevant to each other is the life insurance included in the partial financing. The present value of this $52.32 charge over the three years is either added to the cash purchase or subtracted from the partial financing. Since the lease plans have no life insurance provision, the better view is to eliminate this factor from the study. On an annuity basis (P/A) the present value of the life insurance in the amount of $45 is eliminated from the partial financing cost. Actually, you would buy the expensive decreasing-term insurance, but this is eliminated here to achieve comparability.

The 36-month, closed-end lease includes maintenance and insurance, but you cannot compare alternatives # 1 and # 2 with alternative # 3 (the lease plan) unless you make the adjustments for insurance and maintenance. In addition, the use of an automobile from the twenty-sixth month to the forty-eighth month cannot be included in the study because the lease term in alternative # 3 is for only 26 months.

Since casualty insurance will be required for alternatives # 1 and # 2, the present value of the privately placed insurance is added. The insurance is paid in advance and thus the premiums start at "0" year. Current insurance rates used are based upon the policy that would actually be obtained for an outright purchase.

The maintenance presents a different problem. Since three of the four alternatives have no provision for maintenance and the amount included in the 26-month, closed-end lease seems unreasonably high ($300 per year plus 6.2% sales tax), the maintenance is eliminated from alternative # 3.

The final adjustment is for the present value of an automobile required to be used over the 22-month period after the closed-end lease expires to the end of the year. Using the cost of a two-year-old car and deducting the fourth-year salvage value, the adjustment is a net increase of $1,102 for the use of a car for 22 months ($3,000 − $2,000 present value).

The closed-end lease usually permits the purchase of the automobile at fair market value at the end of the lease, with the price subject to negotiation. (The approximate value would be about 50% of the retail cost.)

Alternative # 4, the 36-month, open-end lease, includes the purchase option for a specific amount at the end of the lease term. (The price is actually included in the lease agreement.) Since this alternative includes insurance, no adjustments are required. The 36-month lease does not provide for maintenance.

The final comparative costs in the lowest time-value of money outlay are:

ALTERNATIVE	PLAN	COMPARATIVE COSTS AT 8%	DELTA (%)
#2	Partial financing	$5,986	0%
#1	Purchase	6,134	2.47
#3	26-month lease	6,777	13.21
#4	36-month lease	6,939	15.92

The percentage increase of each plan over the most acceptable method ranges from 2.47% to 15.92% or, in money, a difference of from $148 to $953. The amount of $953 is obviously, a significant difference.

The rate factor of 8% was chosen as the debt-obligation factor based on the theory that the Smiths were borrowing from themselves. On the other hand, if in your case this is impossible because you do not have the $6,000 available, the debt-obligation factor would be a higher percentage. A 48-month bank *APR* may be used as a substitute for the 8%.

The differences in rates between 8% and 14% are produced by present value computed over an extended period of time. For example, the salvage value of the car at the end of four years is estimated at $2,000. At the 8% rate, the present value is $1,470; at the 14% rate, the present value is $1,184. The delta percent is a minus 19.46%. This would be a substantial difference if the salvage applied to only one option, but salvage actually becomes applicable by adjustment to all four alternatives. Therefore, the results using the 8% are constant although each answer is subject to question as to the proper rate to use.

If a 14% compounding rate had been used, the results would have been more pronounced in favor of partial financing. At 14% the difference is $533; at 8% the difference is $148.

At 14%, the time-value of an outright purchase is $5,060 vs. $4,527 for a partial financing, computed as follows:

YEAR	PURCHASE CASH FLOW	PURCHASE PRESENT VALUE OF CASH FLOW AT 14%	VS.	PARTIAL FINANCING CASH FLOW	PARTIAL FINANCING PRESENT VALUE OF CASH FLOW AT 14%
0	($6,244)	($6,244)		($2,244)	($2,244)
1				(1,461)	(1,282)
2				(1,513)	(1,164)
3				(1,571)	(1,060)
4	2,000	1,184		2,000	1,184
Less present value life ins. (P/A $17 per year)					39
Totals	($4,244)	($5,060)		($4,789)	($4,527)

The lease values are computed as follows:

YEAR		26-MONTH LEASE CASH FLOW	26-MONTH LEASE PRESENT VALUE OF CASH FLOW AT 14%	36-MONTH LEASE CASH FLOW	36-MONTH LEASE PRESENT VALUE OF CASH FLOW AT 14%
0					
1	Rental	($3,281)	($2,878)	($2,613)	($2,292)
2	Rental	(3,281)	($2,525)	(2,613)	(2,011)
3	Rental	(547)	(369)	(2,613)	(1,764)
	Purchase			(2,111)	(1,425)
4	Salvage			2,000	1,184
Subtotals		($7,109)	($5,772)	($7,950)	($6,308)
Adjustments: Maintenance					
1		$ 319	$ 280		
2		319	245		
3 (2 mo.)		53	36		

Purchase			
2	(3,000)	(2,308)	
Salvage			
4	2,000	1,184	
Subtotals	($ 309)	($ 563)	
Grand totals	($7,418)	($6,335)	($7,950)	($6,308)

The final closed-end lease payments in the twenty-fifth and twenty-sixth months are paid in the third year. These payments are reduced to present value as if they were made at the end of the third year. On the other hand, the purchase of the car at the end of the 26 months is brought to present value on the two-year formula. This is done because the rental accuracy range was not significantly different in money if the second year or third year were used; whereas on $3,000 the difference is $283 ($2,308 against $2,025). Since the second year is considerably closer to 26 months than three years, the present value purchase cost was deemed to be at the second year measuring position.

Using 14% as the cost of borrowed money rather than money withdrawn from savings, the results are in order of preference:

ALTERNATIVE	PLAN	COMPARATIVE COSTS AT 14%	DELTA (%)
#2	Partial Financing	$4,527	0%
#1	Purchase	5,060	11.77
#4	36-Month Lease	6,308	39.34
#3	26-Month Lease	6,335	39.94

Here the spread in money ranges from $473 for the difference between the most favorable amount and its nearest competitor ($5,060 minus $4,527). At 8%, the difference from the top to bottom range is $148 vs. $953 as seen in the following:

ALTERNATIVE	PLAN	COMPARATIVE COSTS 8%	14%	DELTA (8% COMPARED WITH 14%)
#2	Partial Financing	$5,986	$4,527	(24.37%)
#1	Purchase	6,134	5,060	(17.51)
#3	26-Month Lease	6,777	6,335	(6.52)
#4	36-Month Lease	6,939	6,308	(9.09)

From the above comparison, it becomes obvious that as the cost of money increases the present time value is lessened. For example, $1 at 8% compounded annually equals $1.08; $1 at 14% compounded annually equals $1.14. In reverse, the higher the time-value factor, the lower the present value. Thus, $1 due in one year at 8% is today worth 93¢. The same formula at 14% makes the $1 worth 88¢ today, making a decrease in percentage of 5.38%. The more it costs to borrow money, the lower the present value of what must be repaid in the future.

Your rate factor depends on what is termed the "opportunity" cost of money (the rate at which a business can earn income on its capital). In other words, the money should be earning you a profit of better than 8%. Otherwise you would be better off in avoiding business risks and leaving the money in a savings account. If savings is not an alternative source of money, the 14% appears to fit more closely the current long-term present-value factor.

Unless you complete the workpaper you cannot tell which alternative is the most favorable. Savings bank rates, tax rates, retail automobile costs, leasing arrangements, tax deductibles, salvage value, and the "opportunity" cost of money are all relevant to the equations.

The paperwork involved in partial financing frequently causes many people to accept a leasing arrangement without actually doing the figures. One solution to this problem is to ask the loan officer's help in completing the questionnaire, then make a copy of the answers for your files. You will find that in purchasing your next car most of the questions can be answered by referring to your copy. Partial financing may be arranged at the dealer's showroom provided the *APR* is competitive.

Since money rates and other variables in the formula can change annually, redo the workpaper each time you plan a change of automobile.

The lease figures are obtainable by telephone from Avis, Hertz, National or local automobile-leasing companies. Ask for their plans and rates for the make and model of car you want. Do not forget to separate basic price, maintenance, and insurance payments from one another before working out the comparative cost workpaper. (The exact sales tax should also be used for your workpaper.)

Banks have made a valiant effort to simplify loan applications. Most banks will gladly fill telephone requests for application forms. The questions which you cannot understand can usually be explained by telephone or during a personal visit. Don't allow lack of initiative to cost you a substantial amount of money.

Even if the outright purchase option (alternative #1) is unavailable to you, you should complete the computations for this alternative in order to have the proper conceptual development of all possible choices. This first option is the easiest to compute, and in any event, you will require these figures for the partial-financing alternative formula.

CONCLUSION

It is possible, through the use of the time-result factor and the formulas presented here to save hundreds of dollars. Leasing companies buy automobiles for the same prices that dealers pay (or less). These companies borrow money to finance their own purchases and you are charged a management fee in addition to an interest factor. There are times when a leasing plan will be better suited to your personal and financial needs than purchasing. The price-spread between the most favorable and least favorable alternatives in the example studied here is $953 at an 8% factor and $1,808 at the 14% rate. The order of preference did not change for the percentage difference as between partial financing and outright purchase. The lease preference order, however, did change. At the 8% factor, the 26-month lease was less costly than the 36-month lease. The contrary was true at 14%, although the difference between the two lease plans at 14% was $27, an insignificant sum for this situation. If your local savings bank rate is not 8% for four-year accounts, by all means use your own time-value factor. However, using 7%, 8%, or 9% will not change the final order of preference.

14
FUTURES

IN 1971, A TEACHER OF BUSINESS LAW at a large, private, urban university circulated among his class of seniors a newspaper advertisement. The ad was sponsored by the well-known McDonald's, a company founded in 1965 with a current annual net income well in excess of $100 million. The advertisement read:

> **Press on. Nothing in the world can take the place of persistence. Talent will not; nothing is more common than unsuccessful men with talent. Genius will not; unrewarded genius is almost a proverb. Education will not; the world is full of educated derelicts. Persistence and determination alone are omnipotent.**

This ad expressed the philosophy of McDonald's chairman and founder, R. A. Kroc. The students who read it were liberal arts and business majors. Business law was an elective course for most of the class. All were of above-average intelligence, and some were members of honor societies like Phi Beta Kappa and Beta Gamma Sigma. These young people were asked individually if they believed in the approach to success set out by McDonald's. They were unanimously *unimpressed* with the contents of the advertisement and some even forcefully denounced the words as nonsense. Nonetheless, each one of those who have by now reached financial security through their own initiative will acknowledge the importance of persistence and determination.* Individuals who have achieved financial success often have great difficulty in convincing young people of

*This is shown clearly in a fascinating work called *Adaptation to Life* by George E. Vaillant, Director of Psychiatric Training at Cambridge Hospital and Professor of Psychiatry at Harvard Medical School.

the indisputable value of "persistence and determination." Perhaps the social cynicism of the late 1960s and early 1970s has played a part in this attitude. Another factor, possibly, is the seeming prevalence in today's culture of youthful multimillionaires whose fortunes were made "overnight" in rock music, films, and other areas of so-called glamour and adventure.

The bankruptcy courts are filled with the victims of "get-rich-quick" schemes, most of which involve borrowing money. The majority of these "inspirations" are not original ideas at all. Money does not manage itself. The accumulation of wealth requires the exercise of continual discipline. Even more important than accumulating wealth is the ability to stay afloat in a sea of financial difficulties; and this, too, requires organization. Study after study of financially secure individuals clearly indicates that a positive, disciplined attitude towards money pays dividends—literally and figuratively—in later life.

The pressure of time has never deterred the active rich (as opposed to the passive rich, who only inherit their fortunes) from the discipline of controlling money. As the legendary law professor replied to the unprepared student, "What were you doing between midnight and 5:00 A.M.?"

PERSONAL ANTI-INFLATION MEASURES

Because most people are living more comfortably today than 10 years ago, you often hear the argument that one can "live with" inflation. "Experience suggests the contrary," says Paul A. Volcker, president of the Federal Reserve Bank of New York. Volcker, a highly respected member of the banking community, is noted for his deep belief in the public dissemination of banking information. In early 1978 he took to the dais to urge an aggressive battle against inflation.

Many outstanding bankers believe the will to fight inflation in this country is not strong enough. Perhaps this is because most people do not really understand how inflation affects the economic system. One fact is clear from every indicator: today's savings will be worth less tomorrow. Why is this so? Why can't tomorrow's money be worth *more* than today's? Excluding the earnings factor, what economic theory insists that the dollar you save today will be worth only between 50¢ and 70¢ in 10 years? Must full employment cause the eventual eradication of your savings? Government officials talk of living with 4.5% inflation as the price for full employment, yet the predicted annual inflation at the beginning of 1978 was somewhere around 6.5%, and in late 1978 was 10%. In other words, the failure of savings to increase in economic value is the price you are personally paying for current monetary policy.

Personal savings are the foundation of our American economy even though the individual's savings of after-tax dollars in this country is only 6.5% compared with 15% in West Germany and 25% in Japan. The national policies of the United States favor the consumer over the saver. Dividends are taxed twice: once at the corporate level and again at the individual level. Interest on savings accounts is taxed at progressive rates.

Tax deductions for savings by those employees without pension plans are generally limited to $1,500 per year (under the Individual Retirement Arrangement). Capital gains taxes have increased substantially through rate increases and through the new preference tax. Interestingly, the government tax revenue picture shows a steady increase in the portion coming from individual salaries and wages and a decrease in the portion supplied by the tax on capital gains.

In the two years following the first major increase in capital gains taxes, the revenues from realized capital gains decreased in the area of $7 billion. These were realized gains. In reality, the tax on capital gains can be deferred until a given asset is sold. By making it uneconomical to sell and diversify investments, the pressure is increased for the wage earner to supply the "missing" tax money. Congress understood this by lowering the maximum capital gains tax rate to 28% in the Revenue Act of 1978.

These are business persons who, despite the admonition of economists, insist that personal savings are the key to economic growth and stability. While your personal effect on government economic policy is limited, nevertheless a successful program of personal savings can make a vital contribution to curbing inflation.

Borrowing money today for asset acquisition and repaying later with cheaper money is one approach to creating personal capital. However, in order for this formula to work, the appreciation of an asset must exceed the interest cost of the money it took to purchase the asset. You must generate the cash to repay the loan obligation. You are creating capital at a slower pace, however, by using your own savings. The borrowing theory is applicable to business needs and is perfectly valid, but it is not useful as an anti-inflationary measure. If you can afford it, a meaningful reduction in your own consumption is the most workable solution.

The government can create capital for you by reducing tax rates, thus allowing you to save money; but this is not what you are supposed to do in a consumption-oriented society. The hope is that a large part of your tax reduction will find its way back into the consumer marketplace. However, for your own economic survival, you must reevaluate your own priorities to make an effective attempt to assist in the war against inflation. Examine your discretionary expenses with the aim of providing funds for increased savings. To help increase savings before spending the discretionary portion of your cash inflow, ask yourself the following questions:

1. Is this purchase necessary?
2. Is it necessary *now?*
3. Is the price fair?

A major shift in consumer resources is a sign that individual price structures are too high. Sellers resist broad price reductions unless market information shows buyer resistance.

CHOOSING YOUR PROFESSIONAL ADVISER

Most middle-income families do not have adequate access to attorneys and do not know how to select the right one. This fact appeared in a report by a committee of the Association of the Bar of the City of New York in support of advertising by lawyers. For many years a person needing professional help in a particular area was advised to call the appropriate local professional organization for a recommended list of available practitioners. However, this system proved totally inadequate. The poor had the Legal Aid Society to assist them, but there was no legal assistance available for a person of moderate means who required a will, the handling of a matrimonial problem, a name change, or redress from a landlord.

In 1977, the United States Supreme Court in *Bates and O'Steen* v. *State Bar of Arizona* held that state bans on advertising by attorneys were unconstitutional because such bans violated the First Amendment (freedom of speech). The Court also decided that the bans deprived people of information about lawyers who might help them. Because of the *Bates* ruling, you now have the opportunity to study the services and fee schedule advertised by any law firm in any state.

You should not hesitate to use a law firm or other professional service on the grounds that they advertise. The ban on professional advertising appears to stem from the days when professions were a form of public service in which the earning of a livelihood was incidental. It may appear to you (and to other established professionals) that advertising by lawyers and other professionals is undignified. However, when the vast majority of individuals require guidance in the area of professional services, advertising appears to be the proper solution. Through advertising you will be able to learn what professionals are available, what services they are selling, and how much these services will cost. If the advertised services are inadequate, false, or misleading, you may be assured that your complaint to the professional associations will be dealt with speedily and forcibly.

The tax law permits, on a trial basis through 1981, prepaid legal service plans. This means that an employer is allowed a deduction for contributions made to a plan providing prepaid personal legal services for employees and their families. This is similar to the deduction allowed for group hospitalization plans.

Major urban law firms are not geared to providing services for persons of modest means. Generally, they are prepared for large undertakings requiring high expenditures of time and talent compensated at rates affordable only by successful corporations and rich individuals. Your own legal problems will usually fall within easily categorized fields requiring routine knowledge which can be readily supplied by an efficient firm advertising its services.

Following World War II there was insufficient manpower to enable the person of modest means to have tax returns prepared at a reasonable price. This created the need for the national tax preparation services which are so successful today. It is interesting that the largest tax preparation service (in its prospectus offering stock to the public) stated that it did not at that time have in its employ *any* certified public accountants or lawyers. This organization, which prepares annually about *10 percent of the individual income tax returns* in the United States, grew because professional organizations failed to recognize a public need. The fees charged by this tax service are extremely reasonable compared with fees charged by professionals; a review of its work shows a competent performance in dealing with persons in middle-class financial circumstances.

In dealing with income tax preparers you are protected by the tax law and the IRS's strict regulations. Therefore, the chances of your employing a negligent preparer are automatically reduced considerably. If you have a complicated tax problem which requires research and specialized knowledge, you should refer the matter to an accountant or a lawyer. If you are a person of very modest means, organizations such as Community Tax Aid will help you without charge.

Choosing a competent professional adviser has never been an easy task. Your first criterion should be whether you feel the individual is relating to you and your problem. Remember that you are *never* bound to an adviser. You are free to pay for the time spent and to go elsewhere. Don't be a "shrinking violet" when it comes to professionals. Ask for—and insist—that fee schedules be in writing. If you think a fee is excessive, never hesitate to question a bill by requesting the time sheets. And if the professional advice you are receiving does not "ring true", do not argue with the adviser, simply move on to a new professional.

INCREASING YOUR FRINGE BENEFITS

Fringe benefits in these days of inflation are an ongoing method of increasing your cash flow on a generally nontaxable basis. Fringe benefits include *perquisites* (perks). These are items which are not direct salary payments but also are reimbursement "extras" for personal or business expenses that are your basic due as part of your job.

The cardinal rule to remember for monetary fringe benefits is that every dollar of your necessary personal outlay paid by your employer increases your cash flow by one dollar. If the outlay is a business expense, your cash flow increases according to your tax bracket. Or, a one-dollar fringe benefit may be equivalent to a one-dollar tax-free increase in salary.

Unless you take the time to analyze completely what your current situation is, there is no effective way of discussing an improvement in your fringe benefits with your employer. If you are working for a small, successful firm there is no economic reason why your employer should not provide the same fringe benefits as are allowed by large companies. In many instances, the absence of these benefits is due to lack of initiative at the executive level.

With the federal, state, and in some cases local governments absorbing more than 50% of the cost of a fringe benefit, a company which fails to provide the maximum benefits it can afford is ignoring the trend of the marketplace. For example, some employers who base pensions on the average of the last five years' wages intentionally raise the employee's salary during the last five years on the job for the sake of increasing the pension. This employer attitude is passed down to long-term employees and serves as a model for improving morale.

It is rare that a small company's shareholders will voluntarily offer fringe benefits unless the primary beneficiaries are the shareholder-officers themselves. For this reason many of the fringe benefits in these companies permit the other employees a "free ride" so that the owning group can have coverage. There is nothing wrong with this policy if it helps you as an employee proportionately.

The most important fringe benefit today is health insurance. New health plans are constantly being brought to the marketplace. If you work for a small company, you should bring these plans to your employer's attention. Fringe benefits are the equivalent of tax-free income, so don't be shy in asking for them. There are many faithful employees of small companies who awaken too late to the realization that their employer has been a believer in the "parity" doctrine (i.e., never pay administrative help more than the rest of the industry). Some unenlightened employers believe that help is easily replaceable, but this is not true today. A small company which pays its administrative help more in the form of direct salary and fringe benefits attracts a more intelligent type of employee, thereby creating a more profitable and efficient operation.

If the employer's answer to improving a fringe benefit is the "wait-for-next-year" approach, you must consider your bargaining position. Forget your mortgage and the orthodontist. The bank doesn't want to own your home, and the orthodontist will wait a couple of months for his or her fee. If you can't receive a fair hearing after presenting a written outline of suggestions for improving your fringe benefits, start looking for a new position. (Obviously you shouldn't reveal this to your employer until you have a new job.)

Fringe benefits are as important as wages, work hours, and working conditions. Extensive bargaining over fringe benefits takes place between unions and large employers. If you are employed by a large company under a collective-bargaining agreement, you can do very little in the area of major fringe benefits to improve your position. Nevertheless, you should certainly take advantage of any available opportunities for educational funding. Many employers will reimburse you for tuition costs of a course of study which is directly or indirectly related to your work. For 1979 through 1982, your employer may provide educational assistance—which is not includable in your income. The plan must not be discriminatory. The educational courses need not be job related.

It is said that equality is one of the great differences between the American economic system and the rest of the world. In the United States there is no barrier to prevent a worker from rising to the management level. In fact, many large enterprises are managed by men and women who started on the "bottom rung" of the ladder. The importance of using educational-funding benefits to achieve financial security cannot be overemphazied. IRS Publication 508 *Tax Information on Educational Expenses* will give you a complete checklist of deductible educational expenses. Use this list in setting up a plan of possible educational benefits which your employer can cover.

Life insurance to the extent of $50,000 a year may be carried by your employer for your benefit in a group plan, tax-free to you. The life insurance of over $50,000 is taxed at term insurance rates. Check your life insurance needs and consider asking your company to participate in fulfilling your family insurance needs. Even if you must reimburse part of the excess coverage to your employer, the aftertax cost to you will be less than your buying this yourself. In addition, group insurance requires no medical examination.

Pension and profit-sharing plans are an essential part of the corporate fringe-benefit package. Large and small companies find that a plan to accumulate funds outside the Social Security system provides employees and their families with a financial security almost impossible to achieve with after-tax savings programs. If you work for a successful company which does not offer a compensation formula of at least 15% of your wages (and in many cases, through combined plans, up to 25%), you should carefully consider the possibility of seeking employment with another company. Foregoing wage increases for a generous pension plan is a common practice. Particularly because of the passage of ERISA (Employee Retirement Income Security Act of 1974), your future benefits are well-protected by law.

Despite the immediate deploring of the red tape involved with ERISA by the business community, the fact remains that this law exists to protect you. The IRS's national office has a special section to assist any company to continue its plan that it is considering dropping due to ERISA's requirements. In its first years, ERISA's complicated nature created major problems for small companies. The IRS and the Department of Labor have made valiant efforts to keep the business community informed, and the large-scale termination of plans by companies is now over. More and more small companies are installing new and generous retirement-income arrangements.

You should find out what other employers in your industry are doing for their employees, then do your best to prepare a written analysis of what your employer *should be* achieving for you. To make it easy for small companies to adopt plans, the IRS has published prototype plans that require minimum additional detail for qualification. You can write to the IRS for a copy of a prototype plan.

Relocation allowances rightfully attempt to shift the burden of an expensive relocation from the employee to the employer. From babysitters to long-distance telephone calls, every out-of-pocket cost involved in your moving expenses should be reimbursed by your company. For examples of the items of expenditures see IRS Form 3903, *Moving Expenses*. Ask your local IRS office for Publication 521 (*Tax Information on Moving Expenses*) and Publication 523 (*Tax Information on Selling or Purchasing Your Home*). These will provide a checklist of possible relocation expenses. (You can also obtain these pamphlets by writing to the IRS, Box 1040, Brooklyn, New York 11232.)

Despite the widespread belief to the contrary, expense accounts are not an alternative form of executive capital improvement. It is the policy of the IRS to examine carefully the expense vouchers of the key executives of major corporations under tax audit. The cavalier attitude of charging everything to an executive expense account is a thing of the past. Corporate executives who charge personal items to their employers are required to make restitution to the employer and are warned that a repetition will incur the harshest penalty the law allows. Due to the intensive study of expense accounts made by the IRS in all its audits, this subject receives widespread attention.

The starting point of understanding expense accounts is the tax law itself. This law states that all ordinary and necessary business expenses within certain limits are deductible if properly documented.

You should first make an analysis of your company's written expense account policy. List all the items it covers and check your company's policy with your friends' company policies to see if your organization is generous in its approach. If you have a CPA prepare your tax return, show him or her the list and ask if there should be any additions. Such omitted items of business expense might include local transportation; gifts on behalf of your employer; baggage charges for display material; cleaning and laundry expenses when traveling; dues to professional organizations; trade and professional magazines related to your work; and home entertainment. You can deduct such items if you pay for them in connection with your work, but this requires *before-tax* money. Therefore, your paying for the item costs you your *after-tax* bracket. If your total tax bracket is 40%, you pay out of your pocket 60% of the expense. If your employer pays, you have improved your cash flow by that 60%.

To get an idea of all the possible expense account items for which you might be reimbursed, read the IRS Publication 463, *Travel, Entertainment and Gift Expenses*. This pamphlet was designed to cover your deductions.

Remember that you must prepare a detailed list of all your expenses. This is not a subject matter that can be covered verbally. Your employer will have to study this list and will probably have to discuss it with the company's accountants. You should realize that some of your proposed reimbursements may seem revolutionary or unusual to your employer. And also remember, you are not supposed to make a *profit* on your expense account. You are, however, to be adequately reimbursed for all reasonable expenditures.

Since the IRS allows you to claim automobile expenses at 17¢ per mile for the first 15,000 miles and 10¢ per mile thereafter, your company should at least meet this standard in its own policy. Tolls and parking are an additional expense. Consider asking your employer to purchase an automobile for your use. If you use a car for business at least half of the time, you would reimburse the company for the non-business use or be charged additional compensation. The automobile would of course belong to your employer. Many employers charge back two-sevenths of the original cost of a car on a four-year life cycle to the employee's salary account. For example, let's assume your company bought a car for your business use which you also use as a family automobile. The car cost $6,000. The annual depreciation over four years is $1,500 a year. This means you would be charged annually with additional salary of $428 ($1,500 × $^2/_7$ for the personal use of the car. This would still be considerably cheaper than owning the car yourself.

Miscellaneous perks include overtime fringe benefits such as dinner money and cab fares. Employer-established child care facilities increase your cash flow at no cost. The company store is an established idea which has been expanded to include cooperative employee buying of non-employer products. Prepaid legal plans are another new idea in fringe benefits, as are extended educational benefits.

If there is an expense for which your employer *would* have reimbursed you but for which you failed to submit a voucher, the IRS will not permit a deduction on your own tax return.

INVESTING: A FINANCIAL WINDFALL

Barrack rooms and dinner tables abound with talk of "the impossible dream", the financial windfall. Lotteries, roulette tables, and other games of chance and sport cater to that dream. There are moments in the lives of the rare and fortunate few when sudden wealth arrives on the scene. But the winning ticket from the lottery or an inheritance brings with it new responsibilities.

Taxes that are to be paid out of sudden riches should *never* be deferred through tax-shelter devices. Payment in the same year of state and local income taxes should be made so that they are an offset against taxable federal income. Consult an accountant or a lawyer for ideas on prepayments to reduce your taxes in the year of your windfall.

If your sudden windfall is less than $100,000 after taxes have been paid, you should consider a savings account with staggered maturities: U.S. government obligations or municipal bonds with an **Aa** rating or better. *Do not* use your sudden wealth for tax-shelter deals. If you want to buy a portfolio of investment-grade stocks, you should purchase a copy of either Moody's or Standard & Poor's listing of well-known stocks.

From either of these books choose high-grade and investment-grade stocks, avoiding the completely speculative grade. A stockbroker can assist you in weighting your portfolio between these two grades. Your investment in a stock portfolio or a mutual fund should not exceed 50% of your capital.

A real estate investment restricted to from 25% to 33⅓% of your windfall would be appropriate only if you have had experience in operating property for income or can participate in a joint investment venture.

A fund less than $100,000 is not, in terms of today's capital, the basis for a great fortune through speculation. Even if you have a business that could expand by using this money, restrict your risk to no more than 33¹/₃% of the windfall. Savings accounts at the current long-term rate of 8.17% double in value in less than nine years. If you want to reduce the income tax impact of the interest you can make gifts to your family.

The approach then to a less-than-$100,000 windfall is one of conservatism. This is not the time to buy a new car, renovate the house, or to take a vacation trip. You should consider the windfall fund an additional financial security and should treat it as such. However, spending the income or interest from your windfall is different from invading the capital. You should use the income as part of your cash inflow, retaining the original fund intact.

If your financial windfall is more than $100,000 you should seek investment advice from either an accountant and/or a tax lawyer who represents wealthy families. (The fees for these professional services are tax-deductible.) The tax specialist will advise you about the wide range of tax-incentive investments available. But remember, if an adviser receives a fee from the sponsor of a proposed investment deal, the adviser cannot be considered independent. An independent adviser charges you exactly the same whether you buy or do not buy into a deal. Before committing any funds to an investment you should get advice from both a tax adviser and an investment counsel.

If you have young children, you might consider seeking an insurance consultant to the advisory group. Try to find a life insurance consultant who will charge a fee whether you buy insurance or not. (A fee for this service would range from about $350 to $500.) It may not be feasible in the state in which you reside to find an independent life insurance consultant. In this case, you may use a life insurance agent and then ask a tax professional to review the insurance proposal.

With a fund in excess of $100,000 the pyramid of financial management is more easily constructed than with a lesser amount. At the base are the high-grade secure investments such as savings accounts, government bonds, and "blue-chip" stocks. At the next level of the pyramid are the medium-grade investments. The top or smallest area of the pyramid is confined to speculations. The portion for each area of the pyramid depends on your age and cash-flow position. In general, a family with minor children whose combined gross income, exclusive of the windfall, is between $25,000 and $35,000 a year would divide the pyramid in the following way:

	QUALITY RATING	%
Base	High-grade	50
2nd Tier	Investment	25
3rd Tier	Medium	15
Top	Speculative	10
	Total	100%

If you are uncertain whether an investment is high grade or investment grade, take the conservative approach and treat it as the lower category.

The four-grade division is found in *Moody's Handbook of Common Stocks*, published quarterly. Standard & Poor's also grades stocks. Some knowledgeable money managers consider stock ratings worthless. However, the point of the ratings approach is to attempt to spread your risk and at the same time exceed the performance of a savings account. A real estate investment may also fall into any one of the four stock-rating categories, depending upon the tenants, location, and other factors.

Your own life experiences are directly related to how you would treat a windfall. If you know that you are a compulsive consumer, you should immediately contact a lawyer and have a spendthrift trust prepared to "save you from yourself." Even if you are not a reckless spender, you should consider the trust form (revocable or irrevocable) as the proper vehicle for carrying out the financial objectives of your windfall. Banks are frequently chosen for trusteeships in sudden-wealth situations, and your local bank's trust department can be of immeasurable help. Unfortunately, many banks have not performed well in recent years in handling the investment needs of wealthy families. You may be co-trustee of your own trust since its primary purpose is to conserve your money, rather than establishing an estate. The bank's trustees' fees are fixed by state law and are deductible to the extent the income of your trust is taxable. This approach is called "the living trust," and it is the most acceptable method of employing your new capital in a productive manner.

FINANCING HIGHER EDUCATION

After the downpayment on your home, your largest single cash outlay will probably be for your children's higher education. Over the past eight years, college tuition costs have increased in private universities by 88% and in public universities by 74%. These figures may seem shocking to anyone not paying tuition bills.

The extent to which students now use loans to finance their education indicates that family priorities have drastically changed in recent years. Whereas previously parents considered it an obligation to finance the major part of higher education for their children, today's family's cash inflow is being used differently. Although there are excellent ways of saving money for a college education (savings accounts, U.S. "E" Bonds, municipal bonds, and insurance), the middle-class family does not seem particularly interested in building college funds. This is borne out by the number of students from middle-class homes who seek educational loans. Currently, the student loan program permits borrowing up to $5,000 per year at about 7% annual interest, with repayment starting after graduation.

Articles in *U.S. News & World Report* (January 30, 1978) and *Business Week* (February 4, 1974), as well as regularly published newspaper pieces, point out the middle class as the victims of the spiralling college costs. Congress is seriously considering a tax credit to help finance higher education. However, some knowledgeable educators believe that the tax credit will *increase* college tuition.

Bright middle-class students are frequently rejected for merit-type scholarships because their families' incomes are above the limits of eligibility. These income limits are considered inappropriate in many instances since they deal with *gross income* rather than the family's *discretionary* cash outflow—a tremendous difference when you are paying college tuition for more than one child in a single year.

The average cost of maintaining a student at a private university is now in excess of $5,200 a year and $2,200 a year in a public university. On this basis, a four-year education would cost $20,800 at a private college and $8,800 at a public college. Interestingly, *Business Week* in February, 1974 predicted the 1978 college costs almost exactly. For 1983 *Business Week* forecasts a $26,000 four-year cost at a private university and $12,000 at a public one. These increases over five years average 4.56% per year for a private education and 6.40% per year for a public one.

Many middle-class families are sending their children of high school age to live with relatives in distant states in order to qualify for the excellent, low-cost public universities in some states. Continued increases in tuition, it is argued, will permit the great universities to cater only to the poor and the rich. In addition, the current debate over the large percentage of uncollected student loans is a cause for concern. Middle-class families do not have the same opportunity to receive grants and loans as low-income families, yet the social policy of the country and available funds do not make any change feasible at present.

Parents using a trust to save for college education must have income-producing property in order for the trust to function properly. This method requires transferring property for 10 years or more to a trust, where the income accumulates at relatively low tax rates. The accumulated trust income is used late to pay tuition. At the end of the trust term, the parent receives the trust property corpus. There are numerous tax problems involved in using the trust vehicle, and a professional adviser should be consulted before embarking on this course of action.

The College Blue Book is a well-known publication listing all types of sources for financing a college education. Another book is *Don't Miss Out, The Ambitious Student's Guide to Scholarships and Loans*, published by Octameron Associates, P.O. Box 3437, Alexandria, Virginia 22302. Most financial advisers recommend that you start saving for each child's education at least by the time that child is 10 years of age. Then, if the funds are not actually required due to some fortuitous event such as loans, grants, and tax credits, you can use the money for other purposes.

COLLEGE EDUCATION WORKPAPER

The inflation rates of college education require the use of an index method of forecasting the future costs. Assuming, therefore, that costs are expected to rise 5% (compounded) a year for both public and private university education, the factors for the next 15 years are as follows:

YEAR	INDEX	YEAR	INDEX
1978	100	1986	147
1979	105	1987	155
1980	110	1988	163
1981	116	1989	171
1982	122	1990	180
1983	128	1991	189
1984	134	1992	198
1985	141		

You will also need to know what amounts, accumulated at current interest rates, will permit the necessary funds to be available for tuition. In order to simplify the interest problem, the yearly cash is assumed to have been saved at the end of the year. If the time span is shorter the interest earned will be lower. However, this is not material in solving the problem, and only makes the mathematics more complicated. An earnings rate must be applied to the accumulated funds. The 5% factor applied to rising college costs is an estimate. Similarly, the earnings rate is also an "educated guess." At the present time, considering yields on tax-exempt bonds, long-term savings bank rates, and the effect of taxation on interest taxable to the children, a rate of 6% on the money accumulated appears to be reasonable. At the 6% earnings rate the following are the annual payment (annuity) factors required to accumulate $1 at the end of a period. This is an annuity from a future amount (A/F).

NO. OF YEARS	ANNUAL COMPOUNDING FACTOR APPLICABLE TO END-OF-YEAR AMOUNTS AT 6% EFFECTIVE RATE
1	1.0000
2	0.4854
3	0.3141
4	0.2286
5	0.1774
6	0.1434
7	0.1191
8	0.1010
9	0.0870

10	0.0759
11	0.0668
12	0.0593
13	0.0530
14	0.0476
15	0.0430

If the inflationary factor is actually less than 5% per year, the result is excess savings. On the other hand, if the factor exceeds 5% annually, the difference will have to be supplied at the time tuition is paid.

For example, the children of Daniel and Louise Smith are eight and 10 at the end of 1978. Assume that college starts at age 18 and that the Smiths will send their children to private universities. How much must be saved annually to finance their education? The 1978 tuition plus living costs at private universities or their equivalent is on the average $5,200 per year.

The following workpaper is *not* a feasibility study to work out whether the Smiths can afford to send their children to college. It determines *how much* is required to finance their children's college education.

OBSERVATIONS ON COMPUTATION OF COLLEGE FINANCIAL REQUIREMENTS

The objective of the Smiths' workpaper is to determine how much is needed to finance the college education of both children. The workpaper is not involved with money priorities, alternative sources of funds, or whether or not the Smiths can afford the cost of a private university education for their children. In addition, the possible rise of the inflation-rate, tuition-costs, or earning rate of the Smiths' money are not material factors in this economic study. The study shows that an annual fund in excess of $4,600 a year must be placed into some earning vehicle (e.g., a savings account) in order fully to fund the children's education.

The first problem is how to ascertain the educational financial needs. Whether the money is available for savings is next. The workpaper starts with the ages of the children. Step 2 determines the years when the tuition will be due. The simplified example assumes tuition is due at the end of the year following that year's savings. At the present grade levels, the older child will enter in the fall of 1987. The educational fund covers six years of which the middle two are double-tuition periods.

		1	2	3	4
1.	Ages of Children				
	A	10			
	B	8			
2.	Future Tuition Costs				

			Index — 1978	100	
			Tuition Cost — 1978	5200	

Year Required	Child A	Child B	Index	Estimated Tuition Cost
1987	X		155	8060
1988	X		163	8476
1989	X	X	171	17784
1990	X	X	180	18720
1991		X	189	9828
1992		X	198	10296
Total Estimated Tuition Costs				73164

3. Funding Required Annually

Year Required	Future Periods	Estimated Tuition Costs	Annuity Factor	Annual Payment
1987	9	8060	0.0870	701
1988	10	8476	0.0759	643
1989	11	17784	0.0668	1188
1990	12	18720	0.0593	1110
1991	13	9828	0.0530	521
1992	14	10296	0.0476	490
Total		73164		

Estimated Annual Payments
Required To
Finance Tuition | | | | 4653

The year 1978 is the index of 100. The 1978 tuition expenses of $5,200 equal the 100 index factor. The inflation-rate table on page 499 indicates the projected inflation rate for the first year of college, 1987, at 155. This means the 1987 tuition is expected to cost 155% of the 1978 figure or $8,060 ($5,200 × 1.55 = $8,060). Each succeeding year is computed using the index number for that year. The middle years with the double costs require using $10,400 (2 × $5,200) as the 1978 cost for two tuitions.

The total tuition costs for educating the Smiths' children at a private university is estimated to be $73,164. From this cost, the Smiths can compute the annual payments required to make up this fund by using annuity factors. The workpaper goes on to show that the 1987 year carries with it the nine periods (1987 minus 1978) from 1978 and each year after adds another period. The annuity factor of 6% for the future periods when the money will be required is multiplied by the expected cost. The total is the payment required annually in order to accumulate the necessary funds. This is called a *present annuity from a future amount*. For example, in order to accumulate $8,060 at 6% over nine years, an annual payment of $701 is necessary. Taxes, if payable, would reduce the annuity factor. In our example, 6% is the earnings after taxes. Each year's funds are computed using the tuition cost multipled by that year's annuity factor. The six separate annuity factors are added together to give the *total annual payment* required to finance the education needs up to the date when the first tuition payment will be due.

The fund available at the date tuition begins would be $53,468. The factor from an annuity table is 11.491 for nine years at 6% ($4,653 × 11.491 = $53,468). The first year's tuition would be paid from this fund. Thereafter the annual payments required are reduced by that year's annuity as indicated in the table following:

YEAR	ANNUITY PAY-MENT FOR YEAR'S TUITION	TOTAL ANNUITY PAYMENT	ESTIMATED TUITION COST
1987	$ 701	$4,653	$8,060
1988	643	3,952	8,476
1989	1,188	3,309	17,784
1990	1,110	2,121	18,720
1991	521	1,011	9,828
1992	490	490	10,296
Totals	$4,653		$73,164

You will notice under this plan that $3,309 is required in the third year to finance the tuition cost of $17,784 for both children.

The economic study estimates both the tuition inflation rate and the fund's earning rate. An error of 25% or less would not materially change the funds needed. In the event that inflation is curbed and interest rates rise, the current payment will create a larger fund than is anticipated.

Determining whether the fund should be in the form of savings, U.S. Bonds, municipal bonds, or other forms of investment is not the purpose of the study. This workpaper is designed to show how the computations are made to determine the current payments in order to create future funds. These financial targets may seem impossible for you to achieve with your present cash flow. If you do not want to saddle your children with tuition loans or burden yourself in the future with refinancing your home, you should give serious consideration to specific-goal budgeting.

The Smiths have to consider seriously whether their cash flow can provide this kind of money to finance education. If not, they must decide just how much can be accumulated for the educational fund. The future-value annuity factor on 11.491 gives a fair representation of the funds that could be available through annual savings up to the college entrance date of 1987. Thus, $2,000 saved each year at 6% for nine years will be worth almost $23,000 ($2,000 × 11.491 = $22,982).

Exercise caution, before putting the funds into a savings account in the name of a child. In some states withdrawals may not be allowed until age 18 without a court's permission. A custodian account under the Uniform Gifts to the Minor Act would be more appropriate. Withdrawals from a custodian account for college tuition payments in most states is considered a proper use of the funds on behalf of the beneficiary. Any of the funds remaining in hand in this type of account automatically belong to the child at age 21. The tax on the interest is includible in both types of account on your child's tax return. However, you must feel comfortable enough financially so that the chance of your needing the money in these accounts is remote. And you must analyze your own future prospects carefully in order to make this decision.

COMPUTERIZING YOUR RECORDS

Money processing or the checkless society is the wave of the future. The burden of handling pieces of paper such as checks and deposit slips will be replaced by perodic printouts or display tubes. Computer terminals will supercede checks. The hardware (computer) is on market and the software (computer program) is being developed. The checking account as you know it will be obsolete. The only reason for a delay in immediate changeover is the need to educate the public. You must be confident with the mechanics of the system. You must accept electronics instead of paper documents. For your switchover to electronics from a paper world be assured that your rights of privacy will be protected through vigorous enforcement of the law with severe penalties handed out to violators. The effect on your life will be almost as dramatic as the eventual changeover to the metric system of measurement.

The new system is simple: everyone who transfers money to you arranges to deposit electronically the money to your bank account. You also arrange to pay your creditors and others electronically. The automatic deposit system is already being used by the Social Security Administration and the Veterans Administration. If at any time your withdrawals exceed your deposits (overdrawn account), the bank charges you interest. If the reverse is true (excess money in your account), the bank either pays you interest and charges a fee for maintaining your account or there are no charges. The bank in the free account situation earns its fee through the use of your excess deposits. At the end of the period (usually a four-week cycle), the bank presents you with a classified bank statement showing each deposit and the source of the funds. On the other side, each withdrawal is shown by date, payee, classification of item, and amount. At the end of the year or shorter time span, the items making up each classification of account together with its total is available. Your budget eventually could be added to the system. At the end of the year, your tax return would be produced after inputting adjustments for bank interest, for casualty losses, your personal exemptions and other noncash items.

This procedure is referred to as the Electronic Funds Transfer System (E.F.T.S.). The elimination of burdensome tasks of checkwriting and making deposits will be an important benefit of E.F.T.S. However, the prime result to you of the checkless society will be better money management.

The 24-hour self-service complete banking centers started by one of the country's largest banks is another step towards E.F.T.S. The cash-dispensing machine outside your local bank is also part of an electronic network designed to serve you more efficiently.

Under the E.F.T.S. system as it may eventually develop, instead of a checkbook, you would own a device similar to a thin pocket calculator. In the memory of this machine would be your checking account number. When you wish to buy from a store, your machine is placed on a terminal which is similar in size to an electric typewriter. This terminal also has an adding machine tape. You activate your bank account by attaching your machine to the terminal. You then key in your P.I.N. (Personal Identification Number) consisting of nine digits. The P.I.N. sets into motion the communication link between the store's and your bank's computers. All you do is key in the amount of your purchase. Your bank account will be automatically charged for the purchase. If you want to defer payment, other key strokes will permit that information to be transmitted to your account. If you desire a classification of your purchase, that data may also be inputted into the system at the same time. The adding machine tape on the vendor's terminal provides you with a receipt.

The use of cash even for small purchases or bus rides will be curtailed by adding features to the vendor's terminal that automatically charges the proper amount after you begin the transmission with your P.I.N.

For example, if your telephone bill is charged automatically, all back-up documentation would be sent to you by the bank, along with the print-out of your entire account. This documentation would be transmitted by the telephone company's computer to your bank's computer. Your bank would print the details of the bill as part of its service. If the telephone company charges you for a long distance call in error, your credit would also include interest on your money. As far as you are concerned, the whole operation of the E.F.T.S. is no more complicated than your present pocket calculator or push-button telephone. In fact, the push-button telephone with the buttons "#" and "*" may eventually be used as a home terminal for E.F.T.S.

SERVICE BUREAU

If you would like to simplify your record-keeping now, you can easily convert your checkbook to a data-processing set-up. You only need to set up account numbers for the chart of accounts discussed in Chapter 3, CASH FLOW. There are a number of computer service bureaus who will computerize your checkbook by classifying your transactions. The expense is usually tax-deductible since it is used to help prepare your tax return. The service bureau will help you establish the account numbers. All you do is mark the account number on each check stub or deposit entry. You can use either two- or three-digit figures. Thus, contributions to charity might be account #660. You would mark the check stub below the name of the charity with the number 660. The computer printout lists all the checks and deposits in date order including payees, names, and amounts with a description of the purpose, obtained from the account number. The listing is then summarized by account classifications. Thus, at the end of the year you have the exact amount received and spent for every category. You can make the necessary adjustments and from that your tax returns can be readily prepared. For computerizing your records on an annual basis, a competent service bureau charges about $250. This would be of particular interest to people who are self-employed, work at part-time activities, or have income from rents. For further information about using a service bureau, write to PDS Corporation, P.O. Box 548, Englewood, N.J. 07631.

The home computer will be the next step after employing a service bureau. Within the next few years complete computers for money managing in the home will be available for the cost of today's electric typewriter.

CONCLUSION

Financial security is a state of mind. Managing money requires persistence, organization, and knowledge. You can supply the ingredients for the first two items. It is hoped that this book has supplied you with the third.

In making financial decisions rarely does the difference between success or failure hinge on a single factor. The factors set out in a written economic study using the now familiar four-column paper will clearly increase your odds towards a proper decision.

The digits zero through nine arranged in conjunction with the four functions of addition, subtraction, multiplication, and division, can show you where you have been, where you are, and where you are going financially.

When you get to the computer stage you won't even need the digits zero through nine, as it uses only zero and one.

The technology of the future will permit you more leisure time. It will be most rewarding to use some of it for managing your own money.

Index